P9-CCY-381

Hemp Today

This sheet of

100% HEMP PAPER

is the first page in the story of a new hemp industry.
A sustainable future starts here.

Paper courtesy of Ecolution, Fairfax, Virginia

Hemp Today

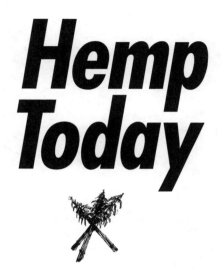

Edited by
ED ROSENTHAL

QUICK AMERICAN ARCHIVES   *Oakland, California*

"Marijuana Economics" Copyright © 1988; "Hemp as Biomass" Copyright © 1992; "Hemp in England" Copyright © 1993; "Hemp Realities," "Hemp in Holland," "Hemp in Hungary," "The Hempstead," and all section introductions and summaries Copyright © 1994 by Ed Rosenthal

"Fiber Wars" Copyright © 1994 by Dave West

"The Schlichten Papers" and "Why Hemp Seeds?" Copyright © 1994 by Don Wirtshafter

"Can Hemp Save Our Planet?" Copyright © 1990 by David Walker

"A Supplement and Answer to David Walker" Copyright © 1990 by Lynn and Judy Osburn

"Cannabis for Paper" Copyright © 1993 by John Birrenbach

"Hemp or Wood: Potential Substitutes" Copyright © 1994 by V.S. Krotov

"Hemp Pulp and Paper Production" Copyright © 1994 by Gertjan van Roekel, Jr.

"Agronomy and Crop Physiology of Cannabis: a Literature Review" Copyright © 1990; "Fiber Hemp in France" Copyright © 1992; "Fiber Hemp in the Ukraine, 1993" Copyright © 1993; "Paper from Dutch Hemp" Copyright © 1994 by Hayo van der Werf

"Hemp Variations as a Pulp Source for Paper" Copyright © 1993 by Etienne de Meijer

"Australia, Eucalypts and Hemp" Copyright © 1994 by Andrew Katelaris

"Tasmanian Trials," Copyright © 1994 by Wolfgang Spielmeyer

"The Tasmanian Hemp Company," Copyright © 1994 by Patsy & Frits Harmsen

"Hemp Breeding in Hungary" Copyright © 1991 by Sebastiaan Hennink

"Fiber Hemp in the Ukraine, 1991" Copyright © 1991 by Sebastiaan Hennink, Etienne de Meijer and Hayo van der Werf

"Hemp in China" Copyright © 1994 by Paul Stanford

"The UK Hemp Project in 1993" Copyright © 1994 by Ian Low

"Hemp Today in the USA" Copyright © 1994 by Mari Kane

"Hemp: from Today into Tomorrow" Copyright © 1994 by Chris Conrad

"Economics of Marijuana Legalization" Copyright © 1993 by Dale Gierenger

"Marijuana and Medicine" Copyright © 1994 by Robert Clarke and David Pate

"Isochanvre" Copyright © 1994 by Chenviotte Habitat

European Economic Community record published in 1989

All rights reserved. Except for use in a review, no part of this work may be reproduced in any form without express written permission of the publisher and/or the copyright holder.

ISBN 0-932551-14-9

First Printing: November 1994

Published by Quick American Archives, a division of Quick Trading Company

Distributed by: Quick Trading Company
                   P.O. Box 429477
                   San Francisco, CA 94142-9477
                   (510) 533-0605
                   Publishers Group West

Printed in the United States of America

This book is dedicated to Jack Herer,
the founder of the modern hemp movement.

Table of Contents

Introduction

by Willie Nelson

FARMERS HAVE A SPECIAL CONNECTION with the earth. When a farmer knows his land and supplies its needs, a harmony exists which results in a bountiful harvest. The vitality of life is everywhere. Fruit trees which grow heavy with their juicy sweetness, the livestock, part of a never-ending herd, and the annuals which start as a bare field with life-plans contained in each seed. A few months later they cover the field in a sea of green then complete their life cycle and ripen with seed. The farming cycle closely follows nature, with humans as the caretakers. Its ancient roots and annual rhythms ground the farmer and the people near the farm.

It was not too long ago that all of us, city and country folk alike, had a farmer relative or friend. We were able to go back to the farm, to help with the harvest or just to be in the fresh air touching soil. This has disappeared in my lifetime. Farmers are a tiny part of this country's population. The family farm has almost faded away.

The experts can probably point out all the reasons. A changing economy, efficiencies, mechanization, we have all heard the list. In the end, however it is figured, the farmer gets the short end of the stick. Not only is the farmer's income declining as he is paid less for his crop, but his natural, recyclable, biodegradable crops are replaced with synthetics that only seem cheaper and more efficient.

If we used more farmed products and fewer synthetics, we would go back to a more sustainable life. There would be more farmers and more industry to use the farm products. There would be fewer toxics and unre-cyclable wastes. This is exactly the story that the hemp people talk about.

Hemp is a healthy crop which helps the soil, smothers weeds and needs no insecticides. It could make the very difference between the survival of the family farm and its extinction. It is much more valuable per acre than corn or other grains and has many markets because it can be used as a wood substitute and for food, feed for animals, clothing and industrial raw material.

Farmers all over the world are taking advantage of the surging market. Yet here in North America, where hemp has thrived since colonial times, farmers are not allowed to grow it. In effect, the government is subsidizing farmers all over the world while penalizing American farmers.

Hemp is intertwined with American history. We grew it to rig the great New England sailing ships, traveled west in Conestoga wagons covered in hemp cloth, dressed in homespun hemp cloth when we got there and wound up wearing hemp jeans. We tied our cargo with hemp rope and fed the poultry with hemp seed. We used hemp to help develop this country.

Our forefathers saw great value in this plant. George Washington said, "Make the most of the hemp seed. Sow it everywhere." We should listen to his advice and let farmers in America supply our industry with hemp.

Willie Nelson

Foreword

by Ed Rosenthal

CANNABIS MAY BE THE PLANT most important to humanity. Almost every part of the above-ground growth has an economic value and is used by industry. It is extremely productive and its products could help conserve scarce resources. Over the millennia, humans have developed thousands of varieties. Each was bred to provide specific products in a particular environment. It is cultivated for its grain-like seed, very strong fiber and wood-like inner core. Plants grown for this purpose are usually referred to as hemp.

Cannabis has shared a long symbiotic relationship with humans. Researchers theorize that it was discovered in the foothills of the Himalayas. Traders and migrating peoples carried the seed in all directions. Both species, *homo sapiens* and *cannabis sativa* have benefitted greatly from this intercourse.

Cannabis has been discovered and lost by societies innumerable times. Each time it is discovered it meets a need. Technology advances, making it obsolete. Its use ends and it is "lost." Then a new use is discovered and it is grown once again. Better or cheaper substitutes are discovered and the plant becomes obscure once more.

The situation in the U.S. was typical. During the colonial era hemp cultivation was important because of its use for rope and sailcloth. Cotton began to dominate the cloth market beginning in the 1790s with the invention of the cotton gin, which made the fiber cheaper to process.

Cheap tropical fibers such as jute and abaca soon dominated the rope and cord market.

Just as hemp cultivation was declining in the U.S., the use of cannabis tinctures as medicine became more common. The 1927 pharmacopia lists five pages of uses for the tincture. The variety which was used for medicine, *cannabis indica*, contains a psychoactive complex of cannabinoids. Delta-9 Tetrahydrocannabinol (THC) is considered the most active. Its structure was theorized by Adams in the 1940s and then the molecule was discovered by Mechoulam in 1974.

In the nineteenth century chemists were able to synthesize the active ingredient in willow, salicylic acid. This led to standardization of the ingredients and the creation of aspirin. Early 20th century chemists' inability to isolate, standardize and synthesize THC led to its decline in use and eventual removal from the U.S. Pharmacopoeia.

Plants high in THC which are grown for their psychoactive properties are referred to as marijuana. The use of these THC bearing plants has been frowned on by society. This has tainted cannabis in all its manifestations and its cultivation is highly restricted.

Restrictive regulation of cannabis in 1937 resulted in the plant's fading from public consciousness. Only small subcultures continued to use it as a medicine and euphoriant from the 1940s to the 1960s. Use was centered in the entertainment and jazz communities and regionally in urban centers and the south. The beats discovered it and began to smoke it in the late 1950s. By the 1960s it was adopted by the new anti-establishment youth, the hippies. Use mushroomed. This eventually led to the re-investigation of hemp as a natural, renewable source of medicine and industrial product.

After cannabis was made illegal and hemp severely restricted in the U.S., most people's consciousness concentrated on the euphoriant aspect. Until recently, hemp remained in the background except for occasional articles in niche journals. In the past few years hemp has become a trendy topic again.

As hemp information was disseminated, a demand was created and a supply was soon found to market to eager buyers. Now industrial users are investigating the easily cultivated agricultural resource.

The regulations concerning hemp cultivation remain so restrictive that it is not grown in commercially in the U.S. Although farming hemp commercially is not feasible, hemp products are permitted.

Small industries have grown up around imported hemp seed and fiber. These new companies include importers, clothing, accessory, food and cosmetic manufacturers, retailers, mail order companies, and fiber board manufacturers. In the near future we can expect new companies involved in spinning and paper manufacturing.

Even with the new industry which is emerging, hemp's future and potential are controversial issues. The editorial focus of this book was to select a balanced group of chapters. Together, they provide the reader with both a background on hemp's recent past, reports on its cultivation and use today, and a roundtable of discussions on its potential.

Hemp has jumped from magazines such as Britain's *The Ecologist* and *High Times* in the U.S., to the press wires, TV, and national journals. Much of this media attention has accepted the "hemp hype" without investigation. Recent books have focused on hemp's past history and its idealized potential. One popular volume even claims that this plant alone can save the world from ecological disaster. The purpose of this book is to investigate the realities of hemp.

The book is divided into four sections. It begins with several articles on hemp's recent history in the U.S and the potential that its proponents saw for it as an industrial crop early in this century. This information is very important because it shows clearly that hemp's elimination as a commercial crop was not due to economic competition but was a result of a harmonic convergence of special interests.

The second section contains different perspectives on hemp's potential. Together with the literature reviews they provide a glimpse of the future directions hemp commercialization may take. These viewpoints are often in conflict, but all of them point to hemp's increasing importance as a raw material for industrial and commercial use.

Most Americans think of hemp in national terms. However, cultivation has continued in Europe and Asia. These reports on the state of hemp from countries all over the world show the crop at a crossroads. While the old markets are evaporating, new ones are emerging that are affecting cultivation and factory production. This gives us a perspective of hemp beyond our borders. Once again we see hemp being rediscovered. However, in this case, it is not just in one country or among one group.

The interest in hemp is worldwide. Reports are included from China, England, France, Holland, Hungary and the United States. Each of these countries has its own hemp program and different goals. These reports give a rounded view of the hemp industry worldwide.

If hemp and marijuana were grown on plants which were not closely related, there is no question that hemp would be legal. If hemp yielded industrial products and a medicinal drug without psychoactive qualities it would still probably be legal. Since hemp and marijuana have been associated in the law since the inception of criminalization in 1937, there is some question as to whether hemp can be legalized in the United States without changing the marijuana laws. That topic is not an issue covered by this book. The economics of legalized marijuana is covered briefly, however.

Even as contraband grown by people with essentially no experience in commercial farming, marijuana has become one of the major crops in terms of gross revenue and even more importantly, net income. It would remain important commercially if it were legalized and taxed. Section four takes a brief view of some commercial models of legalization of marijuana.

The appendix is meant to provide the reader with background material on hemp cultivation, production and industrial uses. Some of this material is a bit dated. However, it is very accurate and should be considered a reliable source.

This book is meant to provide the reader with the information needed to get a clear picture of hemp at the crossroads. Will it help lead us to a greener future or is it just a pipedream? The market will decide in the next few years.

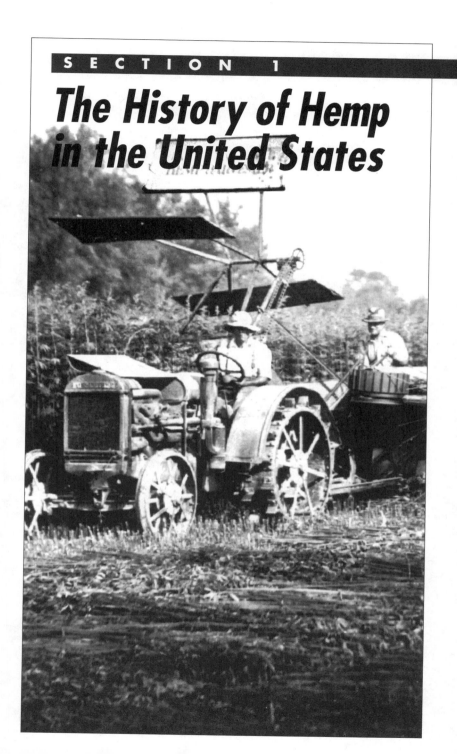

The History of Hemp in the United States

Introduction

by Ed Rosenthal

AT ONE TIME I owned a company which manufactured banjos. At the time I facetiously told friends that I was sending a lobbyist to Washington to make sure that all soldiers were issued banjos, the only musical instrument invented in the U.S. Even as a young entrepreneur I understood the power that the government has to regulate, control or dominate a particular market.

Economic policy and policies influencing economics have controlled the flow of commercial activity in the U.S. since the acceptance of the Constitution, when the federal government assumed the state governments' debts. It is much easier to have the government control your competitor rather than have to share the market.

In the 1930s there were many groups who had an interest in illegalizing, or at least, severely regulating cannabis. The pharmaceutical industry was patenting medicines. They could not patent a plant concentrate whose complex chemical structure had not been elucidated. With *cannabis indica* concentrate off the market, they would be able to patent and market second-best drugs.

Jack Herer, in his book *The Emperor Wears No Clothes*, showed the role that DuPont and Hearst played in pushing intense regulation. The chemical company saw hemp as a threat to the synthetic fiber market, which they had just invented. Hearst saw cheap pulp as a threat to the value of its forest holdings. These companies used their influence and media power to push restrictive legislation.

Dave West's research shows how southern Congressmen who were firmly in the hands of cotton fiber producers helped in the restrictive efforts. His findings add to the body of evidence that there was a concerted effort on the part of special interests to eliminate competition from hemp.

The Schlichten documents reveal several important issues. First, industrialists were aware that America's forests were in danger and not inexhaustible near three quarters of a century ago. However, market conditions and subsidized lumber from the National Forests was reflected in a low price. Today only one million acres of primeval land is left of of eight hundred million only four centuries ago. These letters show that industrialists refused to consider alternatives to the ravaging of the forestlands.

Now that the forests have been cut, the paper mills and chip plants are running out of material, manufacturers are beginning to consider hemp as a raw material.

Fiber Wars:

The Extinction of Kentucky Hemp

by David P. West, Ph.D

THE SCENE IS A DAIRY FARM in east-central Wisconsin, August 21, 1993. On its fifth pass over the farm, the helicopter comes in low and hovers. The farmer's terrified, triple-A, artificially inseminated cow tries to leap the fence, breaks her leg and in three days is dead, calf lost. The newspaper report explains that "Local authorities have been using the National Guard helicopters in the area to search for wild marijuana patches." According to their press release, the Wisconsin Department of Narcotic Enforcement's Project CEASE removed 9.3 million hemp plants this year in Wisconsin. "Hemp," they explain, "is the plant from which marijuana is extracted."[1]

Since 1983, when the program first began, CEASE has employed Sheriff's deputies, the U.S. Army Reserves, National Guard and law officers of the Wisconsin State Division of Narcotics Enforcement to search and destroy "wild marijuana:" 3 tons in '83; 22 in '84; 41 in '85; 104 in '86; 165 in '87; 113.7 in '88 (estimated, "conservatively," to be worth $113.3 million on the illegal market).[2] More recently, plant counts rather than tonnage have been reported: 9.3 million plants pulled up in 1993.

Hemp, cannabis, has become a pariah and neither environmental groups nor professional plant breeders dare association. Plant breeders could contribute some factual information to the discussion of the variation that exists within the genus, *Cannabis*, but researchers in the United States find it virtually impossible to obtain permit number 225 issued by the Drug Enforcement Agency and required to legally grow and conduct research on any cannabis[3] plant. No one in agriculture has been able to obtain this permit for decades because cannabis is a Schedule One narcotic. Ironically, the state where the cow fell victim to the War on Drugs was once the number one producer of hemp.[4] And nobody smoked it.

There is a lesion in our national memory banks regarding the role of this plant in our history.[5] How do we reconcile the heinous character of this plant with the fact that George Washington and Thomas Jefferson were dedicated hemp farmers? (The former said, "Sow it everywhere" and the latter invented a hemp brake.) How is it that hemp was safe enough to be used as legal tender in colonial times, yet the curators of the Smithsonian Institute found it necessary to remove all reference to hemp from their displays?

Hemp is the common name for the fiber-yielding plant botanists call *Cannabis sativa*. "Cannabis" and "canvas" have the same etymological root; hemp canvas covered the pioneer's conestoga wagons later to be turned into Levi's new kind of trouser. Hemp was to navies what titanium is to modern military technology. Napoleon invaded Russia to cut off England's access to Russian hemp upon which the British navy depended. The USS Constitution used sixty tons of hemp in its riggings and sails. Because of its strategic importance, there were laws both in England and the colonies at various times *requiring* the cultivation of hemp. Hemp fiber is resistant to rot, making it the fiber of choice for maritime cordage. In fact, hemp has been humanity's premier cordage fiber throughout most of history; "hemp" was often used generically for fiber from any source.[6] What is the truth about hemp? And why is it growing wild all over Wisconsin and other states and under attack by helicopter? How did this plant, so valued by the Founding Fathers, become an outcast, a pariah?

The real story of hemp is not a story of drugs, but of "Fiber Wars," an age-old battle for markets among alternative fibers. Plant fibers have played a central role in international relations throughout history. European powers rose and fell with the vagaries of the fabric trade. The looms of Antwerp and Bruges ran on Flemish flax and English wool. In the 1700s, an upstart East Indian fiber made from seed hair threatened the British wool industry. Laws were passed banning its importation.

Protectionism would not prevail, however, since the British East India Company stood to gain so much from the new fiber. Bertha Dodge in her historical monograph, *Cotton: The Plant That Would Be King*, explains that "By 1719, this industry had grown to such proportions that the woolen interests, through Parliament, again tried to have the importation of raw cotton interdicted, this time meeting with no success whatever."[7] Cotton became a world power,[8] and is credited as the single greatest force in the early economic development of the U.S.:

> While the immigration of people and particularly capital into the United States played an important part in our growth in the thirty years after 1815, it was the growth of the cotton textile industry and the demand for cotton which was decisive.... The vicissitudes of the cotton trade—speculative expansion of the 1818, the radical decline in prices in the 1820's and the boom in the 1830's—were the most important influence upon the varying rates of growth of the economy during the period. ... The demands for western foodstuffs and northeastern services and manufactures were basically dependent upon the income received from the cotton trade.[9]

Before cotton entered the arena, linen from flax had been the highest valued fabric, its usage tracing into prehistory. Flax lost its preeminence when a series of mechanical inventions shifted the economics of cotton fabric production, and commenced the industrial revolution. The fly-shuttle, invented by John Kay in 1733, speeded up the looms, increasing the demand for thread, a demand met by the invention of the spinning jenny by John Wyatt in 1738. These tools could be concatenated and driven by water or steam in the new, centralized work environment, the factory. Whitney's cotton gin appeared in the 1790's after which the raw cotton to supply the needs of English factories came increasingly from the American south. "The ten bales reaching England in 1784 from the new United States... had become about one-third of a million bales by 1820, over two and a half million by 1860."[10] Whitney's machine, by mechanizing the de-linting of Upland cotton, the American variety, engendered the slave-based plantation system needed for labor-intensive cotton agriculture.

The changes in cotton manufacture transformed fiber economics. Cotton quickly took over markets previously dominated by flax, and to a lesser degree by hemp, in the U.S. and Europe. Flax culture nearly disappeared in the U.S. before 1850. It endured as a cottage industry, each rural household having its own small plot for domestic use. "From a series of papers written between 1787 and 1791, by Mr. Tench Coxe, Commissioner of Revenue... it appears that manufactures from flax and hemp had become an established and very important [cottage] industry; he enumerates, among articles 'manufactured in a household way,' seines and nets of various kinds, twine and pack thread, sail-cloth, tow-cloth, white and checked shirting, sheeting, toweling, table-linen, bed-ticks, hosiery, sewing thread, and seine-thread lace."[11] A coarse fabric, "tow-cloth," made from hemp was used for summer clothing, but "It is doubtful if American hemp will ever again be used for such purposes, not so much because flax linen is a better product, but because the cheapness of cotton has enabled this fiber to supersede both hemp and flax in common manufactures in the domestic economy."[12]

Flax and hemp (and jute and ramie, which we will not discuss) are "soft" bast fibers, fiber found in the stem of the plant. Hemp fiber bundles are longer than those of flax, but flax fiber contains less lignin and is therefore more flexible and makes a finer fabric. The best hemp can be superior to flax for fine fabric. Flax is generally stronger than hemp, which is stronger than jute. Agronomically, hemp's yields are generally twice those of flax.[13] The strength and quality of either fiber are highly dependent on the seed variety, the conditions of growth, time of harvest and manner of retting and other post-harvest handling.

Since antiquity, bast fibers have been obtained by "retting" and "breaking" the stem. Retting (rotting) is the microbial decomposition of the mowed-down stems left lie in the field in the damp fall.[14] Retting can also be done in pools or running water, which produces higher quality, lighter colored fiber, but can also create an odor problem from anaerobic decomposition. The finest grades of hemp, such as the Italian, were produced by water-retting. The Navy preferred water-retted hemp for its riggings:

The Federal Government in 1841 authorized a bounty, which allowed for the payment of not more than $280 per ton for American water-retted hemp, provided it was suitable for naval cordage. Many of the planters prepared large pools and water-retted the hemp they produced. But the work was so hard on Negroes that the practice was abandoned. Many Negroes died of pneumonia contracted from working in the hemp-pools in the winter, and the mortality became so great among hemp hands that the increase in value of the hemp did not equal the loss in Negroes.[15]

Water-retting never caught on in the U.S..

After retting, the fiber is separated from the cellulosic pith (hurds or shives) by "breaking," described as one of the hardest jobs known to man, hence, Thomas Jefferson's effort at bringing a degree of mechanical advantage to hemp breaking. In 1896, Charles Dodge of the USDA Office of Fiber Investigations mentions that "nearly 300 patents have been issued in the United States for machines for breaking hemp, many of which have proved absolute failures...."[16] The hurds are cleaned from the fiber by "scutching" and the fiber is further refined by "hackling" before being spun into twine and rope.

Flax and hemp overlap in many characteristics. Although the plants are botanically dissimilar, without microscopic or chemical examination, their fibers can only be distinguished by the direction in which the they twist upon wetting: hemp will rotate clockwise; flax, counterclockwise. Flax is a dual usage crop, with varieties grown for their stem fiber, and other distinct varieties for the oil in their seed. This is also true of hemp. Both plants produce very similar drying oils in their seed, oils with a high percentage of linolenic acid, used until mid-century in paints. Whereas linseed oil became a major industry, an industry based on hempseed oil was never established in the U.S.[17] The oils are also valued for nutritional and even medicinal qualities.[18]

Flax was called the "pioneer plant" because it was the first crop grown on cleared land. However, it did not do well if grown successively on the same land. As a result, flax moved west with the pioneer migration to Minnesota, North Dakota and the Canadian plains for the oilseed types, and to Michigan and Oregon for the fiber types. The decline in productivity when flax was grown repeatedly led to the belief that flax was "hard" on the soil, and it was not recommended to be grown more than once in ten years on the same land. Eventually, it was demonstrated that the poor performance was due to a *Fusarium* fungus that persisted in the soil and caused plants to wilt. Flax's struggle with a host of pathogens limited its progress.

Weed control in flax was also a problem. Hemp was often used before a flax crop because it left the land free of weeds and in good condition. Hemp, it was said, was "good" to the soil because it could be grown successively and improved the soil with its deep penetrating tap-root. Although hemp demands substantial nutrition for growth, most of the nutrients are returned to the soil when the crop is dew-retted.[19]

Cotton competed more directly with flax than with hemp, as flax had been used for fine fabric and, "The cotton industry had considerable interest in hemp, since it was manufactured locally into baling cloth, rope and clothing for Negroes."[20] But having been displaced by cotton as fabric, flax of coarser grade pursued hemp's non-maritime markets. Until 1872, a duty on imported jute protected flax and hemp. Its repeal was a concession to manufacturing interests that opened the door to a cheaper raw material for bagging and set back the nascent domestic fiber industry. One flax worker saw it this way:

> So a conflict rages between jute and flax, and so evenly balanced are the forces, that flax is able to compete for a portion of the cotton baling; yet jute has a slight preponderance, perhaps altogether due to the advantage of larger capital, and better organization and division of labor, and therefore jute manufacture is successful, and flax milling comparatively depressed. It is a conflict between the seaboard and the interior; between the heavy manufacturer on the one side, and the small manufacturer and farmer on the other.[12]

Today, we have lost sensitivity to the subtlety of natural fibers. But their differences and suitability for specific uses were an aspect of daily life to our ancestors. Since the time of George Washington the government had tried to encourage domestic coarse fiber industries for baling cloth, twines, and cordage. Tariffs protecting the hemp industry were passed in 1789, 1816 and 1861.[22] Hemp was a strategic material in that its principal use was in the shrouds, cables and sails of ships. But most of the hemp used by the Navy was imported from Italy and Russia. In 1824, domestic hemp was pitted against Russian hemp by rigging the *USS Constitution* on one side with American and the other with Russian grown hemp, "and after being thus worn for nearly a year, it was found, on examination, that the Russian rope, in every instance, after being much worn, looked better and wore more equally and evenly than the American." But the commander said, "the difference between them was not so great as to warrant a declaration that the proof was conclusive in favor of the Russian...."[23] Imported hemp continued to be favored by the Navy and domestic hemp was used mostly for twines and as oakum for caulking.[24] Today, aficionados of ship restoration insist on authentic hemp, witness the *Alysha* in Galveston harbor.

In 1878, New Jersey offered a bounty of $6.00 extra per ton of hemp stalks, $7.00 per ton for flax and $10.00 for ramie. But without tariff protection, the labor requirement for these fibers put them at a disadvantage against fibers produced using cheap labor in the tropics. Manila hemp, abaca, from a relative of the banana, took hemp's maritime markets. Rope made of this fiber did not require tarring, floated on water and was cheaper. By 1911, the nation was spending $16,000,000 importing tropical fibers. This drain on the economy had been recognized early on and in response the USDA ran several programs to promote domestic replacements and offered prizes for mechanizations.

Unable to compete with cotton, fiber flax production declined. But oilseed flax culture expanded. Due to chemical properties bestowed by its fatty acid composition, linseed oil was the principal ingredient of paints, varnishes and, after its invention by Frederick Walton in 1863, linoleum. The straw leftover from the oilseed crop yielded an inferior, coarse fiber that was usually burned. The flax industry needed an outlet for this byproduct: "With a present demand for 35,000,000 yards of bagging for cotton, while flax-fiber enough to produce it is thrown away, the effort to extend the production of flax bagging would seem to be worth official consideration."[25]

Displaced by cotton, in going after the baling cloth market flax was displacing hemp, as was cheap jute. Before jute, hemp had been the baling cloth fiber:

> At a time when the country was producing 75,000 tons of hemp fiber, jute was little known in the American market, and this vast product was utilized in the manufacture of bagging and burlaps, the better qualities being employed for cordage. It is doubtful if hemp fiber can be produced sufficiently cheap to compete with jute butts at one and one-half cents per pound, but its larger employment in cordage manufacture would extend its culture, and enable it to recover a part, at least, of the ground it has lost as an American fiber industry. A rough product that could be cheaply produced would be sufficiently good for binding-twine manufacture, and the same quality of fiber could be employed with advantage in the production of cheaper grades of small cordage that are now made from imported jute, because of its [hemp's] superior strength and less liability to deterioration when stored unused for any length of time. More carefully cultivated and prepared it could compete with the hemps of other countries in the manufacture of the finer grades of cordage and with more careful retting, in water, it might be again woven into fabrics.[26]

The usability of the fiber from oilseed flax varieties was a matter of some debate. According to some, "It is futile to expect that fiber and seed can be produced from the same crop."[27] The Office of Fiber Investigations agreed, in 1893: "Seed culture and fiber culture are so distinctly different that the farmer who essays to grow fiber by the same methods he employs in growing seed can only make an ignominious failure and he will do well to avoid the experiment."[28] Yet the market was there, materials were being imported, and oilseed flax had a byproduct. The Flax and Hemp Spinners and Growers Association president, A. R. Turner, was optimistic: "it seems a safe statement to make that it is possible to preserve all the fiber from flax even though it may be sown primarily for seed."[29] But flax fiber from the oilseed crop, as it came to the spinners, was of low quality and often dirty. As a byproduct, the quality of the fiber was given no priority and the method of harvest for seed left the stems tangled and soiled. Cotton producers did not care for it. In 1879, it was reported that the "New York Cotton Board will receive no cotton whatever baled with flax bagging, giving as a reason that flax bagging is so dirty it makes a difference in the price of the cotton."[30] For fiber from oilseed flax to find a market, several technological developments were needed: "The special classes of improved machines demanded by this industry, in establishing an American practice, are (1) a flax-pulling machine to do away with the laborious and costly hand pulling; (2) an economical thresher, to save the seed without injury to the straw; and (3) an improved scutching machine to prepare the fiber for market."[31] Similar technological developments were targeted for hemp, which the USDA was advancing aggressively. In fact, hemp yielded to mechanization more rapidly. In 1905, a mechanical hemp brake was "the first machine having sufficient capacity to be commercially practical that has cleaned bast fiber in an entirely satisfactory manner."[32]

Meanwhile, on other fronts, cotton was not doing so well. After the Civil War destroyed the foundation of southern agriculture, the plantation, the South was led, inexorably, to a debilitating economic dependence on cotton monoculture Gilbert C. Fite, in his book *Cotton Fields No More*, has presented a detailed chronicle of the role of cotton in the agrarian society that replaced the plantation—sharecropping on small, tenant farms:

> Southern farmers...became "trapped" in a cotton economy. Without land or equipment the newly freed blacks, and many whites as well, sold their labor in exchange for a share of the crop which they produced on credit. This system increased the cost of nearly everything they consumed and fastened a yoke of permanent and oppressive debt upon hundreds of thousands of farmers, both white and black...

> To most southern farmers in the 1880s and 1890s, cotton seemed to provide the best, and perhaps the only, means of acquiring [consumer] goods...

> So farmers produced cotton, even though increased production periodically depressed prices and encouraged them to raise even more cotton

in hopes of gaining needed cash or credit. The result was low net incomes and low standards of living...

Moreover, the entire credit structure had been built on the production of cotton. Money was advanced to growers on the crop, and it was the only collateral accepted by most merchants and landowners."[33]

As a result, Fite explains, "the living standard of so many farmers in the South was not a relative matter but one of absolute poverty."[34] Attempts to promote the diversification of southern agriculture were unsuccessful due, Fite says, to "the reluctance of planters to let their sharecroppers and tenants grow any commercial crop other than cotton."[35] Cotton was "good as cash" and sharecropping created an insatiable need for it. Furthermore, the extreme social stratification that had characterized the South before the war persisted with sharecropping. "If the 40,000 to 50,000 large farmers and planters, making up only between 2 and 3 percent of all farmers in the South, enjoyed a fairly comfortable existence in the late nineteenth and early twentieth centuries, most of the others faced extremely hard times."[36] The USDA worked to change southern agriculture with programs emphasizing diversification. Fibers were given considerable attention: "There are several fiber plants, concerning which further authoritative information is most desirable, as their production or utilization will open up new industries, particularly in the South, where there is such a need of diversity in agricultural production."[37] Where cotton reigned, these efforts met with little success and much resistance.

While the South's cotton economy struggled, following the Civil War, hemp culture spread, with active federal assistance, north into Illinois, Iowa, Ohio, New York, eventually to Wisconsin and Minnesota, west to Nebraska and California, and also, briefly, south. In his pastoral account of post-bellum life in the hemp growing region of Kentucky, James L. Allan recalls that "...the long interruption of agriculture in the South had resulted in scarcity of cotton; so that the earnest cry came to Kentucky for hemp at once to take many of its places."[38] Flax fiber also enjoyed a short resurgence. Both fibers were promoted by the USDA's Office of Fiber Investigations, established in 1890. Its first Director,

Charles Dodge, asserted "There is no reason why hemp culture should not extend over a dozen States and the product used in manufactures which now employ thousands of tons of imported fibers."[39]

In 1895, Dodge mentions that "In the past two years there has been an increasing demand for information relating to hemp culture, and experiments looking to its production have been carried on in localities where previously its culture was unknown, notably in extreme Southern States, which are large cotton producers."[40] In 1901, the report tells that "During the past two years hemp has been grown successfully on a small scale near Houston, Texas, and with improved methods of handling the crop it seems probable that it may become a profitable industry in that region."[41]

Hemp growing in the South did not proceed, however. Hemp can be grown in southerly climes, but worldwide the greatest fiber production is in more northern latitudes, between the 30th and 45th parallels, in Russia, Hungary, China and Wisconsin. In contrast to cotton, a southern and even tropical fiber, hemp and flax are the temperate fibers. When grown in the South, it is as winter crops.

U.S. shipbuilding declined after the Civil War and with it the hemp industry, but a new impetus for increasing hemp production came with the invention of a binder for the harvest of wheat and other small grains requiring a strong binding-twine for which hemp was ideally suited. Hemp's success, Dodge's Office of Fiber Investigations recognized, depended on successful mechanization of harvesting, breaking, scutching and hackling. In 1896, they "hoped before another year to bring together for the first time the promising hemp-cleaning devices that have been brought to public notice for an official trial."[42] In 1899, the USDA Yearbook states:

> There is a reasonable prospect of establishing an extensive hemp industry in the United States on new lines, involving the use of either a taller variety or two crops of the short variety, growing the crop on large areas of cheap land, plowing deep, putting on the necessary fertilizers, reaping and breaking by machinery, and using the process of water-retting.[43]

And, in 1902, the Yearbook told how

In Nebraska, where the [hemp] industry is being established, a new and important step has been taken in cutting the crop with an ordinary mowing machine. A simple attachment which bends the stalks over in the direction in which the machine is going facilitates the cutting...The cost of cutting hemp in this manner is 50 cents per acre, as compared with $3 to $4 per acre, the rates paid for cutting by hand in Kentucky."[44]

Hemp culture moved north under USDA auspices. It was first grown experimentally in Wisconsin in 1908. The results were so encouraging that they were repeated and expanded over the following decade. Hemp caught on rapidly among farmers who observed the experiments near Waupon, in east-central Wisconsin, and noticed that it cleaned the fields of weeds. Wisconsin Agriculture Experiment Station researcher Andrew Wright was given responsibility for promoting the growth of the industry. He reported on the progress in 1918:

When the work with hemp was begun in Wisconsin, there were no satisfactory machines for harvesting, spreading, binding, or breaking. All of these processes were performed by hand. Due to such methods, the hemp industry in the United States had all but disappeared. As it was realized from the very beginning of the work in Wisconsin that no permanent progress could be made so long as it was necessary to depend upon hand labor, immediate attention was given to solving the problem of power machinery. Nearly every kind of hemp machine was studied and tested. The obstacles were great, but through the cooperation of experienced hemp men and one large harvesting machinery company, this problem has been nearly solved. *The hemp crop can now be handled entirely by machinery* (italics added).[45]

The future looked promising. The Wisconsin Hemp Order was formed on October 17, 1917, at Ripon, "to promote the general welfare of the hemp industry in the state."[46] The key to the industry's growth was the organization of the central mill located with rail access. In 1921, the USDA reported that

> The organized hemp growers of Wisconsin, working in cooperation with the field agent of fiber investigations [Andrew Wright], have so improved the quality and standardized the grades of hemp fiber produced there that it has found a market even in dull times. The hemp acreage in that State has been kept up, although there has been a reduction in every other hemp-producing area throughout the world.[47]

Mechanization and the mill organization quickly raised Wisconsin to the status of number one hemp producing state. California also initiated hemp production and reported the highest yields: a ton of dew-retted fiber per acre.

Production increased during wartime due to the increased demand by the Navy and reduction in foreign sources, but tended to declined in peacetime, when imported sisal, jute and abaca cut into hemp's traditional markets. In 1901, it was observed that "No horticultural varieties are recognized in this country. Nearly all of the hemp grown here in recent years is of Chinese origin."[48] In fact, it was known that introduced foreign strains had to be grown "for at least three generations (three successive years) in the country where it is to be grown for fiber"[49] to achieve satisfactory adaptation to the local growing environment. In an effort to support the industry in the face of foreign competition, the USDA ran an aggressive hemp breeding program under the direction of Lyster Dewey. Germ plasm was collected from around the world,[50] and breeding selection was initiated in 1912. Several varieties of hemp were recognized by their points of origin:

> that cultivated in Kentucky and having a hollow stem, being the most common. China hemp, with slender stems, growing very erect, has a wide range of culture. Smyrna hemp is adapted to cultivation over a still wider range and Japanese hemp is beginning to be cultivated, particularly in California, where it reaches a height of 15 feet. Russian and Italian seed have been experimented with, but the former produces a short stalk, while the latter only grows to a medium height. A small

quantity of Piedmontese hemp seed from Italy was distributed by the Department in 1893, having been received through the Chicago Exposition....[51]

The American landrace, "Kentucky hemp" is believed to derive from Chinese germplasm. Its hollow, fluted stem was a favored characteristic for good fiber hemp. Dewey initiated his breeding program using the Kentucky landrace together with the internationally collected germplasm. Progress was steady:

1917: "The crop of hempseed last fall, estimated at about 45,000 bushels, is the largest produced in the United States since 1859. A very large proportion of it was from improved strains developed by this bureau in the hempseed selection plats at Arlington and Yarrow Farms."[52]

1918: "Early maturing varieties, chiefly of Italian origin, are being grown at Madison, Wisconsin, in cooperation with the Wisconsin Agricultural Experiment Station. This is the third year of selection for some varieties, and the results give promise of the successful production in that State of seed of hemp fully equal to the Ferrara of northern Italy. "[53]

1919: "The second-generation hybrid Ferramington, combining the height and long internodes of Kymington with the earliness and heavy seed yield of Ferrara, gives promise of a good fiber type of hemp that may ripen seed as far north as Wisconsin."[54]

1920: "The work of breeding improved strains of hemp is being continued at Arlington Farm, Va., and all previous records were broken in the selection plats of 1919. The three best strains, Kymington, Chington and Tochimington, averaged, respectively, 14 feet 11 inches, 15 feet 5 inches, and 15 feet 9 inches, *while the tallest individual plant was 19 feet* (italics added). The improvement by selection is shown not alone in increased height but also in longer internodes, yielding fiber of better quality and increased quantity."[55]

In 1928, Wisconsin saved the Kentucky germplasm when the seed crop in Kentucky was lost due to weather conditions:

> In exceptional flood of the Kentucky River in June and early July, 1928, destroyed nearly all of the seedhemp crop. Fortunately, Wisconsin hemp growers had seed left over from previous years, but studies on hempseed germination conducted in 1927–8 indicated that most of the seed more than 3 years old germinated very poorly.[56]

Wright emphasized the limitation on the Wisconsin industry from the need to obtain seed from Kentucky because the available varieties did not mature seed as far north as Wisconsin. The variety "Ferramington," coming from a cross between the fine, flaxen hemp of northern Italy, and varieties of the Chinese type, showed promise for seed production in Wisconsin. Of Ferramington, Dewey wrote, it "has been tried in Wisconsin, where it gave a very good crop nearly two weeks earlier than the main hemp harvest."[57]

Much of the feral hemp that is the target of CEASE today may be descended from Ferramington and from Kymington another variety, also early maturing which was bred using the Minnesota hemp variety known as "Minnesota 8." Since the fiber crop was cut before seed matured, raising hemp for fiber was a separate operation from seed production. Seed from Kentucky continued to supply the Wisconsin industry until its demise.

While hemp was expanding and mechanizing, flax was in decline. A fiber industry was established in Michigan in 1880 by James Livingston who later expanded it to Oregon. But the spinning of flax into thread for fabric ceased around 1920 after which the fiber was used primarily for upholstery tow.[58] The constant problem for flax was susceptibility to a variety of diseases, including races of wilt, canker, rust and blights. "The story of flax improvement centers primarily about the successful battle against diseases that threatened to wipe out the industry completely."[59]

Flax contributed greatly to the sciences of plant breeding and plant pathology as efforts were brought to bear on the disease problem. Eminent pathologists, like E. C. Stakman at the University of Minnesota, honed their science on the disease problems of flax. A great feat of plant breeding and genetics is commemorated by "Plot 30," preserved at North Dakota State University in Fargo, where a technique for breeding disease resistance into crops was first demonstrated. Although elite varieties with resistance to flax wilt were bred by H. L. Bolley at the turn of the century, the flax industry continued to decline as markets were taken by petroleum-based materials.[60]

The USDA investigated other uses for hemp and flax in an effort to bolster the industries in the face of competition from imported tropical fibers. Both fibers had long been used for paper: the first drafts of the U.S. Constitution were written on hemp paper; bibles are often printed on hemp paper because of its light weight, strength and durability. Paper made from hemp fiber is difficult to rip by hand and does not yellow and turn brittle as does paper from wood pulp. Efforts at using byproduct flax straw met with mixed results. "Flax straw was found to cook with great difficulty, to require a very high percentage of bleach, and to screen badly, but could possibly be used for cheap wrappers."[61] In time, leftover flax straw found a use as cigarette paper. In Europe, today, cigarette papers are commonly made from hemp, often in a blend with flax.

In 1916, a USDA bulletin showed that a byproduct of hemp fiber production, the high cellulose hurds, which were burned as the fuel source in the hemp mills, could also be turned into paper.[62] In 1917, the USDA reported that

> Because of the scarcity of raw materials for paper making and the increasing tonnage of hemp hurds, the matter was placed before a large paper company, with the result that the entire year's output of a hemp-breaking mill has been contracted for by a commercial firm.[63]

Recently, Donald Wirtshafter, hemp activist, lawyer and founder of The Ohio Hempery, has discovered among the archives of the Scripps newspaper family a remarkable 1917 correspondence from a Mr. Ed Chase to E. W. Scripps regarding an invention of one G. W. Schlichten.[64] Schlichten invented a hemp decorticating machine. A decorticating machine is able to separate the fiber from the hurds of unretted stems. The resulting fiber has higher quality and brighter color than dew-retted fiber. Chase has this to say: "I have seen a wonderful, yet simple, invention. I believe it will revolutionize many of the processes of feeding, clothing and supplying other wants of mankind." The cost of Schlichten's operation located at the Timken Ranch in California's Imperial Valley was detailed:

> One of Schlichten's machine's will produce per day (two shifts of eight hours each), as follows:

> Two tons of fiber worth about .... $ 600.00
> Five　"　" hurds　"　"　........................ $　27.50
> One　"　" tops, leaves, etc. worth about................ $　　5.50
> 　　　Total .... $ 633.00

As an aside, it is interesting to note that a ton of *marijuana*, sold as a green manure because of its nutrient content, was worth only $5.50 in 1917. Today, CEASE would no doubt estimate the value at around a million. It is strange that this opportunity was overlooked since the medicinal value of cannabis had been recognized in both veterinary and human medicine since antiquity.[65] In 1917, "medicinal" varieties were recognized as distinct from the fiber types of cannabis. They knew that the fiber crop had no utility for that application. Whereas flax has two major types, fiber and oilseed, hemp has three. The flax industry understood this.

Chase goes on to explain the value of this invention to his employer, Scripps:

ADVANTAGES OF HEMP HURDS
FOR PAPER STOCK

FIRST: We make paper from an annual and thus help to preserve the forests, the streams and the soils.

SECOND: We make paper at lower cost than is possible from wood, for the following reasons:

　A. Wood must have the bark, knots, etc., removed. The hurds are ready for the digester, when, as a by-product, they leave the Schlichten machine.

　B. ...less caustic soda....

　C. Sulphite must be mixed with ground wood pulp; but not with the pulp from these hurds.

Furthermore, hemp paper, Chase says, "is of better quality than newsprint stock."

As optimistic as this report was, it apparently met with an impasse and was not pursued. Wisconsin's hemp industry produced more hurds than were used in firing the boilers. Excess hurds created a fire hazard and were given away to farmers for bedding.[66] By the mid-Thirties, technological innovation which allowed the pulping of Southern pines alleviated the pulp shortage. But why the Schlichten invention was not pursued further in 1917 remains a great mystery.[67]

The Twenties were the apex of the hemp industry in Wisconsin. Mills were operating on both the east and west sides of the state.[68] Andrew Wright, who was responsible for much of the industry's growth, could proudly point out that "Wisconsin has...more hemp mills than all other states combined."[69] The growth of the industry had come as a result of a concentrated effort at mechanization: "By the simple mechanical process of hackling, now being done by very efficient power-driven machines, hemp fiber is reduced to a condition closely resembling the coarser grades of flax and may be spun on flax-spinning machinery."[70] No further progress in this direction was made, however. By 1931, with the nation in collapse, hemp was still pinched between cotton, flax and the tropical imports and Dewey specifically cites spinning machinery as the critical limitation:

Owing partly to the resistant character of the fiber itself and partly to the lack of development of special machinery for spinning hemp, this fiber is not spun as efficiently and cheaply as cotton and jute. The average price per pound of scutched hemp fiber is nearly twice the average price of jute and less than the price of cotton, but hemp yarns are more expensive than those of cotton as well as jute.[71]

It was the step between scutching and spinning which cost. This was a critical technological obstacle that would not be overcome before other, political, impediments would stop hemp's further progress.

Federal assistance had played a major role in overcoming the technological hurdles which had limited hemp prior to the twentieth century and, had the resources been directed to this need, the fate of hemp as a crop might have been radically different. But flax and hemp were struggling for the same fiber markets while cotton was facing loss of its territory to a new threat. The competition between flax and hemp was a minor skirmish on the fringe of the major battle of Fiber Wars.

For cotton, the first decades of the twentieth century were a roller coaster ride of over production and low price. The South was trapped in an economic maze of small, tenant farms, insufficient mechanization, under capitalization and the surplus/low-price spiral of cotton monoculture. "Well, farmers have never made money," Calvin Coolidge said.[72]

That agriculture had not progressed in the South as it had in the North was clear from the Census Bureau Report of 1900. Average investment in farm implements and machinery were: Alabama, $39; North Carolina, $40; Georgia, $44; in contrast to: Kansas, $170; Nebraska, $205; Iowa, $253.[73]

> Between 1855 and 1930 farmers in the corn belt had reduced the man-hours necessary to produce an acre of corn (about 40 bushels) from 33.6 to 6.9 hours. Even the most efficient cotton growers in Texas, who used more and bigger machinery, had only cut the man-hours for an acre of cotton from 148 to 72 in the same period. Thus, while corn growers had reduced man-hours by nearly four-fifths, cotton farmers had cut the needed labor by only one-half. And most cotton growers in the Southeast had not done nearly that well.[74]

The problem was that cotton did not easily adapt to mechanization. In 1903, a historian of the American cotton industry wrote:

> Cotton harvesting machinery would be of incalculable value, but an efficient machine for picking cotton has yet to be invented. It is a difficult problem for the inventor, because picking cotton is something like gathering raspberries, and even American genius has boggled at it. There have been many fruitless efforts, but I am assured that there is not to-day in the United States a single machine with which any planter would even attempt to pick cotton.[75]

It was not just a matter of inventing machines to replace muscle power and increase the efficiency of the process:

> Before complete mechanization of cotton production could occur, other changes were necessary. It was important, for example, to breed a cotton plant on which the bolls would develop higher on the stalk and open more evenly.... Chemicals were required to control weeds and to defoliate the cotton plant before harvest.... Entomologists and engineers needed to join efforts to develop proper pesticides....Before full mechanization of the cotton crop could be achieved, the combined contributions of engineers, chemists, fertilizer specialists, plant breeders, entomologists, agronomists and other scientists were necessary. Full mechanization also required some changes in farm organization throughout much of the cotton belt.[76]

In other words, they had, virtually, to start over with cotton. The development of insecticidal chemicals was particularly critical because the boll weevil had found its way from Mexico in the 1890s and had become the scourge of cotton growers. Today, because of insect pests, cotton remains the most polluting, chemically intensive agricultural crop grown by man.[77]

Flax also amassed a coterie of researchers dedicated to its problems. "The linseed crushers realized that their industry was entirely dependent on the success of the flax crop in the Middle Northwest, where it had made its last stand. It was with the cooperation of the flaxseed crushers and the paint manufacturers that Bolley was encouraged to carry on his notable work in the breeding of wilt-resistant flax."[78] This situation stands in marked contrast to that with hemp, of which Wright wrote, "Wisconsin hemp is, as yet, entirely free from attacks by insects and diseases. Not one report of injuries to the crop from insects or plant disease has been received."[79] In countries where hemp continues to be grown to the present, it has no serious pests.[80] In fact, hemp is recognized as a deterrent to insects. In some countries, the leaves have traditionally been placed in grain and linen as a repellent to insects.[81]

Since cotton was the basis of the economy of the South, and in spite of the need to reinvent the crop, it was to cotton that government efforts were directed as a means to moving the South out of its economic doldrums. As such, the USDA became increasingly an agency for southern economic development. Unfortunately, the agriculture programs exacerbated the problem by increasing yields when cotton surpluses were preventing an adequate price to growers. The situation had improved somewhat for a few years around 1910, but good cotton prices always resulted in maximum planting which resulted in surplus and price depression. The programs generally enhanced the fortunes of the large landowners who needed assistance the least.

Encouragement from the agricultural universities and the USDA for diversification away from cotton monoculture met resistance, in spite of major campaigns waged to persuade farmers to voluntarily reduce their cotton acreage in order to reduce the surplus. These efforts were largely unsuccessful: "The usual cry for reduction of cotton acreage will go up, but experience has proved that this cry will produce no results. Cotton raising is as firmly embedded in the system of the Southern ruralist as sea-faring is to the coast-dweller of New England."[82]

Added to this, a new specter had appeared on the horizon, a new combatant in Fiber Wars. Synthetic polymers made from natural cellulose (first from cotton lint, later from wood pulp) were discovered in the late nineteenth century. By 1905, the first synthetic fiber, rayon, had appeared in England. DuPont introduced rayon fabric around 1917.

Rayon production in the United States increased from 10 to 380 million pounds between 1920 and 1939 and approximately doubled during the war period. By 1941, United States production of rayon was equivalent to 1,350,000 bales of cotton.[83]

Once again technological innovation altered the playing field: in the 30 years after its appearance in the U.S., the number of filaments per 150 denier yarn would go from 12 to 225, "even finer than those spun by a silk worm."[84] Cost per pound of rayon filament yarn would go from $2.92 in 1920–21 to $0.55 in 1944. Rayon had another advantage: waste at the mill was one tenth that of cotton.[85]

Synthetic fibers pushed existing fiber domains against each other, as cotton had a century earlier. Many agricultural products had already met their demise in the chemical laboratory, beginning with natural dyes like indigo. Writing of the chemical revolution, William J. Hale was confident that

> The replacement of cotton and woolen garments by cloth of silk-like fibre [rayon] is proceeding at assured rates. Eventually both cotton and wool will meet their Waterloo as far as finest cloth is concerned. Thus the land given over to the cultivation of cotton and eventually that to the grazing of sheep is slowly but surely passing out of the picture.[86]

Synthetics were not agricultural products, so they were completely outside the pale of agricultural policy, unlike *other* fibers which were vulnerable to changes in agricultural policy when,

> In 1930, hundreds of thousands of southern farmers began to skid from normal hard times to disastrous depression. If observers believed that life could not get worse than it already was for millions of rural residents in the South, they were badly mistaken. A decade of depression was beginning which forced living standards down well below poverty levels experienced for years by many southern farm families.[87]

To counter the immense political power of the moguls of finance and industry, farm cooperatives and populist agrarian political organizations such as the Grange, had arisen. These movements began in the North and West, among wheat and corn farmers. Benefiting by their example, southern cotton organizations[88] had emerged which succeeded in placing elected officials in key positions:

> After the Democrats won control of the House of Representatives in 1930, Marvin Jones of Texas became chairman of the House Agriculture Committee. Born on a cotton farm, Jones had escaped the poverty of the farm by studying law and going into politics.... In 1933 another southerner, Ellison D. "Cotton Ed" Smith, assumed the chairmanship of the Agriculture Committee in the Senate....He was a staunch supporter of legislation that would help cotton and tobacco growers. Another

powerful southerner vitally interested in farm welfare was Senator John H. Bankhead of Alabama.... Besides serving on the Senate Agriculture Committee, he was also named to the important Banking and Currency Committee. The southern position was further strengthened in 1931 when Edward O'Neal, a northern Alabama planter, was elected president of the American Farm Bureau Federation, the nation's most powerful farm organization.[89]

Together, this political block was successful in structuring New Deal legislation to direct public money toward the South's predicament. Ed O'Neal had built a coalition with corn and wheat interests to pressure Congress for legislation addressing the farm crisis. Enacted in 1933, the Agriculture Adjustment Act authorized payments to farmers for not planting seven basic commodity crops: "Three of these basic commodities—cotton, tobacco and rice—were among the South's major commercial crops. While many officials did not consider tobacco a basic commodity, it was included in the bill because of strong political pressure from tobacco-state congressmen."[90] The objective of AAA was explained to cotton farmers in a USDA bulletin: surpluses would be controlled by reducing production, "so that cotton will have the same purchasing power with respect to articles that farmers buy which it had in the period from August 1909 to July 1914."[91] And the taxpayer would pay for the idled land (and still does). Through this and other New Deal legislation, money was redistributed to the South to promote its economic recovery. "By February, 1935 FERA [Federal Emergency Relief Administration] had made rehabilitation loans to 87,350 families of whom 93 percent were in the South."[92] However, the subsidy programs could not overcome the fundamental problem of low cotton prices and the concomitant poverty that resulted from complete economic dependence on one crop: "...between 1936 and 1939 government payments to farmers in...ten southern states rose from about $70 million to $304 million. Indeed, if it had not been for federal payments, southern farmers would have been worse off financially in 1939 than three years earlier."[93]

Because landowners were paid to fallow their land, the burden was transferred to the predominantly black agricultural labor force which was put out of work. This population migrated to northern industrial cities, seeking jobs in the factories and creating the black urban under-class which would explode in the 1960s.

The increasing southern dominance of federal agriculture policy ensured that cotton would receive the research allocation it demanded. And so, in 1933, in a USDA restructuring, the Office of Fiber Investigations was made the Division of Cotton and Other Fibers, and Lyster Dewey's hemp breeding program was terminated. Reporting before his retirement in 1935, Dewey makes his point, matter-of-factly:

> The hemp breeding work, carried on by the Bureau for more than 20 years, was discontinued in 1933, but practical results are still evident in commercial fields. A hemp grower in Kentucky reported a yield of 1750 pounds per acre of clean, dew-retted fiber from 100 acres of the pedi-greed variety Chinamington grown in 1934. This is more than twice the average yield obtained from ordinary unselected hemp seed.[94]

The program had been outstandingly successful, but the need to rein-vent cotton for mechanical handling drew the resources of the USDA, which was also having to divide its activities between agriculture and social welfare programs.[95] Something had to give. Since hemp had few problems, no diseases,[96] no insect threats, most technological hurdles accomplished, there was no large infrastructure dedicated to it. Flax, on the other hand, was still an important oilseed crop—although synthetic materials would soon change that—with serious biological problems, and an influential trade organization, the Flax Institute of America.

The USDA flax program, under the direction of Arthur C. Dillman, was continued. But, "In spite of all the progress made by the plant scien-tists in developing improved strains of flax and their success in fighting plant diseases, the tremendous decline in flaxseed production during the depression years, 1931 to 1938, became a major problem for the [linseed oil] industry."[97]

The same year Lyster Dewey retired, a new supporter of hemp emerged. The National Farm Chemurgic Council was founded in Dearborn, Michigan, in 1935, the brainchild of William Jay Hale, the Dow Chemical Company chemist who had predicted the synthetic replacement of cotton and wool. Hale believed he had a solution to the underlying causes of the farm crisis and the Depression in a new science, chemurgy, "devoted to advancing through applied science the development of new industrial uses for farm-grown materials and the establishment of new farm crops."[98] Hale argued that the farm should be the source of hydrocarbons and raw materials for the chemical industry, rather than non-renewable, fossil sources.[99] Many of the ideas of chemurgy, such as ethanol fuels, are incarnate today in the New Uses Council, dedicated to agricultural diversification. One fruit of the chemurgy movement was the establishment by the Agricultural Adjustment Act of 1938 of four regional USDA laboratories, at Peoria, New Orleans, Philadelphia, and Albany (California):

> "To conduct researches into and to develop new scientific, chemical, and technical uses and new and extended markets and outlets for farm commodities and products and byproducts thereof. Such research and development shall be devoted primarily to those farm commodities in which there are regular or seasonal surpluses and their products and byproducts."

Although hemp was not included in the government program—it had no surplus problem—it was a favorite of chemurgists because it was a potential source of cellulose for the nascent plastics industry.[100] At 67%, hemp exceeds flax in cellulose content.[101] A *Popular Mechanics* article in 1938 raved hemp as the source for 50,000 products, essentially plastics, and called it the "Billion Dollar Crop."[102] Henry Ford, an avid chemurgist, formed a car body of plastic reinforced with hemp fiber.

During the Depression years, protagonists for agriculture, like Hale[103] and George Washington Carver,[104] were struggling against powerful opposition. The struggle was acrimonious. On the other side, big money was fighting, surreptitiously, against a benevolent federal agriculture policy. The use of subterfuge by this faction was exposed when

> A Senate investigation in 1936 found that financial backers of the Farmer's Independence Council included Lamont du Pont...; Alfred P. Sloan, Jr., of General Motors...; and J. N. Pew of the Sun Oil Co.... [Ed] O'Neal branded these men "Wall Street Hayseeds....The Council...went out of existence soon after the Senate exposure.[105]

During this same period, stories appeared in the popular press concerning *marijuana*, said to be the same as hemp. Among African-American, Hispanic and South Asian minorities, the use of cannabis genotypes that produce copious psychoactive resin was popular. In India, where alcohol was illegal, cannabis use was common and ancient, a sacrament in some religious sects. Hashish production in India was under government control. However western society was unfamiliar with it and it was not in demand. As its use spread beyond minorities, cannabis began attracting official attention from the Federal Bureau of Narcotics. Marijuana prohibition took up the slack from declining use of opiates that had been the FBN's *raison d'etre*.[106] While the hemp industry began to take notice of the government's accusations regarding their livelihood, the USDA, with no hemp advocate left in 1937, seemed unaware of any impending threat. The Annual Report simply mentions that

> Helpful information has aided the hemp industry in assisting farmers who have grown hemp during the past year and new companies in processing their hemp. Recommendations have been made to the Navy Department for specifications for American-grown hemp fiber with a view to improving the market for domestic hemp tow.[107]

But a 1936 memo reveals that the "legitimate" uses for cannabis were viewed by the FBN as an obstacle to bringing cannabis within their hegemony:

> The State Department has tentatively agreed to this proposition [regarding international treaties], but before action is taken we shall have to dispose of certain phases of legitimate traffic; for instance, the drug trade still has a small medical need for marijuana, but has agreed to eliminate it entirely. The only place it is used extensively is by the veterinarians, and we can satisfy them by importing their medical needs. We must also satisfy the canary bird seed trade, and the Sherwin Williams Paint Company, which uses hemp seed oil for drying purposes. We are now working with the Department of Commerce in finding substitutes for the legitimate trade, and after that is accomplished, the path will be cleared for the treaties and for federal law.[108]

Apparently, there were no voices from the USDA objecting to this course of action. After Lyster Dewey retired, A. C. Dillman ran the "Other Fibers" part of the Division of Cotton and Other Fibers. He was succeeded by B. B. Robinson in 1946, when he moved on to the Flax Development Committee of the Flax Institute. Robinson, a flax breeder, "selected several promising single-line strains of fiber flax, including his nos. 37, 47, 51, and 54, which have produced a high yield and excellent quality of fiber."[109] Their concern in 1937 was "...what to do to get our farmers to grow more flax." The crop that year had been devastated by drought. At the annual meeting of the Flax Institute[110] "A resolution was approved to inaugurate an aggressive campaign in an effort to get farmers to increase their flax acreage for the 1938 crop. Recognizing the terrific destruction of the 1937 flax crop caused by grasshoppers and crickets, a resolution was passed urging Congress to appropriate sufficient funds to exterminate or control these pests should they occur again in 1938."[111]

In 1937, Representative Robert L. Doughton of North Carolina introduced the Marijuana Tax Act. Matt Rens of the Rens Hemp Company, Brandon, Wisconsin, went to Washington together with others from the industry, as well as members of the medical profession. He argued before a House subcommittee for provisions to protect the industries dependent on hemp. In 1937, nothing was actually known about the chemistry of psychoactive types of cannabis. Stories were told, later revealed to have been concocted, of marijuana-crazed "coloreds" raping and murdering.[112]

The reaction of Western society to cannabis was characteristic of a series of historical social adjustments brought about by contact with non-Western societies and their plants. In the eighteenth century, coffee was the rage and was similarly received:

Coffee houses in England became the centres for a certain intelligentsia and social set. There was so much argument and discussion in the houses that spies returned to King Charles with black stories of the seditious nature of those places. He was advised, and attempted to have them closed. One year there was a royal order to that effect, but within 11 days it was withdrawn because lawyers pointed out that it curbed the basic rights of man. The King then countered with a heavy tax on the drink sold publicly, which resulted in a situation like some other similar governmental prohibitions, tremendous ingenuity being expended to reduce the tax burden and still allow coffee for the houses. [113]

The difference between cannabis and former prohibitions lay mainly in the sophistication of technology available for social intrusion and control by agencies of government. In time, cannabis prohibition would become the principle obstruction to the resurgence of the hemp industry. In 1937, authorities knew that the cannabis being smoked was not originating in the fields of Wisconsin or Kentucky.

The existence of a legitimate hemp industry was not questioned by the proponents of the tax. Provisions were made to allow the hemp industry to continue functioning as a revenue source. Today, although it must be imported, it is still not illegal to possess hemp fiber, or paper made with hemp, or birdseed containing dead hemp seed, or even the whole plant stalk. So long as there is no leaf, or viable seed. Recently, there have been attempts by law enforcement to have existing laws rewritten to make any part of the cannabis plant verboten. There was an initial success in Kentucky,[114] but a recent move to change the Minnesota law failed.[115]

Regarding the fiber crop, FBN Director Harry Anslinger testified, "There is some resin that comes up through the plant but if he is a legitimate hemp producer he will cut it down before the resin makes its appearance."[116] "Some resin" fails to represent the variance in psychoactive potential of different types of cannabis. This obfuscation has been perpetuated to the present by agencies dependent on prohibition to enhance their revenues.

Varietal difference was clearly recognized by those familiar with the crop. That fiber and herbal cannabis are distinct varieties was shown in a photograph in Dewey's 1913 USDA Yearbook chapter on hemp.[117] Wright understood the varietal differences which he characterized in 1918: "There are three fairly distinct types of hemp: that grown for fiber, that for birdseed and oil, and that for drugs."[118] Herbal and oilseed types are poor fiber producers.[119] As with flax, attempts to use one type for the other purpose requires a compromise of quality. The flax community well understood this concept. In 1936, A. C. Dillman had explained,

"Although fiber flax and seed flax—linseed—are quite distinct crops from the standpoint of agriculture and industry, from the standpoint of genetics they are simply of one species."[120]

Fiber hemp is sown thick with a grain drill, a bushel or more of seed to the acre, so the plantings are dense and plants do not branch. Few weeds[121] can compete with a crop of hemp. Densely spaced, the stem of the plant remains small, about the size of one's little finger. The fiber crop is cut before or at time of flowering. Herbal genotypes, on the other hand, are planted with wide spacing so they branch profusely and the flowers are harvested. Due to elevated cannabidiol (CBD) levels, smoking a fiber variety produces a headache and would be a potent discouragement to youthful experimenters.[122] The general populace recognizes this and it is usually treated as a joke. Yet, after 1937, all types of cannabis were labeled drug plants. By 1938, "Other Fibers" at the USDA is fully engaged in the cannabis-as-drug propaganda:

> The Marijuana Tax Act of 1937 requires all growers, importers and processors of hemp to register and be licensed. As a result of growing public opposition to the cultivation of *this drug plant* [italics added], the continuation of hemp culture in the United States may depend upon eliminating as much as possible of the active drug principle from the plant. Preliminary tests indicate a possibility of ultimately obtaining a hemp variety with little or no active drug. Research on this problem is actively under way.[123]

This is the first instance in all of the USDA's reports on hemp that it has been called a "drug plant." Again in 1939, we are told that

> The future of the hemp industry in this country seems to depend largely on the development of strains or varieties of hemp free from marijuana. Coordination of biological, chemical, pharmaceutical, and psychopathic studies lend encouragement to the efforts to free hemp from this destructive drug.[124]

Yet, at this same time, to others the chemurgic prospects for hemp appeared so promising that it was declared "American farmers are promised a new cash crop with an annual value of several hundred million dollars." And, they noted, "the connection of hemp as a crop and marijuana seems to be exaggerated."[125]

Nonetheless, after this time, the literature regarding cannabis is dominated by studies predicated on its identification as a monotypic drug plant. Funding for research on *Cannabis* flowed principally from agencies involved in drug prohibition. A 1942 unpublished memo reported that "Approximately three thousand young plants from our own and government seed (*including known low-marijuana*, partially hermaphroditic and common Kentucky fiber stocks) are now growing in experimental plots and in the greenhouse (italics added)."[126] Researchers, then and now, were precluded by institutional structures from having first hand familiarity with the character they were studying. If Kentucky hemp stood in contrast to "low-marijuana" hemp, then in 1942 "drug-free" hemp was already in the government's possession. It never made it out. One notable early study,[127] lacking a direct chemical assay for the "active drug principle" employed a measurement based on the death of a particular species of fish when exposed to acetone extracts of hemp leaves. The study reported an eight fold variance for potency in samples of Kentucky hemp only. The study failed to include medicinal cannabis varieties as controls. Other work[128] purported to demonstrate that it would take a long time to effectively remove the drug principle from the hemp crop. Such studies undertaken on grants from drug control agencies of the government formed the basis of assumptions by policy makers and became an obstruction to progress of fiber hemp in the United States and, eventually, most of the "First World." The "Second World" never succumbed to this confusion of hemp varieties so hemp breeding and industry continued to advance there.[129]

In Holland where cannabis has been de-prioritized as a criminal matter, research on hemp has resumed. In 1991, Dutch hemp breeders released a hemp variety, "with virtually no narcotic potential."[130] They said it was easy to select changes in THC[131] concentration and that THC and fiber are under independent genetic control. "Fiber content and THC are not interrelated."[132] Furthermore, they demonstrated that recognized fiber and herbal types clearly separate for percent THC.

Recently, Dr. Avram Goldstein in his book, *Addiction*, has acknowledged that "The THC content of the leaves varies greatly; most wild cannabis is derived from plants originally grown for hemp fiber, which contains less than one percent THC."[133] N. W. Simmonds, the British botanist and authority on crop evolution, states that "drug yield is low unless harvest is confined to the upper parts of female plants of special cultivars grown in hot climates, as is the case in the production of Ganja in India."[134] DeMeijer, in Holland has compared hemp varieties in their collection that could be used for papermaking and reported:

> Outdoor screening of 97 populations showed significant variation in the average content of the cannabinoid THC, which ranged from 0.06 to 1.77 in the female inflorescence leaf dry matter. For comparison, THC contents exceeding 10 are not uncommon in marijuana produced by seedless clones of superior [herbal] genotypes in greenhouses and growth chambers. Outdoors, in densely spaced crops, such contents will not occur, even in drug strains.[135]

The simple fact is that the fields of fiber hemp grown in Russia and China have at no time fed the stream of international drug trafficking. Had these fields such potential, would they have gone un-invaded all these years?

Eventually, studies of cannabis in the U.S. were isolated to a laboratory at the University of Mississippi in Oxford, "in localities where previously its culture was unknown, notably in extreme Southern States, which are large cotton producers,"[136] recalling the previously quoted words of Charles Dodge from 1895. Neither Wisconsin nor Kentucky was the seat of any research to restore hemp to the state's economy. All work on the genus Cannabis from that time forth in the United States has served to ingrain into the public mind the notion that the fiber hemp crop is marijuana. Today, discussions of hemp are constantly diverted by the drug issue, as has been this one.[137]

Meanwhile, the replacement of linoleum by vinyl, a petroleum product, was a further blow to the linseed industry, which was struggling to hold on as its other markets shifted to water-soluble paints, also made from petroleum sources. Flax and hemp were juxtaposed dominos in the general historic toppling to synthetic, petroleum-based materials. There is speculation that DuPont Chemical Company was betraying its cognizance of the meaning of the 1937 Marijuana Tax Act when, that year, its Annual Report referred optimistically to "the extent to which the revenue-raising power of government can be converted into an instrument for forcing acceptance of sudden new ideas of industrial and social reorganization."[138]

As the U.S. entered WWII, the hemp industry was in decline from competition with synthetic fibers on the one side and flax straw and the imported fibers on the other. Then Japan's invasion of the Philippines cut off access to abaca and once again the strategic importance of hemp, recognized by Napoleon a century and a half earlier, was impressed upon the nation. Suddenly, it was necessary to set aside all the nasty things which had been said and mobilize for war. Unfortunately, seed stocks of "this drug plant" were very short. The government organized a private corporation, War Hemp Industries, Inc., with its headquarters at 208 South LaSalle Street in Chicago, which set about increasing seed stocks, planting 36,000 acres in Kentucky in 1942. Unfortunately, much of the seed was lost because of bad weather. Seventy one hemp mills were planned in several states, although only 40 were actually built, 12 in Wisconsin.[139] Each mill cost about $350,000. They were designed by Andrew Wright. A film was produced and informational publications were issued by the USDA[140] encouraging farmers to grow "Hemp for Victory," depicting the progress in mechanization of hemp production.[141] Naval stores of fiber were extended by admixing ten percent hemp. Wisconsin farmers were raising 32,000 acres by 1943. In that year, an acre of hemp in Wisconsin averaged $110.59, while corn made $48.29.[142] Overall, 60,000,000 pounds of fiber were produced in 1943 and 1944, combined, which covered the strategic requirement.[143]

Not everyone was happy with this plan. The following press release, reproduced here *in toto*, speaks for itself:[144]

THIS IS AN EXAMPLE OF CRADLE TO GRAVE PLANNING TO THE END RESULT

March 30, 1943

The New Deal Bureaucrats and their fellow "dollar a year" fiber racketeers of the War Production Board are now offering Hemp Marijuana (dope) narcotic to the American people instead of increased food production. The American people are footing the bill.

In one of the most dastardly propositions ever "cooked" up the U. S. Department of Agriculture and the War Production Board are manipulating the proposition of a promotion and scheme to grow and produce hemp from a plant, outlawed by law, that is the fount of the insiduous {sic} drug known as Marijuana, the worst and most serious source of all (dope) narcotic evils afflicting children, in the schools and outside, and grown-ups alike in all walks of life. The fiber itself from this plant is worthless. The seeds from this plant fly far and wide. The resultant wild growth becomes dangerously uncontrollable. In the face of shortage and scarcity of labor, foodstuffs, linseed oil, fibers and other critical materials which are peculiarly being denied us, these corruptors [sic] of American life are now engaged in the promoting of 350,000 acres, erecting 100 buildings and building a large volume of equipment and machinery in a number of Mid-Western States for the production of this narcotic (dope) plant product, all of which must reach the staggering cost of $500,000,000 and end in catastrophic failure. A number of land-grant educational institutions are in on this racket. The Commodity Credit Corporation and the War Production Board and the Defense Plant Corporation, through their own created socalled [sic] "War Hemp Industries, Inc., Agency," something new in the New Deal bureaucratic set-up, are running this (dope) narcotic show with private racketeers as undercover men. Large profits have been made already by them on the seeds by cheating and gipping [sic] the government. The financial "kill" is figured to be colossal for all the participants. The kill to agriculture, industry, (the choicest and most fertile land or soils are being demanded) and health and welfare of the American people is going to reach disastrous proportions from which recovery may never be found possible. Congressman Hampton P. Fulmer, Chairman, Agricultural Committee, and Congressman Paul Brown, overseeing the Commodity Credit Corporation, and certain other members of the Congress, among them Senators Harry S. Truman and Scott W. Lucas, and Donald M. Nelson, Chairman, War Production Board, and John R. Hutson, President of the government Commodity Credit Corporation, Agricultural Adjustment Administration, etc. (the latter active participant) are acquainted with the facts as are being described here and have been presented to them in detail. The power-pressure of the participants in this narcotic (dope) racket is obviously superior to the best interests of the American people even during these dangerous times of their sacrifices and sufferings at home and on the battle front. The truth of the above report is vouched for. Do you want this (dope) narcotic in your community? You are lined up for it. It is to be noted that increased acreage for guayule rubber has been stopped because of the acute food shortages but though rubber scarcities exist yet.

HOWARD D. SALINS, Managing Director
Flax and Fibre Institute of America,
6423 North Newgard Avenue[145]
Chicago, Illinois, U.S.A.

NOTE:—This whole hemp marijuana racket will be dumped out of existence right after the war is over in accordance to with [sic] a statement from Washington, D.C., but obviously not before the "kill" in taxpayers' money has been made and the narcotic has been spread to dope them.

This author's attitude at the resurrection of an old nemesis may be intelligible in light of the decline flax was suffering as synthetics took over the paint markets, and as the use of hempseed for its drying oil was attracting new attention.[146] One thing flax did not need was another competitor.

While the author of this diatribe accuses the War Hemp Industries of wasting strategic resources, according to Walter Wilcox, author of *The Farmer in the Second World War*, "The outstanding example of misused human and other resources in agriculture during the war effort occurred in the Cotton Belt. Although the acreage of cotton dropped some 17 percent during the war, production was maintained at far higher levels than was required for the war effort...Although the acres of cotton fertilized decreased each year [under the USDA quota program], this was largely offset by heavier rates of [fertilizer] application."[147] Pounds of fertilizer used per cotton acre increased from 277 in 1940 every year to 335 by 1945. This resource, Wilcox points out, would have been better used on strategic crops, which short staple cotton was not. Southern legislators fought to get quotas removed from cotton production. When the war began there was a surplus of 12,900,000 bales of cotton. When it ended there were still 11,000,000 bales.

Cotton was continuing to lose markets to new synthetic fibers. Technological progress was stimulated by the war and when it ended synthetic fiber had conquered cotton's biggest market:

> One of the most significant developments during the war in rayon was the sharp increase in United States production of high tenacity rayon for use in tire cords. Prior to the beginning of the war this was not only the largest single domestic outlet for cotton but was a field in which there was practically no competition.[148]

By 1949, rayon had taken two-thirds of this market. Rayon's price had fallen substantially through the war years, so "In November, 1950, cotton cost the mills 45.3 cents a pound, as compared with 32.9 cents for a comparable quantity of rayon staple fiber."[149] And chemists were finding new synthetic fibers: nylon, fiberglass, fibers from milk and corn protein. Cotton was also suffering losses in its second biggest market: bags. "The output of paper for shipping sacks increased from 195,000 tons in 1940 to 667,000 tons in 1948."[150] That same year, cotton's use in bags hit an all-time low: 383,000 bales. Paper was also replacing cotton for "towels, handkerchiefs and napkins, window shades, plastics, twine, and draperies."[151] In the previous century, most paper had been made from recycled cotton rags. Rags accumulated after Charles Herty at the Georgia State Department of Forestry invented a process by which southern pines could be pulped.

After the war, as cotton's dominance diminished, the economic condition of the South gradually improved, due in large part to war reductions in farm population which allowed farm acres per capita to increase to a point where efficiency was possible. Cotton pickers came into increasingly widespread use. The effect of mechanization was "to shift the relative profitableness of cotton from one geographical area to another—from parts of the South where cotton acreages per farming unit are small to other areas, including the West, where acreages per farming unit are large and where irrigation is a factor."[152] Many southern farms finally succeeded in diversifying away from cotton monoculture. Today, pulp is the leading export for five southern states. Southern tobacco growers also prospered as hundreds of thousands of soldiers returned home addicted to nicotine as a result of government assisted cigarette give-aways. This benefitted the flax industry as the leftover flax straw was finding a use in cigarette paper.[153]

The South's hegemony in agricultural policy continued.[154] So, while hemp and flax were desperate for markets, the USDA initiated a program in Florida, in 1943, to study the value of a native fiber-yielding grass, *sansevieria*, also known as bow-string hemp. Programs investigating other long fiber plants were also begun with specific interest in papermaking potential. Although hemp was cited for tear-resistant paper, the selection of species for further research focused on two southern plants: ramie and kenaf. Efforts directed at these plants utilized hemp technology:

> No harvesting machinery has been designed especially for ramie, but several reaper-type harvesters built for other crops can be adapted. The war-time hemp cutter has been combined with the hemp pick-up binder to make a complete cutting and binding machine.[155]

Kenaf was subsequently selected

"...for developmental studies. These include the preparation and use of mechanical pulps, chemi-mechanical pulps, semi-chemical pulps, and high grade bleached chemical pulps. So far as strength is concerned, experimental kenaf bleached pulps have been superior to commercial hardwood pulps and, except for resistance to tear, comparable to soft-wood kraft pulps and superior to softwood sulfite pulps.[156]

Kenaf will not flower if grown in the North. It will produce fiber there, but it is not on the scale of southern production. Yields in research plots have varied from 2.5 ton/acre (Rosemount, Minnesota) to 15 ton/acre (College Station, Texas).[157] "Today [1991] research and development continues, primarily in Texas, Oklahoma, Mississippi and Southeastern U.S.A., with emphasis on development for newsprint manufacture."[158] Reflecting on the difficulties in introducing a new fiber, one researcher candidly revealed his experience of Fiber Wars:

New product development (and this includes improvement of old products) is absolutely essential if plant fibers are to remain competitive with other fibers. Much of this research will be done by governmental institutions and by various associations of producers, ginners, etc., who have a vested interest in cotton.[159]

With the effort to identify new sources of long fibers at the USDA, it might seem that the hemp industry was already history by 1950. Actually, the industry continued in Wisconsin, Minnesota and Kentucky. The Rens Hemp Company operated five mills in eastern Wisconsin. A scutching unit was capable of handling 6000 to 7000 pounds of dry stalks, yielding 800 to 1000 pounds of clean fiber per hour. Approximately a dozen men working two shifts throughout the year were able to handle the production of 4000 acres.[160]

The company still obtained seed from Kentucky which it distributed to growers. The equipment to harvest the crop was owned by the mill alleviating the capital equipment burden to farmers. Matt Rens' son, Willard, kept the business going until the 1957 crop was sold out in 1958. He says,

"I don't think I would have enjoyed being in the business another five years because of the marijuana problem." Now retired and living in Arizona, he is the last man to grow hemp commercially in the U.S..

The tax, he says, was not a big deal. It cost each farmer $3.00, and the company had to buy a special license to be a seed distributor. There was some additional paperwork, but they were never visited by any inspectors. However, he recalls hearing of a mill near St. Paul, Minnesota, that was forced to close in the early fifties. It was an autumn when there was insufficient moisture for dew-retting, so when the stems came into the mill, leaves were still attached. As has been noted, normally hemp returns to the field the bulk of the nutrients it uses for growth when the leaves fall off during the retting process. But, in this instance, the leaves came in and so did the FBN and halted operation for over a year, forcing the mill into insolvency. It had been one of the government's war mills that some entrepreneurs had tried to take private.

Mr. Rens says he never smoked any of the crop, his growers were surprised to learn they'd been growing marijuana, the heinous drug plant. (Truly, what they were growing were the hemp varieties produced by Dewey and Wright.) According to Mr. Rens, the final demise of the Wisconsin hemp industry occurred because it was unable to beat its competition, not directly because of the drug issue. A local newspaper article revisiting the "Hemp King" explained that "Willard Rens operated the plant until 1957, when synthetic fibers took over the market."[161] With no government agency promoting hemp, but one suppressing it, and no alternative uses being explored although recognized uses for hemp were given to undeveloped southern species, the industry languished and died. The emerging fresh vegetable canning industry in Wisconsin took over the hemp acreage.

Need we have lost the domestic hemp industry? The problem was largely one of market development, which would have required a degree of government support and encouragement. But agencies which might have given that support were now dominated by other interests. The crop from Wisconsin was shipped to the east coast to be made into cordage, an economic disadvantage since substantial transportation costs were incurred. This disadvantage undermined hemp's ability to compete with the tropical fibers delivered by ship, other markets having been lost to the synthetics (twines and carpet backing). Clearly, to be economical, the end-use of the crop needed to be located nearer the mills, such as in Wisconsin's paper industry. Mr. Rens says that there was some interest in the fiber for paper in his time, but not the hurds. But this use never developed since supplies of wood pulp in the state had not become limiting, and, in those years, sulfate pulping was developing.

With the final, complete elimination of commercial hemp production, there remained no commercial interests to restrain anti-cannabis political action. The forces of law and order tightened on cannabis with a death grip. In the United States, a plant with any detectable THC is now classified as a Schedule One narcotic, joining a list of chemically synthesized substances which have no redeeming utility.

Fiber seed varieties are recognized as such throughout the world and are certified, as are many seeds farmers purchase.[162] The European Union places an ultraconservative threshold at 0.3% THC to distinguish psychoactive from fiber types. DeMeijer, et al., place a threshold at 0.5%. These criteria, by focusing solely on THC, have the unfortunate effect of limiting germplasm options to those in which economic interests are already vested. Small, et al. showed that Cannabis accessions could be grouped effectively by the ratio of THC to CBD (cannabidiol, non-psychoactive). Fiber types tend to have ratios less than one.[163] Elevated CBD levels are enough to render the plants unusable as smoking material.

The tragic element of this story is that as a result of the pariah status to which hemp was relegated in the U.S., Kentucky hemp is now extinct. The germplasm produced in Dewey's breeding program and all that collected by the USDA is lost. The National Seed Storage Laboratory, located in Fort Collins, Colorado, is charged with the preservation of germplasm as a safeguard against national disaster, such as nuclear war. In the early 1960s, ten bags of hemp seed, the only known remnant of the Kentucky hemp varieties, were transferred there from the USDA. A USDA Yearbook report noted that "Flax and hemp are no longer produced for fiber in this country, but seed stocks of the best varieties that have been developed by research agencies are maintained."[164] Fortunately for flax, a responsible effort was made to preserve its germplasm. Sadly, the hemp remnant was neglected. At the request of the author, NSSL searched and found these bags of hempseed which apparently were never logged in as accessions of the lab. Consequently, they were not properly preserved. The bags are only labeled with numbers whose import was not recorded, so we cannot know which varieties they might have been. The seed was last grown, as far as can be determined, in 1948. It's dead![165]

This completes the extinction of Kentucky hemp and its derivatives. Nor is this germplasm found in the collections of other nations, as far as I have been able to determine.[166] DeMeijer and van Soest, writing of the Cannabis germplasm collection in Holland, say, "Lacking in the collection are fiber cultivars grouped under the name Kentucky hemp which were cultivated until the nineteen-fifties in the U.S.A....It is doubtful whether viable germplasm of these cultivars still exists."[167] All that remains of this genetic resource is the feral hemp which our National Guard is seeking with helicopters (to the chagrin of at least one Wisconsin dairy farmer).

In 1929 three selected varieties of hemp—Michigan Early, Chinamington and Simple Leaf—were grown in comparison with unselected common Kentucky seed near Juneau, Wis. Each of the varieties had been developed by 10 years or more of selection from the progeny of individual plants. The yields of fiber per acre were as follows: Simple Leaf, 360 pounds; Michigan Early, 694 pounds; Chinamington, 1054 pounds; common Kentucky, 680 pounds.[168]

These and the other varieties, Ferramington, Kymington, and Minnesota 8 among them, the entire lineage of Kentucky hemp, our unique *American* hemp, are lost, their only survivors reduced to ditch-weed. When Mr. Rens closed his doors in 1958, the government required that the hemp seed remaining in his possession be sterilized to kill it before it could be sold to birdseed suppliers.

Today, a great deal of attention is given to the loss of germplasm in tropical rainforests. It is in the context of that concern for global genetic resources that the loss of Kentucky hemp should be framed. It is a long way from a wild plant to an agricultural crop. Current policies are driving us backwards.

The process of becoming weedy is a degenerative process from the point of view of plant breeding. Traits selected by the plant breeder through many generations are degraded as natural selection takes over emphasizing weedy characteristics. And hemp has an extremely malleable genetic makeup. The once valuable germplasm has been eroded in the feral state. We cannot know how "wild" this germplasm has become until it can be studied in an agricultural setting.

The loss of this germplasm is a setback to hemp in North America. The situation from a plant breeding point of view is roughly equivalent to turn-of-the-century. If hemp varieties adapted to North America are to be recreated, we will have to start over with the feral germplasm and plant introductions from China, Italy, and the former Soviet block. Since the machinery used in the mills was sold off for scrap metal, for this, too, we will have to look to the East.

Because of the legal definition of hemp as a drug plant, all hemp used in the U.S. is imported. Nonetheless, trade is exploding for articles made with hemp. Beginning as a means to vote against prohibition when public discussion is suppressed, people are rediscovering the attributes of this durable natural fiber. And there is a great deal of interest in hemp's potential for building materials and, of course, paper. Hemp might also be grown for fiber on polluted lands as part of the remediation process.[169] It has also been discussed as a potential source of biomass energy because of its high productivity.[170] For its unique ability to suppress weeds alone, hemp has a place in the crop rotation, particularly in sustainable and organically-oriented farming systems.[171]

Growing public recognition in the United States that cannabis prohibition, rather than the plant itself, is the source of the societal damage for which it is blamed may soon result in the rationalization of laws affecting hemp agriculture. Such changes are already underway in England and Canada. Hopefully, it is not too late to recover Kentucky hemp from the feral populations. A 1975 study of feral cannabis growing in Kansas reported:

> The major hallucinogen, delta-9-THC, occurred in all plant parts and ranged from 0.0001 to 0.06% of plant dry matter in the time study. Concentration was highest in flowers, leaves, petioles, stems, seeds, and roots, respectively (Fig. 1b). Plant parts containing the most delta-9-THC also contained the most CBD, but delta-9-THC concentrations

were ten times lower than CBD in all plant parts. Delta-9-THC and CBD in leaf tissue exhibited similar seasonal changes, except that delta-9-THC fluctuations came about two weeks later than those of CBD and had the lowest concentration (0.004%) in mid March and the highest (0.046%) in early July.[172]

The highest THC level (0.046%) found in the feral hemp was far below the 0.3% internationally accepted threshold for drug potential.

In 1992, a retired IBM employee hobby-farming in Kentucky was arrested for cultivating a Schedule One drug when 5000 cannabis plants were found in his field. The charges were subsequently dropped (after $15,000 in legal fees) when lab results came back showing the plants had 0.05% THC. Such feral plants are the remains of Kentucky hemp. This case confirms that they never did have drug potential. The THC percentage of the feral hemp from Kansas and Kentucky are equivalent, 0.05%, an order of magnitude below the international standard. There is not, nor was there ever, a need "to free hemp of the drug marijuana." The promulgation of the notion that there was constitutes one of the greatest hoaxes ever perpetrated on the American people.

The Schlichten Papers

By Don Wirtshafter

IT WAS AUGUST, 1917. After 20 years of tinkering, George W. Schlichten had finally accomplished his life's work. He had invented a machine capable of separating the fiber from the tough stalks of hemp and other fiber crops. No longer would crops have to be "retted" in the fields for weeks to allow the stalk's pulp to weaken. What's more, the by-products from decortication would produce a superior paper stock.

Schlichten's invention was called a "decorticator." It was clearly the work of a genius. Schlichten solved an age-old problem. Hundreds of inventors, including Thomas Jefferson, had tried to invent an efficient process to separate the useful "bast" fibers from plants like flax, hemp and ramie.

Prior to the decorticator, it took tedious hand work to break, hack and scutch the tough stalks into shape for spinning into yarn. The new technology reduced labor costs by a factor of at least one hundred. Schlichten's miniature refinery could efficiently separate and clean the fiber from any plant, but hemp was clearly his favorite.

The decorticator was about twenty feet long. Dried stalks were fed in one end. The machine first stripped off the green leafy vegetation that was valuable as a cattle feed. The stalks were crushed through a series of fluted rollers and flappers so that the hurds, the woody pith, were broken out. A series of combs and rollers brushed out the short "tow" fibers. The long fibers were then massaged enough to degum them.

The pectin coatings flaked off and were collected for industrial purposes. The final product, called the "sliver," rolled out the far end of the machine. The sliver was ready for spinning into the finest of linens.

Other inventors had attempted to automate this process. Several hundred patents for processing hemp preceded Schlichten's. Some were even called decorticators. None of these prior inventions worked very efficiently. Most turned out a mat of fibers that then had to be combed to straighten out each fiber, a tedious process. Schlichten's decorticator was able to keep the alignment of the fibers in order. It turned out a continuous "sliver" of hemp that was ready to be spun with existing machinery.

Schlichten was born in Germany in 1862 and began work on his invention there. He had put over $400,000 into the decorticator and felt it was time to get a return on his investment. If he could prove a market for the output of his machine, he could get investment in his business. His headache was what he was going to do with the mountain of hemp hurds his machines would create.

In 1916, Schlichten took his first production of hemp sliver to the New York market. It sold for a record price, $100 a ton more than any other fiber had previously brought. The experts pronounced it better than the finest of Italian hemps. A spinning mill owned by J. D. Rockefeller purchased Schlichten's entire crop and paid him to supervise spinning the unfamiliar fibers into yarn. The mill was so impressed that they tried to buy exclusive rights to the invention. They offered Schlichten a considerable sum—half again as much as he really wanted—but Schlichten was not ready to sell out, especially to Rockefeller.

Scripps Confronts the Newspaper Crisis

Early in this century, Edward W. Scripps established a successful chain of penny papers targeted at the working man. Angered by the right-wing Associated Press, he founded the United Press Syndicate (later United Press International). Because of his interest in science, he established research institutions such as the Scripps Institute in San Diego.

Scripps kept archives of his personal correspondence that preserved a remarkable treasure trove of history. His family donated these papers to Alden Library at Ohio University in Athens, Ohio. Included in these thousands of documents is a series of 24 letters concerning George Schlichten and his invention. Almost everything we know about Schlichten comes from this remarkable hoard.

Scripps heard about the decorticator from Harry Timken, president of the Timken Roller Bearing Company and an early Southern California developer. Timken was one of the leading machinists of his time.

When Timken first went to visit Schlichten, he found the inventor busy at work. Schlichten later complained, "He began to fire a thousand questions a minute at me, then I began to dislike his manner of being even bordering on imposing on me: so we kind of had this little tilt."

Timken's impression was more favorable: "I go there expecting to see a long-hair, and what do I find—a business man, the best business man I ever met."

Once Timken saw the decorticator in action, it was all he could ever talk about. He often called it "the greatest invention in the world." In 1917, he persuaded Schlichten to move his experimentation to the Timken Ranch in Imperial Valley, California. With Timken's backing, Schlichten planted 100 acres of hemp and some other experimental crops.

By August, 1917, the hemp crop was almost ready for harvest. It was such a bumper crop that it received national attention. The Hearst, Pathe and Mutual film companies featured footage of the 14-foot-tall plants in their weekly newsreels. Schlichten readied his decorticators to process the tough hemp stalks.

As U.S. entry into World War I approached, newspapers were faced with a national shortage of the wood pulp needed to make newsprint. Prices were rising, and publishers were desperate for an alternative. Scripps was even considering raising the price of his penny papers to two cents.

Schlichten knew he had the answer for Scripps' paper crisis. He was convinced that the mountain of hurds his machine created could make a superior paper at less cost than wood pulp. The previous year he had given hemp hurds to Jason Merrill, a fiber researcher for the Department of Agriculture. Merrill and Lyster Dewey used these hurds to produce the paper for their famous USD.A. Bulletin No. 404 entitled "Hemp Hurds as Papermaking Material."

To prove his technology, Schlichten had to convince a large newspaper syndicate to finance a full-scale run of hemp hurds through an existing paper mill. Based on Timken's recommendation, Scripps' partner, Milton McRae, granted Schlichten an interview on August 3, 1917, at his office in the Scripps Building in San Diego. Also present at the meeting was Edward Chase, Scripps' right-hand man.

The Schlichten Papers

What Schlichten didn't know was that his presentation to Chase and McRae was bugged. Long before the days of cassette recorders and electronic monitors, Schlichten's sales pitch was secretly listened in on and transcribed by McRae's secretary. McRae mailed the eleven-page, detailed transcript to Scripps, who dutifully preserved it in his archives. This early example of industrial espionage preserved for us a candid view of an amazing individual.

Schlichten knew his revolutionary invention would be a target of attack. The first paragraph of the transcript describes Schlichten defending his German name. He said that a prominent man had told him, "For your name, I think we ought to hang you." Schlichten replied, "Oh well, gentlemen, if you think I deserve to be hanged, you don't need to force me to it. I am perfectly willing to be hanged. But my deeds cannot be hanged; what I am doing for the country and for the work [world?] in general—that cannot be destroyed."

Schlichten explained the advantage of his machine was that it worked with dried rather than retted hemp. Previously, hemp had to ret—that is, rot or ferment in the field or in stagnant ponds—for several weeks to weaken the pulp enough that the rot-resistant fibers could be separated. Retting the stalks destroyed most of the properties of the hurds, leaving them scattered in the field and so full of dirt that they were uneconomical to use. Retting also weakened and discolored the useful fibers.

Decorticated hurds were clean and easy to cook into paper. They preserved the natural glues that made paper stick together. When mechanically baled, they would transport efficiently and load easily in a paper digester. They made a superior paper, using far fewer chemicals, at less cost than tree pulp. The long fibers were stronger and cleaner than anything that could be produced by retting.

The eleven-page transcript details Schlichten's sales pitch to the Scripps employees. He went so far as to tell the newspapermen that he thought it was a crime to cut down forests for the small percentage of paper that could be produced. He explained the environmental impact of deforestation and predicted a time when further logging would be prohibitively expensive or even forbidden. At the end of the lengthy interview, it was agreed that Chase would travel to the Imperial Valley to further investigate the potential of the decorticator.

On August 28, 1917, Chase presented his report to Scripps and McRae. It is an undisputed testimonial to the economics of Schlichten's machine: "I have spent many hours with G. W. Schlichten, the inventor of the decorticating machine. Friday and Saturday last I spent with him at the Timken Ranch in Imperial Valley, while a portion of his first crop of hemp was being run through his machine. I have seen a wonderful, yet simple, invention. I believe it will revolutionize many of the processes of feeding, clothing and supplying other wants of mankind."

Chase's six-page letter detailed the cost effectiveness of the decorticator. Each machine could process eight tons of hemp stalks per day. This would be refined into two tons of the valuable fibers, five tons of hurds and one ton of the tops and leaves. Chase saw the invention working and audited its efficiency over a two-day period. He reported that even though the whole arrangement was "temporary, new and stiff," it turned out three tons of fiber. The letter is important verification of Schlichten's genius, because Chase had no reason to lie or exaggerate to his bosses. Chase recommended that Scripps finance the needed full-scale test of hemp hurd paper.

Timken wrote Scripps on September 5, 1917, encouraging him to go forward with the project. "If I go into the Schlichten Decorticator business, you start a paper mill in San Diego and Spreckles starts a bagging factory, we would make a real start in doing something for San Diego and incidentally for ourselves; or rather, primarily for ourselves and incidentally for San Diego. I trust you will give the question of a paper mill very serious consideration and thought."

A Sudden Reversal

Two weeks later, Chase and McRae reversed their position without explanation. On September 17, 1917, McRae wrote a short letter to Scripps describing a two-hour meeting he and Chase had with Harry Timken. The two convinced Timken "beyond a reasonable doubt" that hemp was not economical for making newspapers. McRae then instructed Chase to drop the matter. He promised Scripps a full report later. Nothing additional was preserved in Scripps' rather complete archives.

Stripped of Timken's backing, Schlichten and his machinery fell into oblivion. Almost a year of research has failed to disclose any details of what happened to Schlichten. His name never appears in any historical accounts about hemp. None of the inventors who later tried to reproduce the decorticator credited Schlichten for his early work. He and his invention disappeared from recorded history without a trace.

In the late 1930s, as Schlichten's patents expired, other inventors came up with decorticators. Anton F. Burkardt, Robert B. Cochrane, Karl Wessel and several others patented designs for decorticating machinery. These became the basis for the factories built for the Hemp for Victory campaign of 1943. None of these later inventions seems to have worked anywhere near as well as Schlichten's. The Hemp for Victory technology was shut down soon after World War II ended.

Karl Kaiser invented a portable decorticator that could be pulled by a tractor through the fields. Although five of these machines were built, hemp prohibition prevented their use on any crop but flax. Eventually, these proved uneconomical and fell out of use.

The Marijuana Conspiracy

The February 1938, *Popular Mechanics* magazine featured a story called "New Billion Dollar Crop." It discussed the rapid progress in decorticator technology and how this was certain to revolutionize the hemp industry. This was the first time the word "billion" had been used to describe a farm crop—the potential of this technology was that great.

By then, it was too late. The 1937 Marijuana Tax Act made cultivation of hemp illegal and relegated decorticators to processing flax, which was not nearly as economical as hemp.

Jack Herer is the author of the popular book, *The Emperor Wears No Clothes: Hemp and the Marijuana Conspiracy*. Herer blames special interests like the Dupont Corporation and the Hearst newspapers for a coordinated campaign to panic America into banning hemp from our nation's agriculture. Herer says there was no way Congress would have prohibited growing "hemp"; the plant was too popular as a farm crop and source of ropes and fine linens. Instead, the power barons adopted the name "marijuana" and used racial innuendos and fear of the unknown to trick America into banning this valuable crop.

Herer says the invention of decorticator machines in the 1930s was the cause of these industrialist concerns. The decorticator could have revolutionized industry and sparked an economic upheaval similar to that caused by the perfection of the cotton gin a century before. The power barons feared the rapid advances being made in hemp technology would destabilize their investments in petrochemical- and forest-based economies.

There is one non sequitur in the "marijuana conspiracy" theory as stated in previous editions of *The Emperor*. Prior to the discovery of the Schlichten papers, the earliest known practical decorticators were those patented by Anton Burkardt and Robert Cochrane in 1936, shortly before passage of the Marijuana Tax Act in 1937. These inventions could not have been the motivation for Hearst's yellow journalism and Harry Anslinger's campaign against marijuana, which started almost 20 years earlier.

The discovery of the Schlichten Papers makes it clear that practical decortication technology became available in 1917. The repression of this industrial revolution dates back that far. This explains why the origins of the "reefer madness" campaign that started in the 1920s.

George Schlichten died in Solona, California on February 3, 1923, a broken man. His death certificate details that the contributing factors to his demise were "over exertion and worry." His occupation was listed as "Manufacturer of Textile Fibers." He was working at the decorticator until the end.

The Hemp Advocates

There are now millions of Americans advocating the reintroduction of hemp farming in this country. What they do not understand is that the legalization of industrial hemp cultivation will do us little good unless we quickly develop the technology to harvest and process the bounty. England grew 1500 acres of hemp in 1993. Some of this rotted in the field because there was no way to quickly harvest the crop during their cold, damp autumn.

Luckily, we have a basis to start. Schlichten and the other inventors patented their ideas. As part of each patent application the inventor submits a set of drawings to illustrate the innovation. Schlichten left us eight pages of drawings with his first patent and another page in his second. Whether or not the later inventors built on these drawings is a matter for debate. Patent drawings are usually purposely kept ambiguous so as not to give away construction details to potential competitors.

Schlichten told Timken he did not consider his work a secret. His patent drawings are unusual in their detail. They give us a great head start toward recreating his work. Schlichten knew he and his invention were under attack. Remember his first words, "I am perfectly willing to be hanged. But my deeds cannot be hanged." He must have known how powerful the forces were that his "revolutionary" invention threatened. Perhaps he disclosed so many details in his patent drawings as his way of insuring that his deeds could not be totally squelched.

The publication of a preliminary article in the April, 1994 issue of *High Times Magazine* has sparked a movement of engineers who are determined to recreate this work. If we are going to "save the world with hemp," then our work is cut out for us. Basic technology has been lost. The genotypes of thousands of cultivars of hemp have been destroyed. Our industrial capacity to spin and weave natural fibers has been dismantled. It will take years of work and millions of dollars in investment to re-establish this industrial base. When one considers that the alternative to this commitment is potential global extinction, it's time we got started.

Letter from Edward Chase about G.W. Schlichten

San Diego, Calif.
August 28, 1917

Mr. E. W. Scripps
Mr. Milton A. McRae

GENTLEMEN:

I have spent many hours with G. W. Schlichten, the inventor of the decorticating machine. Friday and Saturday last I spent with him at the Timken Ranch in Imperial Valley, while a portion of his first crop of hemp was being run through his machine. I have seen a wonderful, yet simple, invention. I believe it will revolutionize many of the processes of feeding, clothing and supplying other wants of mankind.

Heretofore, before the fiber could be extracted from hemp, the hemp stalks had to lie on the ground for months to be "retted." The fiber is then extracted by hand or by certain crude machines. To make a long story short, the fiber from retted hemp is of a poorer quality as to strength and so expensive to get into proper shape, that Kentucky hemp is quoted in the Fiber Trade Journals at 16¢ per lb. ($320.00 per ton). The fiber having been extracted from hemp, the residue consists chiefly of "hurds." Hemp hurds are the woody, inner portion of the hemp stalk broken into pieces in removing the fiber. The old machines, handling retted hemp, turn out only small amounts of fiber and small and scattered heaps of hurds. Only about seven thousand tons of these hurds have been available in the United States annually. These have been so scattered as to be useful only as stable bedding, etc., at about one dollar a ton. Hurds from retted hemp, being dirty from lying long on the ground, and of poor quality from decay, are not proper stock feed.

Mr. Schlichten raised five tons of hemp stalks to the acre on a one hundred acre patch on the Timken Ranch. He will pay the growers $15.00 per ton for dry hemp stalks delivered to his machine. They have only to be shocked to dry properly in a few days. Thus the farmer gets $75.00 an acre for this crop which matures in 100 days. The stubble and that part of the leaves and tops which remain on the field (containing in excess of 50% of nitrogen), are wonderful fertilizer. Moreover, the hemp kills all weeds. The farmer's land is left in fine condition for immediate planting of other crops. A second crop of hemp may be raised, but Mr. Schlichten prefers that only one crop be raised on the same land each year.

From each ton of dry hemp stalks, costing him $15.00, Mr. Schlichten gets the following:

About 500 lbs. hemp fiber @ 16¢ per lb.	.........................$	80.00
" 1250 " hurds @ $5.50 per ton	....	3.44
(worth that figure at stock feed or for paper stock)		
" 250 lbs. leaves, tops, etc. @ $5.50 per ton	...........$	.69
From each ton, about	....$	84.13
From each acre, about	....$	420.65
From his 100 acre experimental patch, about	.................$	42,065.00

One of Schlichten's machines will produce per day (two shifts of eight hours each), as follows:

Two tons of fiber worth about	....$	600.00
Five " " hurds " "	....$	27.50
One " " tops, leaves, etc. worth about	....................$	5.50
Total	....$	633.00

This will be at a total cost of less than $200.00—less than $100.00 per ton of fiber for growing the hemp, passing it through the machine and baling the output ready for market. One fairly good machinist and three common laborers at 35¢ an hour are required per machine for each shift.

This new one machine plant (the whole arrangement being temporary, new and stiff), turned out in the two days I was there:

Three tons of fiber worth...	$	900.00
About seven tons of hurds worth..................................	$	38.50
" one and two-fifths tons of leaves, tops, etc., worth...	$	7.70
Total..	$	946.20

Mr. Schlichten will regulate the selling price of the output of his machine so long as his patents protect him. His United States patent, pending, covers the extracting of fiber from any and all fiber-bearing plants by any mechanical process.

Mr. Schlichten will contract with us over a long term of years for all the hemp hurds necessary to make all the paper and paper products we want to make. He will contract not to sell or otherwise dispose of for any purpose any hurds until our orders are filled. He will, within a reasonable length of time, raise and treat hemp so as to supply us the hurds nearby the Scripps Eastern Newspapers.

Advantages of Hemp Hurds for Paperstock

FIRST: We make paper from an "Annual" and thus help to preserve the forests, the streams and the soil;

SECOND: We make paper at a lower cost than is possible from wood, for the following reasons:

A. Wood must have the bark, knots, etc., removed. It must then be cut into small chips, and sieved. Then it is ready for the digester. The preparing of the wood for the digester is a considerable part of the total paper making cost. The hurds are ready for the digester, when, as a by-product, they leave the Schlichten machine;

B. In the "cooking" and "beating" of these hurds, less caustic soda, resin, and probably less clay, will be needed than when ground wood is used;

C. Sulphite must be mixed with ground wood pulp; but not with the pulp from these hurds.

It is Mr. Schlichten's opinion that we can make news print paper of better quality than is commonly used by newspapers, at a cost of somewhere between $25.00 and $35.00 per ton. These figures should include all costs, overhead and otherwise; but best machinery and equipment for first-class ability in operation and management is, of course, presupposed.

Paper has been made from hemp hurds by the U. S. Agricultural Department. You each have a copy of Bulletin #404 of the United States Department of Agriculture. This bulletin is printed on paper made from hemp hurds. This paper is of better quality than news print stock. This paper was made from hurds of retted hemp. For reasons given above, costs would be higher than in making paper from the Schlichten hemp hurds.

You will note from this bulletin that only four tons of hemp hurds were used in the experiments; also that on such a scale it was found practically impossible to arrive at a cost figure which would be susceptible of commercial interpretation. Mr. Schlichten and I think it likely that proper cost figures may be had by running through a news print mill sufficient stock to keep one paper making machine running one full day. I expect to get further information on this point from the Paper Investigations Department of the U. S. Department of Agriculture, but more especially from the paper mill superintendent or the practical paper maker at the mill we shall choose for the experiment. Whatever quantity it be decided to use for such experiment, Mr. Schlichten would have ready, baled for shipment. It would seem that there will be unavoidable loss of time required for freight shipment to some Eastern mill; I would not like to entrust the experiment to any Pacific Coast mill.

The program I would suggest is that I go at once to Washington and get a letter from E. W. Scripps to Secretary Houston. Then I get such a letter from Houston as will obtain for me the co-operation I want at the right sort of a news print paper mill. Then find out what tonnage of hurds should be shipped; wire Mr. Schlichten to ship; be at the mill when the hurds arrive; arrange for keeping of exact costs; have the paper run through; and finally sell the paper and have it run through our newspaper presses.

Meanwhile I shall be finding an A No. 1 paper mill manager or superintendent (a first-class practical paper maker) to whom we could make a proposition so interesting that he would come with us.

Costs of Experiment

Cost of hurds at machine, per ton ....$	5.50
" " baling " " " " about	1.20
Hauling to cars and loading, about	.35
Unloading	.35
Freight to Eastern mill (possibly less)	20.00
Total cost per ton ....$	27.40
If 100 tons be used in the experiment ....$	2740.00
Mill charge, perhaps about 500.00 ....$	3240.00

I would learn what width of rolls the Ohio Scripps papers could use, and sell them the paper. After paying freight from the mill to the newspaper, I think at least $40.00 per ton would be realized; or, from about 50 tons of finished paper, $2000.00

On page 22 of Bulletin #404, paragraph two, you will note:

"The weight of hurds which are capable of being charged into a rotary (digester) is a decidedly unfavorable factor."

(This in comparison with the weight of a cubic foot of wood as now charged into the digesters at the paper mills.) This would not be the case with the hurds from the Schlichten machine. Mr. Schlichten believes these dry hurds in hydraulically pressed bales would weigh about as much per cubic foot as wood.

You will also note that the bales of hurds from retted hemp must be covered, which would not be the case with the Schlichten hurds.

Also, hurds from retted hemp must be screened or sorted, and the various sizes treated separately and differently. None of this work is necessary with the Schlichten hurds.

Market

My recollection is that the latest and best news print machines turn out fifty tons of paper per day. (This figure I shall soon verify.) If this is correct, a one machine mill, if run 365 days, would produce 18,250 tons per annum. I understand the Scripps Eastern papers consume about 27,000 tons per annum. It would seem that the Scripps Eastern papers would furnish a market for a mill in that part of the United States.

The first decorticating machines will naturally operate on hemp raised in the Imperial Valley and in San Diego County, not far from San Diego Harbor, so that hurds will be available for paper for Pacific Coast and nearby newspapers some time before hurds are produced in the East. Our Coast newspapers consume only about five thousand tons per annum (increasing rather rapidly), which is perhaps only about one-fourth to one-third the output of a one machine mill. Our Pacific Coast newspapers are buying under a contract running until August, 1921. I think many other Pacific Coast newspapers are buying under five year contracts, which at any given date would have varying terms to run. Of course we should have to ascertain beyond a doubt that our output could be sold at a good profit before erecting a mill on this Coast. I believe we could make sure of this because I think we could make book and letter papers, card board, box board, tissues, etc., with an increased investment of between 10 and 15% for additional machinery.

San Diego as a Millsite

With the completion of the San Diego and Arizona Ry. (probably about one year hence), San Diego will be the nearest harbor to the Imperial Valley hemp fields. Also a considerable acreage will probably be raised between Del Mar and Escondido.

San Diego Power Rate

The City of San Diego is buying hydro-electric power at one and one-third cents per kilowatt hour. I believe it costs any paper mill. located near a natural water power, that much to harness and handle its own water power. We may be able to get a lower rate.

San Diego Water

The City of San Diego is pumping water and lifting it 400 feet at a cost of 4¢ per thousand gallons. At the mill chosen for our experiment, I shall learn how much we can afford to spend for water and what quality we must have. I am having an analysis made of water taken from the only well in Sweetwater Valley, that being the most reliable and unfailing source for pumping.

San Diego Financing

I believe I could raise in San Diego, on bonds to be issued against our plant and business, a considerable part of the necessary investment. Of course San Diego would have to compete with Los Angeles in securing for us lowest power and water rates, favorable mill site and financial help. Los Angeles people are making extra-ordinary efforts for more factories, and they might offer us such inducements that we should have to go there. Personally I should prefer San Diego, as Mr. Schlichten says he would for his contemplated textile and other factories.

I believe Mr. Schlichten will invite us, and a few other San Diego friends, to go in with him on his hemp growing and decorticating, and other, ventures if we let him know we might like to do so. I think Mr. Schlichten would be glad to be interested in our paper making enterprises if we want him to be. I think we should have him in with us. If he were interested, I am sure he would have very valuable suggestions from time to time re: reducing costs, increasing output, markets, etc.

Mr. Schlichten has asked me to say that the facts as to the costs and profits of the operation of his machine are confidential.

He has said to me that he has put about $400,000 and about twenty years of labor into this machine; that he is now past fifty years of age and wants to move as rapidly as possible in what he believes will be the revolutionizing of many processes. I am sure he would like us to put on all speed consistent with safety, in pushing the paper-making end of it.

Sincerely,

C. C. to: E. B. S.
          J. G. S.
          J. C. H.

Can Hemp Save the Planet?

Introduction

by Ed Rosenthal

IN 1991 DR. DAVID WALKER wrote his report, "Can Hemp Save the Planet?" It was a response to the assertions made by many hemp activists that one plant species, hemp, is humankind's silver bullet for food, health and the environment. Walker analyzed the literature to check many of the assertions in *The Emperor Wears No Clothes*. This critique sparked a debate that continues today.

Walker's study showed that hemp may be a useful economic crop with many unique qualities. However, it faces stiff competition from other crops with which it was interchangeable for various purposes.

Lynn Osburn, the theoretician behind the "Hemp for Fuel" concept, responded with a critique of the article. He defended his findings and explained his theories thoroughly.

Hayo van der Werf's literature review was originally done for the Dutch hemp research program. It is instantly a summary and a resource for further information about hemp and its cultivation requirements.

Don Wirtschafter's report on the seed and its many qualities provides new information about the seed. Both the seed and its oil present possibilities for human and animal nourishment, health and industrial use. The seed is already the most valuable part of the plant on a weight basis. With the development of many new consumer products, demand for seed may increase dramatically.

John Birrenbach's short article on hemp paper provides some illumination on the subject. It is based on older, although still valid technology from the U.S. Dept. of Agriculture.

Hemp Realities, the opening essay, was written to give an overview and broad perspective to hemp and its relationship to its symbiotic specie, homo sapiens. This chapter provides a short, recent history of hemp popularization. It sorts the myths from the realities and provides actual yield figures which give a clearer view of hemp's yield in relation to other dry weight crops.

The authors of every report in this section see a bright future for hemp. As humans develop new uses for it, a larger part of the farm and manufacturing economy will be hemp related.

Hemp Realities

by Ed Rosenthal

IN THE LATE NINETEEN EIGHTIES hemp became a significant issue in the U.S. and all over the world. Over the same period it has been the focus of many new businesses in several new industries. This interest is the result of one individual's tireless campaign to legalize all forms of cannabis. Jack Herer's book, *The Emperor Wears No Clothes*[1] and his six year book tour galvanized a new group of activists. They based legalization not only on the human rights issue of freedom of consciousness, but also on the economic and utilitarian uses of its industrial products and its medical efficacy. His story seeped uphill to business people, farmers and industrialists and finally to university and government researchers.

In 1993 *The Emperor Wears No Clothes* was published in German and French editions. Both translations have become best-sellers. In 1994 the British edition appeared.

Rather than separating the issues of hemp and marijuana, Herer contends that they are inevitably intertwined and have been since the government began regulating the plant. He draws a picture of a sort of harmonic convergence of interests which resulted in a conspiracy to criminalize hemp.

DuPont had just invented the first truly synthetic plastic which could replace natural fibers. Until that time, the synthetics were derivatives of cellulose. Cellophane and rayon both depended on a source of agricultural product. Now the company could make fantastic profits using cheap petroleum to make valuable fibers.

Herer thinks that hemp was the natural fiber most likely to compete with nylon and that DuPont was acutely aware that the prohibition of hemp would create a void for the new synthetic fiber to fill. He cites statements in the DuPont annual report from 1937 as his proof.[2]

The second member of the conspiracy was the Hearst newspaper empire, which had invested significantly in pulpwood forests. If hemp remained legal and its processing was mechanized, then pulpwood would not be able to compete with this annual and the forests would lose their value.

A third group was anti-minority racists who thought that marijuana was a threat to the control of undesirables such as Mexican-Americans and blacks. In essence they felt that, under the influence of this substance, these people might think about self-respect and become "uppity."

He has also named the pharmaceutical companies which were beginning to patent new drugs which they had developed. These formulations represented a much higher profit margin than unpatentable herbal concentrates. Since cannabis was useful for so many ailments, eliminating it as a medical option would force people to use proprietary formulas rather than the cheaper herbal medicines.

Although Herer does not emphasize them in his book, he claims that other members of this group included the entire prohibition bureaucracy, which was soon to be out of work because of the repeal of the 18th amendment. Marijuana represented an intriguing new substance to fight since it was used by minorities, jazz musicians and other avant garde entertainers. It was estimated that over 50,000 people used marijuana in 1937. This fight would take the effort of quite a few agents.

In his chapter, David West cites cotton interests as movers in the criminalization of hemp. West sees it as a regional issue: the southern cotton-producing states vs. the hemp-producing midwest.

The conspirators, Herer claims, set in motion a scheme to prohibit hemp by associating it with marijuana and concurrently running a fear campaign against the herb. Hearst, the media giant, used its vast influence to create anti-drug hysteria. This propaganda fanned fears of violent minorities going on a rampage and middle-class youth seduced and disgraced.

Since the industrial and intoxicating varieties of cannabis were both affected when the government started regulating the plant, Herer feels that they both must be re-legalized at the same time. This is probably more realistic than most "realists" on the issue believe or would like to acknowledge.

If hemp were made legal, leaving marijuana subject to criminal penalties, the hemp fields would become a very leaky bucket. Farmers who gross perhaps $1500 an acre on hemp would have a terrific incentive to grow one or two extremely similar looking plants per acre and double their gross.

This is a sore point, well known but not discussed by hempsters. They must think that no one else has thought of it. Opening up hemp production without a civil regulatory system for marijuana will necessarily lead to a system that fosters corruption.

Herer claims that hemp is, overall, the most useful annual plant, valuable for fiber, paper, food, fuel and fun as well as medicine. The uses and economics of seed are discussed in Section 2. The use and economics of marijuana as a recreational euphoriant are discussed in Section 4. The use of marijuana as a medicine is covered briefly in Section 4, and is well documented in other works such as *Marihuana: The Forbidden Medicine* by Lester Grinspoon and *Marijuana Medical Papers* by Tod Mikuriya.

Hemp Fiber

Hemp fiber has many uses and has benefitted many peoples. Its long history of symbiotic relationships was uncovered by archaeologists, and predates our written history.[3] The fiber might have been discovered when someone noticed naturally retted fiber and used it first as a rope or twine, next as netting and for baskets and finally for clothing.

In Eastern Europe it has traditionally been used by the poor as homespun cloth for everyday clothing. Only the rich could afford linen or cotton. The peasants grew the plant, stripped the fiber, combed it, spun it, wove it, and finally, sewed it. The hemp was produced both for personal use as well as a cottage industry product. The work was done during the winter, when there was little field work.

With the advance of technology hemp became less important. Hemp has always been a labor intensive crop. It has to be cut. Then the fibrous bark has to be separated from the woody inner portion. This was done using hand brakes and required a large supply of cheap labor. Even with the animal or steam driven brakes which were introduced in the nineteenth century, a large labor pool was required for processing as compared with cotton.

Until the invention of the cotton gin, hemp was inexpensive as compared with cotton, which had bolls containing hundreds of seeds that needed to be combed out by hand. The gin mechanized the production of cotton fiber and made it very inexpensive to produce.

Cotton was grown in very low wage sub-tropical countries, often under slavery, while hemp was grown in the northern tier of very low wage countries such as Russia, where the serf system was still intact.

Intensive colonization of other sub-tropical and tropical areas gave hemp competition from other fibers including sisal, jute and ramie. Post-WWII introduction of synthetics led to further precipitous declines in hemp's use as rope and twine as well as replacing hemp's traditional use as canvas.

Hemp reached its peak in commerce in the 1840's and since that time its use has been declining. Part of the reason for this was the lack of interest in developing labor saving machinery for processing it when cheaper fibers were readily available. When I was in Hungary I saw factories with machinery dating from the 1920–30's. It seems that with the invention of the semi-synthetics, work on natural fibers, except for cotton and wool, virtually ceased.

The FAO reports state that there were 6500 hectares (16,061 acres) grown in Hungary in 1988. In 1991 there were only 5000 hectares (12,355 acres), in 1992 3000 hectares (7,413 acres) and only 300 hectares (741 acres) in 1993 (which was a drought year in which yields were very low). Similar decreases in acreage have been reported in other former eastern bloc countries. The first increases in acreage for many years occurred in 1994 in response to demand for the fiber in the west.

Other countries have responded as well. There was some production in the Czech Republic, Slovakia and the Ukraine. France, Holland and England are also increasing hemp production. In China, the world market for hemp is being taken seriously. There is an experimental crop being grown in Tasmania, Australia. In Canada, several farm groups and business people receive government licenses and grow experimental crops. In the United States, at least one group grew a research crop.

Consumer demand for hemp products in the U.S. and west Europe preceded supply and this trend has continued.

Textiles

Hemp produces between 3 and 5 tons per acre. A total yield of 3.5 tons an acre with a 25% fiber content yields 1750 lbs. of fiber and tow. Between one fourth and one half of it, 440–875 lbs., can actually be spun into a textile grade yarn. A cloth spun of number 10 hemp yarn, similar to a jeans fabric, weighs about 400 grams per square meter (335 grams/ square yard). A single acre yields between 500 and 1,000 square meters (600–1200 square yards) of this fabric. Production of 1,000,000 square meters would require only 1,000–2,000 acres (400–800 hectares). One hundred million pair of jeans would require only 200,000–400,000 acres of land.

When I first visited Hungary in 1991 there was little hope for hemp. The Soviet Union had been purchasing most of the material, and with the collapse of the Union and Russia destitute, the primary customer was gone. When I spoke with bureaucrats at the trading company they thought I was a little weird for my interest in the plant. Now, even as the old industry is drying up, new customers are buying more and more hemp.

Although there was not much interest in hemp technology between the late 1930s and 1990, worldwide interest in hemp fiber has picked up. In 1991 Hungary produced only rough canvas and burlap. Now it produces twills and lightweight fabrics. The technology for spinning yarns has improved considerably. Capital investment is the main slowdown in installing automated machinery, which would make current practices much more efficient. In the future it is likely that technology will continue to progress at a rapid pace. This will result in environmentally friendly methods of producing fine yarns suitable for both weaving and knitting.

When considering textiles, initial cost is only one factor that consumers consider. Although the fabrics now sell at a premium, this has not hurt consumer response. As more hemp supplies come on line the price difference between hemp and other fibers will narrow. The hemp textile industry in the U.S. has grown from a near zero in 1990 to an industry with a retail value which I estimate at $15 million or more.

Hemp is a versatile fabric which can be used for many purposes including apparel, accessories, upholstery and architectural purposes. Fair quality hemp yarns which can be knitted rather than woven have already been produced in China. Higher quality yarns are on the near horizon. Much of the hemp cloth produced in China and Hungary is suitable for clothing including shirts and pants. This cloth can be dyed using techniques for natural fibers. These cloths and finished garments made from them are marketed internationally. Because of the limited supply and antiquated factories producing it, hemp textiles now sell at a high premium as compared with cotton and synthetic textiles.

Consumers who have used hemp clothing or accessories who I have spoken with have been quite satisfied with the items and with new processing techniques the quality will improve even more.

Twine and Rope

Hemp twines and ropes are among the strongest. They have many useful qualities such as their resistance to the degradation of salt-water and their increased strength when wet. Even today, they are used on ships in frigid waters because they remain pliable while plastic-based ropes become brittle and crack under extreme conditions.

Hemp is probably the best of the twines for general use as compared with sisal, ramie and other fibers. For many specialized purposes however, the other fibers supplanted hemp, which was more expensive. For the most part, these fibers and hemp have been replaced by synthetics.

As concern over the environment grows, natural fiber ropes and twines will replace synthetics because of the natural's ability to eventually disintegrate in moist or wet conditions. This may become a minimum ecological requirement in some areas for equipment which may be abandoned or lost, and for consumer items.

Hemp twine has become popular among craftspeople who weave and braid with it. In the near future, as the twine becomes available, this use of hemp will increase dramatically.

Hurds

The woody inner core, called hurds, which is removed from the outer bark, has several uses. It is a raw material for paper, fiber and composite board, building blocks, and is a high source of cellulose. The hurds from Hungarian rope and twine processing are currently turned into carpet padding.

Board

Right now hemp hurds could compete on the world market with wood chips if transportation were not a problem. Wood chips have experienced a steady rise in price since 1989. In 1993 they fetched between $50–55 a ton. Van der Werf estimated that hemp hurds were available in the Ukraine for as little as $20 per metric ton. Hurds were also cheaper than the world market for wood chips in Hungary. Perhaps transport by boat-load rather than container would bring transportation costs down to a competitive level.

Traditionally, hemp hurds were used to fuel the processing and drying of the fiber and were not considered to have much value. In the Ukraine hurds are still considered waste material.

In Hungary and other East European countries they are used to make a press board. The technique is simple. The hurds are chopped to about a quarter-inch in length, which also breaks the stems apart and flattens them. They are placed in a mold and pressed cold. Then they are heated and pressed hot and the phenolic binder is injected. They are cooled, released from the mold, and the sides are cut. Each factory I saw produced a single grade of board. One facility's board used finer pieces of hurd, and as a result had a smoother surface, less pitting and a much more finished look. I did not get structural information on the material.

William Conde and Dave Seber from C & S Specialty Builder's Supply Inc. in Harrisburg, Oregon have been working on converting composite board factories from wood chips to hemp. Because of the cost of transportation it is currently uneconomical to produce hemp boards for markets other than for specialized or niche uses. The main factor for the high cost at the mill is transportation of bulk items from Asia or Europe. If hemp were grown near the factory site and shipped short distances the cost at the mill gate would drop dramatically.

Animal Bedding

The French have been selling hurds to the English for horse bedding. The hurds are considered better quality than the standard wood shavings because they absorb more and compost in one fourth the time. The British began hemp production with the assumption that they could replace French hurds with English. With the £ 225 per acre subsidy from the EC they were sure to make a profit.

There is one firm in France which is making houses from hemp hurds. These Iso Chanvre houses are discussed in the Appendix.

Paper

Until the development of the wood pulping process, most paper was made from old rags. Sailing ships used tremendous quantities of cloth and twine. When the sails and rope became too weak to use any longer on ships it was converted to paper. The action of the salt water and sea air on the material may have helped break down the lignin and pectin holding the fibers together. This is essential in making paper. The weakened fibers would have required less beating and chemicals for conversion to pulp.

Sailing ships faded from the scene beginning in the 1820s and continuing throughout the nineteenth century, reducing the quantity of rag available. This was offset in 1880 when a very polluting commercial process was developed for making paper from wood pulp, which was cheap, abundant and needed no farming. As a first use product, hemp could not compete with cheap pulp for most paper needs, and pollution was not a matter of concern in the 1880s.

The hurds can also be used as a replacement for wood pulp in the paper making process. They have both advantages and disadvantages when compared to wood chips.

High technology paper-making research has been mostly geared to using wood pulp. Techniques for processing and handling hurds and for removing lignin from them have not reached this stage of research yet. Even were the research to show positive results, there is no assurance that hemp will be used. If an entirely new facility were required, it might require an investment estimated at $25–$100 million. Redesigning an existing factory would also require a large economic commitment.

In 1993 the Dutch ended a four year, $40 million integrated research program focusing on the development of hemp as a feedstock for paper mills. There were several teams from different disciplines which focused on all aspects of starting up an industry including breeding, horticultural practices, pulping and paper-making. The final reports will not be made public until 1995. However, as a result of the government research several Dutch farmers have taken an interest in growing hemp.

In England Peter Messenger and John Hanson have both milled paper from imported Spanish pulp in small mills in Scotland. There products are fine quality and have been well received by the public. Only a small proportion of the paper milled worldwide is made from non-woody material. In 1993 Messenger was one of two holders of permits in England. He intends to mill the five acres he has grown.

In France hemp is used as a primary ingredient for making cigarette paper. It is manufactured in three factories. Two of them are owned by Kimberly Clarke. One is located in LeMans. Troyez is the location of another factory. The processes they use are proprietary and well guarded. All three mills produce rolling paper for commercial cigarettes, and much of the paper is exported. In the U.S. most pre-rolled cigarettes appear to be manufactured with this paper. Thus every cigarette smoker is inhaling hemp. Hemp acreage has gradually increased so the farms must be doing fairly well economically.

Other Uses

The percentage of hurds in the French papers may be fairly low. The papers have a very high tensile strength, This indicates that the paper may be made with high percentages of fiber. The French sell hurds for animal bedding. As compared with wood shavings, which are usually used for animal bedding, hemp absorbs more moisture and composts in three months rather than a year. This is important on horse farms, which use a lot of bedding.

Hemp hurds can also be used as a raw material for manufacturing cellulose based products. When rayon was first produced from plant matter, hemp was one of the materials used as feedstock.

Hemp for Fuel

Herer and Osburn claim that hemp is four times as productive as trees. However, looking at Table 1 it is apparent that there are many plants which can produce a higher biomass on an annual basis. They include annuals, perennial and trees. The biomass in hemp, consisting mostly of cellulose and hemicellulose must be used in energy intensive processes in order to convert them into useable fuels unless the stalks were used in a stationary furnace producing heat and electricity. If alcohol is produced energy must be expended to separate it from its solution in water. To get high production of natural gas, the temperature must be maintained high enough for the microbes to have a high rate of metabolism.

Even if some plants yield less per acre, there may be economic advantages to growing them for biomass. Trees and other perennials need much less energy and labor input per unit of harvest. Growing them may be much less harmful to the ecology than keeping fields in annual crops for several reasons. Less energy is expended by not having to plant and harvest each year. Instead, much larger yields are harvested every few years. The soil is disturbed less. Leguminous plants decrease the amount of fertilization required.

Other plants, including annuals such as sugar beets, produce easily fermentable sugars and starches which can be converted to ethyl alcohol very efficiently.

The idea of using hemp for fuel or burning any crop for fuel, including trees, is not really viable except in very special situations. In order to grow the crop a farmer must supply energy inputs such as seed, fertilizer and machinery to plant and harvest and economic inputs including the cost of land. The difference between the energy input and the energy and economic output is the sun's energy which the plants convert into tissue.

Herer and Osburn claim that farmers can earn a profit on this energy difference. If this were so, electric power stations or methanol plants could start by using biomass waste which is now a problem to dispose of. Newsprint contains a very high percentage of cellulose and is an ideal candidate for burning since there is a glut resulting in low prices. Hemp producers cannot match the low prices of waste paper. Even if paper prices rose due to recycling demand there would be other sources of fuel for recycling.

Two sources of wood is scrap from current deconstruction and from dump mining which would separate scrap wood, paper and other cellulose debris from recyclable metals and plastics. Yard wastes, which present collection problems and are no longer allowed to be dumped, have high cellulose content and could also be considered for biomass. If collection programs were instituted probably close to 5 billion dry tons of yard wastes could be collected.

Water hyacinth, a noxious weed, is harvested to prevent it from clogging lakes and waterways. When dried it yields up to 16 tons per acre. Rather than spraying roadsides with herbicides, weeds could be mowed and dried for energy production. Farm animal wastes could be easily converted to methanol. Even stale edible oils resulting from frying food could be used to power diesel engines. All of these energy sources could be utilized with relatively little energy input as compared with farming.

Herer and Osburn claim that hemp is a very drought tolerant crop which needs little fertilizer and can be grown on marginal soil. My travels in England and Hungary have given me some first-hand experience on this matter.

In England I visited a field in Essex in 1993. The soil was a rocky clay loam, considered ideal for hemp. One end of the field had not been fertilized. The plants there had a canopy of less than six feet while in the

ABOVEGROUND, DRY BIOMASS YIELDS OF SELECTED PLANT SPECIES OR COMPLEXES

SPECIES	LOCATION	YIELD (ton/acre-year)
ANNUALS		
Sunflower & Jerusalem Artichoke	Russia	13.5
Sunflower hybrids (seeds only)	California	1.5
Sorghum	Puerto Rico, New Mexico, Iowa, Kansas, North Dakota, Mississippi	7—30
Forage sorghum (irrigated)	Kansas	12
Forage sorghum	North Dakota	7.5
Sweet sorghum	Mississippi	7.5—9
Exotic corn (137-day season)	North Carolina	7.5
Silage corn	Georgia	6–7
Kenaf	Florida, Georgia	8–20
PERENNIALS		
Water Hyacinth	Florida	16
Sugarcane	Mississippi, Florida, Texas, Hawaii, California, Louisiana, Puerto Rico, Philippines	12–50
Sudangrass	California	15–16
Alamo switchgrass	Alabama	6.5
Carthage switchgrass	Kentucky	7.7
Switchgrass	Indiana	7.2
Alfalfa	New Mexico	8
Bamboo	Alabama	7
Cinnamomum camphora (dominant species) & other species	Japan	6.8
Castanopsis japonica (dominant species) & other species	Japan	8.3

SPECIES	LOCATION	YIELD (ton/acre-year)
Hybrid poplar (short rotation)		
Stubble crop (1 year old)	Pennsylvania	8
Stubble crop (2 years old)	Pennsylvania	8
Stubble crop (3 years old)	Pennsylvania	8.7
Red alder (1–14 years old)	Washgton	10
Eucalyptus sp.	California, Spain, India Kenya, Ethiopia, South Africa, Portugal	8.3–24.1
MISCELLANEOUS		
Algae (fresh water pond culture)	California	8–39
Tropical rainforest complex (average)		18.3
Subtropical deciduous forest complex (average)		10.9
World's oceans (primary productivity)		6

fertilized area the canopy was ten feet. Anyone who has grown cannabis, whether hemp or marijuana, knows that the species is a heavy feeder. Furthermore, hemp does best in a rotation with other crops. Some of the crops used in the rotation are maize, wheat, oats, peas, alfalfa and potatoes. Hemp cannot be grown on the same field continuously without fertilizer. Hemp should be grown on a given field only once every two to four years.

In 1991 Hungary got its normal rainfall. When I visited the fields in September of that year the canopy was about ten feet tall. In 1993 Hungary experienced a drought. The number of plants per square meter was very low and the plants were no taller than four feet.

Herer and Osburn claim it would take 6% of the land mass of the U.S. to supply its energy needs by cultivating the crop. The arable land area of the U.S. consists of only 21% of the total land.[4] If hemp were to be grown on 6% of the land it means it would have to be grown on 28% of the arable land. Each piece of arable land would have to grow hemp more often than every four years.

Some arable land such as that devoted to perennials, orchards, dairy or niche farms could not be used for hemp cultivation. This means that new farmland would have to be put under plow, putting considerable stress on the environment. If farmland devoted to dairy, orchards and perennials and niche land were removed from the land available to grow hemp, each piece of non-specialized farmland would probably have to have a hemp crop every other year, a highly improbable situation.

The idea of using marginal land to produce a bio-mass crop is not viable. Consider that with both prime and marginal land a farmer adds the same inputs: tractor, fuel, seed and fertilizer. At harvest prime land produces more than the marginal land so the cost of production per unit will be less on prime land even with the increased cost of the land. The more valuable the crop, the more important this becomes to the producer as small differences in production yields can result in sharply increased earnings.

Much marginal land is currently devoted to wildlife or natural preserve. Much of it is marshy or wet, or on hilly terrain. Draining or tilling this land can create severe erosion problems. Converting it to farmland would be an ecological disaster.

Herer and Osburn say that there is only one plant which is adaptable to conditions in the temperate climate range which can produce biomass. They do not consider that farmers are not interested in a plant just because it adapts to a wide variety of conditions. Farmers look at the micro-conditions of the particular land they are to plant to decide what crops they should grow. Often they grow different crops on one area of a single farm than another, because environmental conditions differ.

Farmers are not interested in which plant will grow under many conditions. Instead they try to figure out which regimen of crops they can use to make the most profit on their land. If a plant performs second best economically in a wide variety of conditions, the farmer is likely not to choose it, but instead to select the best performer.

Herer and Osburn do not realize that solving our energy crisis will take an integrated approach, using many different technologies in order to supply our nation's needs. Energy conservation, solar energy, especially passive water and space heating, electricity from windmills, tidal power and solar batteries, and waste to energy and other technologies can all help to meet our energy requirements and get us off the petroleum addiction.

Energy production would yield a low profit to farmers. Burning should be used as only the last step in a recycling program. After the plant is recycled as paper and cardboard several times, it could be burned or converted to other energy forms. It would be dangerous to rely on one species or even one method for virtually all energy needs.

Seed

Cannabis seed may have been the first part of the plant used by humans and the first to be selected for. Even before the beginning of domestication of plants humans harvested grains. Hemp seed is one of the easiest to gather and it has a very high proportion of oil, which was highly regarded in the lean world of neolithic humans. The oil contains many fatty acids which are essential to human health according to Udo Erasmus, in his book *Fats that Heal, Fats that Kill*. The seed also contains a high proportion of amino acids in ratios appropriate for human consumption. This seed could substitute for meat in much the same way as soybeans.

When I visited Hungary in 1993 I examined feral hemp seed which I found growing near Budapest. These plants had seeds approximately the same length as domesticated plants, however they were oblong rather than rounded. They weighed much less than domestic seed. On some plants the seed dropped off the branches when they were shaken briskly. On other plants the seeds stayed securely on the branch. If once domesticated plants will revert to their original state when left to go feral, these differences in seed morphology may indicate that seed size and retention were selected for by the farmers.

Hemp seed and hemp seed oil have many uses which are described in another article in this book.

A typical seed crop yields twenty to thirty bushels per acre. Since there are 44 pounds in a bushel, this is approximately 900–1300 lbs. per acre. Wholesale prices quoted for hemp seed in the U.S. vary between 20¢–90¢ per pound. Farmers would realize a discount from a gross of between about $375–$1200. This would be a high gross for acreage which usually grows grains. If oil is pressed with a yield of 25% oil by weight, it would produce a yield of 14–21 gallons per acre. The oil currently sells for between $50–$100 per gallon.

The high protein mash, which is usually used as an animal feed supplement can be used as a food.

The Future

Hemp's continuing relationship with humans is assured. After two centuries of decline, the plant has been rediscovered. Environmentalism and other social trends are having a positive effect upon the market and there is a good prospect for hemp's use as a building material. The seeds and their contents also have a high value. The uses of seed products will increase into cosmetics, human nutrition and medicinal qualities.

In the next few years the nascent hemp industry will enlarge many times. Eventually production will have to begin in North America to meet demand for fiber and chips, which are costly to ship. The northern tier growing areas are most likely to benefit from this resurgence in cultivation. Factories and mills will relocate to these areas to minimize transport costs.

Cultivation by American farmers will redistribute farm income. The high profit crop will be grown throughout the midwest. Farm implement makers and seed companies will supply farmers' needs. Specialized farm machinery makers and seed breeders will increase both productivity of the farmer and the plant's genetic structure, increasing both yield and fiber production as a percentage of yield.

On the world scene, there will be a resurgence of hemp cultivation for both textiles and wood chip substitutes. As western and Asian forests are depleted, production of hemp will increase to help meet the demand for wood substitutes.

Eventually, with so much hemp in consumer goods, hemp may actually be used as a bio-fuel as the last stop for carbon products which can no longer be recycled but are useful only as a source of energy.

Can Hemp Save Our Planet?

by David W. Walker, Ph.D.

"IF ALL FOSSIL FUELS *and their derivatives (coal, oil, natural gas, synthetic fibers and petro-chemicals) as well as the deforestation of trees for paper and agriculture (e.g., Brazilian and Indonesian rainforests), are banned from use in order to save the planet, preserve the ozone layer and reverse the greenhouse effect with its global warming trend; then there is only one known renewable natural resource able to provide all of the following goods and essentials such as paper and textiles, meet all the world's transportation, home and industrial energy needs, and clean the atmosphere—all at the same time—our old stand-by that did it all before: Cannabis hemp...marijuana!" (Herer, 1990, p. 11)*

Hemp has been a crop of enormous economic and social value for most of the recorded history of humanity. Jack Herer in his publication *The Emperor Wears No Clothes* (1990) advocates the expanded cultivation of hemp for environmental, economic and social purposes. The objective of this manuscript is to review scientific literature pertinent to the arguments raised by Herer in his book. The literature search was limited to those publications which could be located in the Louisiana State University Library System. There is a great deal more literature on *Cannabis*, hemp, and marijuana which is undoubtedly available in other libraries. Further, most of the contemporary research on the subject of hemp cultivation is reported in Romanian, Bulgarian, and Russian. Those works were not reviewed by this author.

TRADITIONAL USES OF HEMP:
Hemp as a Source of Fiber

A strong, lustrous, and durable fiber is obtained from the inner bark of *Cannabis sativa* (Ash, 1948; Dempsey, 1975). Hemp fiber is particularly valued because the individual fibers may be quite long (3–15 feet) and are very durable and strong (Purseglove, 1966). Since hemp is one of the strongest vegetable fibers known to humanity, sturdy vegetable fibers from several other species have become known as hemp (Ash, 1948; Dempsey, 1975). For example, Manila hemp, sisal hemp, New Zealand hemp, Mauritius hemp, and sunhemp are derived from species other than *Cannabis sativa* (Ash, 1948). *Cannabis sativa* is commonly referred to as true hemp or simply hemp.

Robinson (1943) asserted that the yields of hemp fiber per acre were twice as great as those of flax. Recent yield data, however, indicate that the average worldwide yields of hemp and flax are comparable. For the three-year period beginning in 1985, the worldwide average yields of hemp, flax, and jute were 597 kg/ha (533 lbs/A), 566 kg/ha (505 lbs/A), and 1440 kg/ha (1284 lbs/A), respectively (Anon., 1988).

Uses of hemp fiber. Soft fibers obtained from the inner bark of plants are known as bast fibers (Ash, 1948; Hill, 1952). Bast fibers may be separated into fine flexible strands which can be used in textiles, as cordage, and in paper (Hill, 1952). Hemp has been used since ancient times for spinning into cloth and cordage (Ree, 1966). Hemp is still a popular textile in some parts of the world such as South Korea, where in the 1960s it was estimated that one-third of the population wore hemp garments because of their exceptional durability (Ree, 1966). This cloth is described as coarse and stiff having an average life span of about 3 years (Ree, 1966). Although some authors assert that hemp is not suitable for use in finer textiles (Kirby, 1963), others state that the finer grades of hemp fiber may be spun into yarns which may be used to produce soft and lustrous fabrics (Dempsey, 1975) or coarse linen (Hill, 1952).

Bast fibers are also obtained from flax, jute, and ramie (Hill, 1952). In modern times, and in decades past, advocates of expanded hemp production have called hemp fiber "the strongest vegetable fiber known to man" (Malyon and Henman, 1980). On the other hand, several reports state that hemp fiber is less flexible and elastic than flax (Hill, 1952; Kirby, 1963). Hill (1952) adds that hemp lacks flexibility and elasticity because it is more lignified than flax. Furthermore, Kirby (1963) and Berger (1969) believe that another limitation of hemp fiber's use in finer textiles is that the fibers are not easily bleached or dyed. Christie (1987) reported the relative fitness of hemp, flax, ramie, and jute for use in textiles. Relative to hemp, ramie had greater tensile strength and flax had greater cohesiveness. According to the report, both flax and ramie had greater durability, fiber length, fineness, uniformity, and color than hemp. Flax, ramie, and jute had greater pliability than hemp (Christie, 1987). Christie's data would favor flax and ramie over hemp for use in textiles. Unquestionably, other evaluators may arrive at different conclusions.

Hemp has been and is used for a wide variety of other purposes. One of hemp fiber's more important characteristics is that it is unaffected by water (Berger, 1969). Ropes, sailcloth, and canvases used by navies and maritime interests were primarily manufactured from hemp before the introduction of Manila hemp and sisal hemp (Haarer, 1953; Malyon and Henman, 1980). Hemp has also been used to make carpet, twine, sacks, bags, webbing, nets, and tarpaulins (Berger, 1969; Hill, 1952; Kirby, 1963). According to Haarer (1953) and Kirby (1963), ropes and binder twine made from other vegetable fibers such as abaca and sisal are as good, if not better, than those manufactured from hemp fiber. Haarer adds that jute has replaced hemp as a source of fiber in the manufacture of carpet, wrapping twine, and sacking fabrics. Sisal hemp and abaca have replaced hemp as a material for making cordage because, according to Kirby (1963), such fibers are stronger and more suitable.

Extracting fiber from hemp stalks. After harvest, the fiber must be removed from the hemp stalk. The labor intensive nature of this process, called retting, has apparently contributed to the decline of hemp production and utilization (Malyon and Henman, 1980). There are three methods of retting: dew retting, snow retting, and water retting (Kirby, 1963). Dew retting was the most widely used retting process in the U.S. prior to marijuana prohibition though it is considered to produce fiber inferior to water retting (Haarer, 1953). Dew retting was mechanized to a large degree during World War II (Haarer, 1953). In this process, fungi act to degrade the cut stalks as they lay in the field; morning dew provides the required moisture for the maintenance of fungal populations (Christie, 1987). During the decomposition, the stalks must be turned over in order to expose the entire surface to microbial degradation (Hackleman and Domingo, 1943), hence the need for mechanization. Over-retting, allowing too much degradation, quickly reduces the strength and quality of the fiber (Hackleman and Domingo, 1943). Snow retting is practiced in the Soviet Union and resembles dew retting with the exception that the moisture required for decomposition is provided by snowfall rather than dew (Kirby, 1963).

Water retting, which is practiced in Europe and the Far East (Christie, 1987) involves placing the cut stalks in a pool or tank of water which favors decomposition of the stalks by bacterial action (Haarer, 1953). Finer and better-quality fibers are obtained from water or tank retting (Christie, 1987). These fibers are more suitable for processing into finer textiles. Unfortunately, this process is quite labor-intensive adding significantly to the cost of hemp fiber production and processing (Malyon and Henman, 1980). Ash (1948), reported that numerous chemical-retting processes have been tested and found to be unsuitable for adoption on a commercial scale.

After retting, the fiber must be physically removed from the stalks by breaking. Essentially, the woody pulp in the core of the stalk must be broken so that the fibers may be removed. Even today, this process is accomplished entirely by hand in most production areas adding enormously to the cost of hemp production and processing. An experienced hemp breaker can break only 100 to 200 pounds of hemp daily (Dacy, 1921).

Economics of hemp production for fiber. Domestic hemp production was at its greatest in the middle portion of the nineteenth century (Dempsey, 1975). During the Crimean War (1854–1856), access to Russian hemp was limited and domestic production did not keep pace with demand. Consequently, industry began to use abaca and other fibers obtained from tropical plants. The development of steam-driven ships reduced the need for sailcloth, for which hemp was uniquely well-suited, having a negative impact on the hemp production (Malyon and Henman, 1980). Hemp production in the U.S. gradually declined until World War I when it increased temporarily (Dempsey, 1957). In World War II access to jute and abaca was denied when the Japanese military occupied production areas and controlled shipping lanes in the Pacific (Ash, 1948). During that period of shortage the U.S. federal government engaged in a intensive and ambitious campaign to increase domestic production of hemp fiber. The revival of hemp production was short-lived, however, and demand for domestic hemp waned when shipments of lower-priced abaca, jute, and sisal were resumed (Ash, 1948; Dempsey, 1975).

Since World War II, worldwide production of hemp also has declined due to competition from sisal, jute, and abaca. The costs associated with hemp production and processing, primarily the labor-intensive activities of retting and breaking, has made the utilization of hemp less competitive (Berger, 1969; Haarer, 1953). In France, which has developed a hemp paper industry, hemp production for textiles is practically non-existent (Malyon and Henman, 1980). Even in previously-important hemp producing nations, such as Italy, hemp production has suffered from lower-priced, imported tropical fibers (Kirby, 1963). Further, the prohibition of marijuana has had a negative impact on hemp production in Western countries (Haarer, 1953).

Improvements in hemp production and processing technology could make the crop more competitive with tropical fibers (Ash, 1948). Even though mechanical breakers were developed in the early part of this century (Dacy, 1921), this technology has not been widely adopted in contemporary production areas for reasons which are not entirely clear.

A distinct improvement in the production of hemp which facilitates mechanical harvesting of the crop has been the development of dioecious varieties of hemp (Dempsey, 1975). Hemp is a mostly monoecious crop, plants which produce only male or only female flowers. This trait confounded efforts to mechanically harvest the crop because male plants reach maturity and die several weeks before female plants. By the time female plants have the most-desirable fiber characteristics, male plants have long since died and begun to rot. Dioecious plants mature at roughly the same time and mechanical harvest is more practical (Dempsey, 1975). Dioecious varieties are presently being grown in some western European countries, but most of the worldwide production still appears to depend upon monoecious varieties.

Hemp Fibers as a Source of Paper

Some of the first papers ever produced were apparently made from hemp fibers (Isenberg, 1956). The fibers of hemp are still used as a raw material for paper (Berger, 1969; Hill, 1952). Both hemp and jute are used to produce scuff- and tear-resistant papers (Clark, 1965). Isenberg (1956) asserts that most of the hemp fiber used to produce paper is obtained from discarded textiles or cordage.

Malyon and Henman (1980) describe a relatively new paper industry based in France in which hemp is produced solely for the purpose of manufacturing high-quality, durable paper. Even though hemp production for fiber has declined substantially in France, hemp production for paper increased through at least 1977 (Malyon and Henman, 1980). The secret to the French hemp paper industry was the development of a mechanized breaking process to remove the fibers from the woody pulp of the hemp stalk. Malyon and Henman (1980) add that this process appears to be cost-effective only when undertaken on a fairly large-scale basis. The authors asserted that the French were quite convinced that their hemp paper industry was an unquestioned success. Further discussion of hemp as a source of paper will be covered later in the section entitled "New and Proposed Uses of Hemp."

Hemp as an Oilseed Crop

"Hemp seed can either be pressed for its vegetable oil, leaving a high-protein seed cake as a byproduct or it can be sprouted (malted) and used like any other seed (in) salads or cooking." (Herer, 1990, op. 9)

Finally, hemp seed contains 30% (by volume) oil. This oil makes high grade diesel fuel oil and aircraft engine and precision machine oil. (Herer, 1990, p. 44)

Major production of hemp as an oilseed crop is limited to the Soviet Union (Haarer, 1953) with some production in Turkey, Taiwan, Romania, China, Japan, Hungary, Czechoslovakia, and France (Vaughan, 1970).

The extracted oil is used much like linseed oil in paints, varnish, and for the manufacture of soap (Hill, 1952; Purseglove, 1966; Small et al., 1975). The oil is a drying oil which absorbs oxygen and dries into thin elastic films (Hill, 1952). Dempsey (1975) writes that the oil is also edible. After the oil has been extracted, the remaining oil-cake is used as a livestock feed (Small et al., 1975). The oil content of seeds and seed yields are discussed in a later section on the use of vegetable oils as an energy source.

Hemp Seed as a Protein Source

"The marijuana hemp seed...is the second most 'complete'—with the eight essential amino acids—vegetable protein source on our planet. Soybeans alone have a bit more protein. However, hemp seed is many times cheaper and its protein potential is more efficiently utilized by the human body than soybean. In fact, the marijuana seed is the highest in content of enzymes, edistins (globulated oils), (sic) and overall amino acids of any food on our planet, including the soybean." (Herer, 1990, p. 41)

"The marijuana seed's combination of amino acids, enzymes, and edistins (sic) make more food protein and nutrients available to the human body than any other food on Earth." (Herer, 1990, p. 42)

Only one report stating the protein content of hemp seeds was found and no reports describing the amino acid composition of hemp seeds were located. The only report found (Purseglove, 1966) stated that the seeds contain 22% protein. Soybean seeds were reported to contain 34% protein (Whigham, 1981) and 32–42% protein (Payne, 1983). Peanut kernels reportedly contain 21 to 36% protein (Woodruff, 1981) and 25 to 28% protein (Payne, 1983). The seeds of another legume, chickpea, consists of 20 to 28% protein (Payne, 1983). Legumes such as chickpea, peanut, and soybean generally include greater quantities of protein than the seeds of plants from other families. Sunflower seeds contain 15–20% protein according to Monk and Kresovich (1987), while Payne (1983) reports that they consist of 27% protein. The proportion of cotton seeds which is protein is 23% according to Parnell (1981) and 17 to 21% according to Payne (1983). Flax seeds consist of 24% protein (Dybing and Lay, 1981). Oilseed rape is 20–25% protein and sesame seeds are 25% protein (Payne, 1983). Contrary to Herer's (1990) proclamations, the protein content of hemp seeds does not appear to be exceptional.

Apparently, hemp is unique in that 65% of the storage proteins found in hemp seeds are globulin edestin (St. Angelo et al., 1964; St. Angelo et al., 1966; Stockwell et al., 1964). The value of edestin to human/mammalian nutrition could not be determined. Other references to edestin were not found.

Hemp as Birdseed

"Hemp seed was—until the 1937 prohibition law—the world's number one bird seed, and also the birds' favorite." (Herer, 1990, p. 9)

There are several reports in the literature stating that doves and bobwhite quail fed extensively on hemp seeds when these seeds were available (McClure, 1943; Robel, 1969). In fact, when hemp seeds were abundant in Iowa they represented the primary source of food for doves (McClure, 1943). Further, captive doves prospered on a diet consisting solely of hemp seeds (McClure, 1943). Carr and James (1931) indicated that hemp seeds seem "to be a remarkably well-balanced grain" and that pigeon squabs fed diets of hemp seeds made impressive weight gains while on the diet. Purseglove (1966) adds that hemp seeds are used in both bird and poultry feed. This evidence verifies the claim made by Herer (1990) that hemp seed are evidently a very good food for birds.

Hemp as a Livestock Feed

The fact that an oil-cake may be derived from the waste products of oil extraction from hemp seeds was briefly mentioned in the section on hemp as an oilseed crop (Small et al., 1975). This oil-cake is used as a livestock feed in areas where hemp seeds are produced for their oil.

Recent research was conducted to evaluate hemp waste, presumably resulting from fiber extraction, as livestock feed during periods of severe feed shortages (Jain and Arora, 1988). The authors analyzed the refuse for nutrient content and found it contained 17–18% crude protein. In order to improve the palatability of the hemp refuse, water-treated refuse was compared to untreated refuse. Both water-treated and untreated refuse were then used in four different livestock rations in concentrations of 0, 15, 30, and 45% refuse. The various rations were then fed to crossbred bulls and their daily consumption of the rations was measured. The palatability of hemp refuse was not improved by the water treatment. Feed consumption by bulls fed water-treated refuse was significantly lower than that of bulls fed no hemp refuse. Bulls fed rations consisting of 15% untreated hemp refuse ate as much as those bulls fed no refuse. However, when the concentration of hemp refuse in the feed exceeded 15%, decreased consumption was apparent (Jain and Arora, 1988).

NEW AND PROPOSED USED OF HEMP:
Hemp Hurds as a Source of Paper

"Hemp is 77% cellulose, a basic chemical feed stock (industrial raw material) used in the production of chemicals, plastics and fibers." (Herer, 1990, p. 44)

"Hemp hurds are also the most efficient source of cellulose." (Herer, 1990, p. 46)

"The fragments of dried stalk that remain are hurds, which are 77% cellulose and can be made into dioxin-free paper, non-toxic paints and sealants, industrial fabrication materials, construction materials, plastics and much, much more." (Herer, 1990, p. 13)

"...and this process would use only ¹/₅ to ¹/₇ as much polluting sulfur-based acid chemicals to break down the glue-like lignin that binds the fibers of the pulp." "Hemp is only 4% lignin, while trees are 18–30% lignin. Thus

hemp provides four times as much pulp with at lease five to seven times less pollution..." (Herer, 1990, p. 21)

"The problem of dioxin contamination of rivers is avoided in the hemp paper making process which does not use chlorine bleach (as the wood pulp paper making process requires) but instead safely substitutes hydrogen peroxide in the bleaching process." (Herer, 1990, p. 21)

After the fiber has been removed from hemp stalks, the remaining woody material is commonly referred to as hemp hurds. Herer (1990) makes a persuasive case for using hemp hurds as a source of paper pulp based on two contentions. First, Herer asserts that hemp hurds contain exceptional quantities of cellulose and produce much more biomass than any other agricultural plant species. The production of a substantial quantity of cellulose would be a desirable trait for a new major source of paper pulp since cellulose is the essential raw material for paper. The issue of biomass production will be discussed in the following section on using hemp as an energy source. Herer's second argument for using hemp hurds as a source of paper pulp is based on the premise that hemp hurds contain less lignin than other sources of paper pulp. A lower lignin content should reduce the amount of processing required and, presumably, produce less pollution.

As was discussed in a previous section, hemp fibers have long been used as a source of paper. Two sources report that hemp *fiber* is 67% cellulose (Berger, 1969; Kirby, 1963). Another source states that the fiber is 70% cellulose (Purseglove, 1966). Christie (1987) declares that hemp contains 65% cellulose and 16% hemicellulose. According the Christie's data, the total cellulosic content of hemp plants is 81%, a figure very similar to that reported by Herer (1990). The proportion of cellulose in hemp hurds is less well known. West (1921) describes inconsistencies between several reported studies describing the composition of hemp wood. Even by their most conservative estimates hemp wood is 52% cellulose. But West discounts a report that hemp wood contains as much as 71% cellulose. The original articles upon which West's conclusions were drawn could not be located. Comparing these rough estimates to those of other paper sources, coniferous woods such as longleaf pine and

Douglas fir contain about 60% cellulose (Clark, 1965). Deciduous woods, such as Aspen poplar and white maple are a little greater than 60% cellulose (Clark, 1965). Several non-woody plants which could also be used as sources of paper pulp have comparable quantities of cellulose. For example, depithed sugarcane is greater than 60% cellulose (Alexander, 1985; Clark, 1965). Retted flax, a product comparable to hemp hurds is 64% cellulose and 17% hemicellulose, respectively (Christie, 1978). Moreover, jute fibers contain 75% cellulose according to Christie (1987). Flax and jute, therefore, contain quantities of cellulosic material comparable to that of hemp. Bamboo contains between 44 and 62% cellulose (Clark, 1965). Straws from cereal grains contain 43 to 54% cellulose and rice straw is 43 to 47% cellulose (Clark, 1965).

The lignin content of annual plants is much lower than that of woody plants, the conventional source of paper pulp today. Lignins are polymers of phenolic acid which harden the cell wall, comprised of cellulose and hemicellulose, into an inelastic and enduring material resistant to microbial degradation. An essential requirement of producing paper pulp is the process of delignification, removing the lignin from the cellulose (Hunsigi, 1989). It is the process of delignification which accounts for most of the pollution originating from pulp mills. Hunsigi (1989) confirms that annual plants are lower in lignin than woody plants and would require lesser amounts of chemicals for cooking and bleaching. The wood from trees and other woody plants generally contains 20 to 30% lignin, whereas fibers from non-woody, annual plants consists of 10 to 20% lignin (Hunsigi, 1989).

Reports of the amount of lignin in hemp are widely variable. Christie (1987) states that hemp fibers contain only 8% lignin. On the other hand, it has been suggested that male plants have a lignin content of between 13 and 16 per cent of dry weight, while the lignin content of the female plants is between 23 and 25 per cent (Kirby, 1963). The amount of lignin found in the studies cited by West (1921) ranged from 22% to 30%. Herer's assertion that hemp contains as little as 4% lignin seems disputable. It is possible that this kind of genetic variability for lignin content may exist with the species *Cannabis sativa*, but that variability, to the best of my knowledge, has not been documented in scientific literature. Clouding the issue even further is the research of West (1921) which found that four chlorinations were necessary to prepare a lignin-free crude cellulose extract; three chlorinations were insufficient. Obviously, further research specifically addressing this characteristic of hemp fiber and hemp hurds is warranted.

Other bast fibers share the same desirable characteristics of hemp according to Hunsigi (1989). These include kenaf, mesta, flax, esparto grass, and reeds. Hunsigi adds that all these plants generally have lignin contents in the vicinity of 15 percent. A waste product of sugar extraction from sugarcane called bagasse, widely suggested as a source of paper pulp, contains about 20% lignin (Hunsigi, 1989). Abaca is about 11% lignin, while bamboo contains 23% lignin (Hunsigi, 1989). Eucalyptus, a species with incredible biomass production potential, is 28% lignin (Hunsigi, 1989). In addition, retted flax reportedly contains 2% lignin, while jute contains 11% lignin (Christie, 1987). It appears likely that several non-woody plant species probably contain less lignin than hemp.

At the time of his writing, Clark (1965) reported that over 300 paper mills worldwide used non-woody materials for paper manufacturing. The use of non-woody, annual fibrous plants was much more common in countries where pulpwoods derived from trees were limited (Clark, 1965). Further, the production of fiber crops for paper pulp is much more widespread in developing countries (Hunsigi, 1989). On the other hand, Isenberg (1956) indicated that at the time of his writing 95% of the paper in the world was made from wood.

According to Hunsigi (1989) interest in the use of agricultural fibers as a source of paper pulp has been renewed due to concerns about the environmental impacts of using trees as the primary source of paper products. The production of paper from plant fibers is not at all limited to hemp. Hunsigi contends that paper can be manufactured from any plant material containing cellulose, the chief component of plant cell walls. Hunsigi estimates that of the one-quarter million known plant species, about 400 species from the plant families, Gramineae (Poaceae), Leguminosae (Fabaceae), and Malvaceae, have the greatest potential as sources of paper pulp (Hunsigi, 1989). The use of agricultural fibers has its drawbacks, though. As compared with forest-based pulp sources, fibrous crops typically have low-bulk density requiring larger storage facilities. Further, the supply of agricultural fibers is generally seasonal, which can increase the cost of operating and maintaining processing facilities (Barnard, 1984). Many of these fibers are at least somewhat perishable meaning that they may require controlled storage or rapid processing. Hunsigi (1989) adds that removing the fibers and converting them into paper pulp is presently a labor-intensive process. These problems are clearly characteristic of most, if not all, agricultural fibers, hemp not withstanding.

Hunsigi (1989) has ranked these potential paper species in order of importance with sugarcane first followed by bamboo, straws (including rice, rye, wheat, sorghum, maize, and barley), kenaf, mesta, *hemp*, abaca, sisal, henequen, jute, ramie, flax, and sunhemp. Hunsigi predicts that sugarcane bagasse will become the predominant source of non-woody paper pulp in the near future. Clark (1965) also contends that sugarcane bagasse is an excellent non-woody source of paper pulp. Further, another bast fiber, kenaf has received a great deal of research interest during the past two decades (Hunsigi, 1989) suggesting that this plant may also become much more important as a source of paper pulp. Although bamboo is a photosynthetically-efficient grass, Hunsigi (1989) cites problems with the flowering of bamboo as having restricted its use as a raw material for paper. Hunsigi adds that "plant fibres like hemp, flax, kenaf, and mesta need to be used more intensively either singly or in a (mixture) for the production of specialty thin papers such as cigarette paper, tea bags, currency notes, etc. This would, perhaps, more than compensate for the high costs involved in the transport, handling, and storage of these bulky materials." Many more plant species are mentioned by Hunsigi (1989), Clark (1965), and Isenberg (1956) as being potential sources of raw material for paper pulping.

Plants as a Source of Energy

"Biomass conversion through pyrolysis (applying high heat to organic material in the absence of air or in reduced air) will make charcoal to replace coal." (Herer, 1990, p. 44)

Processes for using biomass as an energy source. Before discussing the potential value of growing hemp as an energy crop, the technology available for converting plant biomass into energy should be addressed. The processes could be used to produce not only liquid petroleum fuels, but petroleum-based products such as plastics, cellophane, polyvinylchloride (PVC), etc. Presently, four biomass conversion technologies are either available now or may be technically feasible in the near future. First, ethanol can be produced from food crops with high sugar or starch content (Anon., 1981; Coombs, 1983). Crops such as sugarcane, sugar beet, maize, cassava, pineapple, sweet sorghum, and potatoes are considered to be the most promising (Anon., 1981). In addition, the yeast-based fermentation process used to produce ethanol has already been developed on a commercial scale (Anon., 1981; Coombs, 1983). In fact, this technology is the most well-established of the four processes for converting biomass to energy. The resulting liquid fuel, ethanol, is reasonably compatible with the spark plug-type internal combustion engine, but cannot be used to operate diesel engines (Coombs, 1983).

In another method, lignocellulosic material from trees, grasses, and agricultural crops can be converted into ethanol (Anon, 1981). According to a United Nations report (Anon, 1981), grasses, shrubs, fast-growing trees such as eucalyptus and poplar, some hardwood tree species, and latex-bearing plants could supply the raw cellulose and lignin required for this process. Apparently fast-growing water plants such as water hyacinth and sea kelp, as well as algae, could also supply the needed raw material (Anon., 1981). This process first involves the hydrolysis of cellulose into fermentable sugars. The subsequent fermentation and distillation of the resultant sugars is identical to that describe above for high sugar/high starch crops (Anon., 1981).

In the third process, methanol, commonly known as wood alcohol, is produced from wood, crops, and grasses (Anon., 1981). Presently, methanol is commercially synthesized from natural gas. The production of methanol from biomass is envisioned as a three-step process (Anon., 1981). First, the lignocellulosic material is converted into a synthetic gas via a high temperature thermochemical conversion (Anon., 1981; Coombs, 1983). In the second step, the gas is cleaned and the carbon monoxide to hydrogen ratio is adjusted. Finally, the synthetic gas is liquefied and catalytically converted to methanol. The latter two steps use well-established technologies, while the first step requires additional development (Anon., 1981). Furthermore, as of 1981, biomass conversion to methanol had not been performed on a commercial scale. Coombs (1983) states that the thermochemical conversion of biomass to methanol is preferable to other known processes for the production of liquid fuel from plant biomass because the properties of the raw materials are much less exacting than those of materials used for the production of ethanol via the yeast-fermentation system.

Finally, a fuel very similar to diesel fuel can be obtained from vegetable oil crops (Anon., 1981; Coombs, 1983). Examples of plant species from which vegetable oil may be extracted include oil palm, coconuts, soybeans, sunflowers, cotton, rape, groundnuts (Anon., 1981) and, of course, hemp. The oil is simply squeezed out of seeds and can be used as a fuel in diesel engines with relatively little additional refinement (Anon, 1981). As mentioned previously, the waste product is an oil-cake which can be fed to livestock. There is one major drawback. The international price of vegetable oil as a food is about 3 more expensive than the price of diesel fuel when crude oil is selling for $30 per barrel (Anon., 1981; Monk and Kresovich, 1987). The use of vegetable oils as a diesel substitute, therefore, is not economically viable at the present time.

Of these four processes, hemp could serve as a raw material for latter three. The long-term potential for deriving significant, sustainable quantities of liquid fuel from plant materials appears to be greatest for those processes which depend upon cellulose rather than sugar, starch, or oil (Anon. 1981). This is partly because most of the world's stored biomass reserves are in the form of cellulose. On the other hand, it must be recognized that liquid fuel production from cellulose still has some technological barriers to overcome before large-scale commercial production can be economically feasible (Anon., 1981). Coombs (1983) argues that probability for developing efficient and economically viable thermoconversion processes is greater than the probability that the use of vegetable oils or sugar and starch crops can be made economically feasible. These predictions about the future of biomass conversion technology are in favor developing energy crops based on cellulosic production potential.

Biomass Potential of Hemp

"Remarkably, when considered on a planet-wide, climate-wide, soil-wide basis, cannabis is four to 50 times richer in renewable biomass/cellulose potential than its nearest rivals on the planet—cornstalks, sugarcane, kenaf, trees, etc." (Herer, 1990, p. 9)

"Hemp is the best source of plant bulk for biomass fuel, to make gas, charcoal, methanol, gasoline, or even used to produce electricity." (Herer, 1990, p. 13)

"In 1916, the U.S. Department of Agriculture wrote in special bulletin No. 404, that one acre of cannabis hemp, in annual rotation over a 20-year period, would produce as much pulp for paper as 4.1 acres of trees being cut down over the same 20-year period, ..." (Herer, 1990, p. 21)

"Depending on which U.S. agricultural report is correct, an acre of full grown hemp plants can sustainably provide from four to 50 or even 100 times the cellulose found in cornstalks, kenaf, or sugar cane—the planet's next highest annual cellulose plants." (Herer, 1990, p. 44)

"'Illegal' hemp is earth's #1 biomass resource; it is capable of producing 10 tons per acre in four months." (Herer, 1990, p. 44–45, 47)

As discussed previously, a large part of the argument for using hemp as a biomass energy crop and as a source of pulpwood is based on the presumption that hemp produces enormous quantities of biomass and cellulose. A 1916 USDA publication by Dewey and Merrill states that one acre of hemp will produce as much lignocellulosic biomass for paper as four acres of pulpwood. Their calculations are based on a pulpwood yield of 0.185 tons/acre/year and a hemp hurd yield of 2.5 tons/acre/year. Osburn (date not available) asserts that "Farmers must be allowed to grow an energy crop capable of producing 10 tons per acre in 90–120 days." "Hemp is the number one biomass producer on planet Earth: 10 tons per acre in approximately four months." The source or basis for Osburn's assertions cannot be obtained from the article. It, therefore, would seem reasonable to verify these data with reports of biomass yields from hemp and other possible sources of paper, including pulpwood.

Based on 1985–87 data, a very good yield of hemp fiber in European nations ranges from 1400 to 2100 kg/ha (1250 to 1870 lbs/A) (Anon., 1988). Various estimates suggest that the total biomass yield of hemp plants is from four to five times that of the fiber yield (Berger, 1969; Dempsey, 1975; Dewey and Merrill, 1916; Kirby, 1963; Wilsie et al., 1944; Purseglove, 1966). It could, thereby, be concluded that a good biomass yield from hemp plants grown for fiber would be in the range of 5,600 to 10,500 kg/ha (5,000 to 9,400 lbs/A or 2.5 to 4.7 tons/A).

Dempsey (1975) describes the various components of the total hemp plant biomass yield. He estimates that a good yield of green hemp plants would be about 40,000 kg/ha (36,000 lbs/A or 18 tons/A). The yield of green stems would be approximately 28,000 kg/ha (28 mt/ha, 24,976 lbs/A, or 12.49 tons/A). These green-weight yield data are similar to Osburn's 10 tons/A estimate. The total hemp plant dry weight would be about 16,500 kg/ha (14,700 lbs/A or 7.4 tons/A). Of that dry weight, about 10,500 kg/ha (9,400 lbs/A or 4.7 tons/A) would consist of dried stems (Dempsey, 1975).

The best yields of wood (assumed to be green weight, not dry weight) from traditional pulpwood species grown in northwestern Europe are in the range of 10 to 12 mt/ha/yr (4.5 to 5.4 tons/A/yr) and may be as great as 13 to 17 mt/ha/yr (5.8 to 7.6 tons/A/yr) in Ireland (Cannell, 1988). Intensively-cultivated plots of Salix have yielded 8 to 10 mt/ha/yr (3.5 to 4.5 tons/A/yr) in Sweden (Cannell, 1988). In southern Europe, *Eucalyptus* trees can yield from 29.4 to 66.5 mt/ha/yr (13 to 30 tons/A/yr) (Hunsigi, 1989). *Populus* grown in Italy yield about 14 mt/ha/yr (6 tons/A/yr) of wood and irrigated stands of fast-growing species such as *Platanus* can yield 15 mt/ha/yr (6.7 tons/A/yr) in Greece (Cannell, 1988). The biomass production potential of hemp is, accordingly, greater than that of trees grown for pulpwood.

Several non-woody annual species have even greater yields. Cassava, sweet potato, kenaf, and mesta can yield up to 20 mt/ha (9 tons/A) (Barnard, 1984; Hunsigi, 1989). Good yields of sweet sorghum are in the range of 35 mt/ha (15.6 tons/A) (Barnard, 1984). The biomass production potential of these non-woody species is similar to that of hemp. Napier grass will yield 66 mt/ha/yr (29 tons/A) (Hunsigi, 1989). Finally, good biomass yields of sugarcane are about 75 mt/ha/yr (33 ton/A/yr) (Barnard, 1984). Hunsigi (1989) reports sugarcane yields of 104 mt/ha/yr (46 tons/A/yr). Clearly, sugarcane and napier grass produce much more biomass than hemp and have much greater potential for biomass production.

The efficiency with which certain plants are able to capture light energy and use it to assimilate carbon dioxide into carbohydrates is the most important factor in selecting plants with the greatest biomass production potential (Anon., 1981). Many tropical grasses such as sugarcane, sorghum, and maize (corn) have a pathway for photosynthesis commonly known as C_4 photosynthesis which is much more efficient than the pathway common to most other plants, especially dicots like hemp. As Alexander (1985) states in his book *The Energy Cane Alternative*, "together with certain of its tropical grasses relatives, sugarcane is the finest living collector of sunlight known to man." Given that these plant species share with hemp the potential for multiple product use and that some of them are widely adapted, especially sorghum, many believe that biomass production will rely heavily upon plant species which utilize the C_4 pathway of photosynthetic carbon fixation (Monk and Kresovich, 1987).

Sugarcane shares with oil palm and coconut another characteristic which favors their utilization as a biomass crop. Most other energy crops are only available on a seasonal basis, whereas these three crops can be made available on a nearly continuous basis. Of course, sugarcane is adapted to tropical and subtropical climates while oil palm and coconut can only be grown in the tropics. It seems likely that any type of energy crop grown in temperate climates would be available only on a seasonal basis. This fact could mean that long-term storage facilities would have to be constructed. Moreover, some crops would require immediate processing, while others could be stored for significant periods of time. Especially in temperate zones, dependence upon a single crop as an energy source would also seem quite unlikely, in part because, most crops cannot be grown successively and must be rotated with other crops (Barnard, 1984). Hemp's requirement for rotation will be discussed later.

Hemp as a Source of Vegetable Oil for Energy Uses

"Biomass can be grown for fuel at about $30 per ton or seed crops can be pressed for oil; the left over seed cake makes a high protein raw food resource." (Herer, 1990, p. 45)

"Finally, hemp seed contains 30% (by volume) oil. This oil makes high grade diesel fuel oil and aircraft engine and precision machine oil." (Herer, 1990, p. 44)

Hemp seeds are generally reported to consist of 30 to 35% oil (Dempsey, 1975; Haarer, 1953; Purseglove, 1966). Robinson (1952) maintains that the oil content can vary from 20 to 34%. On the other hand, Small et al. (1975) found little difference between drug and fiber varieties of hemp for oil content. They indicated that a Russian variety known as 'Olerifera' contained 40% oil, while most of the other varieties were 30% oil. It was their opinion that a "good oil variety" would be one that produced greater yields of seeds rather than contained a larger proportion of oil (Small et al., 1975). For comparison purposes, flax seeds reportedly contain 36% oil (Dybing and Lay, 1981) and sunflower seeds consist of 40–50% oil (Monk and Kresovich, 1987).

According to Dempsey (1975), a good yield of hemp seeds would be in the range of 600 to 1100 kg/ha (530 to 980 lbs/A). Purseglove (1966) said that if hemp were grown solely for seeds at a wider spacing, yields of approximately 1350 kg/ha (1200 lbs/A) could be obtained. Other oilseed crops with comparable yields include soybean (2700 kg/ha or 2400 lbs/A), groundnut (1300 kg/ha or 1160 lbs/A), rapeseed (1000 kg/ha or 900 lbs/A), and sesame (800 kg/ha or 715 lbs/A) (Barnard, 1984). The oil extracted from the seeds of any of these species could be used as a liquid fuel.

Overall Potential of Plants as a Source of Energy

"Farming only 6% of continental U. S. acreage with biomass would provide all of America's energy needs and end dependence on fossil fuels." (Herer, 1990, p. 44–45)

We clearly possess the ability to produce energy from plant biomass. The overall potential for producing a significant proportion of our energy needs from energy crops is overstated by Herer. These limitations become more apparent when we consider that only 9% of the earth's land surface is arable (Thomas et al., 1973). Estimates are that 21% of the land area in the United States is agriculturally productive. Some nations have a larger proportion of arable land (France 35%, India 42%, Denmark 62%) while others have much less (China 11%, Soviet Union 9%) (Thomas et al., 1973). Most of the surface area of the planet has been explored and most experts do not believe significant amounts of agriculturally productive land will be discovered in the future. In fact, deforestation of lands presumed to be arable may have contributed to the "greenhouse effect" and, regrettably, much of this land was productive for only two to three years before the soil developed a consistency not unlike concrete.

The Food and Agriculture Organization of the United Nations has estimated that if the entire world production of cereals, root crops, and sugar crops had been converted to ethanol that "less than 83 percent of the world's 1978 automobile gasoline fuel needs and only 6 percent of the world's total commercial energy needs" would have been met (Anon., 1981).

Producing Hemp Without Cannabinoids

"If you really want to save the planet with hemp, then you would find a way to grow it without the narcotic top and then you can use it." (Dr. Gary Evans of the USDA as quoted in Herer, 1990, p. 12)

"...hemp grown for biomass makes very poor grade marijuana. The 20 to 40 million Americans who smoke marijuana would loath to smoke hemp grown for biomass, so a farmer's hemp biomass crop is worthless as marijuana." (Osburn, date not available)

The drug and fiber types of *Cannabis* are sufficiently distinct that some scientists have contended that hemp was not a single species but actually two or more species (Small et al., 1975; Small and Cronquist, 1976). Although the plant morphology is somewhat different, the primary distinction of interest is in the quantity and types of cannabinoids produced. That is, the drug types produce large quantities of the psychoactive tetrahydrocannabinol (THC) whereas the fiber types are generally believed to produce very little, if any, THC (Small et al, 1975). The cannabinoid content of *Cannabis sativa* is now known to be genetically controlled ((Beutler and der Marderosian, 1978; Small and Cronquist, 1976; Turner et al., 1985). The population, though, is high variable for this trait (Small and Beckstead, 1973). These findings simply mean that it is possible to breed fiber-type hemp plants which have either no THC or a great deal of THC. In fact, Small et al. (1975) state that "the often advanced opinion that fibre varieties of *Cannabis* do not have drug properties is not always correct." On the other hand, the modern French hemp paper industry is apparently based on varieties of hemp which contain very little, in any THC (Malyon and Henman, 1980).

Climatic Range, Soil Tolerance, and Management Requirements of Hemp

For a plant species to be widely grown as a source of energy or paper pulp, that species must be adaptable to a wide range of climatic and soil conditions (Barnard, 1984). Generally speaking, hemp is widely adapted to a variety of climates ranging form the temperate zone corn belt in the U.S. to the plains of India to the mountains of Columbia. Fiber production from hemp requires about four months of frost-free weather, whereas seed production requires a growing season of about five months (Ree, 1966; Robinson, 1952).

"Hemp seeds put down a 10 to 12-inch root in only 30 days, compared to the one-inch root put down by the rye or barley grass presently used by the U.S. government." (Herer, 1990, p. 47)

Even though hemp is said to have a vigorous root system (Malyon and Henman, 1980), reports to the contrary can be found. Haney and Kutscheid (1975) found that male plants had much weaker root systems than female plants which accounted for the early mortality of male plants. Berger (1969) stated that root development was widely variable depending upon soil type. The development of a strong taproot was possible in deep soils, but in soil conditions which were unfavorable a more shallow system of lateral roots prevailed (Berger, 1969). Berger adds, "Although this root system is in itself strong, it must be regarded as relatively weak in comparison with the extent and speed of growth of the hemp plant above ground."

"Hemp is easy on the soil, an ideal crop for the semi-arid west and open range land." (Herer, 1990, p. 45)

A desirable characteristic of a potential energy crop would be the ability to grow in poor soils which would not sustain food crops so that energy crops would not compete with food crops for valuable land resources (Barnard, 1984; Coombs, 1983). Hemp apparently does not meet this criterion. Most production advisories clearly state that hemp should be planted on the most productive soil (Quimby, 1973; Robinson, 1952). Soil aeration is unquestionably a major factor determining the productive potential of hemp in a particular soil (Berger, 1969; Haney and Kutscheid, 1975; Ree, 1966). Hemp cannot tolerate poorly drained, wet soils (Wilsie, 1944), nor will it grow well in soils which dry out too quickly (Kirby, 1963). Furthermore, hemp will not grow well on acidic soils (Kirby, 1963) and prefers a neutral or slightly alkaline soil (Berger, 1969). Hemp grows best in well-drained clay-loam or silt-loam soils (Berger, 1969; Dempsey, 1975). The soil should be deep and fertile (Berger, 1969), and preferably contain sizable quantities of organic matter (Dempsey, 1975).

In addition, hemp is not recognized as a drought-resistant crop (Berger, 1969; Hackleman and Domingo, 1943; Kirby, 1963; Ree, 1966).

Hemp requires ample soil moisture throughout the growing season (Dempsey, 1975; Ree, 1966). In addition, hemp grows best in regions with an annual precipitation of approximately 700 mm (27 in.) (Ash, 1948; Berger, 1969; Kirby, 1963) with about 125 mm of rainfall per month during the growing season (Dempsey, 1975). Hemp is, therefore, adapted to subhumid, rather than semi-arid climates, as suggested by Herer (1990).

Reports by Dewey and Merrill (1916) state than hemp is easy on the soil and requires little fertilization. Contemporary literature does not support this claim. According to Kirby (1963) "... it has been stated that no other crop reacts better than hemp to proper husbandry and proper fertilizing." Intensive management and fertilization is required for hemp because the plants produce an enormous amount of biomass in a relatively short period of time (Berger, 1969). This is coupled with the fact that the "root system is relatively weak and sensitive" (Berger, 1969). Further, hemp removes immense quantities of nutrients from the soil. Research during World War II found that hemp extracted more nutrients per hectare than cotton or flax (Dempsey, 1975). Further, it "removes 2 to 3 times as much nitrogen, 3 to 6 times as much phosphorus, and 10 to 22 times as much potassium per hectare" as cereal grain crops (Dempsey, 1975). Hemp requires liberal fertilization because a large quantity of readily-available nutrients must be accessible to sustain rapid growth (Berger, 1969; Dempsey, 1975). This problem is less severe when hemp is grown for fiber if retting and breaking of the stalks occurs in the fields (Dempsey, 1975; Haarer, 1965). In these situations, most of the nutrients are returned to the soil for utilization by subsequent rotation crops (Berger, 1969). However, this production practice would not lend itself to chemical retting and mechanized breaking. Furthermore, harvesting hemp for paper pulp or as an energy source would mean that very few of these nutrients would be returned to the soil but rather would be part of the biomass product. Production of hemp as an energy crop will, therefore, require intensive fertilization. But as Hunsigi (1989) points out, this is likely to be the case with any fiber crop grown for biomass (Hunsigi, 1989). Summarizing, Herer's contention that hemp is easy on the soil and be grown successfully on poor soils is questionable.

Contemporary experience in Italy has demonstrated that hemp can be grown successively on the same land without detriment (Berger, 1969). Production recommendations, however, generally suggest that rotation with other crops would be desirable (Dempsey, 1975). Crops which leave a substantial amount of nitrogen and organic matter should, ideally, precede hemp (Dempsey, 1975).

"Hemp seeds sown free from airplanes flying over eroding soils could reclaim land the world over." (Herer, 1990, p. 47)

Haney and Kutscheid (1975) reported on an extensive survey of naturalized hemp stands in the midwestern U.S. They found that hemp seeds will not remain viable in the soil for much longer than 2 years. If hemp was eliminated from a site, the seeds had to be re-introduced before hemp could become established again. Further, seeds had to germinate early and grow rapidly in order to colonize a site. Almost all of the sites where hemp was found growing had been repeatedly disturbed by cultivation, mowing, waste disposal, and/or stream channeling. They reported permanent establishment of hemp required disturbing the soil in a particular site at least once every 4 to 5 years (Haney and Kutscheid, 1975). It seems unlikely, therefore, that aerial distribution of hemp seeds would result in the successful establishment of the species on eroded or marginal soils.

"Hemp needs no chemicals, has virtually no weed or insect enemies— except for the U.S. government and the DEA." (Herer, 1990)

At least in the U.S., hemp has relatively few insect pest or pathogens (Dempsey, 1975; Robinson, 1952). The few pests which occasionally attack the plant probably could be controlled with environmentally-safe insecticides based on *Bacillus thuringenesis*, a pathogen specific to certain insect larvae. The few other recognized pests of hemp could be controlled by appropriate crop rotation.

Because hemp is capable of rapid growth and germinates early in the spring, it can successfully compete with most weed species (Haarer, 1953; Hackleman and Domingo, 1943; Wilsie, 1944). Hemp has, therefore, been used to reduce weed populations in thoroughly-infested fields. Herer's assertions concerning this aspect of hemp cultivation appear to be valid.

"Furthermore, recent studies indicate that depletion of the ozone layer threatens to reduce world soya production by a substantial amount—up to 30% or even 50%, depending on the fluctuation of the density of the ozone shield. But hemp, on the other hand, resists the damage caused by increasing ultraviolet radiation and actually flourishes in it by producing more cannabinoids which provide protection from ultraviolet light." (Herer, 1990, p. 42)

The initial research on the tolerance of hemp to UV-B radiation suggested that drug-type hemp plants produced cannabinoids upon exposure to excessive levels of UV-B radiation which thereby protected the plants against the harmful effects of UV-B exposure (Pate, 1983). Subsequently work found that even though the drug-type plants responded to excessive levels of UV-B exposure with increased cannabinoid synthesis, fiber-type varieties, which did not produce cannabinoids in response to UV-B radiation, were also quite tolerant of UV (Lydon *et al.*, 1987). The authors concluded that cannabinoids do not contribute to the UV-B tolerance of hemp (Lydon *et al.*, 1987). Unquestionably, the mechanism by which hemp is able to tolerate UV-B radiation warrants further investigation.

Conclusions

In general, utilizing non-woody plants for paper pulp and converting plant-derived biomass into liquid fuels seems to be an ecologically-sound approach to solving some of the problems facing the people of this planet. It seems very unlikely, though, that humanity can depend upon any single plant species to save the planet from ecological and environmental destruction. Reliance upon a single plant species as our sole source of energy and fiber would be imprudent and perilous. Weaning out society from fossil fuels and pulpwood will require utilizing several plant species which are well-adapted to each specific production area. Hemp alone will not save the planet. But hemp, used in combination with many other plant species, such as sugarcane, sorghum, and flax, may play a vital role in saving our planet from catastrophe.

Clearly, additional research on the biomass potential of hemp and the chemical composition of hemp hurds and seeds is urgently needed. This species is commonly dismissed as a viable crop simply because of the American-imposed prohibition on its cultivation. Furthermore, plant scientists studying the adaptation of plants to increased levels of UV-B radiation unquestionably should investigate the mechanism by which hemp plants tolerant this type of stress in order that such tolerance might be imparted upon other economically and socially important species.

A Response to Dr. Walker

by Lynn and Judy Osburn

First, we wish to thank Professor David W. Walker for the many hours of research involved in preparing *Can Hemp Save Our Planet?* His excellent work revealed many sources we had not heard of. It is as exciting to have a Ph.D. confirm so much of the material in *The Emperor Wears No Clothes*, as it is to have the scientific literature.

Unfortunately, references pertaining to the hemp-for-energy section of *The Emperor* were left out in the rush to meet the printing deadline. Therefore Dr. Walker did not have access to the scientific literature "Energy Farming in America" is based upon, and further explanation is necessary.

When we first read Dr. Walker's manuscript, we also saw the need for clarification of many other points. Again we thank the professor for bringing these to our attention.

Under the heading "Hemp seed as a protein source," Professor Walker states that the protein content of hemp seeds does not appear to be exceptional, citing the comparative protein content of various food seeds. However, he was unable to locate reports describing the amino acid composition of hemp seeds, the basis of Herer's claim that hemp seed is the second most complete source of vegetable protein. Dr. Walker states, "Apparently, hemp is unique in that 65% of the storage proteins found in hemp seeds are globulin edestin." But he was unable to find literature on the value of edestin to human/mammalian nutrition.

Globulins are one of seven classes of simple proteins (as adopted by the American Society of Biological Chemists). Edisten is contained in this class. [Simple proteins are protein molecules not attached to other types of molecules, such as the coloring agent in hemoglobin; nor produced from natural proteins by the action of reagents.] Globulins are found in seeds and animal blood, edestin being found in seeds and serum globulin in blood. (E. Wertheim, *Textbook of Organic Chemistry*, 1945, gives "edestin in hemp seed" as the textbook's example of the common source of edestin.)

Proteins are divided into two broad classes: fibrous, which are sturdy and tough and are used for support and protection in cartilage, ligaments, tendons, muscles, hair, hooves, skin, horns and feathers: and globular proteins. "The really important proteins, however, are the *globular proteins*. In these, the polypeptide chains are not merely straight lines, but exist in complicated loops and twists which are never quite the same in any two different proteins. It is the globular proteins that do the main work of living and among them are the powerful and mysterious substances known as enzymes." (I. Azimov, *The Chemicals of Life*, 1954)

Globular proteins serve life functions that require mobility and hence solubility. (Fibrous proteins are insoluble in water, globular proteins are water soluble.) Globular proteins make up all enzymes, many hormones, antibodies, albumin in eggs, hemoglobin and fibrinogen which the body converts to the fibrous protein, fibrin, the blood clotting agent. (R.T. Morrison, *Organic Chemistry*, 1960)

Funk and Wagnalls New International Dictionary lists the castor-oil bean and hemp seed as sources of edestin. It also states the word edestin comes from the Greek "edestos," meaning edible. (1984)

From a nutritional standpoint, proteins can be divided into two classes: proteins containing human tissue proteins in approximately the relative quantities to be found in our bodies; and proteins in which one or more *essential* amino acids—one of the eight amino acids the human body cannot manufacture from other amino acids—is lacking (e.g. corn and gelatin), or in which there is a preponderance of one or more of those amino acids needed by the body in only a small quantity (e.g. the chief protein in wheat flower). (*Textbook of Anatomy and Physiology*, Kimber, Gray, Stackpole, 1943)

Regarding human protein requirement: "Qualitatively, it is considered desirable to secure amino acids similar to those of human tissues, both as to kinds and relative quantities of the various kinds." (Id.)

Plasma, the fluid portion of blood which supplies nutrients to tissue, contains three protein types: serum albumen, serum globulin, and fibrinogen, which together compose about 80% of plasma solids. (*Gray's Anatomy*, 1978) Globulin is the third most abundant protein in the human body, after collagen and albumin. (Pearson & Shaw, *Life Extension, A Practical Scientific Approach*, 1982)

All seeds contain albumen (albumen is also called albumin by chemists ("albumin, n. Any of a class of albuminous or protein substances found in blood; albuminous, adj. . . . consisting of albumen or albumin"). Albumen is the nutritive material that fills the space in a seed between the embryo and the seed coats. (*Funk and Wagnalls New Practical Standard Dictionary*, 1945)

Fibrinogen is a complex protein found only in animals. (*Webster's Twentieth Century Dictionary*, 1948; *Funk and Wagnalls Dictionary*, 1947) No vegetable protein contains fibrinogen.

Since hemp seed is unique in its high content of edestin, a larger percentage of its protein is readily available in the form found in blood plasma.

Because all seeds contain one of the three plasma proteins, albumen, and no seeds contain another, fibrinogen, it is reasonable to conclude that the possession of the edestin protein would tend to satisfy the *Textbook of Anatomy and Physiology*'s criteria for the quality of protein required for human life. That is, the hemp seed contains human tissue proteins in similar quantities found in our bodies—or in the plasma which delivers nutrients to our tissues. This conclusion is supported by the fact that hemp seed cake was one of the principal livestock feeds up until this century, and by the findings of Cohen & Stillman, *Therapeutic Potential of Marijuana*, 1976, and the *Czech Tubercular Nutritional Study*, 1955. More research is needed concerning the amino acid content of the proteins in hemp seed.

Under the heading "Hemp as a livestock feed," Dr. Walker cites poor results when hemp waste, "presumably resulting from fiber extraction," were used as livestock feed. *The Emperor* makes no claims regarding hemp *hurds* (the waste product from the fiber industry), however,

Dr. Walker did find verification concerning the use of hemp seed cake derived from the waste products of oil extraction from hemp seeds.

We would not expect hemp hurds to make good feed since they are mainly comprised of cellulose—necessary for making paper, and the source of hydro-carbon for fuel. Sawdust has also been rumored to have been unsuccessfully tried as livestock feed supplement.

Under the heading "Hemp hurds as a source of paper," Dr. Walker lists several sources regarding the cellulose contents of hemp *fiber* and other plants suitable for paper-making. The figure we gave of hemp hurd's 77% cellulose content came from *Popular Mechanic's* "New Billion Dollar Crop," February, 1938: "... the woody 'hurds' remaining after the fiber has been removed contain more than seventy-seven percent cellulose, and can be used to produce more than 25,000 products, ranging from dynamite to Cellophane." Since publication of Jack's book we have located additional sources regarding hemp fiber cellulose content. *Encyclopedia of Textiles* (1960) states "cellulose is about 77% of the composition." *Long Vegetable Fibers*, (Ludwig Weindling, 1947), lists hemp fiber's content at 77.8%. (Dewey and Merrill, 1916, mention the chemical similarity between hemp fiber and hemp hurds as related to chemical processing.)

Overall, hemp's cellulose content generally compares with that of other bast fibers, except jute, which has a lower cellulose content. However, hemp's efficiency as a source of cellulose is based on its nationwide production capabilities. Because it adapts to much more of our country's climatic conditions, hemp has the ability to produce a greater amount of cellulose in our latitude than any other plant. (See *Hemp as Biomass* section of this article.)

Jute is comparable with hemp in yield per acre. (Weindling) However, jute's cellulose content is lower than that of hemp or flax. "Chemical analysis shows jute fiber to be composed of a modified form of cellulose known as lignocellulose (a compound of cellulose and lignin), or bastose. Due to this fact it can combine directly with dyestuffs, whereas fiber of greater cellulose content, such as flax and hemp, cannot do so as readily. This valuable characteristic is responsible for the utilization of jute for carpet yarns, for which it is often dyed with brilliant colors. Unfortunately, however, jute cannot be satisfactorily bleached; the bleached fiber in time loses its whiteness, and the strands disintegrate, but experiments along these lines are continuing." (Weindling, 1947)

Further: "For successful cultivation, jute requires a warm, humid climate, plenty of rainfall during the growing months, and rich loamy soil; good clay or sand soil being best. After the plant has become well rotted, it is not injured by floods and will even grow luxuriantly when half submerged in water." Jute grows in a section of Bengal which receives close to 100 inches of rainfall per year. Weindling also states that both jute and flax are more exhausting to the soil than hemp.

Jute would be unsatisfactory for many paper uses because of the difficulty in bleaching it. As for biomass for other uses, (we will discuss energy in the next section) jute would be limited to tropical regions of the country.

Flax has a cellulose content similar to hemp. And, like hemp, flax grows in a variety of temperate climates, but does best in regions where moderately cool, damp weather prevails throughout the summer months. (Weindling) However, the yield per acre of flax is about half that of hemp. Weindling reports from 450 to 550 pounds per acre. The *Encyclopedia of Textiles* states: "The flax plant grows from 2 to 4 feet tall ... [Compared to hemp's 7 to 10 feet—even taller reports from other sources.] The yield per acre varies greatly in different parts of the world, from a low of 280 pounds per acre to a high of between 800 and 1000 pounds..." Flax also requires careful soil preparation. (Weindling)

Kenaf produces as much bulk as hemp, but is restricted to warm, humid areas. Kenaf's cellulose content is about the same as jute—lower than hemp. (*Encyclopedia of Textiles*)

Weindling reports an annual fiber yield from ramie from 500–600 pounds per acre. Ramie grows in a moist warm or temperature climate. He also says ramie's "strength, durability and high yield per acre have been enthusiastically and at times inaccurately described..." Although ramie will flourish on any good, well drained land, capable of retaining moisture throughout the growing season, dry heat or severe cold will kill the plant. (Weindling)

The fibers of sunn hemp, another bast fiber, "when viewed externally by the naked eye or even under a microscope...are similar to true hemp. The feature distinguishing sunn hemp, which may be found upon detailed examination of a cross-section, is the presence of a very thick layer of lignin between the cells. It is not as strong or durable as [true hemp]..." Sunn hemp requires moderate to heavy rainfall. The average fiber yield per acre is 500 or 600 pounds. (Weindling)

As Dr. Walker points out, any plant can be used to make paper or textiles. However, the other fibers have found little commercial practicality and therefore statistics regarding production are difficult to find.

Dr. Walker's findings on the lignin content of hemp vary somewhat from Jack Herer's claim. The variance is of little importance, since the comparisons regarding lignin made in *The Emperor* were made against wood-based paper making. Indeed, several annuals compare with hemp in lignin content. And therefore those annuals, like hemp, would require less chemicals than wood during the paper-making process. But, as stated above, they have other drawbacks in the majority of climatic regions of our country. (Hemp's adaptability to varied climates will be discussed in the *Biomass Potential of Hemp* section.)

Also, *The Emperor* refers to the lignin content of hemp hurds, which presumably is lower than the total lignin content of the strong fiber.

Professor Walker distinguishes annual plants from woody plants in his manuscript's lignin section. Stanford Research Institute (1979) does not use woodiness to differentiate annuals from perennials or trees. SRI's definition of woody plants is: plants that produce persistent woody material, and includes standing vegetation not suitable for lumber. Bast fiber plants contain woody material (Weindling, Kirby and other sources refer to the woody portions of bast fibers) and hemp falls into a category between low-moisture herbaceous and woody.

As the professor points out, many different plant species have great potential to replace wood in paper-making. The different climate regions will find the most suitable agricultural fibers when the needless cutting of forests is finally halted. As we will see in the hemp as biomass section, hemp happens to be the most suitable on an overall basis for the United States. That is not to say our tropical regions should neglect the potential of high yield tropical plants.

Dr. Walker points out several drawbacks in the use of agricultural fibers for paper-making. First, the low bulk density compared to wood requires larger storage capacity. According to congressional testimony by a John Deer Co. researcher in 1978 harvesting equipment is available for agricultural biomass. Hay cubers, used to compress alfalfa into dense cubes for compact storage and transportation would make storage of agricultural pulp and biomass comparable to that of wood. Additionally, dried cubes require no controlled storage or rapid processing, another drawback Dr. Walker points out.

In answer to the problem of the seasonal supply of agricultural fibers, hemp's season is extended due to its earlier in short season areas and later in long season regions. (sources cited in biomass section) Also, wood harvesting is subject to seasons where snow halts production.

Finally, Professor Walker states, "Hunsigi (1989) adds that removing the *fibers* and converting them into *paper pulp* is presently a labor-intensive process" (emphasis added). Hemp fibers are removed for textiles, a product with a value high enough to make the process economical. It is the *hurds* left over from the process which we advocate should be used for paper-making.

Dr. Walker states, "Kenaf has received a great deal of research interest in the past two decades suggesting that this plant may also become much more important as a source of paper pulp." Unfortunately, hemp prohibition has eliminated modern research into hemp.

Plants as a Source of Energy

In discussing the technology available for converting plant biomass into energy, Dr. Walker states the fermentation process used to produce ethanol is the most well established. Actually, the technology involved in pyrolysis, also known as fractional distillation, is used by the petro-chemical corporations in converting ancient fossilized biomass into fuels.

Dr. Walker's research centers mainly on biochemical (anaerobic distillation and fermentation) conversion, which cannot produce enough energy for our nation's needs. (*U.S. Energy Atlas*, Cuff & Young; Congressional testimony, from *Brown's Second Alcohol Fuel Cookbook*, Michael H. Brown.) Fermentation conversion is best suited for the chemical feedstock industry and "biomass resources are in a position to compete immediately, with profits reinvested in further improvements....

Now is the time to substitute biomass-derived chemicals for petrochemicals." (*Science* magazine, June, 1981, "Chemicals from Biomass: Petrochemical Substitution Options.")

In describing methanol production, Dr. Walker points out that the final two steps use well-established technologies, while the first step requires additional development. (citing Anon., 1981) The initial development has been worked out in pilot plants known as gasifiers, by various government agencies, private firms and universities, including Georgia Tech. "The concept of producing methanol from wood is not a new one. Methanol obtained from the destructive distillation of wood was the only commercial source until the introduction of the synthetic process in 1977" (R.M. Rowell & A.F. Hokanson, *Methanol from Wood: A Critical Assessment*, from *Progress in Biomass Conversion*) Hagen, 1976, lists natural methanol production in 1930 at 12.9 thousand tons, peaking in 1940 at 14.1 thousand tons, then declining through 1960. By 1965 natural methanol production was totally replaced by synthetic methanol (at 25.1 thousand tons in 1930 increasing to 3229 thousand tons in 1977).

The work in pyrolysis at Georgia Tech, in cooperation with Tech-Air, was initiated in the late 1960's. Research centered on agricultural and wood wastes. The successful results led Tech-Air in 1972 to design and build a field test pyrolysis facility to process forestry wastes to produce charcoal, oil and combustible gas. In 1975, the American Can Company acquired Tech-Air because of the can company's interest in pyrolysis for use in a total resource recovery facility for municipal waste, as part of their Americology Division. (J.A. Knight, *Pyrolysis of Wood Residues with a Vertical Bed Reactor*, from *Progress in Biomass Conversion*) "The Georgia Tech/Tech-Air pyrolysis process is versatile and flexible. The distribution of the energy among the products—charcoal, oil and gas—can be varied by control of the operating conditions, primarily air-to-feed ratio, of the reactor, ... The system has been tested extensively with municipal refuse." (Id., citing Bowen *et al.*, 1978)

The crude gas produced from this destructive distillation technique can then be scrubbed and processed using standard syngas technology. The methanol production from wood waste as the resource material yields approximately 100 gallons methanol per oven dried ton (ODT) of feed material. (*Methanol From Wood, A Critical Assessment*, P.M. Rowell & A.E. Hokanson, from *Progress in Biomass Conversion*; 1976 National Academy of Science; *Fuel Alcohol, an Energy Alternative for the 1980s Final Report—Appendix*, U.S. National Alcohol Fuels Commission, 1980).

We are in agreement that "the thermochemical conversion of biomass to methanol is preferable to other known processes for the production of liquid fuel from plant biomass." And that "the long-term potential for deriving significant, sustainable quantities of liquid fuel from plant materials appears to be greatest for those processes which depend upon cellulose rather than sugar, starch or oil." (Walker, page 7) However, most likely because Dr. Walker lacked the unabridged "Energy Farming in America" and the accompanying references, he failed to consider the vast potential of pyrolitic conversion of biomass into charcoal to fuel electricity generators. The U.S. National Fuel commission's 1980 *Final Report* lists the advantages of biomass over coal for electricity production;

Availability—biomass is renewable and available locally.

Technical—biomass is easier to burn and gasify.

Environmental—biomass is at least 10 times lower in sulfur content. Therefore no abatement procedures necessary for sulfur and nitrogen; coal has higher content of ash with no value, biomass ash content is lower and has value as fertilizer; coal conversion mobilizes toxic trace metals and coal tars are highly carcinogenic; coal mining is destructive while biomass production improves land; coal production increases CO_2 in atmosphere, biomass does not.

Economic—small scale use of biomass results in lower shipping costs and less difficult conversion; centralized large scale use of coal is required to offset the high cost of environmental control.

Biomass Potential of Hemp

Dr. Walker found general confirmation of Osburn's ten ton per acre yield for hemp. And he did not even consider in his statement; "Various estimates suggest the total biomass yield of hemp plants is from four to five times that of fiber," that those estimates (at least Dewey and Merrill's) are the yield of hurds compared to fiber yield. Total stem weight comprises 60% of the overall weight of the hemp plant. Thirty percent of the weight is contained in the leaves. (Kirby and Weindling) The remaining 10% is contained in the roots, which would not be harvested for energy production. So the fiber yield plus five times that number would comprise two thirds of the total available hemp biomass harvest.

In the paper-making section we itemized the various limitations of bast fiber crops other than hemp. Now we will list what the sources say about hemp.

Dr. Walker states that fiber production from hemp requires about four months of frost-free weather, and seed production requires about five months (citing Robinson, 1952).

Vegetable Fibers, R.H. Kirby (1963) confirms what modern marijuana cultivators have experienced. Kirby explains that northern and southern varieties of hemp have adapted to differing climates—from short and cool to long and warm. Then: "... as had been mentioned, there are so many types of [true] hemp and these are able to adapt themselves so effectively to different climates and terrains, that it is difficult to define what are the best climatic conditions for hemp."

"This plant can endure considerable changes in temperature, and this is one reason why it is so widely distributed in both the northern and southern hemispheres. Frost for any long period will destroy young hemp plants, but once the plants are ready for harvesting they do not seem to suffer from the cold."

California high-altitude growers have reported flowering plants surviving temperatures down to ten degrees Fahrenheit.

Weindling (the same source cited concerning the climatic limitations of other bast fibers) writes: "The hemp plant grows best in a temperate, humid climate, but it is hardy and will endure a change to heat and dryness; this hastens maturity at the expense of growth."

As explained in this manuscript's paper section, there are several bast fibers capable of equalling hemp fiber production on a per acre basis. But with the exception of flax, whose production rate is only half of hemp's, the regions they can be successfully grown in are limited. To repeat, they should also be grown for paper and energy in suitable regions, but we cannot fuel our nation from the states of Hawaii and Florida.

Dr. Walker lists plants with an even higher yield rate than hemp. The plants he lists are high-moisture herbaceous plants. (Additionally, kenaf has a limited growing area and sorghum is not as drought tolerant.) According to Stanford Research Institute, woody and low-moisture herbaceous plants are most suitable for pyrolitic conversion into fuels. The biochemical process high moisture plants are suited for cannot supply our nation's energy needs. (*U.S. Energy Atlas*, Senate hearing from *Brown's Second Fuel Alcohol Cookbook*) In discussing biomass, we have always acknowledged that sugar cane produces more biomass per acre, but it is a high-moisture sugar based plant. As the professor states, the energy potential from cellulose based processes is greater than that of sugar, starch or oil based production. SRI research indicates sugarcane is not suitable for pyrolysis conversion. However, sugarcane is ideal for bio-chemical processing into chemical feedstocks, and "Now is the time to initiate vigorous, broad based programs to substitute biomass-derived chemicals for petrochemicals." (*Science* magazine, June, 1981) (Seven percent of our petrochemicals are used in the chemical feedstock industry. [Id.])

Dr. Walker disputed the potential of biomass to replace all our energy needs. Due to his lack of resources regarding pyrolitic conversion, he relied on data from biochemical (anaerobic digestion and fermentation) research. As we previously stated, biochemical conversion cannot supply America's energy needs. However, our figure of 6% of the continental U.S. acreage's ability, when cultivated for biomass, to provide all of America's energy needs is, by no means, an extrapolation. It is taken straight from the 1984 textbook, *Environmental Chemistry*, by Stanley E. Manahan. Additionally, *U.S. Energy Atlas* states the total biomass grown annually is roughly 5 billion dry tons. "Assuming that each dry ton will yield 15 million BTU, the energy yield would be 75 Quadrillion BTU (75 Quads) which is roughly the total need for raw energy annually in the United States at present." It goes on to say that if cultivation is concentrated on high yield crops, the theoretical maximum energy yield may be placed higher than 75 Quads. The *U.S. Energy Atlas*'s projection is considerably lower than the *Environmental Chemistry* textbook's—but even according to the *Atlas*'s much less technical overview, we can supply all our nation's energy needs through pyrolitic conversion of biomass.

Soil Depletion

We would expect hemp to deplete the soil more than flax or cotton, since it produces much more vegetative matter (biomass). Dr. Walker came up with additional sources stating most of the nutrient is returned to the soil during the retting process. But, as he points out, field retting would not occur in a harvest for paper or energy. However, the N, P, K vital to plant growth can be recovered at the pyrolysis reactor in the form of nitrogen gas, and phosphorous and potash from the ash residue.

Rotation is the best plan for any crop, although we have located many old sources claiming crop rotation is unnecessary for hemp. One from an 1867 edition of the "Illustrated Historical Gazetteer of Missouri" states: "I can raise on my land hemp for twelve or fifteen years in succession, without manure or rest. In regard to wheat, I think our soil is not so well adapted to that product as it will be after it has been cultivated for some years. Owing to our light soil, rye does better than wheat."

Weindling writes: "In the cultivation of some of the other long vegetable fibers no crop rotation is practiced, but flax should be invariably rotated with other crops."

Dr. Walker states that it seems unlikely aerial distribution of hemp seeds would result in the successful establishment of the species on eroded or marginal soils due to the fact that hemp is a disturbance plant. We thank him for this correction concerning aerial distribution and will modify the next edition accordingly. However, erosion is a soil disturbing process. That is the reason wild hemp stands occur in run offs and gullies.

Conclusions

We heartily agree with Dr. Walker's conclusion that additional research on the biomass potential of hemp and the chemical composition of the hurds and seeds is clearly and urgently needed, along with study of hemp's adaptation to UV radiation. And it is never a prudent move to base an economy on a single source. Sugar cane, jute and kenaf should be grown in tropical regions for chemical and fiber production. When hemp prohibition is ended the historical hemp fiber growing areas in the eastern United States will re-emerge as part of a hemp multi-industry complex. The northern plains will once again flourish as the nation's energy farming states. Medicinal and recreational grade hemp will be grown on less productive mountainous areas. There is still no other single plant which can serve the wide variety of needs than hemp can. We must stop burning fossil fuels and cutting forests. Hemp can do more to save our planet than any other American crop.

A Review of the Literature
Agronomy and Crop Physiology of Fiber Hemp

by H.M.G. van der Werf

THE ORIGIN OF HEMP lies in central Asia or China; it was grown in China as early as 2800 BC (Dempsey, 1975).In the past hemp was an important fiber crop, its importance has been gradually declining in the course of the 20th century (Table 1). The decline was most pronounced countries having a market-based economy.

Most hemp growing countries grew one or more varieties which in general were selections from indigenous varieties. In Europe the two main types of hemp used to be Russian hemp and Italian hemp (Heuser, 1927).

Russian hemp reached Europe by a Northern route, through Russia. Italian hemp reached Europe through Turkey and the Mediterranean region. Russian hemp has good early vigour (rapid growth in spring), is early ripening and short (1.5 to 1.8 m). The plant is strongly branched and has a high seed yield. Italian hemp has poor growth in spring, it is late and tall (3.5 m). Italian hemp does not branch much, fiber yield and quality are high, seed yield is poor (Marquart, 1919; Heuser, 1927).

Havellandischer hemp, an early German variety, is based on Russian material. Kuhnowse hemp, a late German variety, is based on Italian hemp (Heuser, 1927). The so-called Fleischmann or Kompolt hemp from Hungary is based on Italian material (Hoffmann, 1957).

TABLE 1 —
HEMP AREA IN 1,000 HA, 1910–1988. Data FAO Yearbooks.

Country	1910[a]	1925[b]	1948–52	1969–71	1979–81	1988
Africa	–	–	1	0	0	0
America N	–	–	1	0	0	0
America S	–	–	4	4	4	4
Asia	–	–	–	–	287	171
Bangladesh	–	–	–	7	3	1
China	–	–	–	–	123	53[F]
India	–	–	190[F]	156	132	90[F]
Japan	–	–	4	1	0	0
Korea N	–	–	10[F]	7	8	15[F]
Korea S	–	–	10	5	1	1[F]
Pakistan	–	–	16	10	10	8[F]
Syria	–	–	4	1	0	0
Turkey	–	–	12	8	9	4[F]
Europe	–	–	275	86	59	63
Austria	23	–	0	0	0	0
Bulgaria	3	4	21	10	5	1
Czechoslovakia	–	12	5	2	1	0
France	14	5	5	0	3	1[F]
Germany	0	3	6	2	0	0
Germany E	–	–	4	2	0	0
Germany W	–	–	2	0	0	0
Hungary	63	14	23	12	7	7[F]
Italy	79	112	58	1	0	0
Poland	–	43	14	16	3	3
Romania	6	36	64	26	35	50[F]
Spain	9	7	6	0	0	0
Yugoslavia	15	–	70	17	4	1
USSR	653	858	558	202	140	100F

a: Marquart, 1919. b: Heuser, 1927. F: FAO estimate.

THE HEMP PLANT
Sex Expression of Hemp

Hemp is a dioecious plant, monoecious individuals however do occur. Monoecious varieties have been obtained through breeding. The morphology of the inflorescence of hemp may be either feminine—leafy, stocky, no branches; or masculine—few leaves, strongly branched. Each of these two types may present only female flowers, only male flowers, or flowers of both sexes in different proportions. Hoffmann (1957) presents denominations for each of the six combinations. Plants bearing both male and female flowers are graded into one of five classes depending on the proportion of male flowers.

Male plants die shortly after anthesis. Female plants live 2 to 4 weeks longer than male plants, until the seed is ripe. In a dioecious crop the number of female plants is 10% to 50% higher than the number of male plants (Hoffmann, 1957).

Anatomy of the Stem

The stem of mature hemp may be divided into a vegetative and a reproductive section. In the lower vegetative part leaves are opposite, in the upper reproductive part leaves are alternate. In fiber hemp vegetative internodes are 3 to 4 times longer than reproductive internodes (Verzar-Petri *et al*, 1981).

The stem tissues outside the vascular cambium (to be called "bast" in this review) consist of the epidermis, the cortex and the phloem. In the phloem are sieve tubes and phloem fibers or bast fibers.

The tissues inside the vascular cambium (to be called "core" in this review) are the pith and the xylem. The xylem consists of vessel members, ray and parahadeal parenchyma cells, and libriform fiber (Esau, 1965).

Hemp presents both primary and secondary bast fibers. Secondary bast fibers are shorter than primary bast fibers (2 versus 20 mm), have a thinner cell wall and are more lignified (Hoffmann, 1957).

According to Heuser (1927) length of core fibers is almost constant at 0.5 mm, length of primary bast fibers varies from 10 to 100 mm, on average 35 to 45 mm. Bast fibers are 18 to 25 μ wide, in the lower part of the stem much wider. The diameter of the lumen is about $\frac{1}{3}$ of that of the fiber.

According to Bredemann (1940) the length of primary bast fibers is largest in the middle of the stem, decreasing to top and base. Likewise, Bredemann (1940) states that bast fiber content is highest in the middle of the stem. Heuser (1927) and Arnoux (1969) find the bast fiber content increasing from the base to the top of the plant.

After 17 years of breeding, Bredemann (1952) increased the content of bast fiber in the stem of a hemp population from 12% to 29%. Concomitantly the fraction of bast in the dry matter of the stem had increased from 29% to 48% (core decreasing from 71% to 48%) and fiber content in the dry matter of the bast had increased from 45% to 72%.

Hoffmann (1957) states that breeding for high bast fiber tends to favour secondary bast fiber over primary bast fiber, unless secondary bast fiber is monitored during breeding to prevent this.

Horkay (1982) assesses the high bast fiber varieties of the Hungarian Kompolt breeding program. She found the higher the bast fiber content, the larger the ratio of secondary fiber cells to primary fiber cells.

Height and Diameter of the Stem

Hemp varieties differ in height, late varieties are taller than early varieties (Heuser, 1927; Verzar-Petri et al 1981). Height of hemp plants is very sensitive to growth conditions. Poor conditions such as drought, deficient soil structure or lack of nutrients will limit plant height (Heuser, 1927; Dempsey, 1975). Plant density has a definite effect on plant height. In early maturing, short varieties plant height increases with plant density; in tall, late-maturing varieties plant height decreases as plant density increases (Marquart, 1919). All other authors (Heuser, 1927; van der Schaaf, 1963 and Jakobey, 1965) find that plant height decreases with increasing plant density. Presumably these authors did not investigate short varieties.

Stem diameter decreases with increasing plant density. The height to diameter ratio of the stem increases with increasing plant density (Heuser, 1927; van der Schaaf, 1963).

The diameter of a hemp stem is largest at about ⅓ of its height; within an internode diameter is largest in the middle of the internode and smallest at the nodes. The form of a section through a hemp stem is circular at the base of the plant, hexagonal half-way and square in the upper part (Heuser, 1927).

According to Heuser (1927) the bast fiber content of a hemp plant has a strong positive correlation to its height/diameter ratio. Bredemann (1927) however does not find this strong positive correlation.

THE HEMP CROP
Soil Requirements and Fertilization

Hemp grows best on loose soil (Marquart, 1919; Heuser, 1927). In Germany hemp does particularly well on the nitrogen-rich lowland bog ("Niederungsmoor") soil, especially in a rotation with potatoes, as hemp prevents deterioration of the soil structure (Heuser, 1927). Hemp is particularly sensitive to water logging (de Meyer et al., 1990) it requires a well-drained soil (Friederich, 1964; Dempsey, 1975).

According to Heuser (1927) hemp is very sensitive to drought. Dempsey (1975) states that hemp needs ample water especially during the first six weeks of its growth. Drought and high temperatures towards the end of the growing season will hasten the ripening and cause short plants.

Marquart (1919) stresses the important need of N and K of hemp. Heuser (1927) and Dempsey (1975) both stress that hemp needs much Ca.

Bredemann (1945) and Mathieu (1980) present extensive data on the uptake of nutrients. The nutrient content at flowering is much higher than at seed ripeness (Table 2).

Rivoira and Marras (1975) found highest stem yield at 150 kg of N/ha after a dry spring and at 225 kg of N/ha after a wet spring.

Bast fiber yield however was highest at 75 kg of N/ha in both years. Plant density at harvest decreased with increases in the level of N fertilization.

TABLE 2 — NUTRIENTS IN HEMP, KG/HA.

A crop yielding 6 ton of stem dry matter and 0.7 ton of seed dry matter (Bredemann, 1945).
A crop yielding 10 ton of stem and leaves dry matter (Mathieu, 1980)

Nutrient	Highest nutrient content during vegetation in shoot + root kg/ha (Bredemann)	Nutrients Harvested		
		Bredemann		Mathieu
		kg/ha	kg/ton dm	kg/ton dm
N	211	111	15.2	9.0
K₂O	241	124	17.0	15.0
CaO	259	108	14.8	15.0
MgO	43	22	3.0	1.5
P₂O₅	62	36	4.9	2.5

For France, Anonymous (1982) recommends a soil pH of at least 5. A yield of 10 ton/ha of stem dry matter would require 1000 to 1500 kg/ha of lime, 80 to 120 kg/ha of N, 80 to 120 kg/ha of P_2O_5 and 160 to 200 kg/ha of K_2O.

In Denmark, Nordestgaard (1976) obtained maximum bast fiber yield at the highest N rate applied (140 kg/ha).

For the Netherlands, Friederich (1964) recommends 120 kg of N/ha, 80 kg of P_2O_5/ha and 160 to 180 kg of K_2O/ha.

In six trials in the Netherlands Aukema and Friederich (1957) compared 100, 150 and 200 kg of N/ha. Both stem and bast fiber yield were highest at 200 kg/ha. Bast fiber content in the stem, however, decreased with increasing N-fertilization

Sowing Date and Depth

Thousand kernel weight of hemp seed ranges between 9 and 25 g (Marquart, 1919). According to Hoffmann (1957) the thousand kernel weight is between 18 and 22 g; for monoecious varieties it is about 16 g.

For Germany, Heuser (1927) advises to sow in the second half of April or the first half of May. In his trials, earlier sowing reduced yield, probably owing to a lower plant density caused by frost damage. Providing soil humidity is sufficient, the crop will emerge in 3 to 5 days.

For Italy, Rivoira and Marras (1975) find sowing in early April better than sowing in early May. The former sowing date will extend the duration of the biological cycle by 10 to 15 days.

Tschaneff (1959) advises sowing in early March for Bulgaria.

In the Netherlands, hemp should be sown around the 15th of April according to Friederich (1964). Earlier sowing may cause more weed problems.

On non crust-forming soils hemp should be sown at the depth of 4 to 5 cm (Heuser, 1927). Spaldon and Laskos (1964) advise a sowing depth of at least 4 cm, up to 6 cm in dry years and for late sowing.

Sowing Rate, Plant Density and Row Width

Heuser (1927) investigated the effect of five sowing densities ranging from 42 to 174 kg/ha on hemp yield. Yield of above-ground plant dry matter was maximum at 82 kg seed/ha. Stem yield however was maximum at the highest seed rate, as the fraction of both leaves and seed in the above-ground plant dry matter were negatively correlated with seed rate. Bast fiber fraction in the stem increased with seed rate. Unfortunately no data on plant density were given for this experiment. Heuser does state however, that 80 kg of seed/ha will result in a plant density at harvest of about 260/m² on a mineral soil and about 160/m² on a moor soil. This difference is attributed to the more rapid growth on the nitrogen-rich moor soil which enhances inter-plant competition.

A reduction in the number of plants failing to reach maturity can be obtained by promoting homogeneous conditions for germination and early growth. Marquart (1919), sowing the same amount of seed at row widths ranging from 8 to 30 cm, found plant density at harvest to increase with decreasing row width. In these experiments a reduction of row width probably led to a more homogeneous distribution of plants, thus reducing inter-plant competition. Broadcast sowing of the same amount of seed led to a very low plant density, probably as a result of large differences in germinating conditions and moment of emerging.

In Italy, Rivoira and Marras (1975) used 60 kg of seed/ha in several experiments. Plant densities at harvest varied from 40 to more than

200 plants/m². One of the factors affecting plant density was nitrogen fertilization. Particularly in trials in which nitrogen caused a large yield increase, plant density at harvest decreased with an increase in nitrogen applied. Castellini (1962) gives a usual seed rate for Italy of 40 to 50 kg/ha, this will yield about 200 plants/m² at emergence. At harvest 120 to 150 plants/m² will be present.

For France, Anonymous (1982) advises to use 50 to 70 kg of seed/ha, this will result in about 250 plant/m² (shortly after emergence, probably).

In Hungary, 80 to 90 kg of seed/ha is recommended. This will yield an initial plant density of over 300 plants/m². At harvest plant density is about 150 plants/m² (de Meyer et al., 1990).

In Denmark, Nordestgaard (1976) used 100 kg of seed/ha. Number of plants/m² decreased from 420 at emergence to 360 at harvest.

Danell (1965), comparing seed rates of 40, 60, 80 and 100 kg/ha in Sweden found highest yield of stem and bast fiber using respectively 100 and 80 kg/ha.

In the Netherlands, Aukema and Friederich (1957) tested seed rates from 60 to 130 kg/ha in four trials. They found no consistent effects on yield of bast fiber or above-ground dry matter. Van der Schaaf (1963) compared 50, 70 and 90 kg of seed/ha in one trial. Yield of bast fiber was highest at 50 kg seed/ha. Du Bois (1984) conducted 3 trials on different soil types during one year comparing seed rates of 20, 40, 60 and 80 kg/ha. A sowing density of 20 kg/ha resulted in 74 plants/m² at harvest, 21% of which were diseased; 80 kg of seed/ha resulted in 214 plants/m² at harvest, 39% of which were diseased. The lowest sowing density resulted in the highest stem yield.

Marquart (1919) indicates that a row width of 25 cm or more may cause weed problems, unless the crop is cultivated.

Heuser (1927) recommends a row width of 20 cm as most suited. A row width of up to 30 cm can be used without reducing quantity and quality of bast fiber yield too much. Rivoira and Marras (1975) advise a row width of 15 to 18 cm. Anonymous (1982) advises a row width of 15 to 17 cm.

In the Netherlands, Aukema and Friederich (1957) found both a higher stem dry matter yield and a higher bast fiber content at 10 cm row width compared to 20 cm row width.

Weeds

Under favourable circumstances hemp will grow rapidly and suffocate weed plants. Under the canopy the microclimate is warm and humid, this will promote the germination of weeds, which will die before reproducing (Heuser, 1927).

Sown at 4 to 5 cm depth, the passage of a light seed harrow in a dry soil shortly after emergence will kill weeds without harming the crop (Heuser, 1927).

Lotz *et al.* (1991) found that hemp reduced growth and reproduction of the weed *Cyperus escolenthos* to a much larger extent than other crops such as maize or winter barley.

Diseases and Pests

Marquart (1919) states that diseases and pests have been rare so far in Germany. He mentions the following diseases:
- *Cuscuta Europaea*, "gemeine Seide."
- *Orobanche ramosa L.*, branched broom rape.
- *Phytium de Baryanum Hesse*, damping-off, which will cause "Wurzelbrand": brown soft lesions on young stems.
- *Peziza Kaufmaniana Tisch.*, forms sclerotia
- *Botrytis infestans Hasze.*
- *Bacillus cubonianus Macch.* will cause many longish, somewhat protruding white-gray spots with a fissured surface, up to 10 cm long.
- *Peronospora cannabina Otth.*, false mildew, causes yellow spots on the upper side of the leaf and a black-gray mold on the under side.
- *Phyllosticta cannabis Speg.*, a leaf spot disease.
- *Septoria cannabis Sacc.*, a leaf spot disease.
- *Septoria cannabis Peck*, a leaf spot disease.

Marquart mentions several insects.

Heuser (1927) mentions that diseases and pests are very rare in hemp.

Hoffmann (1957) mentions: *Alternaria sp.*, *Rhizoctonia solani khn.*, *Phytium de Baryanum sp.* (= *P. ultimum*, Trow.), *Botrytis cinerea* and

Sphaerella cannabis (= *Mycosphaerella cannabis,* Wm. A. Roeder). Of these, the latter two also damage fully grown plants. *Sclerotinia sclerotiorum* causes similar damage. As both *Botrytis* and *Sclerotinia* damage the bast fiber, and *Botrytis* in particular occurs more and more frequently, Hoffmann recommends to take these two diseases into account in breeding programs.

Hoffmann further mentions the strongly increased incidence of a hemp anthracnosis which reduces quality and yield of hemp. This anthracnosis is caused by *Colletotrichum atramentarium* (Berk & Broome) Taubenhaus (= *C.coccodes,* Wallr. Hughes).

Hoffmann mentions two insects: *Psyloides attenuata,* the hemp flea beetle and *Pirausta nubilalis,* the European corn borer, which may cause damage in hemp.

Lack of copper may cause a disease-like condition called "gummi"-hemp: the xylem in the plants has lost its rigidity, causing the plants to lodge severely.

Dempsey (1975) mentions the following diseases "not wide spread, occur sporadically, caused by seed- and soil-borne fungi."

- *Septoria cannabis [Lasch] Sacc,* leaf spot.
- *Pseudomonas cannabina* [Lutic and Dowson], stripe disease.
- *Botrytis cinerea Fr.,* gray mold.
- *Sclerotinia sclerotiorum [Lib] Mass.,* hemp canker.
- *Macrosporium cannabium,* brown leaf spot.
- *Phytium sp.,* damping-off.
- *Fusarium sp.,* wilt.

The author mentions Russian varieties resistant against *Botrytis* and *Botryosphaeria morconii.* Fibramulta 151 is said to be resistant against *Fusarium.*

Orobanche ramosa, branched broom rape, is one the principal pests of hemp in France, the USSR and USA.

Ditylenchus dipsaci [Kuhn] Filipjev, the bulb or stem nematode, has been reported in Italy, Germany and Russia, but not to an alarming degree.

Friederich (1964) mentions that a large row width or the use of too much seed will cause a large number of small backward plants which will lodge and be infested by *Botrytis*, forming a source of infestation. According to Friederich, *Botrytis* is the worst disease in hemp in the Netherlands. Meyer and de Meyer (1990) report severe yield losses in hemp grown in the Netherlands caused by *Botrytis* and *Sclerotinia*.

Harvest Timing

According to both Marquart (1919) and Heuser (1927) lodging is very rare in hemp, so it should not complicate harvesting. Marquart (1919) advises to mow hemp for fiber when the stem and the lower leaves of the female plants begin to yellow, while the lower leaves of the male plants are already falling. Heuser (1927) does not give a clear definition of the optimum harvest stage. He mentions that after flowering female plants continue to increase in diameter (+7% to 34%) and in bast fiber content (secondary fiber). Lignification of bast fibers occurs during and after ripening of the seed. Hoffmann (1957) mentions that harvest for fiber generally occurs at the end of female flowering.

According to Spaldon and Laskos (1964) in Czechoslovakia the highest yield of long bast fiber will be obtained when the crop is harvested when 75% to 100% of the male plants are shedding pollen on half or more of their inflorescences.

In southern Hungary male flowering begins in early July, technical maturity (i.e., harvest for fiber) takes place in the beginning of August (Jakobey, 1965).

In Italy flowering starts in the beginning of the July and the highest bast fiber yield is attained during the last decade of July or in the beginning of August. Hemp for fiber is harvested during full flowering. The seed is ripe one month later and the crop can be harvested for both seed and fiber (Rivoira and Marras, 1975).

In France, harvest for fiber takes place by mowing the crop at the end of flowering. The end of flowering occurs around August 20 or later, depending on the variety. The crop then lies on a 5 cm-long stubble and reaches a humidity of 14% to 18% in 4 to 8 days. A crop mown with a mower crusher will dry more rapidly. When the crop is sufficiently dry it is baled. Harvest for both fiber and seed occurs when the seed is ripe, this will be between September 5 and 30, depending on the variety (Anonymous, 1982). In one trial in the Netherlands, van der Schaaf (1963) harvested Fibrimon 21 on August 10 and 24 and on September 7. Highest stem and bast fiber yields were obtained on September 7.

Yield Components and Yield Level

Marquart (1919) analysed whole plant dry matter of several indigenous varieties of hemp. A crop of Italian hemp consisting of plants with a mean length of 298 cm yielded 12 ton of whole plant dry matter/ha. The crop consisted of 10% root, 72% stem, 14% leaves and 4% seed. Similar data are given for other varieties.

In a seed rate trial, 42 kg of seed yielded plants with a mean length of 185 cm and an above-ground dry matter yield of 7.8 ton/ha. The crop consisted of 63% stem, 22% leaves and 15% seed. In the same trial 174 kg of seed/ha yielded plants 176 cm long, a 7.7 ton/ha above-ground dry matter yield and plants consisting of 72% of stem, 15% of leaves and 13% of seed (Heuser, 1927).

On July 25 a hemp crop in which female plants started flowering consisted of 40% leaves and inflorescenses and 60% stem. On September 9 when female plants started ripening, the crop consisted of 37% leaves and inflorescenses and 63% stem; when the crop was ripe for mowing, on the 25th of September, it consisted of 23% leaves and inflorescences and 77% stem (Bredemann, 1945).

According to Marquart (1919) yields of dry hemp stem vary from 3 to 10 ton of dry matter/ha in Germany. In Italy a hemp crop yielded 11.5 ton of stem dry matter when harvested at the end of July (Rivoira and Marras, 1975). Averaged over 11 trials conducted from 1959 to 1963 in Sweden, Fibrimon 21 yielded 8.7 ton of stem dry matter/ha (Danell, 1965). Averaged over 8 trials conducted from 1965 to 1969 in Denmark, Fibrimon 21 yielded 8.9 ton/ha of stem dry matter (Nordestgaard, 1976).

In the Netherlands Aukema and Friederich (1957) obtained 11 ton/ha of above-ground dry matter on sandy peat soils. On clay soils above-ground dry matter yields range from 9 to 14 ton dry matter/ha. Friederich (1964) obtained 10 ton of straw/ha with Fibrimon 56.

For trials conducted from 1987 to 1989 Meyer and de Meyer (1990) report yields ranging from 8 to 13 ton of stem dry matter/ha.

Discussion and Conclusions

The economical importance of fiber hemp has been diminishing steadily in the course of this century. Within Europe, hemp barely survives as a crop in France and Hungary where a few thousand hectares are grown. In Romania and the USSR hemp is more important (50,000 and 100,000 hectares respectively).

The currently available French and Hungarian varieties do not perform satisfactorily in The Netherlands, as they are too early and too susceptible to diseases. Hemp grown in The Netherlands for paper pulp does not necessarily have to be harvested early or to produce seed. Later varieties may yield more stem, as leaf area duration will be longer and no assimilates are diverted to the inflorescenses. The potential of late varieties may be investigated in field trials in which the varieties currently used are prevented from flowering by means of a long day treatment. Late disease resistant varieties may be obtained through breeding.

The anatomy of the stem is the key to a definition of quality of hemp stem material as a source of fiber. Hemp stems contain three types of fiber: primary bast fibers which are long and low in lignin, libriform fibers which are short and high in lignin and secondary bast fibers which are of intermediate length and lignin content. Variability of fiber characteristics within each of the three types of fiber does not seem to be large relative to the differences in fiber characteristics existing between types of fiber. Quality of hemp stem therefore will depend mainly on:

a) the size of the fiber fraction in the dry matter of the stem
b) the proportion of each type of fiber in the total fiber fraction.

At the crop level genotype and plant density seem to be the main factors determining the size of the fiber fraction and the proportion of each of the three types of fiber in the stem. The effect of these factors can be investigated in field experiments.

Literature data on fertilization of hemp are not sufficient to formulate a fertilization advice which would take the soil fertility status and other crops in the rotation into account. For the time being it seems best to fertilize hemp according to the uptake of minerals. Considering the data collected by Bredemann and Mathieu, nutrients harvested per ton of above-ground dry matter can be estimated at: 15 kg of N, 5 kg of P_2O_5, 17 kg of K_2O, 3 kg of MgO and 15 kg of CaO. Fertilization trials might allow a more accurate fertilization strategy; this type of research, however, does not seem to be a priority.

Sowing dates recommended in the literature vary. Optimum sowing date will depend much on the specific spring weather conditions in each country. Yields obtained so far in The Netherlands range from 8 to 13 tons of stem dry matter/ha. These results were obtained with crops sown in the second or third decade of April. As hemp shows good growth at low temperatures, earlier sowing might result in earlier crop establishment and higher yields. Sowing date trials should be conducted in the research on agronomy of hemp as they will reveal the potential and hazards of earlier sowing.

The literature has shown a high plant density to be desirable. Although the effect of plant density on whole plant dry matter yield generally was insignificant, a high plant density decreased the fraction of leaves and inflorescences in the plant, thus increasing the stem fraction. Furthermore, a high plant density resulted in a higher fraction of the more valuable bast fiber in the dry matter. Literature data from Germany, Italy, Hungary and France all indicate that plant density shortly after emergence generally was at least twice as high as plant density at harvest. Data obtained in The Netherlands show even more severe self-thinning. The plants which die during the growing season not only represent a loss of dry matter, but may also hasten the occurrence of fungal diseases in the crop.

In a hemp crop, the individuals which die during the growing season are the small ones. Any measure reducing variability in plant size will therefore probably contribute to a reduced mortality. A more homogeneous plant size may be obtained either through breeding or by agronomic measures. Both approaches seem worth pursuing. Apart from reducing mortality, less variability in plant size would probably be beneficial as well during harvesting and processing (better separation of leaves and inflorescences from stem material). To which extent a reduced variability in plant size will reduce mortality (self-thinning) may be investigated in field trials by creating hemp crops differing in plant size variability through hand thinning, the use of precision sowing versus conventional sowing and by varying inter-plant distances through a varying row width.

Weed control does not seem to be a problem in hemp. Herbicides are not needed, provided the crop has a high plant density. Research in this field therefore does not seem to be a priority.

Diseases or pests were not a large problem in hemp according to the literature. In general this may be due to the more continental climate of the countries in which hemp was and is being grown. *B. cinerea* and *S. sclerotiorum* are less of a problem in a dry summer. Furthermore, in The Netherlands crop rotations are shorter than in most hemp growing countries. In general disease problems are more frequent in shorter crop rotations. Finally, statements in the literature on the lack of diseases in hemp may be the result of a lack of thorough investigations into the status of diseases in hemp. Fungal diseases are an important problem in hemp in The Netherlands. Hopefully more disease-resistant varieties can be bred to solve this problem. At the agronomical level the effect of applying a fungicide once or twice will be investigated.

The plant development stage in which fiber hemp is harvested varies from one country to another, it lies between flowering and seed maturity. Fiber yield continues to increase after flowering. When varieties become available which flower very late or not at all, the development stage at which the crop is harvested will be before or at flowering. Therefore, an extensive investigation into the optimum harvest stage of fiber hemp in The Netherlands does not seem a priority at this moment.

Yields obtained so far in field experiments in the Netherlands range from 8 to 13 tons of stem dry matter/ha. Yields obtained in other European countries are somewhat less. Perspective for increasing yield level seems present. Measures that may contribute to increased stem yields are: earlier sowing, late varieties and less variability in plant size resulting in less self thinning.

It may be concluded from the literature reviewed that the following experiments are most likely to contribute to an answer to the question:

How much and what kind of fiber can hemp yield in the Netherlands?

Field experiments:

- Sowing date and yield and quality of hemp
- Plant density and yield and quality of hemp
- The potential of a non-flowering hemp crop
- Inter-plant variability and self thinning
- Reduction of damage by *B. cinerea* and *S. sclerotiorum* using fungicides

Acknowledgement

The author would like to thank A.J. Haverkort, P.W.M. van den Brink, M. ten Cate, W. Meijer and A. Termorshuizen for their constructive comments on the manuscript.

Hemp as Biomass?

by Ed Rosenthal

JACK HERER, in the book *The Emperor Wears No Clothes*,[1] introduced the idea that hemp could be used as fuel in place of petroleum to energize America. He is supported by Lynn Osburn, who claimed in his monograph, "Energy Farming in America",[2] that energy needs could be met by converting six percent of the land mass to hemp cultivation. The total land mass in the U.S. is approximately 3,540,000 square miles. About 21% or 743,000 square miles is considered arable. Six percent of the total land mass would be about 212,000 square miles or 28% of all agricultural land. Since the most useable land for hemp plantations is found in the midwest, a significant portion of the land throughout the midwest corn and grain belts, 40% would be dedicated to hemp production.

The new crop would have a significant impact on other markets, too. Since the acreage of corn and grain would decline in order to plant the land with hemp, prices for these commodities would climb. Acreage of cotton, which is in direct competition with hemp fiber, would also decline, resulting in some economic dislocation in parts of the south, southwest and west.

Osburn envisions harvesting the hemp biomass and converting it through pyrolysis to charcoal, which is useful for stationary power generation, to petroleum-like distillates, and to the gasses hydrogen and carbon monoxide, which combine to form methanol, which can be used as auto fuel.

Unfortunately, most of the statistics which are available regarding hemp cultivation are either old and do not reflect advances in agricultural technology, or are from foreign producers with only marginal applicability to American farms. However, there is enough information available to make some extrapolations.

At the turn of the century, it was reported that farmers could expect to harvest between 20 and 30 bushels (one bushel = 44 lbs.) of hemp seed and about 5 tons of stems from one acre of land. Based on recent reports from Holland, England and Hungary I do not think that these the older studies are accurate. These countries have had yields within the ranges that van der Werf reported.

Hayo van der Werf's literature review of European yields found that the average yield was somewhere between 3½ and 4½ metric tons per acre.[3]

Hemp proponents often claim that hemp could be grown on marginal land and would not affect the production of other crops. This is simply not true. Hemp needs a rich, fertile loam and high nutrient levels for high productivity. This limits its production to areas which are already being farmed. The midwestern corn and wheat belts would be ideal sites for large cannabis plantations.

If hemp were grown on marginal land, it would cost more to produce. The farmer would use the same inputs, seed, labor, machinery, fertilizer. The marginal land would produce less and the cost per unit would be higher.

In order to induce farmers to grow hemp, it must appear more profitable or beneficial than growing another crop. No matter what the government energy policy, farmers must be willing to grow it for personal gain.

The feasibility of using cannabis as an energy source also depends on the costs of using substitute material. There is quite a bit of waste material that could be used. For instance, nut companies have shells, dairy farmers have manure and many other agricultural processors have other waste materials. Collected wastepaper and scrap wood could also be used. Yardwaste has been a problem for many landfills. It contains a high amount of cellulose. Since there is a cost involved in dumping waste, using it as fuel would have a savings value by eliminating the material as well as in its energy value.

The cost of buying the energy would certainly be less than the cost of planting and harvesting a crop just to burn. Osburn estimates an unrealistically low cost of $30 a ton for dried hemp in bales in the field. Hemp fiber sells for up to $550 a ton. Hemp stem can be used as substitute for wood chips which currently have a value of $50–60 per ton.

Dave Gold, the author of *Solar Gas*,[4] constructed a still with grants from the U.S. and California Departments of Energy. Although he used corn mash and solar energy to make alcohol, he claims that cat-tails would make the best bio-mass crop.[5] They produce a higher yield per acre than many other crops and they use marginal land, which is not useful for other crops. He states that the roots are also edible, yielding a high quality protein flour. Water hyacinth, a weed which must be harvested regularly to prevent it from choking many American waterways, also has potential as a biomass fuel.

Although there are some corn-to-alcohol manufacturers in the U.S., the overwhelming majority of biomass to fuel plants have had only marginal economic success. A few have had more success. Vermont Light and Power uses softwoods, and a private power generator in California's Central Valley uses almond shells to generate the electricity it sells to the regional power company. Most of the other plants have not been able to compete with cheap oil and gas. However, the increasing cost of dumping may make biomass conversion more attractive in the next few years.

Osburn envisions a pyrolysis process in order to produce gas for cars and other mobile engines, but the biomass could also fuel stationary electric generators. The value of this fuel is less than a pyroletic product, but production is cheaper, too.

Hemp has many commercial uses, most of which have not been investigated. We know that its fiber, the sheath surrounding the stem, can be used as a fine natural fiber for cloth or high quality paper. The pulp can be used to make newsprint.

The seed is 30–40% oil which has burning qualities and viscosity similar to #2 heating oil, which is also used as a diesel fuel. Hempseed oil has also been used as an industrial oil fairly interchangeably with linseed oil. It can be used as a cooking oil too. The oil can be "cracked" to produce gasoline using methods similar to petroleum refining. Once the oil is pressed from the seed, the remaining mash contains about 35% protein and is useful as an animal feed.

Sixty bushels of hempseed weigh about 1000 lbs. If 35% of their weight were oil, the total yield would be 350 lbs. of oil, or approximately 40 gallons. If this has a wholesale value of $0.60 a gallon (for energy), the farmer would realize $24 from the sale of oil. The mash would probably have a value of $150–250 a ton, based on the value of corn. At $200 a ton, the 650 lbs. would be worth about $65. The total value of the sixty bushels of hempseed would thus be approximately $84. Hemp yields about 22 bushels per acre.[6]

Presently seed is selling for between about $0.13–1.00 per pound wholesale in various world markets. The oil fetches between $40–100 a gallon. In short, hemp seed is a more valuable commodity when used for purposes other than energy, than when they are grown to burn. When cannabis is grown for seed, the fiber of the mature plant deteriorates to a lower quality and has much less value, so that the fiber and shives from seed plants is not as valuable as from plants grown solely for fiber.

Presently there is no market or processing facility in the U.S. for the fiber. However, machinery could be imported which would remove the fiber from the woody stem. Some paper mills might be able to use it. Since there is a growing demand for hemp paper and cloth in the United States, hand and custom processors would begin to work with it were it available.

An acre of hemp yields about a ton of fiber. Hemcore is offering it, for £ 320 sterling or $550 per ton.

The remaining 3½ tons of material would have a value of $50–60 a ton, or $175–210 per acre.

The total value of an acre used for fiber and core would be $750, considerably more than the value of an acre of corn or wheat. All of the uses for hemp other than energy place a high value on it. Using hemp as a resource for energy, would not yield the farmer a profitable return. If society cannot make a profit burning its waste cellulose, how can it be profitable to grow a plant to burn?

None of these projections takes into account the new uses for hemp once it is available for industry. It will be a raw material in the manufacture of plastics, composites, papers and cloth, as an absorbent fiber, and as a replacement for synthetic fibers and cotton. Rather than growing the crop mainly as a source of fuel, farmers will realize its economic value by harvesting its seed and fiber.

Hemp or Wood:
Potential Substitutes

by V.S. Krotov

THREE MAJOR FACTORS are restraining the development of the pulp and paper industry of the Ukraine:

1. The capital costs for the construction of new production facilities are high, with payback time often exceeding the normative service life of the main process equipment.
2. The current obsolete equipment causes environmental problems, as it has a high consumption of raw materials, water and energy and a relatively low yield of finished products. Over 10% of the raw materials, the pulping chemicals, and almost all bleaching agents are discharged into the environment.
3. Ukraine is sparsely wooded, and a lack of traditional raw materials hampers the development of its pulp and paper industry. Forests take up only 13.2% of its territory, and logging covers about one third of its pulp requirements. At the same time, Ukraine's agriculture generates millions of tons of fibrous products: cereal straw, sunflower and corn stems, flax, hemp and others.

In this paper fiber hemp as a raw material for paper pulp will be compared to poplar.

(Note: This article appeared in the Journal of the International Hemp Association, *Vol. 1 No. 1, June 1994)*

Pulping of Non-Wood Raw Materials

In principle, all fiber-containing by-products can be used for pulping, but their processing in the pulp and paper industry is more expensive than the processing of wood. Agricultural by-products are more bulky and dispersed over larger territories than wood, making their transport and storage more costly. Other factors increasing the costs of pulping of non-wood raw materials using existing technologies are:

- heterogenous morphology of the raw material containing stems, leaves, spikes, seeds etcetera, and the presence of non-fibrous impurities (e.g. soil),
- high ash content of raw materials and especially the presence of silicon compounds,
- lower pulp yield as compared to wood pulping.

The negative effect of these factors on production and environmental safety can be minimized by additional expenses for the preparation of raw materials, the removal of silicon and the disposal of wastes. However, the extra costs involved would make non-wood pulp more expensive than wood pulp.

Poplar or Hemp?

The development of a competitive pulp industry in sparsely wooded countries requires:

1. Setting up plantations of fast-growing plants with a high yield of fibrous raw materials,
2. The development of a new technology adapted to the specific characteristics of local raw materials, including agricultural by-products.

For the conditions of Ukraine, the choice of plants to be grown on plantations and to be used for pulp and paper is limited to fast-growing poplars or hemp. The technology for growing poplar in short rotation (12 years) plantations has been developed by one of the Ukranian

Research Stations. In the south of Ukraine, Toropogritsky's poplar is recommended for growing. The annual increment of such poplar plantations on irrigation areas of the Kherson Region varies from 20 to 40 cubic meters/ha, depending on fertility, planting pattern and irrigation practice. Taking an average annual increment of 30 cubic meters/ha, and a poplar wood density of 420 kg/cubic meter, we obtain an amount of wood of 12.6 ton per ha per year. A feasibility study for such poplar plantations has shown that the costs of the wood were four to five times higher than those of aspen wood logged and delivered to the Kherson Pulp and Paper Mill from Central European regions of Russia.

Hemp is promising as a raw material for pulp and paper. Southern hemp is most suitable for growing under the conditions of Ukraine, since it is hardy, suffers little damage from pests and diseases, and can be grown in monoculture for many years. At present is yield of dry stems is 8–10 ton/ha in many areas, which is four to five times more than the average annual increment in Ukranian forests and approaches the increment of the most productive plantations of fast growing poplars.

Perspectives

The Ukranian Institute of Bast Crops (UIBC) at Glukhov, Sumy Region, has bred hemp cultivars containing practically no psychoactive components. Until the present the hemp selection was aimed at breeding varieties for the textile industry, i.e. the selection work took into account the bast portion of the stem, as well as the content of THC. In the pulp and paper industry, the entire stem can be used. Based on its large experience, the UIBC expects it can breed cultivars yielding 12–14 ton/ha of dry stems. In this case the stem yield is comparable to the wood yield of the best poplar hybrids. As opposed to hardwoods such as poplar, hemp can meet all the requirements of the paper industry for short- and long-fibered pulps for practically any paper or board grade.

In 1992, UIBC compared the labour costs of growing and harvesting hemp to those of poplar. Proceeding from the present average yield of 6 ton/ha for hemp and from an annual increment of poplar of 12.6 ton/ha, the costs were comparable. Thus, hemp plantations are more efficient that poplar plantations as a source of raw materials for the pulp and paper industry. However, the advantages of hemp can be realized only if a new technology allowing pulping of the entire stem is developed. Such a technology has been developed at the Ukrainian Pulp and Paper Research Institute.

Hemp Paper Production

by John T. Birrenbach

SINCE IT IS NOT THE INTENT of this report to give a detailed history of paper making, I provide this short synopsis, with notes as to the use of hemp, of the paper making processes history.

Since the earliest time man has used things upon which to record his ideas. From drawing in caves to the use of tree bark and now paper, man has sought to record his ideas so that they may be preserved.

The first, generally regarded, preparation of paper from plant fibers is about 500 BC.[1]

The use of hemp fibers is noted in 105 AD in an announcement by Ts'ai Lun to the Emperor of China.[2]

During the next 1,700 years many different materials were used to make paper. With the advancement of modern textile manufacture the use of scraps, mainly cloth and fiber textiles, for the production of paper became the norm.

In the early 19th century the need for a sustainable source of raw materials to make paper was necessary. Until the 19th century the raw materials used were in limited supply, and paper was only manufactured in areas where textile mills were present.[3]

In 1863 the first claim of making paper from wood is made by Augustus Stanwood and William Tower in Gardiner Maine. With the invention of the wood pulp process the decline and the eventual end of recycled rag paper was certain.[4]

By the mid 20th century the use of tree paper had become the norm, and the use of other materials in paper production is now labeled as specialty papers. It is also clear by the early 1900s that the use of trees for paper production can be only a transitional material at best as tree production can not be sustained.[5]

In the early 1980s environmental groups began to bring pressure on the U.S. Government and companies producing paper from trees to stop the practice. At the same time the use of recycled paper, and the search for an alternative source of raw materials capable of supplying the U.S. with its paper needs continues.

In summary,

- the use of trees in the production of paper is only a recent development.[6]
- the pressure from environmentalists and the public against the use of trees to make paper is not likely to be reduced, but rather increased.
- the use of recycled paper can not supply the United States with its paper requirements.
- the need to find an alternative crop that can safely produce paper is imperative.

Production of Hemp

As it is necessary to discuss the production of hemp as it relates to the production of hemp hurds, the raw material sought for the purpose of this report, I include a short synopsis on the production of hemp and its processing into the basic raw materials the plant produces. This synopsis is necessarily sort as the purpose of this report is to discuss the use of hemp hurds as a paper-making material, not the cultivation and processing of hemp.

To understand the production of hemp it is necessary to understand the plant itself.

The plant *Cannabis Sativa L.*, is composed of a main stalk that can grow to a height of over 18 feet, and a root structure that can reach depth of over 2 feet. Extending from the main stalk are leaves and branches, on the branches grow leaves and flowers. The plant is naturally dioecious,[7] but in some varieties there is monoecious or dual sexing present.[8]

The stalk of the plant *Cannabis L.* is composed of a woody inner core surrounded by an outer bark composed of fiber. The outer bark contains the fiber commonly separated and used in the production of rope, cloth and other fiber products. The woody inner core contains a small percentage of short fibers.[9]

During the decortication, or fiber separation, process the inner core is broken into small pieces, these small pieces are called hemp *hurds*. These hurds correspond to shives in flax.[10]

Hemp is commonly grown in a variety of manners depending on the end use of the hemp. If hemp is grown for seed it is commonly grown in rows approximately 1–2 feet apart, similar to corn, this allows for branching and maximum seed production. If hemp is grown for fiber it is generally grown in rows as close together as 2–3 inches.[11] The hurds from hemp grown for any reason may be used as a raw material for the production of paper.[12]

Ideally hemp cultivated for paper would be grown in a manner consistent with that of fiber production. By cultivating hemp in this manner the largest volume of hemp hurds would be collected. Additionally by cultivating hemp in this manner the fiber would then be available for sale to textile manufacturers.

During the previous 5,000 years hemp hurds, with the exception of some relatively obscure uses, were basically a useless and uncollectible material that was commonly left in fields or burned for fuel.[13]

The Composition of Hemp Hurds

The inner surface of the hurds usually bears a layer of pith, consisting of thin walled cells nearly spherical or angular, but not elongated. They are probably of little value for paper, but they constitute less than 1% of the weight of the hurds. The principle weight and bulk consist of slender elongated woody cells. The outer surface is covered with fine secondary fibers composed of slender elongated cells, tougher than those of the wood but finer and shorter than those of the hemp fiber for commerce.[14]

Retting

Nearly all the hemp previously cultivated in the United States was dew retted. This would no longer be the case. In almost every instance of modern commercial hemp cultivation retting is now conducted in ponds. Hurds from water-retted hemp are cleaner and softer than those from dew retted hemp,[15] and are therefore, more highly sought by the textile industries. Additionally water-retted hemp hurds should also be of a more uniform nature and more highly sought by the paper maker. It can be assumed that a retting process designed for maximum paper production could be invented.

Yields

Yields of hemp production world wide range from a low of $2\frac{1}{2}$ tons to a high of 6 tons of hemp stalk per acre. Percentages of fiber vary from 19–40%. This leaves approximately 60–80% hurds remaining as a source of raw materials in the production of paper.[16]

Yields of hemp hurds are between 1.5–4.8 tons per acre.[17] This becomes a sizable amount of material that could be used in the production of paper.

These yields have increased from less than 2.5 tons of hurds per acre when the original study was conducted by the U.S. Department of Agriculture.[18]

Many of the problems associated with the processing of hemp that were outlined in the *U.S. Department of Agriculture Bulletin #404* have been overcome with the advance of technology.[19]

The major drawback to using hemp hurds as a source of raw materials was the collection process. During the period before the original report was prepared, there was little use of mechanical decorticators.[20] This made collection of hemp hurds nearly impossible. This is no longer a problem since the invention of many specialized machines that can process tons of hemp per day.[21] These facilities could be located centrally for the ease of collection of the raw materials produced.

Presently there is very little use for hemp hurds. With exception to the production of particle board or methanol fuels and farm bedding there is no use for hemp hurds other than paper production. Historically, the hurds were used as fuel for processing hemp.

Currently there is no supply of hemp hurds in the United States. To supply all the raw material necessary to provide paper, the United States would need to cultivate 17–21 million acres of hemp. This would produce the necessary 54 million metric tons of raw material necessary to produce virgin paper each year.[22] The United States has 1 billion acres of farm land. Approximately 1% of the available farm land found provide all the paper now produced, in the United States, from trees on an annual basis.[23]

Shipment of hemp hurds could be facilitated by the construction of paper mills near the decortication mills. The decortication mills in turn could be located close to the fields where hemp is cultivated. The proper installation of hemp cultivation in selected areas could facilitate the shipment of raw materials to the processing facilities.

Cultivars of hemp with little (0.01% Tetra-Hydrocannabinol) or no psychoactive substances have been developed in the Ukraine.[24] This alone should be incentive enough to begin cultivation of hemp on a commercial scale.

If laws were introduced so that farmers, like those in France, Italy and Spain, could cultivate low potency varieties of hemp, many farmers would take advantage of cultivating hemp.[25]

Currently the major cannabis crop still grown in the United States is commonly called *sinsemilla marijuana*, or seedless marijuana. This material is highly prized on the illicit drug market because of its seedless nature and high potency. With the introduction of large scale commercial cannabis cultivation on the pollen produced by the non-psychoactive plants would pollinate the illicit marijuana, thus producing seed and reducing its value on the illicit drug market. The seed, collected by the illicit grower, would produce a lower potency marijuana than that of the previous generation from which it was collected. This would in effect cause the eradication of outdoor grown marijuana in the United States at the same time adding a valuable farm crop and reducing the destruction of the forests.

Clearly with the re-introduction of hemp as a farm crop all paper used by the United States in a given year could be grown by the American farmer. In addition by cultivating an additional 1–2% of the farm land we could establish ourselves as the provider of pulp for paper to a considerable size of the portion of the world. This would reduce the current trade deficit experienced by the United States.

It is clear from the evidence available that the cultivation of hemp is a simple matter. In the traditional farm belt of the Midwest, hemp requires no herbicides, irrigation, pesticides or complicated cultivation or harvesting techniques.[26] As such hemp would be comparably cheaper to cultivate than corn, and require less physical care to reach a harvestable crop. It can be assumed that with the state of current technology that in comparison to other crops hemp would be an inexpensive crop to cultivate.[27]

It can also be assumed that given the current state of technology that it would be relatively inexpensive to process the crop into the three (hurds, fiber and seed) raw materials that can be produced from hemp.[28]

Hemp Pulp and Paper Production

by Gertjan van Roekel, Jr.

THE USE OF FIBER HEMP (*Cannabis sativa L.*) for pulp and paper dates back more than 2,000 years. The oldest surviving piece of paper in the world was discovered by archeologists in 1957 in a tomb near Sian in Shensi province, China (Temple 1986). It is about 10 cm square and can be dated precisely between 140–87 BC. This paper and similar bits of paper surviving from the next century are thick, coarse, and uneven in their texture. They are all made of pounded and disintegrated hemp fibers. Paper historians agree that the earlier Egyptian papyrus sheets should not be referred to as paper, because the fiber strands are woven and not "wetlaid" (Hunter 1957). The Chinese paper-making craftsmanship was transferred to Arabic and North-African countries, and from there to Europe. The first European paper making was reported in the first half of the 16th century (Hunter 1957).

Until the early 19th century, the only raw material available for paper making was rags. Rags are worn-out clothes. Since at that time clothing was solely made of hemp and flax (sometimes cotton), almost all paper in history was thus made of hemp and flax fibers. With the industrial revolution, the need for paper began to exceed the available rag supply. Although hemp was the most traded commodity in the world up to the 1830s (Conrad 1993), the shortage of rags threatened the monopoly for hemp and flax as paper-making fibers. This was the major incentive for

(Note: This article appeared in the Journal of the International Hemp Association, *Vol. 1 No. 1, June 1994)*

inventors and industries to develop new processes to use the world's most abundant (and cheap) source of natural fibers; our forests.

Currently, only about 5% of the world's paper is made from annual plants like hemp, flax, cotton, sugarcane bagasse, esparto, wheat straw, reeds, sisal, abaca, banana leaf, ananas and some other more exotic species. The world hemp paper pulp production is now believed to be around 120,000 tons per year (FAO 1991), which is about 0.05% of the world's annual pulp production volume. Hemp pulps are generally blended with other (wood) pulps for paper production. There is currently no significant production of 100% true hemp paper.

Renewed Interest in Hemp Paper

The recent renewed interest in hemp as a paper-making fiber seems to originate from a strong environmental motive. All primary forests in Europe, and most in North America have been destroyed, amongst others for paper production. Now we accuse the nations which still have primary forests of not guarding theirs.

In Europe all trees harvested for paper making were intended for that purpose, so there seems to be no valid reason to switch to a non-wood or "tree-free" fiber source. This of course is a little different in the Americas and in Asia and Australia, where primary forests are cleared at a huge environmental cost. In these regions hemp has a number of advantages as an alternative source of paper-making fiber. Hemp does not need pesticides or herbicides, and yields three to four times more usable fiber per hectare per annum than forests. And last but not least; paper recycling was invented to make up for the mistake of cutting down our primary forests. Technically speaking, one doesn't need to recycle hemp paper, because it is a renewable raw material.

One disadvantage of using hemp or other annual plants as fiber source is that the present pulping technology has been optimised for tree-fiber pulping, so some adjustments in the pulping processes need to be made when applying this technology to hemp fibers. Before going into technical details, we will first examine the technology of pulp and paper making.

Pulping and Paper Making

Paper making is essentially the rearranging of elementary fibers from whatever source (a tree, a hemp stalk, an old pair of jeans or even a scoop of algae) into a flat thin sheet.

Elementary fibers are the basic building blocks of trees and many plants. The average paper making fiber is about 2 mm long and about 20 micrometers (0.02 mm) thick. All fibers are assembled of chains of cellulose molecules, arranged as a rigid structure. These building blocks are glued together with other biological components (lignins, pectins), which give a certain flexibility and strength to the tissue, so that the tree or plant can bend at high stresses, doesn't break in a storm, and is able to carry its seeds and fruits. The following explains what is needed to process a fiber source into paper (Smook 1982):

Pulping (from fiber source to pulp):

- *Cleaning:* all non-fibrous components need to be removed from the raw material, and the remaining fibers must be cleaned of dirt, rocks and other contaminants.
- *Fiberizing:* the elementary fibers are taken apart by either chemically removing the glue that holds them together, or mechanically tearing the fiber structure apart. From this step on, the material is referred to as "pulp."
- *Cutting:* especially hemp fibers are too long to give a homogeneous paper sheet, so the fibers have to be cut to the right size.
- *Classification:* the fibers suitable for use in paper are separated from the ones too short, too long, too wide, too thin, too crooked, too dirty and too old. Fibres can be classified by weight (centrifugal and gravitational processes) and size (various sieving processes).
- *Bleaching:* optimally, the suitable fibers may be bleached to a higher "whiteness." The whiter a sheet, the better the contrast with the ink. Old-style pulp mills use chlorine compounds with hazardous side-effects. Modern pulp mills use oxygen-based bleaching (compounds like oxygen, ozone and peroxide). Hemp pulp can be bleached with relatively harmless hydrogen

peroxide. For some applications bleaching is not required; for instance in packaging paper and board.

- *Refining:* this is a separate process step in which the fiber surfaces are "roughened." The greater surface roughness of a fiber, the better it adheres to other fibers in the paper sheet and the greater the strength of the paper.

Papermaking (from pulp to paper):
- *Dilution:* in order to lay the fibers evenly into a homogeneous sheet, the pulp is diluted with large amounts of water (sometimes up to 200 times as much water as fiber pulp).
- *Formation:* the fiber-water slurry is poured on a fine mesh wire. Most of the water will fall through the wire, leaving the fibers to settle into a flat sheet.
- *Drying:* in the next steps, the wet sheet is dried by subsequent pressing and steam heating.
- *Sheeting:* finally, the formed sheet is cut to the required size.

These processes are essentially the same for manual paper making and for modern paper machines, with the difference that the old paper maker put out one handmade sheet per minute, and the state-of-the-art Fourdrinier newsprint paper machine puts out 15,000 square meters a minute: a 10 meter wide sheet at 90 kilometers an hour!

Remainders of the Hemp Pulp Industry

Although there are thousands of non-wood paper mills in the world, only a few of them use hemp as a fiber source. At present 23 paper mills use hemp fiber, at an estimated world production volume of 120,000 tons per annum. Most of the mills are located in China and India, and product moderate quality printing and writing paper. Typically, these mills do not really have a fixed source of fiber, but they simply use whatever can be found in the region. About 10 of the mills are located in the western world (U.S., U.K., France, Spain, eastern Europe, Turkey), and these mills produce so-called specialty papers such as:

- *cigarette paper:* even popular American cigarette brands have a 50% hemp cigarette paper and filter. Some countries still have legislation prescribing the use of hemp in cigarette paper, because other fibers (like spruce) generate hazardous fumes when incinerated (!).
- *filter paper* (for technical and scientific uses)
- *coffee filters, tea bags*
- *specialty non wovens*
- *insulating papers* (for electrical condensators)
- *greaseproof papers*
- *security papers*
- *various specialty art papers*

These papers can generally only be produced from special fibers like hemp, flax, cotton and other non-wood fiber sources. The average hemp pulp and paper mill produces around 5,000 tons per annum. This should be compared to a "normal" pulp mill for wood fiber, which is never smaller than 250,000 tons per annum. The only reason the remaining mills can still produce at this extremely small size is that there is a very special use for the pulp. This partly explains the high price for a hemp pulp: about U.S. $2,500 per ton versus about U.S. $400 for a typical bleached wood pulp. The remaining mills in the western world are unable to cope with western environmental regulations because of their small size and archaic technology. Some mills survive by shipping their waste water to a large wood pulp mill nearby, others have to close down. There is a clear shift in capacity towards countries that do not as yet take environmental problems very seriously.

One reason for the high price of hemp pulp is the inefficient pulping processes used. Another reason is that hemp is harvested once a year (during August) and needs to be stored to feed the mill the whole year through. This storage requires a lot of (mostly manual) handling of the bulky stalk bundles, which accounts for a high raw material cost.

Classical Pulping Technology

Most mills predominantly process the long hemp bast fibers, which arrive as bales of cleaned ribbon from preprocessing plants located near the cultivation areas. The bales are opened and fed into the spherical tank, called a digester. Water is added (5 to 10 times the fiber weight), together with the cooking chemicals to remove the "glue" components lignin and pectin from the fibers. Most mills use sodium hydroxide and sulphur cocktails.

The fibers are cooked for several hours (sometimes up to eight hours) at elevated temperature and pressure, until all fibers are separated from each other. After cooking, the cooking chemicals and the extracted binding components are separated from the fibers by washing with excess water. This is where most of the pollution waste emerges from the process. Often wastes are discharged as such into the local surface water.

The remaining clean fibers are then fed into a Hollander beater, which is best compared to an industrial size bathtub, with a large wheel revolving around a horizontal axis at one point in the tub. The wheel pumps the pulp round and round, and meanwhile cuts the fibers to the right length, and also gives the fibers the required surface roughness for better bonding capacity. This beating goes on or up to twelve hours per batch. Some mills add bleaching chemicals in this beating process, other mills pass the pulp from the beating machines to separate tanks for bleaching. These separate bleaching treatments often use chlorine compounds, which are also discharged into the environment. The bleached pulp is then ready to be pumped to the paper machine, or can be pressed to a dryness suitable for transportation to a paper mill elsewhere. The processing time of more than twenty hours make this process very expensive, as the costly equipment and handling must be depreciated over a very low throughput.

Necessity for New Technology

New applications for hemp as a paper making raw material require a new pulping technology which must be able to use hemp from wet storage. Some new technologies have been developed, albeit in laboratory or on pilot scale. The next item in this series about hemp pulping and paper-making will discuss these new technologies and their benefits.

Hemp as a Pulp Source

by E.P.M. de Meijer

THE FEASIBILITY OF NONWOOD PULP production by means of hemp (*Cannabis sativa L.*) is currently under investigation in the Netherlands. Research ranging from breeding to pulp technology and market survey is carried out at several institutes of the Agricultural Research Dept. (DLO). This effort is part of a comprehensive search for profitable new nonfood crops for Dutch agriculture. This article reports on some results of the screening of a germ plasm collection for variation in characters relevant for the introduction of *Cannabis* as an arable pulp crop. Selected genotypes are presently used for breeding experiments.

Establishment & Maintenance of the Collection

A collection of approximately 200 populations was established at Centro for Plant Breeding & Reproduction Research-Agricultural Research Dept. (CPRO-DLO) over the past five years.[1] It comprises fiber and drug strains and wild or naturalized populations from a worldwide geographic origin ranging between 28° and 58° latitude.

Apart from cultivars of which seeds were commercially available, each population has been regenerated to obtain sufficient seeds for evaluation trials. Some research is being carried out to identify optimal conditions for long-term storage of the collection.

Evaluation Topics

The main objectives of the breeding research are an adaptation of stem quality to the requirements for pulp production and an increase of stem yield to make hemp competitive with other arable crops and traditional sources of pulp. Because of legal implications, contents of narcotic compounds in *Cannabis* need to be low. Furthermore, the crop should be a poor host for soil pathogenes. These topics are important in the germ plasm screening, besides various morphological, physiological, and biochemical traits for a general characterization of populations.

Stem Quality

The bar and wood core of dicotyledoneao possess distinct properties. For a detailed characterization of stem quality, these two fractions and their constituent fibers need to be discriminated. The bark fibers of *Cannabis* are the traditional fibers of commerce used for cordage and textiles. The woody core has usually been considered waste. The present research focuses on the utilization of entire stems. Therefore, the germ plasm evaluation covers bark as well as woody core properties.

Within the bark, a distinction is made between primary and secondary fibers. Properties of the distinguished stem fractions are summarized in Table 1. For bark, the chemical properties concern the extracted fibers, whereas for woody core, the contents of the entire tissue are given.

When compared with conifer fibers, the woody core fibers of the hemp stem are much shorter, which has a negative effect on paper strength.[2] The length of secondary bark fibers is comparable to that of conifer fibers. Primary bark fibers are much longer, which makes them suitable raw material for a range of high-quality paper grades. Because of its low a-cellulose content, the potential utilization of the woody core seems restricted to mechanical pulps,[3] whereas the bark of hemp is already used in chemical pulps for specialty papers.

The collection screening comprised the estimation of the mass fractions of primary and secondary bark fibers and woody core in the stem

TABLE 1.
CHEMICAL AND MORPHOLOGICAL PROPERTIES OF THE
DISCRIMINATED STEM COMPONENTS OF *CANNABIS* *

PROPERTIES	PRIMARY BARK FIBER	SECONDARY BARK FIBER	WOODY CORE TISSUE
a-cellulose	60–72[3,4]	—	36–41[3,4]
Hemicellulose content (%)	11–19[3,4]	—	31–37[3,4]
Lignin content	2.3–4.7[3,4]	—	19–21[4]
Fiber length (mm)	(1)–9–(34)[5] (10)–40–(100)[9]	2[9,10]	0.26–0.44[7] 0.55–0.57[8,9,12]
Fiber width (mm)	(16)–30–(67)[8,9,11,12]	17[11]	14–16[7] 26–27[8,12]
Fiber wall thickness (µ m)	—	—	0.7–3.4[7]
Fiber lumen width (µ m)	—	—	17[5]

*For footnote information, see Footnote Section.

dry matter. For the woody core, dimensions of the fibers were also assessed. The laborious determination of chemical characters was omitted, as there seemed little prospect for finding variation among populations. Only small differences were previously found within a set of French and Italian hemp cultivars in contents of a-cellulose, hemicellulose, and lignin measured in bark and wood separately.[4]

Variations in stem composition were observed in field-grown stems of 92 populations of very distinct origin and domestication. This illustrates what hemp fiber breeding in this century has achieved. Total bark fiber content ranges from 12% in wild populations and drug strains to 28% in modern cultivars. With increasing total bark fiber content, populations show a gradual decrease of the woody core fraction from 74% to 52%, and an increase of the secondary and primary bar fiber fraction from 1% to 10% and from 10% to 23%, respectively. Selection for increased bark fiber content was discontinued beyond a level of about 30%. This was due to the inevitable increase of the relatively short and coarse secondary bark fibers that negatively affected rope and textile quality.

The average length of woody core fibers of 98 evaluated populations ranged from 484 μ m to 607 μ m. Resulting differences between populations were, however, not statistically significant. The average diameter of these fibers did differ significantly; they ranged from 25 μ m to 38 μ m. The lack of variation in woody core fiber length indicates that for paper pulp production, breeding should give priority to a continued replacement of woody core by bark fiber, rather than to the improvement of woody core properties.

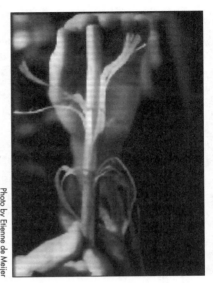

Photo by Etienne de Meijer

Tissues of the hemp stem: woody core, secondary bark, and primary bark.

Stem Production

In field experiments in the Netherlands, maximum yields were obtained from 14 to 16 metric tons of stem dry matter per hectare (one hectare = 2.47 acres). In *Cannabis*, there is large variation of dates of anthesis (full blooming) and seed maturity that depends primarily on origin latitude. Field-grown populations that are acclimatized to and grown in the Netherlands (52° latitude) flower at the end of June. Populations that are imported from higher latitudes flower earlier, and for those from lower latitudes, anthesis is delayed up until mid-September. In general, late-flowering populations have larger stem yields. Therefore, besides selection for vigorous growth, this variation in life-cycle duration enables an increase of stem production by simply organizing the production of seed for sowing at a much lower latitude than the latitude of cultivation.

Narcotic Compounds

The presence of narcotic compounds is generally considered an important reason for the decline of hemp cultivation in the course of this century. Outdoor screening of 97 populations showed significant variation in the average content of the cannabinoid THC, which ranged from 0.06% to 1.77% in the female inflorescence leaf dry matter.[5] For comparison, THC contents exceeding 10% are not uncommon in marijuana produced by seedless clones of superior genotypes in greenhouses and growth chambers. Outdoors, in densely spaced crops, such contents will not occur, even in drug strains. Although high bark fiber content does not necessarily exclude high THC content, most fiber cultivars have very low THC content and thus possess no psychoactive potency.

Soil Pathogenes

Although hemp itself is generally considered to tolerate continuous cultivation on the same field for periods of five to 10 years, host-characteristics for soil pathogenes are imported with regard to other susceptible

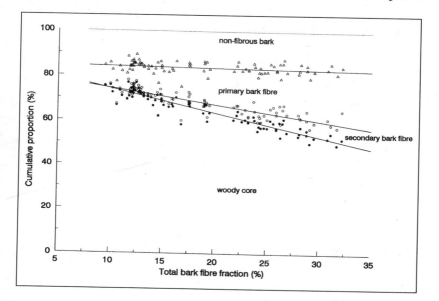

crops in the narrow rotations of the Netherlands. Reactions of *Cannabis* to the root-knot monatodes *Meloidogyne hapla* and *M. chitwoodii* are currently being studied and results indicate that *Cannabis* is a moderate host for *M. hapla* and a poor host for *M. chitwoodii*.[6]

One hundred and forty-eight populations of the *Cannabis* collection were screened for resistance to *M. hapla*. Significant variation in host characteristics was found. The results of the test agreed sufficiently with nematode infection and multiplication on a naturally infested arable field, which indicates that there seem to be good possibilities for breeding highly resistant cultivars.

Conclusion

There is sufficient variation within the genus *Cannabis* for further genetic improvement of quality and yield of hemp fiber as a nonwood source of pulp. Fiber cultivars with negligible low contents of the narcotic compound THC are already commercially available. As a relatively low-input crop that can be grown at a wide range of latitudes, hemp seems very suitable for mass production of nonwood cellulose. The poor host characteristics to plant-parasitic nematodes, which can even be improved by breeding, make hemp also suitable for more intensive agricultural systems with narrow rotations of susceptible dicotyledonous crops. However, the main factors for a successful introduction of hemp as a pulp source are not botanical or agricultural, but industrial and political considerations.

Why Hemp Seeds?

by Don Wirtshafter, J.D.

MANY PARTS OF THE WORLD grew *Cannabis sativa* for its valuable fibers. Others places concentrated on its psychoactive properties. In either case, wherever hemp was cultivated, the nutritious and delicious seeds of the plant were prized as food. Cultures from around the world had their local recipes. The most common way to use the seeds was to grind them into a porridge called "gruel." The seeds were also used to press an edible oil. Many cultures also developed fancy treats for traditional celebrations.

In parts of China, toasted hemp seeds are still sold like popcorn in movie theaters. Street vendors will fill your hand with a cup of freshly toasted seeds for a small coin. In the Ukraine's hemp growing regions, ancient hemp seed recipes are still shared. The Japanese use ground hemp seeds as a condiment. Polish cooks continue to bake them into holiday sweets.

Today, there is a resurgence of interest in using hemp seeds for human nutrition in the United States and Western Europe. *The Hemp Seed Cookbook* was written in 1991 by Carol Miller and this author. It contains information on hemp seed nutrition and 22 recipes for using the seeds. There is so much demand for the seeds, they are currently in short supply.

Hemp Seed Nutrition

The author commissioned a nutritional analysis of one batch of sterilized hemp seeds and hemp seed oil. The work was performed by several laboratories and is compiled in this article. These results confirm that hemp seeds are an extremely valuable human food with unique properties that deserve attention.

Where possible, the results of this testing program are compared to the Recommended Daily Allowances (RDAs) set by the U.S. Department of Agriculture.

A complete mineral assay was performed on the sterilized hemp seeds. It can be seen that hemp is especially high in the most needed minerals: Calcium, Magnesium, Phosphorus, Potassium and Sulfur. It is also

ANALYSIS OF HEMP SEEDS

	RESULTS	U.S.R.D.A.
Moisture	5.7%	
Fat	30%	
Protein (N x6.25)	22.5%	
Ash	5.9%	
Energy	503 Calories/100g	
Carbohydrates	35.8%	
Carotene (Vit. A)	16,800 IU/lb	5000 IU/day
Thiamine (B1)	0.9 mg/100g	1.2 mg/day
Riboflavin(B2)	1.1 mg/100g	1.7 mg/day
Pyridoxine (B6)	0.3 mig/100g	2.0 mg/day
Niacin (B3)	2.5 mg/100g	20 mg/day
Vitamin C	1.4 mg/.100g	60 mg/day
Vitamin D	<10 IU/100g	400 IU/day
Vitamin E	3 mg/100g	30 IU/day
Insoluble Dietary Fiber	32.1%	
Soluble Dietary Fiber	3.0%	
Total Dietary Fiber	35.1%	

low in heavy metals like Strontium, Thorium, Arsenic Chromium. Heavy metals must be avoided in a healthy diet.

The vitamin results were disappointing until you see that hemp's vitamins compare favorably with other grains. Vitamins are mostly provided by fresh vegetables. You would have to eat over a pound of hemp seeds to meet your RDA in many vitamins. The heat from the sterilization process may affect the vitamin content. This will be the subject of further research. The fresh green leaves of the hemp plant could not be tested for nutrition. They are used in the Indian beverage called Bhang, a frothy concoction of hemp leaves, spices, milk and honey or sugar.

Protein

Hemp seeds contain up to 24% protein. A handful of seed provides the minimum daily requirement for adults. Our testing confirms that hemp is a high quality protein containing all eight essential amino acids in the correct proportions that humans need. The basic proteins in hemp are easy to digest. Soybeans contain a higher total percentage of protein, but these are complex proteins that many people find hard to digest.

Widespread use of hemp seed for protein could nourish much of the world's hungry. Because hemp seeds are so digestible, many scientists suggest their use for nutrition blocking diseases and treating malnourishment.

All this is not to mention that these seeds taste great. Hemp seeds can be used as a protein and flavor enhancer in any recipe. Once the seeds are cleaned and roasted, they can be substituted for up to ¼ of the flour in any recipe. Less oil should be used than is called for in your recipe because hemp seeds contain so much of their own oil.

Hemp Seed Oil

The hemp seeds we tested contain 30% oil by weight. Varieties of hemp bred for high oil content contain up to 40% oil. This is said to be the most unsaturated oil derived from the vegetable kingdom. Hemp oil is

MINERAL ASSAY OF STERILIZED HEMP SEEDS

ELEMENT	LEVELS	U.S.R.D.A.
Aluminum	54.	
Antimony	1.75	
Arsenic	0.3	
Barium	6.48	
Beryllium	0.04	
Boron	9.5	
Cadmium	0.28	
Calcium	1680.	800-1200 mg/day
Chromium	0.65	
Cobalt	0.53	
Copper	12.	
Germanium	2.67	
Iodine	0.84	.080-.150 mg/day
Iron	179.	18 mg/day
Lead	0.027	
Lithium	0.062	
Magnesium	6059.	300-400 mg/day
Manganese	95.43	
Mercury	<0.001	
Molybdenum	0.51	
Nickel	5.0	
Phosphorus	8302	800-1200 mg/day.
Platinum	9.23	
Potassium	6170.0	
Selenium	< test limits of 0.02	
Silicon	13.8	
Silver	0.40	
Sodium	22.0	
Strontium	7.33	
Sulfur	2394.	
Thorium	8.12	
Tin	2.6	
Titanium	1.78	
Tungsten	1.84	
Vanadium	0.84	
Zinc	82.0	15 mg/day
Zirconium	1.23	

eighty-one percent the poly-unsaturated essential fatty acids (EFA's) that are needed by, but not produced in the human body. Further, the proportions of these oils in hemp matches the ratios that were previously determined to be most beneficial to human nutrition.[1] The addition of hemp seeds to our diets can help supplement our deficiencies of these needed nutrients.

The natural oils consist of three fatty acids bound on a glycerine molecule in what is called a triglyceride. Of the dozens of fatty acids that we normally consume, only two or three have proven to be essential to sustaining human life. Originally these were called the Vitamin F's. Perhaps because scientists found it impossible to put Vitamin F in a vitamin pill, the name was changed to the Essential Fatty Acids (EFAs) in the 1950's. They are a recognized part of the Recommended Daily Requirement: 3 grams/day of the Omega 6 Linoleic Acid (LA) and 2 grams/day of the Omega 3 Linolenic Acid (LNA). No requirement for the third oil, the Super Omega Six, Gamma Linoleic Acid (GLA) has been set.

Some scientists blame the prevalence of degenerative diseases in our society on the lack of essential fatty acids in the modern diet.[2] The present craze for "fat free" diets misses the boat on EFAs. Some oils do plug up your system, but other oils are mandatory for sustaining life. Further, without oils in your diet, you do not get the fat-soluble vitamins, A, D, E and K. Unless you are consistently eating the correct, extremely fresh foods, the "no fat" diet will eventually leave you devoid of these needed nutrients.[3]

The EFAs are used in a variety of body functions. They act as the lipids in the membranes of all body cells. They prevent build-up of arterial plaque. They are the precursors of the prostaglandins that are needed by our immune systems. At least 200 articles a year studying the EFAs are published in the scientific journals.

Because of the increased public awareness of EFA deficiencies, consumption of therapeutic oils that provide the EFAs has markedly increased. Flax oil has become a six million dollar per year industry. It is popular because it is rich in LNA. LNA deficiency is much more common than LA deficiency. Flax oil is primarily used to treat cancer and arteriosclerosis. The EFAs are able to decrease arterial plaque.

Dr. Andrew Weil, author of *Natural Health, Natural Medicine*, recently contrasted flax oil to the edible grade of hemp oil in the

April/May, 1993 issue of *Natural Health Magazine.*

Most flax oil is not delicious. There is great variation in taste among the brands currently sold in natural food stores, but the best of them still leaves much to be desired. I have been recommending flax oil as a dietary supplement to patients with autoimmune disorders, arthritis, and other inflammatory conditions, but about half of them cannot tolerate it. Some say that it makes them gag, even when concealed in salad dressing or mashed into a baked potato. These people have to resort to taking flax oil capsules, which are large and expensive. Udo Erasmus, author of the classic book, *Fats and Oils* (Alive, 1986), says that the problem is freshness. Unless you get flax oil right from the processor and freeze it until you start using it, it will already have deteriorated by the time you buy it.

PROTEIN SCAN OF HEMP SEEDS

AMINO ACID	mg/g seeds
phosphoserine	0.9
aspartic acid + asparagine	19.8
glutamic acid + glutamine	34.8
threonine	3.7
serine	8.6
proline	7.3
glycine	9.7
alanine	9.6
valine	3.0
cystine + cysteine	1.2
methionine	2.6
cystathionine	0.9
isoleucine	1.5
leucine	7.1
tyrosine	5.8
phenylalanine	3.5
tryptophan	0.6
ethanolamine	0.4
lysine	4.3
histidine	2.5
arginine	18.8

Hemp oil contains more EFAs than flax oil and actually tastes good. It is nutty and free from the objectionable undertones of flax oil. I use it on salads, baked potatoes, and other foods and would not consider putting it in capsules. Like flax oil, hemp oil should be stored in the refrigerator, used quickly, and never be heated.

Unlike flax oil, hemp oil also provides 1.7 percent gamma-linolenic acid (GLA). There is controversy about the value of adding this fatty acid to the diet, but many people take supplements of it in the form of capsules of evening primrose oil, black currant oil, and borage oil. My experience is that it stimulates growth of hair and nails, improves the health of the skin, and can reduce inflammation. I like the idea of having one food oil that supplies both omega-3s and GLA, without the need to take more capsules.

If you have a chance to try hemp oil, a long-forgotten, newly redis-covered food, I think you will see why I am enthusiastic about it.

Therapeutic use of Evening Primrose Oil, Borage Oil and Black Currant Seed Oil has been accepted by naturopathic physicians and the general public. All are sources of Super Omega 6, Gamma Linoleic Acid (GLA). The problem with these oils is that they are currently only avail-able in a solvent extracted form, not the much preferred cold pressing. Healthy bodies can process LA into GLA. This is why GLA is not officially considered an Essential Fatty Acid. Systems under stress from auto-immune diseases, alcohol abuse or other imbalances cannot make this transition so supplementation with GLA can prove beneficial.

None of the previously available nutritional oils combine the needed EFAs in anywhere close to the proportions that scientists have deter-mined is ideal. One would have to carefully use a combination of these oils to get the optimal combination. Hemp oil is just coming on the mar-ket. It has a perfect 3:1 ratio of LA to LNA and a healthy GLA compo-nent (1.7%) as well. Its no wonder that Udo Erasmus in his new book, *Fats that Heal, Fats that Kill*, pronounced hemp to be the "the most per-fectly balanced, natural EFA-rich oil available" and "nature's most per-fectly balanced oil."[4]

These therapeutic oils all share one difficulty, they are so reactive that they have no shelf life. The better an oil is for you, the more quickly it will degrade. Unless properly protected, the good oils will go rancid in a mat-ter of days. This is why our modern, junk food diets are so devoid of EFAs. Food engineers design "convenience foods" to be low in EFAs so that their products can sit for years without going rancid. Manufactures start with saturated fats (coconut and palm oils) or they artificially saturate the oils through the hydrogenation process. Hydrogenation produces the harmful trans-fatty acids that should be avoided in a healthy diet.

The shelf life problem is why you will not quickly see hemp seed treats sold in cellophane packages. Once you toast or grind the seeds, the rancidity reactions begin. Hemp seeds are safe for bakery goods that will be consumed within a few days, but not for any product that must sit longer. The Food & Drug Administration issued a cease and desist order against one company that tried to cellophane wrap hemp granola bars.

For years, no one had been able to figure out how to put EFAs in a bottle or a pill and make them last. In 1986, advanced seed oil companies began using technology that could extract oils in the absence of heat, light and air. This proprietary technology uses inert gases and vacuums to cold press an oil without contaminating it with oxygen. By keeping the oxygen away from the oil, the process avoids starting the chain reactions that create rancidity. Finally, the reactive oils, like hemp, can be pressed into a product that can be kept in the bottle for up to one year without going rancid.

The hemp oil that is available now is rather expensive, about three times the cost of flax oil. This is because the seeds have to be imported and the pressing technology is so expensive. Still, when one compares the grams of GLA per dollar, it turns out hemp is already a better deal than many of its competitors such as Evening Primrose Oil. The price is sure to go down with increased production and competition. When the government finally allows us to grow hemp seeds domestically, we will be able to produce a high quality hemp oil that will compete in price with corn oil.

Other Products from Hemp Oil

Skin cells readily absorb EFT's, but not saturated oils. A coconut oil based skin cream will only coat the skin surface, offering some moisture protection simply by blocking the loss of additional moisture. A lotion rich in EFAs can be absorbed into the skin cells replenishing the lipids damaged by sun rays and/or dry air. Hemp oil is especially effective in saving sunburned skin, preventing it from peeling.

Hemp oil was known in ancient times as linum, the root word for liniment.[5] (True, flax is also generally and taxonomically known by this name. It is wonderful to untangle the ways the oil and fibers of these plants have intertwined through history.) There are many ancient recipes for making soothing rubs from the oil, or even from the roots of the hemp plant. It makes a wonderful massage oil except for its irritating ability to permanently stain your bed sheets a light green color.

FATTY ACID BREAKDOWN OF HEMP OIL

COMPONENT NAME	CARBON CHAIN	% OF TOTAL FATTY ACIDS
Palmitic Acid	C16:0	6.1
Palmitoleic Acid	C16:1	0.3
Heptadecanoic Acid	C17:0	0.2
Stearic Acid	C18:0	2.1
Oleic Acid	C18:1	12.0
Linoleic Acid	C18:2	56.9
Gamma Linolenic Acid	C18:3	1.7
Linolenic Acid	C18:3	18.9
Arachidic Acid	C20:0	0.5
Eicosenoic Acid	C20:1	0.3
Behenic Acid	C22:0	0.3
Erucic Acid	C22:1	0.2
Lignoceric Acid	C24:0	0.3
Nervonic Acid	C24:1	0.2

ANALYSIS OF HEMP SEED OIL

Moisture	0.19%
Vitamin A	8,700 IU/lb
Vitamin E	<1 mg/100g
Phosphatides	0.03%
Chlorophyll	6 ppm
Fat Stability AOM	5 hours
Free Fatty Acid	0.94%
Insoluble Matter	0.01%
Iodine Value	166.5
Saponification Value	192.8
Specific Gravity	0.9295 at 20° C
Unsaponifiable Matter	0.28%
Smoke Point	165° C
Flash Point	141° C
Melting Point	(-8° C)

Both flax and hemp are known as the drying oils. Their high EFA ratios are put to use in industry. As these oils go rancid, they get hard. Our ancestors learned to take full advantage of these properties.

Hemp is the preferred base for house paints. It was known for soaking into the wood, preserving it. During the hearings for the 1937 Marijuana Tax Act, a representative of the Sherwin Williams Co. testified that in 1935 his company imported 135,000 pounds of hemp oil for use in paints and varnish. This is in addition to what the company grew in its large Texas plantation. Old-time house painters still complain that the paint companies ruined paints in the wake of the 1937 prohibition by switching to a flax (linseed) oil base. Flax oil only forms a skin on top of the wood, encouraging rot and leaving the paint liable to peeling. Older painters also say the fumes from hemp oil were not a problem, but that modern oil paints can give them headaches.

Hemp oil makes a wonderful varnish for wood. The oil penetrates into the surface bringing out the best of the wood's grain. It also serves to harden the lumber's surface making it resistant to scratching and other abuse. Hemp oil can be boiled to quicken its drying time.

Hemp was also the base for early printing inks, but flax, because it dries more quickly, became the preferred ink base. When you hear of the new, non-toxic soy based inks, understand that soy oil is only 50% LA and 9% LNA. Hemp, at 57% LA and 19% LNA, is a far superior drying oil that needs far less processing to make a quality ink. At least one modern entrepreneur has begun making hemp based ink and using it to print articles on hemp-based paper.

Cleaning Hemp Seeds

Just like any other produce you bring into the kitchen, hemp seeds need washing before use. Small stones, sticks and foreign seeds inevitably make their way into the product. This foreign matter is easily separated because the hemp seeds will readily float. We wash our seeds in a tall, two quart water pitcher.

Put up to one pound (three cups) of seed into the pitcher and fill with water. Stir the seeds in the water with a spoon. Let this settle for 10 seconds then pour off all of the floating seeds into a colander. Pour carefully to leave the residue at the bottom of the pitcher. Add some more water to the pitcher and then pour off again to capture any remaining seeds.

Rinse the seeds again through the colander. Seeds can then be dried in a pan for grinding or you may go directly to the toasting process described below. Of course, if you like to chew, eat the seeds without any further processing.

Using Whole Roasted Hemp Seed

To roast hemp seeds you first need to wash the seeds according to the previously given instructions. You can immediately roast the wet seeds or the seeds can be dried and roasted later. It is best to use a heavy skillet on top of the stove. This takes about ten minutes, stirring constantly, on high heat. Others use baking sheets in a low temperature (250–300° Fahrenheit) oven. This takes 20–30 minutes. You will know they are done when the popping of seeds slows and they begin to smell like roasted nuts. Avoid roasting the seeds so much that they burn.

After hemp seeds have cooled, they are ready to grind. We use a hand cranked Corona flour mill, but any grain grinder, nut grinder or coffee mill will work. For a buttery texture you may want to grind the meal twice.

For people who have trouble with the coarse hulls of the seeds, most can be removed with the following technique. First roast the seeds as above. Then blend small quantities of the seeds for a few seconds in a blender, coffee grinder or Corona mill set very wide open. This breaks the seeds in half releasing the meal. Most all of the hulls can then be separated by screening. The metal colander we use is perfect for letting the meal through but keeping the half shells of the hulls behind. Then grind the finished meal in the Corona mill.[6]

Why Sterilized Seeds?

The only hemp seeds you can legally purchase in America have been pre-cooked under government supervision. This makes them legal to possess, but compromises their value considerably. The problem is that this cooking destroys much of the nutritional potential of the seeds and leaves them prone to rancidity.

Allowing the sterilized seeds into commerce was a compromise worked out during congressional hearings for the 1937 Marijuana Tax Act. Representatives of the American bird food industry testified before the House Ways and Means Committee that parakeets would not sing unless they were fed hemp seeds. Pigeon growers had been unable to find a substitute for hemp seeds in their feed. Bowing to pressure from Harry Anslinger, the infamous Commissioner of Narcotics, the producers agreed to pre-cook their seeds past the point of germination.

Legal hemp seeds are either heat sterilized or steam sterilized. Steamed seeds are far superior in freshness. Contrary to popular conception, none of the companies that currently supply legal seeds use irradiation to treat their products.

The only purpose for the sterilization is to keep the seeds from growing into new plants. The cooking does not affect the level of THC which is already almost nonexistent in the live seeds, especially if the dust is rinsed off the seeds before use.

The word "sterilized" creates misconceptions. The seeds are not cooked to the point of killing bacteria, i.e., boiled for 15 minutes. Instead, the seeds are brought to a temperature of 160° Fahrenheit for five minutes and then cooled. This is hot enough to alter some of the enzymes necessary for photosynthesis. If the seeds were cooked further, the seed coats would break, allowing the reactive oils in the seeds to quickly go rancid.

As it is, the shelf life of the cooked seeds is considerably compromised. The heat opens micro fissures in the hull that allow oxygen to penetrate into the delicate kernels. Live seeds can sprout after being kept in a drawer for five years. The cooked seeds can go rancid in a few months, especially if not refrigerated.

Robert Stroud, known as the "Birdman of Alcatraz," became an expert on birds during the long years he avoided execution on California's death row. His 1939 book, *Diseases of Birds*, still stands as an authority in its field. Stroud explained how nutritious hemp seeds were, but expressed frustration with the "sterilized" seeds that were coming on the market as a result of the 1937 Marijuana Tax Act.

> "I want to make it perfectly clear right now that anything said in these pages about the virtues of hemp seed apply to fresh, unsterilized hempseed—most assuredly not to the rancid trash now on the market ... Because the seed is rich in the reproductive vitamin, an unlimited supply of it should be kept before the hens making eggs to insure a high percentage of hatchability ... The oil of hemp seed becomes rancid very quickly and what was once a valuable food becomes deadly poison. For this reason, hemp seed must always be used with care."

This is still important advice. Taste hemp seeds before you cook with them. If the seeds are old enough to have lost their nutty flavor or taste rancid, please discard them. Many people are buying their seeds from animal feed stores that do not pay attention to the freshness of their products. Rancid oil feels scratchy at the back of the throat. Tasting for rancidity is an acquired skill that you should learn to protect yourself from all sorts of spoiled foods.

The 1937 compromise agreed to by the bird food industry created many problems. Principally, the seeds could no longer be grown in this country. The seeds are now grown overseas, mainly in China. This greatly increases the price and lowers the quality of the currently available seeds. There are no organically certified seeds available at this time.

Because the seeds are imported, they must be fumigated to kill all insects and other plant pests. Every spice, every grain of rice, any foodstuff that is brought into this country goes through this process. Hemp is no exception. The fumigant used is *methylene bromide*. This chemical works like carbon dioxide, suffocating all living matter. It is inert enough that it does not react with the seeds and dissipates into the air.

The real problem with *methylene bromide* is that it travels up to the upper atmosphere where it becomes an ozone depleter. The *methylene bromide* used as a fumigant is a tiny fraction of what is used for tenting houses and agricultural fields, but is still of concern. Hemp seeds must be tested for the bromide residues of fumigations before they are used for human food.

Are these Seeds Really Legal?

Sterile hemp seeds are specifically excluded from the definition of "marijuana" and are not controlled substances under federal law. Public Law 91-513, Section 102(15). The term "marihuana" is defined as:

> "...all parts of the plant Cannabis sativa, whether growing or not, the seeds thereof, the resin extracted from any part of such plant: and every compound, manufacture, salt, derivative, mixture or preparation of such plant, its seeds or resin; BUT SHALL NOT INCLUDE the mature stalks of such plant, fiber provided from such stalks, oil or cake made from the seeds of such plant, any other compound, manufacture, salt, derivation, mixture or preparation of such mature stalks (except the resin extracted therefrom), fiber, oil or cake OR THE STERILIZED SEED OF SUCH PLANT, WHICH IS INCAPABLE OF GERMINATION." (emphasis added)

These exceptions to the definition of marijuana are what has allowed the resurgence of the American hemp industry.

The importation, sterilization and commercial distribution of hemp seeds is regulated by the Drug Enforcement Administration pursuant to the Controlled Substances Import and Export Act, U.S.C. 952 Et. Seq. and 21 C.F.R. 1311. In calendar year 1990 approximately 60 tons of seeds were imported into this country, mostly for use as birdseed.

The seeds themselves contain almost no Tetrahydrocannabinol (THC), the most psychoactive principal in marijuana. THC is concentrated in the female flower top and leaves. Tiny quantities of THC are found in the dust of these parts that inevitably ends up being packaged with the seeds. The varieties of hemp grown for seed are genetically low in THC, so the residue that comes with commercial seeds is hardly worth smoking.

The DEA recognizes that legal, sterilized hemp seeds contain detectible quantities of THC. The DEA's official testing procedure requires laboratories to test for the viability of hemp seeds taken into evidence. Viability testing (rather than THC analysis) determines whether or not the material constitutes a controlled substance.

National Reports

Introduction

by Ed Rosenthal

HEMP HAS BEEN AN ECONOMIC CROP worldwide for thousands of years. At the beginning of 1990 its long history seemed to be coming to an end. Production was at its nadir. The traditional customers and users stopped purchasing and the hemp industry was mired in regulation.

Now, just a few years later, the industry is rebounding with increased acreage, new production facilities producing new products, and most importantly, it has a new set of customers and end users.

The reports in this sector show hemp in transition from a declining crop to its rediscovery and renewed resource. The more recent the documentation, the more optimism in the report.

Hemp is a growing industry in Europe and Asia. Acreage is increasing all over the world and the plant is being used for many new products. After a near hiatus in the U.S. and de-emphasis of research elsewhere, vigorous investigation for product development has begun again.

Most of the reports in this chapter come from the main producing countries. The Ukraine and Hungary continued research and production for the COMECON market. Just as the industry was about to cease, the western market appeared. China had a healthy cannabis industry. When western buyers appeared, the Chinese were able to supply both cloth and paper.

In France the industry has shown a steady increase over the years. Production is centered around supplying rolling paper factories. Recently the French have been exporting their seed both for use and sowing. It is probable that we will see French hemp cloth soon.

The reports show that these four countries never lost their hemp industry. They continued to profit from hemp after it was eliminated as an economic crop in the U.S. Now that it is becoming popular again the industry infrastructure is being revitalized in order to meet increasing demand.

New countries are entering the market. Reports from Australia, Canada, England, Holland, Poland, and the United States show an industry in resurgence. It becomes obvious that hemp production is increasing worldwide.

Other countries are investigating or making first attempts at the new hemp market. We did not receive any reports from Kazakhstan or Southeast Asia, but we have heard that they are beginning to produce hemp again. In Kazakhstan there is an ambitious effort to harvest the feral hemp growing on the vast plains. They estimate a yield of one and a half tons per acre. Since the only cost is harvesting, this could be a very profitable enterprise.

Logistics problems must be overcome. Is the machinery available to harvest and transport the stalk to a port? How valuable is the low fiber content feral stalk? What grade is the fiber? Do they have a market for it?

Polish cloth appeared in the U.S. in 1994 for the first time. The canvas had a soft feel and was very competitively priced. Cultivation of hemp is illegal in Poland, and the fiber was imported from Russia. According to commercial sources, we can expect more cloth and paper from Poland.

Recently, some fourteen inch wide handloomed cloth has been imported from Thailand and Laos. The cloth was probably produced by tribal hill people and may be a byproduct of marijuana cultivation. Rather than throwing the plant stalks away, they are stripped of their fiber.

All of these developments indicate a burgeoning market for hemp goods. Since this market has been reborn, it has been consumer driven. Rather than industry educating consumers about a product, consumers have been looking for hemp goods. Today the market centers around cloth, paper and seed, the industrial market is likely to grow much larger. When hemp is used as a wood substitute for composite production, paper, bedding and other uses, the volume will be very large, dwarfing the cloth market.

The seed has tremendous potential as a poultry feed, one of its traditional uses. That market is small as compared with the potential for the human consumption as a processed product. The oil has potential use in human nutrition as well as for industrial products, in much the same way that linseed oil was traditionally used.

The first experimental commercial hemp plot was grown in the U.S. this year as described in the report "The Hempstead." Farmers in the U.S. will probably soon be cultivating hemp for its industrial uses throughout the midwest, supplying fiber, hurd and seed to resource hungry industries.

Hemp in Australia

Australia, Eucalyptus and Hemp

IN MANY COUNTRIES around the world, the impact of decades of neglect and thoughtless exploitation of the natural environment is beginning to show. Despite much rhetoric to the contrary, it remains that our country continues to suffer severe degradation of the land, air and water due to thoughtless agricultural, forest and water management policies.

Australia enjoyed unparalleled prosperity for decades, based on the production of wool and wheat. The agricultural base has broadened to include sugar cane, many fruits and cotton for domestic consumption and export. The fragile soils of the Australian continent were not suitable for chemical methods of farming, neither were they able to withstand the impact of imported domestic cattle and sheep. Intensive herbicide and pesticide dependent cultivation methods lead to high costs and decreasing returns.

One of the most profound problems has been that of water management. Even though Australia has lush tropical rain forests in the northeast, it is the driest continent on earth. Large scale damming of rivers and sinking bores for irrigation have led to severe salination due to evaporation, concentrating trace amounts of salt present in artesian water. This has been compounded by clearing of tree cover. The most shameful

(Note: This collection of articles appeared in the Journal of the International Hemp Association, Vol. 1 No. 1, June 1994)

aspect of policy here is to allow the clear-felling of old growth forest to be chipped for Kraft paper.

The roots of Eucalyptus trees reach deep into the subsoil to extract water. After clearing of trees, the water table rises, bringing buried salt to the surface. In some parts of the inland river system thousands of hectares have been permanently lost to a smothering layer of salt. Excess phosphates from chemical fertilizers have entered the waterways. With flow rates seriously reduced by irrigation, the protective flushing effect is lost and there have been several outbreaks of toxic blue green algae.

Fortunately, there have been small improvements. Forward thinking people have formed a "land care" organization to plant trees and practice more sustainable farming. There is a growing movement in Australia to introduce fiber hemp for the production of fabric and paper as well as developing a ligno-cellulosic ethanol fuel industry. Despite recent developments in Europe and England, where fiber hemp cultivation under licence is in progress, little cultivation is taking place. The legislative power to regulate hemp is held by each state government. Modest progress has been made in Tasmania by the "Hemp for Paper" Consortium.

In New South Wales, the most populous state with the most suitable agricultural land and climate, there has been a complete refusal by the authorities to allow fiber hemp trials, despite the support of Universities, agricultural firms and farmers. Economic projections have indicated that hemp will be a highly profitable crop, provided we can convince the government to follow the United Nations policy on fiber hemp and permit industrial scale trials.

Andrew Katelari
Bio-logical Products, 3 Luton Place, St. Ives 2076, Sydney, Australia.

Tasmanian Trials

During the 1992-93 growing season, the University of Tasmania at Hobart, carried out field trials together with the Tasmanian Hemp Company to investigate the production potential of fiber hemp in Tasmania.

The dioecious Hungarian cultivar Kompolti was sown in a replicated field experiment at a rate of 50 kg/ha of seed. Sowing dates were November 2, 16 and 30 and the experimental plots were harvested about 4 months later.

All crops emerged rapidly within a week of sowing, and full ground cover was reached soon. Weeds were effectively smothered, so no extra control methods were required. No significant pest or disease damage was observed.

Irrespective of sowing time, plants started to form inflorescenes in the middle of January, which slowed down vegetative growth in favour of reproductive development. Yields were 8.0, 8.4 and 6.1 ton/ha of stem dry matter. Delta-9-THC content was measured in young leaves and female inflorescences several times during the growing season, and it was always well below the legal limit of 0.3%.

If better adapted (i.e., later flowering) varieties were used, yields of 10 to 12 ton/ha of stem dry matter could probably be obtained in Tasmania.

Wolfgang Spielmeyer
University of Tasmania, Hobart, Australia.

The Tasmanian Hemp Company
In the beginning

"What happens to those beautiful native forests in Tasmania?" was the question posed in a Dutch living room in 1988 when we were sharing photographs and experiences. After explaining that a good proportion ended up as woodchips for Japan which we then bought back as paper, a friend said that he had seen something on Dutch TV about hemp for paper. I was brought up as a logger's daughter in Tasmania, and began to feel very angry with myself for not having seen beyond trees for paper.

So began our long search to track down this curious phenomenon. Our lives are now totally dominated by hemp, despite the warnings of a visiting Dutch Hemp Project leader not to let it do so.

Frits' niece helped us to locate the Dutch university students researching hemp and our knowledge (and Frits' translation skills) began to improve dramatically. Since then, we have visited the Dutch Hemp Project's pulp researchers and the research farm and hosted two of the top researchers for a whirlwind tour here in 1993.

The Tasmanian Hemp Story

Our achievements, apart from notoriety and positive public education throughout Australia, include three annual licensed trials of low-THC hemp supervised by the University of Tasmania. Frits harvested our 1994 trial between a morning rehearsal and evening orchestral concert with the Tasmanian Symphony Orchestra at the end of March. Our bureaucrats are nervous about the venture, but have not yet put a stop to our endeavors, although they suggest that we should walk before we run. In our opinion we have walked for too long: the world can't wait for sensible solutions and our campaign has broadened from hemp for paper to hemp for just about everything! Tasmanian farmers are most interested and the general public is supportive. The only abusive phone call we ever had was from an elderly ex-employee of one of Australia's pulp and paper manufacturers who claimed the Dutch were "decadent"!

We set up the Tasmanian Hemp Company to help our negotiations with government and business. We had already founded the Hemp for Paper Consortium Incorporated, a small non-profit community association aiming to spread information on the agricultural, industrial and environmental benefits of a hemp industry. I began by submitting a plan to the Tasmanian Government in February 1991 for an environmentally sound pulp mill based on hemp. This was in answer to a call for expressions of interest in a Northern Tasmanian Pulp and Paper Mill. Frits' translations of Dutch research as well as information gathering since 1988 provided the basis for the submission.

The later establishment of the company was seen as a practical example of promoting an industrial approach to hemp, a lead which the consortium had hoped would be taken up by business people in Tasmania. This did not happen, however, mainly through lack of government interest. Considering the enormous obstacles placed in the way of the Hemp for Paper Consortium Incorporated when lobbying for licenses to grow hemp, it is little wonder that others have not wanted to venture in.

Our company is the first importer of hemp fabric to Tasmania. We are sewing this into clothes which we sell, to promote products that could be produced from fiber grown here. Our biggest step will be achieving a commercial licence to grow hemp here in Tasmania, for which we began negotiations with the Tasmanian government officials recently.

It is interesting to note that our licence applications now need to go through the Poppy Advisory Board of Tasmania. Tasmania is the only Australian state which grows opium poppies. The poppy officials are nervous of Tasmania's "clean" image being ruined by the media painting Tasmania as the drug state of Australia, where we also grow hemp. They insist that the low THC content of our crop will not get in the way of a good story.

Our Objectives

Long-term: to develop hemp as a new crop and a sustainable industry which will help overcome Australia's problems of soil degradation, pollution from agricultural chemicals, and controversy over the use of native forests.

Short-term:
a) to provide organically grown hemp for export to existing markets,
b) to set up separating machinery in Tasmania as a first step to down-streaming, so that companies in Tasmania interested in either the bast or core fiber can be supplied (e.g. to replace expensive, imported Kraft pulp; to provide horse bedding),
c) to set up a small integrated pulp/paper/textile/fluff mill in Tasmania.

Patsy & Frits Harmsen, Directors
Tasmanian Hemp Company, 430 Tinderbox Road, Tinderbox,
7054 Tasmania, Australia.

China, Hemp and Paper

by D. Paul Stanford

HEMP (*CANNABIS SATIVA*) originated in central Asia, and is indigenous to Kazakistan, Pakistan, Nepal, the Kashmir region of India and Tibetan region of China. All archaeologists agree that hemp was one of the first known plant species to be purposely cultivated by human beings. Hemp is the only one of the originally cultivated plants to be dioecious, or have separate plants for both the male and female of the species. Carl Sagan, the Cornell astronomer and well published science writer, speculated in his book, *The Dragons of Eden*, that hemp was the very first plant to be "grown."

Beginning by at least 10,000 BC, or twelve thousand years ago, the inhabitants of two regions in Asia began cultivating hemp. On the western flank of hemp's indigenous region, in the Mesopotamian valley between the Tigris and Euphrates Rivers in present day Iraq, and, at the same time, on the eastern flank in the Huang He (Yellow River) valley in China, the peoples there settled into the first agricultural civilizations and began growing hemp.

In China's traditional culture, hemp's multitude of uses had economic and spiritual significance. Artifacts unearthed from sites in China dating back over 12,000 years ago indicate that hemp was cultivated since the remote beginnings of agricultural settlements. The ancient Chinese called their country, the "land of hemp and mulberry." The mulberry bush was prized because it is the food of the silkworm, and silk is one of China's most venerated products. Only the most powerful and rich could afford silk though, and hemp was what everyone wore most every day.

Hemp was cultivated for food and oil from the seed, fiber for cordage, stitching, textiles and clothing from the stalk, medicinal concoctions from the female flowers, and for its prodigious leaf production to go back into and build the soil. Hemp's deep tap root draws up subsoil nutrients that are then available for the next crops in rotation. Hemp grows so quickly that it shadows all other plants, so the undergrowth dies off without sunlight, thereby acting to organically clear the cultivated fields of unwanted species (weeds).

Hemp was well known by the people of eastern Asia prior to the invention of writing, or in prehistoric times. Its Chinese name, "ma," is the most basic of verbal sounds, meaning mother in every human language, but in Chinese it is also synonymous for horse and as an inquisitive query (much like a verbal question mark.) The individual elements, or strokes, of the Chinese character for hemp represent a home inside which hemp fibers are hanging from a rack. The character is also used in combination with several other characters to give its influence to several other word's meanings, such as the Chinese words for: numb, clever, anaesthetic, linen, indifferent, troublesome, sparrow and the name of game Mahjongg; each of these words contain the character for hemp.

According to traditional Chinese tales, paper was invented by Ts'ai Lun, a eunuch scribe of the imperial court, in 105 AD, in the then capitol of China, LouYang, on the Yellow River. This story is a fable, since paper fragments made from hemp have been found in graves in China dating back to the first century BC (over 200 years prior to the mythical invention.) It is not known why Ts'ai Lun gets credit for the invention of paper, since these artifacts predate him. But the legend has it that prior to paper's invention scholars had to be physically fit since they had to carve and carry about their writing on wooden tablets and bamboo slips. These records were very heavy. Patiently weaving the fibers to a textile finish was not practical given the volume required for record keeping.

No one knows exactly how the method was finally discovered, but it eventually became popular the world over. Paper was first made using 80% bark of the hemp stalk and 20% bark of the mulberry bush.

The perfect representative invention of China's civilization to the other "barbarian" peoples is this paper from the "Land of Hemp and Mulberry." The mixture is pulped by crushing the fibers, then placing them in a vat of water with quick-lime (calcium carbonate). The fiber is screened from the water through a silk mesh, the screens are left out to dry and then the dried paper is peeled from the screen.

In the landmark Japanese book of the fifth century AD, *A Handy Guide to Papermaking*, the author K. Chohoki states, "hemp and mulberry... have long been used in worshipping the gods. The business of paper making therefore, is no ignoble calling."

Hemp paper quickly gained popularity for written communication and art. The Chinese kept the secrets of paper making hidden for many centuries. It spread from China to Japan in the fifth century AD, to Samarkand by 751 AD, Baghdad by 793, Cairo in the 10th century, Spain by the 12th century, Italy by the 13th century, and Nuremburg in Germany, where movable type was invented, in 1390.

The legend of paper's invention in China is that when Ts'ai Lun first announced this new discovery, he was scoffed at and jeered out of the imperial court. No one would realize and recognize the break-through. Ts'ai Lun decided the only way to popularize his invention was through hype. He said that paper would bring the dead back to life.

Shortly thereafter, with the help of friends, Ts'ai Lun pretended to die. He had himself buried in a coffin that had a hollow reed attached so he could breath. While he was mourned for several days, he waited below the earth. Then his conspirators announced that if some of his paper were burned on his grave, he would rise from the dead. A skeptical crowd gathered to watch the event. After a quantity of Ts'ai Lun's paper had been burned, they exhumed the coffin. To the great surprise of all present, Ts'ai Lun sat up and thanked them for their devotion and faith in him and his invention. The resurrection was considered a miracle which was attributable to the power of his paper.

Paper burning at funerals became a wide spread tradition in Chinese culture. It is still continued today. In fact, hemp has several connections to funeral rights in Chinese culture, some of which continue even today in post-communist China. White is considered the color of mourning for the dead in China and other East Asian countries. In China today, families and friends of the recently dead wear a white hemp fabric collar in mourning. Throughout East Asia and Greater China (Hong Kong, Taiwan, People's Republic of China, Malaysia and Singapore) the belief and practice of burning paper money and paper home models is a standard way for people to provide their departed relatives with these items in the after-life. Ancestor worship is the main "religion" of traditional China. It is thought that without these traditional paper offerings and other food offerings, the departed will fade away and dissolve in their after-life.

In traditional China (mainland China prior to the communist revolution, Malaysia, Taiwan,) since prior to the 3rd century BC until today, the dead are mourned in a belief system known in China as the "Wu Fu," literally Five Clothes or Five Levels of Mourning. All the levels of the Wu Fu involve hemp. The Wu Fu are five levels of mourning that people were expected to conform to when a relative, especially the patriarch of the family, has died. The Wu Fu was embodied in the law, which prescribed punishment for those who failed to observe mourning for elder kin. The level that one performed the mourning rituals at depended how closely one was related to the deceased. If the departed was one's father or husband (the first level and closest in Chinese patriarchy), then the survivor was expected to wear coarse, unhemmed hemp clothing, hemp sandals, hemp head-dress and carry a hemp stalk for 27 months. At the second level of the Wu Fu, if the deceased is one's grandfather, brother or direct uncle, then one must wear coarse hemmed hemp clothing, hemp head-dress, hemp sandals and a hemp mourning staff for one year. At the fifth level, for a distant uncle or in-law, one would wear hemp fabric with a silky finish for three months.

The earliest traces of hemp fabric have disappeared. From archeological research, hemp cords have been found twisted together and imprinted on the sides of pottery dating back 12,000 years. The oldest remnants of fabric are made from hemp and are from a burial site in China dating back to 1000 BC. The ancient Chinese must have discovered that the twisted strands of hemp fiber were much stronger than individual strands. This must have been followed by the invention of spinning and weaving fibers into cloth, an innovation that ended reliance on animal skins as the sole material for clothing. The ancient Chinese also used hemp fiber to make their shoes.

The Chinese were urged to plant hemp from their earliest written records. The "Shu King," a book from 2350 BC has several instructions regarding hemp. Hemp cultivation has been encouraged, esteemed and extolled for its many uses throughout history.

Chinese military forces were given a technological military advantage over their opposing forces with the discovery that hemp fibers provided much stronger bowstrings for archers in combat than the bamboo ones previously used. The hemp bowstring was so important that Chinese royalty set aside large portions of land exclusively to cultivate hemp for this purpose; thus, hemp was the first agricultural war crop.

During the long history of China, hemp was used throughout every canton of the country, from prehistoric times until today. It clothed the people from head to foot, provided a numerous variety of other products, and came to symbolize a power over evil and disorder.

Because illness was considered to be caused by evil spirits, the cure had to involve driving the evil spirit out. Hemp stalks were carved into snake-like figures and these were used to exorcise the evil spirits. Hemp leaves were often applied directly on wounds to aid in healing.

A Chinese emperor, Shen-Nung, who lived in the twenty-eighth century BC, is considered the founder of Chinese medicine. His book on medicine included cannabis flowers for several ailments.

Hemp in China Today

Today, China produces the largest commercial hemp crop. China used hemp as the primary fiber for clothing until the early 1980s. China never ceased producing paper from hemp. Though hemp fiber's use declined from 1890–1990, it has increased in this decade. Cannabis drugs were prohibited in China in 1961, but there has never been a campaign to imprison hemp growers and I have witnessed many people just growing their own on tiny plots. Hemp grows abundantly around most temples.

The Chinese system is, of course, a socialist one, so the planning of many businesses there, especially the industrial ones, is directed by the government. The Chinese business and government leaders have had many scientists undertake research on nonwood paper fiber production. Their research has shown that, though hemp is by no means the exclusive nonwood fiber for utilization in paper making, hemp is the best, most productive, economical and ecological fiber.

Hemp pulp is used to strengthen other fibers that would otherwise not be strong enough on their own to make paper. Hemp pulp is added to post-consumer recycled waste, which is both domestic and imported from North America, and other straws and reeds. Generally, between 5% to 25% hemp content is common in paper used domestically in China. Some 100% hemp paper is manufactured for very thin specialty paper and currency. Most Chinese hemp pulp contains the whole stalk; both bast and hurd fibers are pulped together in their natural percentages for paper.

Fiber hemp in China is designated by color. There are red, yellow and green varieties of hemp fiber. The properties of the three types of fiber are identical, only the color is different.

Hemp is cultivated today in China for three uses: textile, paper and seed production. The bast fiber is used primarily for textiles. When the bast is stripped from the stalk in China it is still mainly done by hand in the fields. Most hemp is dew retted, meaning the stalk is left in the field for up to three weeks to allow bacterial action to break down the leaves and stalks for easier removal of the valuable bast fiber. This, however, limits the usefulness of the hurds to barnyard animal bedding. The whole stalk is used for producing most domestic paper.

The seed crop is roasted for domestic snacks, used to produce oil in the fields (80% of Chinese people work in agriculture) and almost 40% are exported. In 1992 over 600 tons of hemp seed was imported into the United States by six companies. The companies are licensed by the Drug Enforcement Agency to sterilize the seeds with heat processing within 48 hours of landing.

Hemp textiles today are regarded by most Chinese as old-fashioned. The trend there is to emulate Western styles, including cotton and synthetic textiles, and many complain that hemp fabrics wrinkle too easily. Until the late 1980s, hemp textile products were in decline and almost vanished.

Matthew Ng, of Hong Kong, working under the label, "Stoned Wear," began manufacturing garments made with 55% hemp fabric in Southern coastal China for export in 1989. These were first imported into North America in 1990 by Joint Venture Hempery, run by Alex Shum of Vancouver, B.C.

An educational and business research center was opened in Shandong province in 1989 near the base of Tai Shan, the Eastern sacred mountain of China, to preserve and revive the cannabis fiber industry. The Hemp Textile Research Institute, in Taian first produced fabric on a commercial scale in 1990. Tai Shan has the highest concentration of religious sites in the world. It is the home of Confucius (Kong Si), the highly esteemed philosopher whose writings were among China's most influential. The long path to the summit of Tai Shan is lined with Confucian, Taoist and Buddhist temples. I visited the Hemp Textile Research Institute in the summer of 1990. At that time the quality left much to be desired. It has gradually improved and several companies have imported hemp fabric from them.

When I first visited the hemp paper mill in Hunan province in 1989, their facility, on the shore of the Dong Ting Hu, China's largest lake, was quite primitive. It too has grown and developed with time.

Though hemp grows throughout China, mostly for local consumption, there are five principle regions were hemp is cultivated for nationwide and international demand. China, removing itself from contact and dialogue with the Western, corporate oriented governments, never accepted the mythological demonization of hemp perpetrated in the rest of the world. With modernization, China is poised to remain at the forefront of the hemp industrial vanguard for at least the next five years. China's long, cultural and historic association with hemp will continue.

Hemp in England

by Ed Rosenthal

SINCE THE DEFEAT of the Spanish Armada in 1588 until WWII the British navy ruled the world. Their ships were the source of immense wealth as they came into port with tribute from colonies and profit from war and trading. For more than two centuries the navy's ships depended on wind for power. Steamships were not introduced until the 1830s.

The sails and rigging of the largest sailing ships weighed 50 to 100 tons. The rigging was made from long strand hemp fiber and the sails were made from heavy hemp canvas. Hemp was used because it was the strongest natural fiber, gained strength when wet, did not become brittle and crack in extreme cold environments, and lasted the longest. Without hemp, the great sailing ships of the late eighteenth and early nineteenth century would have set, without sails.

An acre of hemp yields 3–5 tons, averaging about $3\frac{1}{2}$–5 tons.[1] About 25% of that is fiber, and 75% is the hurd,[2] the brittle, woody inner portion. About half of the fiber is long strand and can be used for twine or cloth. One acre yields slightly less than half a ton of fiber which can be spun to twine or yarn. A one hundred ton ship's rigging required about 200 acres of hemp. A fleet of 50 ships required 10,000 acres or $15\frac{1}{2}$ square miles.

Of course, sailing ships are obsolete and the use of hemp began declining with the invention of the cotton gin, which made cotton cheaper to process than hemp. Tropical fibers from extreme low wage colonies made hemp uncompetitive in the natural fiber market. Even in the early nineteenth century hemp was grown and processed in very low wage European states such as Russia. In the U.S., by 1840 most hemp grown in Kentucky was used to make cloth to cover cotton bales.[3]

The British used much more hemp than they could grow so they depended on Russia for 90% of their sail cloth. According to Jack Herer, the War of 1812 was fought in part over hemp as a trade issue.[4] This shows that the domestic hemp industry in Britain was not that important a supplier. Nevertheless, throughout England there are many place names in which hemp is used.

Cannabis' symbiotic history with humans has been one of discovery resulting in cultural or technological change, replacement by other materials which seemed to be better for specific purposes, loss and rediscovery for other purposes. Its renewed life in the early nineties even as traditional uses were coming to a dead end, is a continuation of this process which Abel[5] claims has been going steady on and off for 12,000 years.

For construction the world powers had many sources of cheap lumber once the European forests had been depleted. The Americas, Africa, Asia, Australia and New Zealand. New sources continue to open up as multi-national lumber companies prepare to deforest Siberia and other north Russian territories. Even so, lumber's value has risen over the past few years as U.S. supplies have been limited by legislation, regulation and depletion.[6]

Dave Seber from C & S Specialty Builder's Supplies in Harrisburg, Oregon thinks that hemp grown near fiberboard factories would be competitive with wood chips. A typical board factory uses about 1500 tons a day and operates about 250 days a year. That comes to 375,000 tons a year. A yield of $3\frac{1}{2}$ tons of stalk per acre yields about $2\frac{1}{2}$ tons per acre of hurds. It would take cultivation of about 150,000 acres, or 234 square miles to feed one mill. The British farmers are growing 1% of one board factory's yearly production.

When I first heard that Her Royal Majesty's Home Office had decided to allow regulated cultivation of hemp in Great Britain, I called the person most responsible, named Robert Lukies. He had become interested in growing when he noticed that the horse bedding being imported from France was composed of hemp hurds.

Lukies teamed up with some people at his local farm supply

Ian Low, one of the founders of Hemcore holds a cannabis plant. The hurd is being used for animal bedding, and the fiber is being used to manufacture cloth and paper.

and commodity company and formed the Hemcore Corp. This company induced thirty farmers to try growing hemp. The farm supply people had been buying hurds from the French, and were selling them for horse bedding. Ian Low, one of Hemcore's officers, claimed that the hurds absorbed more liquid than wood shavings and composted in one quarter of the time. He told me their decision to grow was based solely on sales of the hurds and was surprised to find the high value of fiber.[7]

The government made several demands. All the fields must be invisible from the road and the seed would have to be EC approved. The EC standard is that there must be as much CBD as THC and may contain no more than 0.3% THC.[8] As long as they harvested the crop the EC farm subsidy kicked in at £225 or about $340 an acre.[9] They had figured on the hurds and the subsidy and found a profitable crop. With sale of the fiber, the crop is destined to be a high income producer. The question is, can they can sell it all?

The fields were on a rocky clay loam soil on slightly rolling land in Essex about an hour ride by rail or car from London. The seeds are the grade B French which have about 25% male while the rest are female or hermaphrodite. They were planted at the rate of 400 seeds per meter (40 per square foot) and about 250 per meter were harvested. The yield per acre turned out to be about three tons. The plants reached a height of eight to ten feet and were in full flower when harvest began.

The seeds were planted in May and harvest began in early September. Because of rains there were several delays and the harvest finally ended in early October.

There has been no hemp industry in England for thirty-two years so there are no manufacturers who have experience using the goods for commercial or consumer products. Two hemp advocates, John Hanson and Pete Messemger, have made several runs of paper using small mills in England to make paper from hemp. However, they were using Spanish produced pulp to make the finished product. The pulp looks like heavy blotter paper and does not require nearly as much processing to get to finished paper.

The first pulping trial at a British factory resulted in clogged

Photo by Ed Rosenthal

A monoecious (hermaphroditic) bud. Since all the plants contain both male and female flowers they all flower at the same time rather than consecutively. All the plants are the same quality and ripen at the same time. The seeds came from France. In actuality about 25% of the plants were male.

The English hemp crop has drawn a tremendous amount of publicity. On this day one film crew and two print reporters were in the fields. This was a ten acre plot.

machines which had to be disassembled in order to clean them out. I suspect that the raw fiber and hurds were cut too long and the strands of fiber became intertwined around the machinery parts. These mistakes will be remedied in the future.

Spinning yarn may be a different story. There is not a soft bast fiber spinning industry in England at present. How will the domestic weavers get the fiber spun?

Many buyers have shown interest in the products including some paper mills, a bio-regional organization, craft supply distributors and foreign trading companies. Their fiber and hurd prices are somewhat higher than world prices but domestic buyers prefer to support the domestic industry.

I had no problem getting to photograph the fields but although promised a view of the cutting and mowing, never got to see it. I did see the cut stems dew retting in the fields. They told me that they had a developed their own decorticator and other processors but would not let me take a peek at their inventions.

In a recent interview Low told me that Hemcore expects to expand acreage next year, since the first year's experiment had proven successful, despite some problems.

The UK Hemp Project in 1993

by Ian Low

PULLING, RETTING, GRASSING, breaking, scutching and hackling were going on in East Anglia in Elizabethan times. There was even a law which enforced hemp growing on pain of a fine. The hemp produced was quite coarse and was used for smocks, sheets, bolsters, fishing nets and rope. All over the area there are village names to remind us of the long hemp growing tradition such as Hempstead, Heckfield and Bleach Green. So in 1993 when Hemcore was formed by two East Anglian businesses to redevelop the hemp crop in the area, we were treading a well-worn path, albeit one that hadn't been walked for 50 years.

The reasoning behind our move into hemp production involved a common mixture of circumstances and opportunities, in detail:

Market Openings: for the fiber into paper and textiles, for the core of the plant as livestock bedding, for the seed as fishing bait and bird seed.

Growing Opportunities: with farmers looking for alternative crops to remove the pressure from over production in most of the main arable crop markets.

Environmental Benefits: which were commonly seen as coming from hemp cultivation, both in the growing crop and in the replacement of synthetic or imported products in the market place.

(Note: This article appeared in the Journal of the International Hemp Association, *Vol. 1 No. 1, June 1994)*

The Project

In 1992 my partner Robert Lukies and myself set up a trials program covering as many different varieties of hemp as we could obtain. These trials were taken through to harvest at Hatfield Broad Oak in Essex and the resulting plants were trial processed.

Following the successful outcome of these trials, a decision was made to go ahead with a commercial venture. An application was made to the British Home Office for a licence to grow 600 ha (1,500 acres) of hemp in 1993. After considerable discussion a licence was granted on February 18, 1993, and our plans went into action for establishing a new U.K. hemp industry.

In March 1993, Hemcore Ltd. was formed. It is owned by Harlow Agricultural Merchants, a large East Anglian Merchanting Company and Robert Lukies, who farms and runs a seed processing business in Essex. During March and April, 30 growers were chosen and sites were approved by the Home Office.

The Growing Crop

Drilling took place during the first week of May at approximately 50 kg/ha of seed, drilled 2–3 cm deep on 10–18 cm row widths. We found it important to obtain as fine as possible a seed bed with minimum compaction and used conventional cereal drills for sowing. No agricultural chemicals were used in the growing of the crop, but we did find it very responsive to fertilizer. We used fertilizer rates of about 120 kg/ha of nitrogen, 100 kg/ha of phosphate and 160 kg/ha of potash.

The impressive growth rate of the hemp crops is already well known and our crops certainly lived up to expectations, average heights reached were 3 m with some up to 3.5 m. Maximum heights were reached in early to mid August. There were noticeable plant losses between establishment and full growth, with final plant populations ending at around 180 per m^2.

In July and August, a number of incidents occurred where people stole cuttings of our contract crops. It is extremely doubtful whether they were rewarded for their troubles, but they were certainly of considerable nuisance value and caused the authorities some concern. One particularly troubled crop was harvested in early August to get it out of the way, otherwise harvesting did not begin until September.

The Harvest

September and early October were very wet in East Anglia in 1993. This proved a considerable test of our pioneering harvest plans. Whilst we tried different machines and methods, the mainstay of our operation hinged on a modified rape swather and John Deere Round Balers. We are particularly grateful to the latter company for their wholehearted support. Although weather conditions delayed a large proportion of the baling until mid October, we were delighted by the condition of the crop, and in the end every hectare of every field was cleared. Following such a steep learning curve, we intend to put into practice for the '94 harvest a number of new plans that give us a lot of confidence for the long-term future of hemp production.

The Market

I will not go into detail on processing, as a large amount of what we are doing is at the prototype state and all of it is confidential. Suffice to say that we have at the moment two products coming out of the factory, fiber from the stem sheath for paper and possibly for the textile trade, and the core of the stem which is going into the livestock bedding market. Both products have created a lot of interest and there seems at the moment to be good demand.

Summary

1993 was a year of considerable achievement for Hemcore. The ripples from what we have done have gone round the world. We succeeded in a difficult year to grow and harvest 600 hectares of hemp and we will build on this in 1994. We have continued to do extensive variety and agronomic trials and these too will be extended this year. Processing caused us many more problems than we originally envisaged. Marketing will also present a challenge as the present volumes are only satisfying a small niche market. We have made it clear from the outset that Hemcore's philosophy, unlike that of much of the agricultural world, will be to satisfy market leads, not to be output driven.

Fiber Hemp in France

by H. M. G. van der Werf

AT LE MANS three organizations are involved with hemp:

The Fédération Nationale des Producteurs de Chanvre (FNPC) conducts research concerning the agronomy and processing of hemp and breeds new hemp varieties.

The Comite Economique Agricole de la Production du Chanvre (CEAPC) organises the production contracts between hemp growers and hemp buyers and markets the seed.

The Cooperative Centrale des Producteurs de Semences de Chanvre (CCPSC) contracts growers for hemp seed production, buys the seed and markets it.

Mr Jean-Paul Mathieu is the director of each of the three organizations. On my visit to Le Mans I spoke with him and with Mr Olivier Béhérec, the hemp breeder.

Area of Hemp

In 1992, 3,950 hectares (ha) of hemp was grown in France: of this area, 370 ha was for the production of seed for sowing. About 2,650 ha was grown in the region of Troyes (eastern France), 1,250 ha of hemp was grown in the region of Le Mans (western France), and 50 ha was grown in the South-west of France. In 1992, 200 ha of hemp was grown for the production of high quality seed for sowing, on another 170 ha second quality sowing seed was produced. This seed is cheaper but will produce a crop containing about 70% monoecious plants and 30% male plants, whereas hemp grown from high quality seed will contain very few male plants and will consist almost exclusively of monoecious plants.

Breeding

The FNPC has bred a number of monoecious hemp varieties. Fibrimon 21, Fibrimon 24 and Fibrimon 56 were bred in France in the 1950s by crossing the same parental populations as described for this purpose by Bredemann *et al.* (1961). The numbers added to the names of the French cultivars indicate lateness, the higher the number, the later the cultivar.

In 1965 a collection of 100 fiber hemp accessions was evaluated for stem quality, productivity and also for future availability. The original intention of this screening was to select optimal parents for the production of hybrid F1 cultivars (heterosis breeding) without domestic maintenance of the parents. Out of these 100 accessions 30 were retained and crossed with Fibrimon. At a later stage the idea of heterosis breeding was left and the best performing hybrids were backcrossed with Fibrimon and stabilised to new true breeding monoecious cultivars. Three of these cultivars are presently commercialised as a replacement for the Fibrimon cultivars. These cultivars are Fédora 19, Félina 34 and Fédrina 74, the dioecious parents used in making these cultivars were respectively JUS-9, Kompolti and Fibridia. Another more recent cultivar is Férimon 12, which is an early maturing selection from Fibrimon 21. Cultivar Futura 77 is derived from the same hybrid offspring as Fédrina 74 but it was selected for a somewhat later date of flowering.

In recent years the breeding program has focussed on reduction of the THC content. All varieties have less than 0.3% THC in the inflorescence, meeting the EEC requirement. All varieties exist in two THC levels: between 0.3 and 0.1% and below 0.1%. The two versions are strictly similar except for the THC content. For example Fedrina 74 exists in a version containing 0.20% THC and another version containing 0.07% THC. For some varieties, the low-THC version is not available for sale.

Photo by Ed Rosenthal

M. Matthieu, who has headed the French research projects for nearly two decades checking out an experimental variety.

The seed of the varieties containing less than 0.10% THC are sold only in France. Varieties containing no THC (0.001%) have been obtained by crossing existing varieties with a special variety containing an "anti-THC gene." Agronomic characteristics of these varieties are still inferior to those of the THC containing varieties. Mr Mathieu thinks that this can be overcome and expects that THC-free varieties with good agronomic characteristics will be obtained.

Rotation, Soil Requirements and Fertilization

In the rotation hemp is an easy crop: it does not require any pesticides apart from a seed dressing, it suffocates weeds and leaves a good soil structure. Furthermore it can be grown during 2 or 3 consecutive years in the same field.

Hemp will perform well on many types of soil, as long as the pH is not below 5. Crop growth can be very much impaired by water logging and by compaction of the tilled layer. Crusting soils may cause problems as the emergence is easily hampered by a crust.

A crop yielding 8 t/ha of stems (at 16% humidity) will contain 65 to 80 kg of N, 20 kg of P_2O_5 and 120 kg of K_2O. Recommended fertilizer gifts (depending on fertility status of the soil) are: 100 to 140 kg of N/ha,

80 to 120 kg of P_2O_5/ha and 160 to 200 kg of K_2O/ha. Too much N may cause lodging.

Sowing

Hemp is sown in the second half of April or in the beginning of May. Earlier sowing increases risks linked with slower germination such as poor emergence due to a crusting soil or more severe competition from weeds. About 400 seeds/m² are sown, this will result in about 300 normal-sized plants/m² at harvest. A plant density at harvest of at least 200 plants/m² is desirable for several reasons. The higher the plant density, the shorter the crop. In order to be able to harvest the crop using machines which are currently used in other crops, the height of the crop should not exceed 2.5 meters. Otherwise problems may arise with the use of the mower-conditioner, a machine which breaks the green stems so that they dry more rapidly. The mower-conditioner does not work well with the thicker stems which are obtained from hemp grown at a low plant density. Furthermore, at a high plant density the proportion of bark in the stem is high and in the processing factory the bark separates more easily from the wood in fine stems such as are obtained at high plant densities.

When hemp is grown for the production of seed for sowing the plant density is 10 to 20 plants/m².

Harvesting

Currently no harvesting equipment specially designed for hemp is in use in France. In the past a special machine (a "pick-up égreneur") was used after the hemp had been mown and dried to pick up the stems and separate the grain from the stems. These machines have been largely abandoned as they were expensive due to their low capacity (30 ha per harvest season). The pick-up égreneur is used only for hemp grown for the production of sowing seed now. In 1986 a machine which separates hemp stems into wood and bark in the field was developed. The prototype did perform satisfactorily from the technical point of view, but it was too expensive, so this technology has not been a success. Currently two harvest methods are used for fiber hemp. Both methods only involve machines which are used in other crops as well.

a) The crop is mown at the beginning of September using a cutter bar or a mower-conditioner. The mower-conditioner is used most frequently, the distance between the crushing rolls is kept relatively large, in order to limit losses of grain. The hemp is laid down in a swath and will take about 4 days (mower-conditioner) or about 8 days (cutting bar) to dry (14 to 18% humidity in the straw). Once the hemp is dry it will be baled. The grain is separated from the stems in the processing factory.

b) Around the 15th of September a combine harvester set at 1.50 meters mowing height cuts off the tops of the plants and threshes them. After that, the crop is mown using a mower-conditioner and baled once it has dried. This method decreases fiber yield but will result in a higher seed yield.

Method a) is most used in the Le Mans region, method b) is more popular in the Troyes region. In both regions big round bales are most popular, high density square bales do not work with hemp.

An average hemp crop will yield 6 to 8 t/ha of stem (16% humidity) and 600 to 1000 kg of grain (10% humidity). Bark content in the stem is 35 to 40%, this is high relative to the bark content of about 30% which is obtained in the Netherlands with the French varieties. The lower bark content in the Netherlands may be due to the lower plant density and the higher yield level in the Netherlands.

Processing

In France two factories process hemp bales. If present, the seed is separated from the stems, the stems are then separated into bark and wood by means of a hammer mill. The details of this separation technology were not revealed as it is secret. One of these processing factories,

"Les Papeteries de Mauduit" (part of the Kimberly Clark group) is at Le Mans and processes both hemp and flax. Both hemp bark and flax fiber produced in this factory are pulped and made into paper at another factory of the "Papeteries du Mauduit" at Quimperlé (Brittany). The other hemp processing factory "La Chanvriäre de L'Aube" is a cooperative situated at Bar sur Aube near Troyes. This fac-

Photo by Ed Rosenthal

Hemp stalks drying in the field. After the bundles dry they are processed in the cigarette rolling factory.

tory sells hemp bark to pulp factories in the United Kingdom, Germany and Italy. Both factories also sell the woody core. These woody core is either used in particle boards or sold as litter for pets.

The FNPC has investigated the potential of enzymatic retting as a new way of utilising hemp in the textile industry. In this process hemp stems are not separated by means of a hammer mill as this would shorten the fibers too much. Instead stems are separated into bark and wood using adapted flax breakers. The bark tissue is then cut into 30 cm-long pieces which are carded prior to undergoing the enzymatic retting. The enzymatic retting process dissolves pectins and thus separates fiber bundles into finer strands of fiber cells. The product which is obtained can be spun like cotton or flax. The hemp fibers thus obtained are more hygroscopic and less supple than flax fibers. At this moment the FNPC is looking for 85 million FF to set up a retting factory which would process 3500 tons (metric) of hemp bark per year.

Prices

Some indications of prices were supplied. One ton of hemp straw (16% humidity) is worth about 500 French Francs (FF). One ton of hemp bark (at 10 to 12% humidity) was worth 2000 to 2200 FF at July '92 market prices. The market is very poor as a result of large surpluses of flax tow. Normally one ton of high quality hemp bark should fetch 3000 FF, hemp bark of lesser quality (e.g. containing too much woody core) about 2500 FF. One ton of woody core (not cleaned or processed) is worth 200 to 300 FF. Grain (10% humidity) was worth about 250FF/100 kg. Generally prices range from 200 to 400 FF/100 kg of seed. Seed for sowing is sold at 1600 FF/100 kg within France and for 2000 FF/100 kg to countries abroad.

Concluding Remarks and Relevance for the Dutch Hemp Research Program.

In France hemp is a small crop. At this moment the economic feasibility is severely handicapped by low prices of flax byproducts (tow) which are used in the same pulps and paper products as hemp. The Fédération Nationale des Producteurs de Chanvre however thinks hemp has a future in France, and works vigorously to promote hemp.

Mr. Mathieu thinks economic prospects will improve as flax prices are bound to rise. He also feels that the general attitude towards hemp is positive, as it is a crop which requires a low fertilizer input and which is grown without pesticides. Furthermore, as pulping of trees is increasingly criticised, annual fiber crops are looked upon positively.

The optimism of the FNPC is reflected in their breeding program aiming at producing commercial THC-free hemp varieties and in their efforts to develop technology to open up the textile market for hemp fiber.

The breeders in the Dutch Hemp Program try to make very late varieties which will produce high stem yields. Mr. Mathieu challenged this approach by pointing out some disadvantages linked to it. A late variety does not yield any seed, so neither the sale of the seed nor the EEC subsidy for the seed enter in the financial result of the crop. Conservation of a late variety is difficult as artificial drying is expensive and ensiling may affect fiber quality. An early variety may yield 800 kg/ha of seed which corresponds to 1,500 Dutch Florins (Dfl) – (seed + EEC support). Stem yield of an early variety might be 3 ton/ha less, which corresponds to Dfl 500,–, yielding an advantage of Dfl 1000/ha for the early variety. Even though these are rough estimations, it might be very much worthwhile to add an option to the Hemp Research Program by enlarging the breeding program to include the breeding of an early dual purpose variety.

The harvest of an early hemp variety yielding both stem and seed does not necessarily take place earlier in the season, as the seed requires time to fill and ripen. At harvest, however, the crop is in a different development stage, having fewer leaves and possibly a dryer stem, and the stem yield is also lower. Field drying of a fully vegetative high yielding late variety may be difficult, whereas for an early dual purpose hemp it might be an option worthwhile considering.

In conclusion, the visit to Mr. Mathieu and Mr. Béhérec of the FNPC was very interesting and stimulating. Interesting, to learn about their work in breeding and agronomy which is based on several decades of work with hemp. Stimulating, to meet colleagues who work with hemp in the "real world" and who show thus that hemp is not only a crop of academic interest but may also be of economic significance to farmers.

Hemp in Holland

by Ed Rosenthal

HOLLAND IS A TINY COUNTRY and is one of the most populated in Europe. It has cold oceanic weather. In spite of these handicaps, its agricultural industry is among the world's largest in terms of export profit. They must be doing something right.

The Dutch are able to compete with low wage countries that have better weather by using high technology to grow high value crops. Ornamental plants, bulbs and flowers comprise a large part of their exports. They also are large producers of sugar (sugar beet) pork, dairy, fresh vegetables, potatoes and grain.

In 1989 Holland embarked on a $10 million four year integrated research program to develop hemp as a crop for use in a non-polluting paper industry. The government has enlisted its agricultural department research center which utilizes the talents of some of the country's brightest applied researchers. The final report is expected to be released to the public in late 1994.

The program was started initially to deal with the problem of microscopic nematodes which attack potatoes. Rather than using nematicides which pollute the ground water and are now banned, the fields are on a three year rotation with other crops such as corn, wheat and sugar beets. Agronomists felt that introducing another crop so that the fields would have a four year rotation would reduce nematode damage. After investigating the potential of several plants, they settled on hemp as the most promising.

To increase the number of breeding periods in a year plants were grown in greenhouses as well as fields. The blackout curtains were used to force plants into flowering by shortening daylength. The four year research program ended in 1993.

One of the researchers looking at some of the 100 accessions. The varieties were being tested for quality, yield and suitablity to the Dutch environment.

Photo by Ed Rosenthal

A field of vigorous hemp varieties for research. As a result of this program hundreds of acres were cultivated in 1994.

Research is being conducted on both agricultural and industrial aspects of hemp papermaking at the same time. First the researchers collected seeds from around the world, over two hundred accessions. Each variety was grown in the test plots to find ones best suited to Dutch conditions. Geneticists and morphologists conducted this research. Chemists and paper makers attempted to develop economical ways to harvest and treat the fiber using only non-polluting systems, which will revolutionize the industry.

I visited the processing lab half way through the research program. The only hemp paper they said they had produced looked like an unbleached paper coffee filter. It seemed to me that they were still having trouble separating the pectin and lignin from the cellulose, which must occur before quality paper can be made. Among the methods they had tried were use of hydrogen peroxide (H_2O_2) and ozone (O_3). Both of these are highly reactive non-polluting techniques.

I was not permitted to photograph the paper lab even though I was given an extensive tour. Grinding machines reduced the material, both fiber and hurd, to extremely small particles. I suspect chemical reactions

Photo by Ed Rosenthal

The plants were grown in rows about four inches apart in rows spaced 20 inches wide.

were tried both before and after physical processing. Researchers reported progress throughout the term of the project.

The Dutch program shows what promise hemp has as a high profit crop. They estimate that it will take them another five to seven years to go start a commercial paper-making industry. In the meantime several farmers have decided to grow hemp commercially.

Paper From Dutch Hemp?

by Hayo M.G. van der Werf

FROM JANUARY 1990 until December 1993, a total of 12 research institutes in the Netherlands spent Dfl 17 million (US $9 million) on a hemp research program. The objectives of this program was to establish whether fiber hemp can be of economic interest to farmers and to the pulp and paper industry in the Netherlands. The major research disciplines within the program were: plant breeding, crop physiology, plant pathology, harvest and storage technology, pulp technology, and economics and market research. This research yielded a large amount of factual information, which was recently summarized in two reports in Dutch (Bakker et al. 1993, Van Berlo 1993).

One of the major results of the program: a business concept, outlining the required specifications for a viable hemp-paper business to be set up in the Netherlands, is summarized in this article (Van Berlo 1993).

THE BUSINESS CONCEPT
Pulp Markets

Market research has shown that both high-value and low-value markets are relevant for fiber hemp grown in the Netherlands. High-value pulp markets consist of applications in Light-Weight Coating paper (LWC),

(Note: This article appeared in the Journal of the International Hemp Association, *Vol. 1 No. 1, June 1994)*

sanitary papers and tissues, and 'fluff,' which is used in the production of diapers. In the Netherlands, the size of each of these three markets is about 10,000 ton/year. Low-value pulp markets consist of applications in the production of massive and corrugated cardboard. In the Netherlands, the market for hemp pulp for cardboard production is about 160,000 ton/year. Pulp quality specifications, such as whiteness and purity, are lower for low-value markets than for high-value markets.

The high-value market is the eventual major objective, but initially pulp will be made for the low-value cardboard market, because it does not require top quality specifications. Pulp technology will be gradually optimised, and pulp production for high-value markets will then be possible. First the LWC market will be approached, and finally the sanitary paper, tissue and fluff markets. The low-value market will continue to be served, as the high-value market probably can not absorb all the pulp produced.

Initially, when pulp is produced for low-value markets only, a market price of Dfl 600/ton of pulp is expected. After several years, when pulp will be produced for both high- and low-value markets, a price of Dfl 1,000/ton is possible.

Hemp Production

A hemp-growers cooperative should be set up by arable farmers in the north-east of the Netherlands. In the first year, the members of this cooperative will grow 2,5000 hectares (1 hectare of ha = 2.47 acres) of fiber hemp. Over a period of 6 to 7 years, this area will expand to 11,000 ha and the cooperative will consist of a total of 1,000 to 1,100 farmers. In the crop rotation, hemp will replace cereals. Initially a yield of 10 ton/ha of stem dry matter is expected. After 5 years, improved cultivars will be available and an average stem yield of 12 ton/ha is expected. Initially farmers will get Dfl 130/ton of stem dry matter, this price will increase to Dfl 180/ton as pulp production is geared more to high-value pulp markets. In addition, the European Union (EU) supplies a Dfl 1,700/ha subsidy to hemp growers. The crop is harvested in September by contractors who will use modified silage maize harvesters. The crop is ensiled on the farm and sodium hydroxide is added to the chopped stems for preservation.

Provided the EU maintains its Dfl 1,700/ha subsidy, and if an average yield of 12 ton/ha at a price of Dfl 180/ton is obtained five years after the start of the project, the farmer's gross margin (financial yield minus direct costs) will be Dfl 2,343/ha. This is more than the gross margin of wheat and less than that of potato.

Pulp Production

The pulp factory will be set up stepwise. It will start at a production capacity of 20,000 ton/year of pulp. Ensiled hemp will be brought from the farms to the factory and separated into bark and core using a flotation system. Both fractions will be pulped using chemo-mechanical pulp technology. The resulting pulp will meet the requirements of the low-value market. At this scale, pulp technology and waste water treatment technology will be further optimised.

The size of the factory will then be increased to 40,000 and finally to 90,000 ton/year by adding parallel chemo-mechanical pulp lines. As the pulping process will be more sophisticated, pulps for the high-value markets will be produced. A total investment of Dfl 127 million would be required for a pulp factory producing 90,000 ton/year for both high- and low-value markets.

Financing

In order to be economically feasible, the pulp factory should reach a capacity of at least 40,000 ton/year. This would require an investment of Dfl 57 million. Three sources could contributed to this investment:

a) *Shares.* Shares are owned by the hemp growers (Dfl 500/ha), other farmer cooperatives, banks and paper factories. Shares should finance 50% of the total investment.

b) *Subsidies.* Subsidies from several sources should supply 25% of the total investment.

c) *Low-interest loans.* These should be supplied by national and regional governments, and make up the remaining 25% of the total investment.

Based on this financial structure and on the other assumptions outlined above, the shares would yield a return on investment of 16% with a pay back time of 4.8 years.

Feasibility of the Business Concept

A committee, consisting of representatives of farmers, the paper industry, farmers cooperatives and of the provincial and national government, was asked to give its advice on the business plan. This committee concluded that some of the assumptions the business plan relies on are uncertain, which make it impossible to decide on its feasibility. The committee recommends further research to resolve the uncertainties. This research should include setting up a pilot plant producing 1,000–5,000 ton/year of pulp, and growing the hemp required to supply the pilot plant. The pilot plant would allow improvement of the pulp technology and a better estimate of the costs involved. This additional research would take about 2 years and cost Dfl 8–10 million. Currently, funding for this pilot research is being solicited from the paper industry and the national and provincial governments.

Hemp in Hungary

by Ed Rosenthal

IN 1991 THERE WERE about 6500 hectares growing in two eastern areas. The hemp crop was considered a mere remnant of a once thriving industry. In the previous ten years there was a precipitous decline in production as hemp became a specialty item. The Soviet army used hemp in the far north, where the extremely low temperatures made plastics and synthetic fibers brittle and unuseable. The empire's dissolution and Russia's subsequent near bankruptcy abruptly eliminated Hungary's principal customers.

In 1993 hemp was planted on only 300 hectares, less than half the 650 sown in England. Total sales were way down. There was tremendous optimism in the industry, however.

A number of American hempsters had made the pilgrimage to the spiritual home of hemp in Central Europe. Spinning tales of hemp to gold and pent-up demand in the West, these mendicants to a land of legal hemp wore always trendy deep pockets.

The guided tour included visits to farms, where the converted can sought enlightenment in the large fields of low THC hemp. They walked, touched, smelled and fondled it. They lived their fantasy and dream.

Since they were there to do business, the hempsters visited factories where they saw the stems decorticated and the fiber processed into yarn or twine. Then the potential investors were given complete inspections of the textile factories in Pesc and Szeged. There were optional visits to pressboard factories, both operating and closed. The complete tour took about one week.

There is now a rush for Hungarian fabric and twine as various companies jockey for "control" of the Hungarian supply. At the same time, all these new upstart hemp importers are nervous that a big buyer will come in to the market and make them irrelevant.

Processing techniques also need to be upgraded. Presently, the Hungarians can spin a number 8 yarn. This is a medium weight garment fabric. If they could spin a number 10 yarn which is somewhat finer, it could be knitted rather than woven and T-Shirts and other knits could be manufactured. It is a given among hemp entrepreneurs that there would be an incredible demand for these products.

In '93 the draught was quite severe. Two years ago the plants were ten feet high and there were 250–300 plants per m^2. The yield was about 10 tons per hectare. In 1993 there were perhaps 150 plants per m^2. The plants were only three to four feet high. The yield was very low.

How much do the Hungarians have to grow to supply the mills? If the mills were to produce enough fabric for 25,000 pair of jeans each month, about 50,000 m^2 of 400 gram twill used for jeans. They would use 20,000 kilograms or 20 metric tons of fiber per month. A total of 240 metric tons a year. Figure that 10% of the total yield is actually spun into yarn and then woven for fabric. The total yield required would be 2400 metric tons and with a yield of 10 metric tons per hectare, 240 hectares would be required. Additional acreage is needed for twine, and seed, which is not grown on fiber hemp. Seed hemp is sewn much further apart and develops thicker stems with a lower fiber yield, which is much coarser and less valuable.

Even with these sales, the industry would remain considerably downsized. The U.N. Food and Agriculture Organization estimates that Hungary planted 23,000 hectares each year between 1948–52 and 12,000 hectares between 1969–71. What can they do to increase their industry? Do paper and composite board play a future in Hungarian hemp? Rumors abound of mysterious investors funding paper mills and upgrading the composite board factories with an eye to importing to the European Community. There are also stories of proposals to develop new varieties using targeted smart scientific breeding programs.

Dave Seber of C & S Specialty Builder's Supplies in Harrisburg, Oregon has been studying composite boards for several years. He told me that a single factory in the U.S. uses up to 1000 tons of chips a day. A field yielding 10 metric tons per hectare would produce about 70% or 7 metric tons hurd. The factory would use the yield from about 200 hectares a day. On a yearly basis nearly 50,000 hectares are needed just to feed one mill.

Paper is another item which can use incredible amounts of biomass. Even a small paper mill can process many thousands of tons per year. This would help to restore the viability of hemp as an agricultural crop and at the same time time develop a new ecologically sound paper industry.

In the next few years there will be a maturation in the hemp industry as more companies get involved. The Hungarians are just beginning to respond to the market. As the industry grows the Hungarians are becoming much more savvy and may make a much larger commitment to the growing market.

Hungarian Hemp in Photos

Text & Photos by Ed Rosenthal

HEMP IS GROWN in Hungary for seed, fiber and hurd and then is processed into cloth, twine, board, and paper. The industry was on its rosad to recovery when these pictures were taken. Rather than using new equipment the old was slightly upgraded. Now that investors are involved in Hungary new spinning factories are being built. The key to making cloth is to get as fine a fiber as possible. The finer the thread is spun, the thinner the fabric will be. The main use for hemp cloth during COMECON days was as canvas, a relatively coarse cloth.

Plants grown for seed in the south eastern part of the country. The plants are grown 30 cm apart in rows about a meter apart. This allows each plant to develop a canopy and many flowering branches for higher seed production.

Seed plants are harvested after the great majority of seeds are mature but before the pods open . The plants were 10-12 feet tall and completely covered the space.

When grown for fiber, the seeds are drilled 300-400 per meter. They are cut and bundled using a mower set a few inches off the ground. In 1993 Hungary experienced a drought and the plants were stunted. There were only about 175 per meter and they were only three to four feet tall.

The bundles are stacked and left to dry in the field.

After drying the plants are retted in water in large cement holding tanks. Bacteria begin to eat the vegetation quickly separating the fiber from the hurd. Before the fiber has lost much strength, the stems are dried.

The plants are placed in a decorticator which turns the stems over a wheel.

Since the fiber is pliable and the hurd is brittle, the hurd breaks into pieces and separates from the fiber.

The fiber goes through the scutching and hackling processors which comb the fibers parallel and remove any hurd still attached to the fiber.

Then the fiber is combed finer and finer until it suitable for twisting into yarn.

The fiber coil is divided into thinner tapes...

and then twisted individual strands are braided into twine.

Thicker twines
and ropes are cre-
ated by braiding
thinner twine.

Polished twine runs through a hot wax bath.

It is wound into consumer sized balls.

The factory manager shows the trading company representative bins of twine ready for wrapping.

At the cloth factory thin yarn is woven into hemp cloth.

These factories use very old equipment and have a limited capacity.
More modern factories are planned.

Hemp board is made using a giant press. First the hemp hurds are placed on a moving conveyer and evened out so that they are uniform density throughout. The hurds are pressed using a cold hydraulic press. This flattens them. Then they are injected with phenolic resin under a hot press.

The factory manager showing the U.S. representative some of the board. Close-up you could see some of the stem and and fiber. It had an imperfect but pleasant look. This was a result of the antiquated machinery.

Even with the old machinery and turmoil around privatization factory production is increasing substantially. New spinning equipment will produce high value yarn which can be used for finer fabrics.

Hemp Breeding in Hungary

by Sebastiaan Hennink

ON 8 AUGUST 1991 Dr. I. Bócsa from the Agricultural Research Institute (GATE) in Kompolt Hungary visited a group of hemp researchers in The Netherlands and presented a lecture concerning the recent history of hemp breeding in Hungary.

Last decade no breeding for new varieties took place in Hungary. The industry does not need new varieties and research results. Besides the area under cultivation has drastically declined. Currently only maintenance takes place of the existing varieties. This is necessary, because without selection its characteristics will be lost in a few generations. The bast fiber content will be reduced 50% in approximately 5 generations. In about 10 generations this level will be reduced to the level of the original landrace (13–14%). Breeding started with the original landrace 'Kompolti' (dioecious) in 1952. The current bast fiber content is about 36–38%. A further improve of the current bast fiber content is not wanted. The extra created fibers will consist of secondary bast fiber which negatively influences quality for textile production. Instead it was decided to increase the stem yield. In the 1960s a hybrid variety was developed called 'B-7' (Figure 1). This hybrid is a cross between 'Kinai' (dioecious) and 'Kompolti' (dioecious). This variety is still the best fiber variety in Hungary and is a standard in variety and agronomical trials, however it was never commercialized. The costs for seed production of 'B-7' were too high. From the female parent 'Kinai' all male plants must be removed before pollen delivery. For the production of hybrid varieties

FIGURE 1.

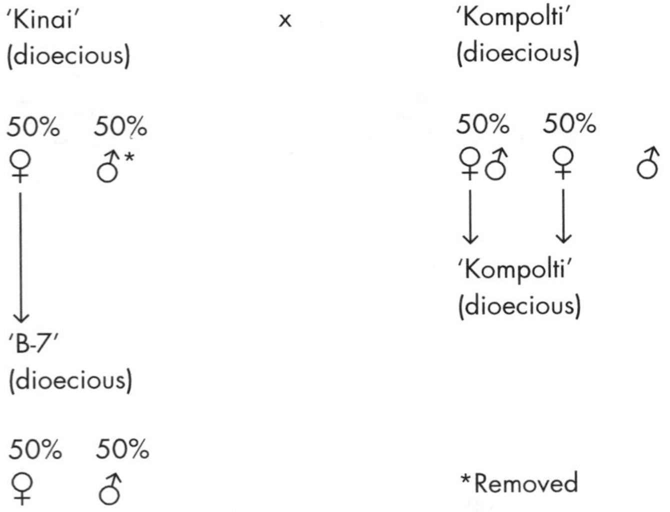

| 'Kinai'
(dioecious) | x | 'Kompolti'
(dioecious) |

'Kinai' (dioecious)	x	'Kompolti' (dioecious)

'Kinai'   x   'Kompolti'
(dioecious)   (dioecious)

| 50% | 50% | | 50% | 50% | |
| ♀ | ♂* | | ♀♂ | ♀ | ♂ |

↓   ↓   ↓

'B-7'   'Kompolti'
(dioecious)   (dioecious)

| 50% | 50% |
| ♀ | ♂ | *Removed

a search started for male sterility. This is never found but it appeared to be possible to create populations consisting of almost entirely female plants. This so called 'unisexuality' is analogous to male sterility. These unisexual populations are obtained by a cross between dioecious female and monoecious plants (Figure 2). The male plants from the dioecious population are removed before pollen delivery. The monoecious plants are the pollen donators and the seeds harvested on the dioecious female plants form the unisexual population. The monoecious population can be maintained by harvesting the seeds on the monoecious plants. The obtained unisexual population consist of 90% females, 8% plants with unisexual flowers and less than 2% male plants.

The first commercial variety that used this principal was 'Uniko B.' This hybrid variety is a cross between 'Kompolti' (dioecious) and 'Fibrimon 21' (monoecious). The F1 unisexual population is still expensive to produce and therefore the F1 generation is multiplied and the F2 generation sold. This F2 population consist of approximately 70% female and 30% male plants so seed yield is high. By using the F2 generation the heterosis effect of this hybrid is not fully used compared to the

FIGURE 2.

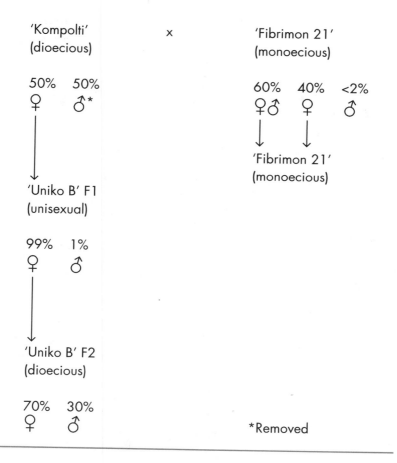

'Kompolti'   x   'Fibrimon 21'
(dioecious)   (monoecious)

50%   50%   60%   40%   <2%
♀   ♂*   ♀♂   ♀   ♂
                            ↓   ↓
                          'Fibrimon 21'
                          (monoecious)

'Uniko B' F1
(unisexual)

99%   1%
♀   ♂

'Uniko B' F2
(dioecious)

70%   30%
♀   ♂   *Removed

F1. Since the old variety 'B-7' still produced the highest yields new methods for creating hybrid varieties were researched. Out of the dioecious variety 'Kinai' a monoecious selection was made (Figure 3). By crossing the dioecious and monoecious 'Kinai' as previous described 'Kinai' unisexual was created. This 'Kinai' unisexual was and still is used as female parent for the production of the hybrid variety 'Kompolti Hybrid TC' (Figure 3). In this hybrid variety 'Kompolti' is used as male parent. 'Kompolti Hybrid TC' is still the best fiber variety of which commercial available seeds can be produced. The latest hybrid variety that has been

FIGURE 3.

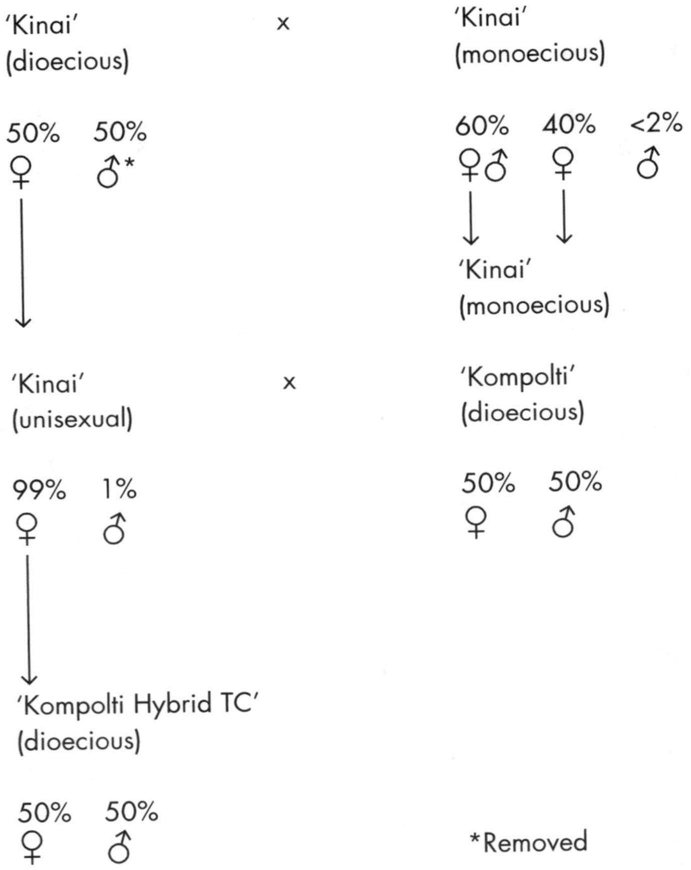

'Kinai'   x   'Kinai'
(dioecious)   (monoecious)

50%   50%   60%   40%   <2%
♀   ♂*   ♀♂   ♀   ♂
| ↓   ↓
| 'Kinai'
| (monoecious)
↓

'Kinai'   x   'Kompolti'
(unisexual)   (dioecious)

99%   1%   50%   50%
♀   ♂   ♀   ♂
|
|
|
↓

'Kompolti Hybrid TC'
(dioecious)

50%   50%
♀   ♂   *Removed

created is 'Fibrico.' This variety is produced the same way as 'Kompolti Hybrid TC' but instead of 'Kompolti,' 'Kompolti Sargaszaru' is used as male parent. 'K. Sargaszaru' contains a chlorophyll mutant that colours the stem yellow at the end of the growing season. The fibers are softer and do not have to be bleached during processing. The stem yield is however, lower than the original 'Kompolti.' In this hybrid 'Fibrico' an attempt is made to combine the good fiber characteristics of 'K. Sargaszaru' and the vitality of 'Kinai.'

In Hungary it was chosen to develop dioecious varieties instead of monoecious for the following reasons:

- The yield of monoecious varieties are lower, caused by inbreeding effects.
- The selection of monoecious varieties demands highly skilled personnel, which gives problems when temporary personnel is used.
- Within monoecious plants female flowers are earlier fertile than pollen is released. Introgression can occur from other (wild) populations.
- The fiber quality of monoecious hemp is lower.
- In dioecious hemp selection is possible before flowering (between male plants) so that selection can take place more efficient.

The varieties created by Dr. Bócsa are recognized worldwide for their good characteristics and are used by many other breeders.

Hemp In The USA

by Mari Kane

IT NEVER CEASES TO AMAZE ME that the modern American hemp movement has come as far as it has despite the fact that cannabis is still illegal to grow. Marijuana prohibition laws are so vehemently enforced that growers often lose their assets and property immediately upon arrest. Licenses to grow hemp are not issued by the Drug Enforcement Agency (DEA), so hemp cannot be grown by American farmers. Consequently, all of the raw material being used by American hemp companies comes from overseas sources. Such an enormous trade deficit in hemp is an affront to the free market system as it automatically puts American hemp businesses at a disadvantage. The problems posed by prohibition laws—cost, availability, and content control prevents hempsters from competing on a global level. Yet, they are persevering in spite of the obstacles.

The United States government's suppression of information about hemp as a raw material has been so thorough that when Jack Herer released his book, *The Emperor Wears No Clothes* in 1985, it hit like a bombshell. Documented revelations about hemp scattered in the wind to be absorbed by eco-warriors, pot-heads, free-marketeers, and image makers across the country. Now considered to be the bible of hemp, *The Emperor* has sold over 225,000 copies in the USA, 50,000 copies in Europe, and is now in its 10th printing, and is in three languages with four more foreign language editions planned for Fall of '94. This loosely designed, paperback book has taught hundreds of thousands of people to believe in hemp as the plant that will "save the planet." Most hemp entrepreneurs cite *The Emperor* as their crystallizing inspiration for starting a hemp business.

With decades of myths and misinformation to overcome, hempsters use education as a major part of their marketing strategy. The Hempstead Company actively promotes hemp on the college circuit in affiliation with The Save the Earth Foundation, which provides funding for environmental research. Newsletters such as *The Greenleaf News* from The Institute for Hemp, *The Hemp Times Quarterly* by Legal Marijuana/The Hemp Store, and *Pakaloha* from the Hawaiian Hemp Company combine hemp history and legalization editorial with in-house mail order information.

Hempsters often resemble missionaries driven to save the earth and create jobs by reviving hemp as a raw material for industry. They preach the history of hemp in America and quote passages from *The Emperor*, describing the limitless possibilities for integrating hemp into our daily lives. Another favorite topic is the 1930's-era Anslinger/Mellon/Dupont/Hearst conspiracy to prohibit the cultivation of hemp for their own material gain. This hemplore is especially effective in winning public support now that people have a greater understanding of the corrupt nature of the Federal government and its ties to big business.

In the depths of a world wide recession, the decision to go hemp is as much an economic choice as it is an ideological one. "Green," "Environmentally Friendly," and "Sustainable" seem to be the hottest catch words of American manufacturers today. The public is increasingly on the alert about environmentally safe products and are discriminating between big polluters and the socially responsible. This is why hemp is an advertiser's dream. It's fresh, hip, earthy, and has enough mystique to arouse the curiosity of even the most jaded cynic. And by combining great design with ecological quality, hemp companies will soon have it made in the marketplace.

Of the fifty or so hemp enterprises now in operation in the United States, roughly 50% are engaged in the garment or accessory trade. This is one reason fabric is at a premium and availability can be scarce. 15% of hemp businesses are import/wholesale, 13% are non-manufacturing retail/mail order. 8% of hemp companies make cosmetics and food from seed oil, and 6% make paper or paper products. Only a scant 4% are using hemp in luggage, while only one company (that I know of) is using hemp for upholstery.

"New" and "Unique" was what designers Matthew and Carolina Chang had in mind when they decided to use hemp in a new line of clothes called "Stoned Wear." In 1989 their company, Joint Venture, imported the first load of hemp clothes to America since the passage of the 1937 Marijuana Prohibition Tax Act. The company was instrumental in prodding the Chinese factories to process the hemp fabric necessary for its overseas manufacturing operation, thus laying the foundation for the now burgeoning Chinese hemp business. At the time, Chinese factory machinery was so antiquated that pure hemp could not be spun, and so Joint Venture opted for a 55% hemp/45% cotton blend. This percentile blend is still being followed by newer designers, such as Two Star Dog who also manufacture in China.

Pure hemp canvas was first imported the the United States in 1990 by House of Hemp in Portland, Oregon. The intended market for the fabric was originally industrial, as tarpaulins and awnings, but as the word of hemp quickly spread the House of Hemp became the main source of hemp to garment and luggage makers across the country. For three years they held the monopoly on pure hemp canvas and supplied manufacturers with bolts of fabric until many of them found their own direct sources.

The word "sourcing" may not be a legitimate verb found in the dictionary, but it has great meaning in an industry where all of the raw material is imported from other countries. Availability is the biggest consideration a new hemp company faces, for without a secure connection business falters, (as it did for a time in 1993 when many sources went dry).

Between 1993 and 1994 several new importers joined the hemp sourcing game. Hemp Traders in Los Angeles, California, and Hemp Textiles International of Bellingham Washington, began importing Chinese fabric in a variety of blends and weaves. American Hemp Mercantile in Seattle, Washington, and Quick Trading in Oakland, California, are providing a main line to pure hemp from Hungary. US Textile is now importing Polish fabric made from hemp grown in the Ukraine.

1993 was also a boom year for American hemp businesses, not in terms of gross sales, but in regard to the sheer number of start-up companies. It was as though the seeds were sown in '92, sprouted in '93, and are poised and ready to bloom in '94.

Like the rest of corporate America, the great majority of growth is in small businesses. Indeed, 90% of the hemp companies now in operation have staffs of ten or less, not counting overseas manufacturers, and most of those are cottage industries of three or less. Because of their microscopic size, some small manufactures have joined forces, in order to share marketing resources and manufacturing costs. With increased purchasing power they hope to compete with larger companies that have factories here or abroad.

One example is a hemp collective in Sonoma County, California, 60 miles north of San Francisco. This group consists of Hemp Essentials of Cazadero, Got it Covered of Santa Rosa, and the hemp cluster of Cannabis Clothes, Hemp Hemp Hooray, and Simply Hemp, located in Occidental. Their purpose for uniting is to share marketing resources and combine their purchasing power. Though they may not agree on the best bio-degradable dyes, they do believe in creating jobs in local communities, some of which have been hit hard by corporate layoffs and real estate slumps.

The hemp garment industry once consisted primarily of baggy shorts and pants, but in the past year the design element has really kicked in. Designers with a conscience are choosing hemp as an alternative to cotton and synthetics, and are putting out some wonderful stuff. All Points East of Carmel, California, has created a line of stitch-resist batik clothes more vibrant and detailed than any tie-dye. The Hawaiian Hemp Company of Pahoa makes clothes with the loose muu-muu fit and clean lines typical of Hawaiian style. Hemp Heritage of Guerneville, California, draws inspiration from the Victorian era with frilly bloomers, camisoles, and petticoats that seem to belong in a Merchant/Ivory film production. Two Star Dog of Emeryville, California, are riding the 'grunge' wave in fashion by creating looks that fit an urban lifestyle. Mindful wear in Sonoma, California, draws heavily from Asian and Middle Eastern influences in their line of women's wear. The only thing stopping biggies like Esprit and Levi Strauss from buying into hemp is cost and availability, two factors which would be solved by domestic cultivation and production.

The oil from the hemp seed is a resource being exploited in many ways. The foremost hemp seed oil baron is Don Wirtshafter of the Ohio Hempery, who in 1989 developed a method by which oil could be pressed in a vacuum, thereby eliminating oxidation during processing. The dark green oil is full of essential fatty acids and protein, rich in hazelnut flavor, but like flax oil, must be kept refrigerated and cannot be brought to a high temperature.

Wirtshafter's seed stock comes from China, but upon entering the country these seeds must be sterilized, lest they fall into the wrong hands and planted in the ground. The steam sterilization process cracks the shells, starts oxidation, and encourages rancidity, which shortens the oil's shelf life. According to Wirtshafter, the freshest seeds are found "over there," while the technology to press them remains in this country. Where an 8 oz bottle of hemp seed oil sells for $20.00, he estimates that price could be competitive with vegetable oil if domestically grown seeds were used.

Hemp seed oil is also being used in the production of cosmetics such as Hemp Seed Salve by Ohio Hempery, Hemp Seed Lip Balm by Carol Miller of Hemp Essentials, and Hemp Seed Soap made by Alison Kiplinger of Conscious Connections in Concord, California. All of these items enjoy brisk sales in retail outlets as they are relatively inexpensive and externally consumable.

Food products is a market made for hemp seeds and is being led by Alan Brady at Hempen Trail of Boulder Creek, California. This hemp seed gourmet gives demonstrations on cooking with hemp seeds and is now manufacturing a hemp seed ice cream. Don't laugh, it's not bad.

Currently, there are three players in the hemp paper industry. Ecolution in Virginia and American Hemp Mercantile in Washington state are both importing 100% hemp paper from Eastern Europe. The paper is available in a number of different weights, suitable for offset or web printing as well as writing, although the supply is limited at present.

John Stahl of Evanescent Press in Leggett, California produces handmade art papers from imported and domestic hemp (local growers donate stems anonymously), and blends it with kenaf, a relatively new commodity on the non-wood paper market. For months, he has been carefully following guidelines set by the Drug Enforcement Agency to secure his future "industrial grade" hemp plantation against the threat of potential thieves. The precautions, such as security fences and lighting, have been installed and are ready for inspection. Of course, there is no way to know how long the Federal red tape will take to iron out.

Stahl ultimately plans to convert a paper mill and equip it with pulping technology developed in the Ukraine. If successful, his project could cost-effectively produce a massive amount of non-wood paper from hemp grown on his own property. He is definitely the man to watch in the coming years.

Two other hempsters to keep an eye on are Bill Conde and Dave Seber of C & S Specialty Builder's Supplies in Harrisburg, Oregon. For the last few years they have worked to develop the technology to produce composite board from hemp fiber that is two to three times stronger than wood. They also have plans to make glue from hemp hurds to provide an alternative to the toxic petroleum-based binders now on the market.

The problem is, to fulfill these dreams they need a reliable supply of domestic hemp stems. If hemp were grown in the Pacific Northwest and loggers were retrained as farmers, there would not be the depressing unemployment and vast deforestation now commonplace in the region. But when President Clinton attended a Timber conference in Portland in 1993, did he want to know about hemp as an alternative to wood? No. The powers that be are unable to accept what other countries have proven—that hemp can be used to build homes.

But the attempt to produce building materials from imported hemp is hopelessly infeasible. All one has to do is imagine the financial and environmental cost of transporting a constant stream of hemp across the ocean via petroleum burning barges and the folly becomes blatantly obvious. As expensive as wood has become, composite board made from imported hemp would be far more costly. So the hemp lumber industry remains stuck in the mud until hemp cultivation is decriminalized.

One curious aspect of the American Hemp Industry is that many movers and shakers are ex-growers of sinsemilla. Having raised the weed and enjoyed the fruits of its bounty, cannabis farmers have an emotional, and dare I say, spiritual involvement with the plant. Their fervent motivation to bring hemp back into mainstream agriculture is born of this connection. The irony is that when growers become entrepreneurs in the legal hemp trade they voluntarily stop growing or dealing in order to avoid being a target of the authorities. In essence, working with hemp is causing people to clean up their act.

With all the hype and glory about hemp's potential to "Save the World" it is inevitable that counterfeiters would start misrepresenting it with fibers such as cotton, flax, and abaca. This unscrupulous practice threatens to taint hemp's new image and ruin its progression into the mainstream economy. Now, a heated call-to-arms for content labeling is transforming the business and bringing it into regulatory line with other major industries.

Since the counterfeiting problem was first recognized, there have been not one but two plans put forth to standardize the labeling of hemp products. Hempsters can choose between the IFH (Institute for Hemp) label or the True Hemp label designed by the newly formed True Hemp Certification Council. Both entities are constantly on the alert for manufacturers who misrepresent products as hemp. They will politely confront corporate presidents with their complaint and if no agreement is reached they will use fax machines and modems to mobilize action against the offending company.

It is quite possible that the two certification programs could coexist and eventually complement each other. One thing everyone agrees upon is that something has to be done to protect cannabis hemp in the infancy of it's re-introduction to American society.

In November of 1994 voters in six states will be asked to vote on hemp initiatives. Many of these measures are extremely far-reaching and if passed, will make hemp cultivation legal for persons 21 and over whether it's being grown for personal or industrial use. The passage of these laws is crucial to the hemp movement because domestic cultivation is the key to growth in the American hemp industry. Without it we will be forever confined to expensive fabric and sterilized seed, with no hope of ever getting the paper, lumber, and biomass energy industries off the ground.

The Hempstead

by Ed Rosenthal

In 1994 the Hempstead Co. became the first commercial group to grow hemp in the U.S. in recent times. It was cultivated on a half acre field of land leased from the government with the cooperation of the United States Dept. of Agriculture Desert Research Facility. Other groups in the area, presumably including local universities, encouraged the project. Several commercial companies had pre-purchased the crop. Sales were not a problem.

The site was the old Timpkin Ranch, where Schlichten first developed his decorticator. For the last two years the fields had been used for kenaf research. Since kenaf and hemp fields look quite similar, no suspicions were aroused regarding the new crop.

DEA regulations for hemp are very strict. They call for barrier fences, guard towers, and constant surveillance. This field under the USDA's wing was protected only by a three strand barbed wire fence 200 feet from and in the plain view of the state highway. The field was guarded only 12 hours a day. There were no intrusions or attempts of breaches of security. Narcotics agents inspected the field periodically and had no complaints. The biggest problem was Canadian blackbirds and white tail doves eating the newly planted seeds.

Chris Boucher, Brian Ambrose and David Martyn assembled support for the project and then applied for the permit in September of 1993. The permit was granted and the seeds were in the ground on March 22, 1994.

The plot was planted with Kompolte TC, developed by Dr. Botsch in Hungary and Futura 77, from Le Mans in France, as well as several hybrids. The clay silty loam is a rich soil considered ideal for cannabis because it holds water but drains well. Seeds were drilled 400 per square yard (480 per m²) with a modified corn planter. There were six separate plots which were being tested for method, either flat seeding or rows. At harvest there were an average of about 196 plants per square yard (235 m²).

Chris Boucher of the Hempstead Company in the hemp field.

The land is about 140 feet (43 m) below sea level and has an ambient temperature of 95° Farenheit, (35°Centigrade) with temperatures sometimes soaring to 120° F (49° Centigrade).

The plants started flowering after 50 days. At 60 days the plants reached an average height of 40 inches (101 cm). At day 118 they were 96 inches tall (243 cm).

The three corporations planning to use the research crop for product development had agreed to purchase the entire crop. Dexter Textiles, of Windsorlocks, CT wanted to process the fiber into nonwoven textiles at first, and later planned to spin the fiber into yarn and weave it into cloth.

Gridcore Inc., of Long Beach, CA was going to process the hurd into high density composite board with superior strength.

International Paper, a major player in the paper industry, was set to use both fiber and hurd for papermaking.

Although this project was coordinated with federal agencies and was under federal auspices, fate stepped in between the planting and the harvested crop.

Things began to unravel on July 5, when Ron Kiczinski and two associates held a press conference. They announced that they were about to sow marijuana seed with the purpose of supplying Dennis Peron's Cannabis Buyers Club with high quality "medical grade" marijuana. Shortly thereafter, as they were planting seed in front of press and the Modoc County Sheriff's Department they were all arrested.

Dennis Peron has been a gay rights and marijuana activist for over 20 years. In March 1994 he opened up a 2,000 square feet space in which patients with documented illnesses could obtain marijuana safely. Over 800 clients were being serviced by August. Because of the need for a reliable, steady source of chemical-free medication, the pair sought to challenge the marijuana laws as far as cultivation for medical use was concerned.

Two days after the ill-fated press conference, the agent in charge for the state of California told the hemp farmers that he had gotten phone calls from the state authorities. They claimed that, because the hemp did test positive for a minute amount of THC (the psychoactive ingredient), its cultivation was in violation of the State Health and Safety Code. Unlike the European Economic Community, which has set standards for the amount of THC allowed to be present in hemp, the State of California only tests for presence or absence of THC. If there is any THC present, the State may declare the crop illegal, despite the fact that there is no psychoactive potential. Shortly after the agent's discussion with the farmers, state equipment entered the federally owned field, cut the hemp and mixed it into the soil. The entire commercial end of the crop was destroyed.

The hemp farmers are considering a suit against the state for damages resulting from the illegal raid. Despite the state's action in destroying the crop, a tremendous amount of research was completed before the plants were destroyed. Seeds were bred and collected for an enlarged seed bank. A more ambitious program is being planned for 1995, with plantings in January, March, April and May.

Fiber Hemp in the Ukraine, 1991

S. Hennink, E.P.M. de Meijer, H.M.G. van der Werf

AS A RESULT OF THE RENEWED INTEREST for hemp cultivation in the Netherlands many aspects of hemp became subject of a comprehensive feasibility study. Technological aspects of the Dutch program are maybe unprecedented, but the agronomic and breeding research is certainly not. Hemp has a long history as a fiber and oil crop in a large part of Europe and Asia and a lot of useful information about this crop can be obtained from breeders and agronomists abroad, especially in Eastern Europe and the Soviet Union. Therefore we were very pleased to have the opportunity to visit the All Union Scientific and Research Institute of Bast Crops in Glukhov.

Probably our trip was the first one in its kind to the Soviet-Union since the mission of Friedrich c.s. in 1964. We were impressed by the hospitality of our Soviet colleagues, interpreters and everybody else involved in our visit. We hope that a continuation of this contact in what ever form will be possible in the future.

In this report our impressions of the activities and strategies of the institute are summarized. We hope that it will be of use to researchers involved in the hemp program in the Netherlands, and that it gives evidence of a correct understanding from our side to the Soviet colleagues.

Hemp in the Soviet-Union

Currently the basic product of hemp in the Soviet Union is the bast fiber which is used for the production of tissue (canvas) and rope. The woody core of the stem is mainly used for the production of chipboard. Also the seeds are harvested for their content of edible oil, the oil cakes are used as fodder. Depending on the primary product of the crop (seed or fiber), different methods of cultivation are practiced (plant density and harvest time are different), while the same varieties are used for both purposes.

About 30% of the total hemp area is primarily used for the production of seed (seed reproduction and oil seed). Also the stems of these crops are harvested but they are of inferior quality.

Before the revolution an area of 960,000 ha of hemp was grown on the present Soviet Union territory. Average straw yield was 3–4 tons/ha. Fiber yield did not exceed 0.3 to 0.45 tons. (Reported weights of straw and fiber include respectively 20% and 13% moisture.) Average seed yield was 0.7 to 0.8 tons/ha. Hemp was cultivated for the production of rope and many kinds of tissue which were exported to Western Europe. A sufficient quantity of hemp seed oil, mainly used as edible oil and for production of paint, was produced to supply the domestic needs.

At present an area of about 60,000 ha of hemp remains, mainly in the Ukraine and western parts of Russia.

The All Union Scientific and Research Institute of Bast Crops

The All Union institute of Bast Crops was established by the Soviet government in 1931. During the 60 years of its existence the institute has investigated breeding, agronomy, mechanization, processing and economy of fiber hemp. Primary processing of hemp is one of the most recent subjects.

The institute consists of five departments:

1. *Department of selection and genetics* deals with the subjects: Establishment and maintenance of a collection of landraces, evaluation methods, breeding, elite seed production, heredity studies

(especially heredity of fiber characteristics and sexual type) and bio technology.

2. *Department of agricultural technology*, studies the agronomy of hemp: fertilization, crop rotation and plant density.
3. *Department of mechanization and harvesting.* Subjects: Design, construction and testing of machinery, production of prototypes.
4. *Department of technology and quality standards.* Subjects: Retting processes, post harvest conservation, environmental effects of retting, quality standards for factories, price level proposals for hemp products, organization of labor.
5. *Department of large scale processing.* Main subject: design of machines for the hemp industry.

Besides these departments which concentrate on hemp there is also a laboratory for selection of flax connected with the institute.

The institute owns an experimental farm of 100 ha for the implementation of new techniques.

SOVIET HEMP VARIETIES
The Collection of Soviet Hemp Varieties

In the past the institute gathered the local hemp varieties of the Soviet-Union, selected landraces were introduced for cultivation in other territories than the region of origin and/or used in breeding programs.

Accessions are multiplied under outdoors conditions, a space isolation of at least 1 km is taken into account. The "most typical" plants according to date of maturity, shape of flowers, bract morphology, stem diameter and stem length are selected. Seeds of at least 100 female plants are harvested to guarantee the populations integrity. Accessions are regenerated every two years.

Landraces

In former times, between 32° and 60° Northern latitude, when hemp was a common crop in large parts of the present Soviet territory, several local forms (landraces) existed. The characters of the local varieties are the result of a long process of unconscious selection by peasants during harvesting and threshing. This selection was favourable for the early maturing plants in the population.

At present the commonly used classification of Soviet hemp varieties is still based on geographic origin:

- Northern hemp (from the Leningrad region), characteristics: adapted to short day length and low temperatures, height not more than 70 cm, vegetation cycle 70 days, production about 2 tons straw/ha and low seed yield. The fiber content is natural which means 12–15%. This group of hemp is of no practical use at present and was only grown by peasants before the revolution. It was cultivated for the production of tissues for clothing and the production of oilseed.

- Middle Russian Hemp, (central Ukraine) characteristics: 110 to 125 days from sowing to seed maturity. The yield of straw is 5–6 tons/ha, seed yield 0.5–2 tons/ha (average of 1 ton). At present fiber content and fiber yield of the selected varieties derived from this group are respectively 30% and 2 tons/ha.

- Southern Russian hemp (South Ukraine, Caucasus and Asiatic republics, also including far eastern hemp). Vegetation cycle of 140 to 160 days. Yield of straw is usually more than 8 tons/ha, stem length sometimes reaches 7m. Fiber content 25%. Seed yield poor, usually less than 0.5 tons/ha.

The Siberian local variety Yermakovskaya, belonging to the middle Russian group, is still used in field trials as a standard because of its excellent fiber quality. Characteristics are: A short vegetation cycle of 105 days, a yield of 4–5 tons straw/ha and 0.7 tons of seed. Fifteen percent of fiber of high textile quality (thin). The content of the narcotic compound THC in this variety is higher than 0.2% which is the tolerated maximum content in the Soviet Union.

Modern Varieties

The main objectives of the hemp selection and breeding program are: high stem yield, seed yield, fiber content and fiber quality, monoeciousness, low narcotic potency, and acclimatization of southern hemp types to northern conditions.

Besides the aforementioned landraces a so-called "intermediary" group of varieties was created. This group of varieties combines a long vegetation period, and a good yield of straw, fiber and seed. Although this hemp is late flowering (southerly maturing), it is adapted to cultivation in areas where originally only middle Russian landraces were cultivated. Intermediary varieties were bred by hybridization of selections of southern and middle Russian hemp and afterwards family group selection. Senchenko bred US-1 (Krasnodarskaya x Northern hemp) which combined good fiber and seed yield, resistance and earliness. In the 1970s US-6 was the main variety; its characteristics were: 24% fiber of good quality, 120 days vegetation cycle, good straw yield, 0.8 ton seed yield. Initially the intermediate varieties were dioecious like the landraces from which they were derived.

Nowadays dioecious varieties are completely replaced by monoecious varieties. Although dioeciousness has biological advantages it is considered to be undesirable from the economic point of view. Monoecious (in Russian "Odnodomnaja") varieties are preferred above dioecious because they are homogenous which allows an easier harvest mechanization.

Another strategy, already attempted before World War II, was to create dioecious varieties in which maturation of male and female plants takes place simultaneously. Although these attempts were successful, the desired characteristic disappeared after two or three cycles of multiplication. Classification and genetics of the several sexual types which occur in monoecious Cannabis populations have been subject of intensive study by Dr. Migal in the last 10 years. US-9 was the first monoecious Soviet hemp variety. It contained a fiber content of more than 30%, but suffered from an insect plague called *Psylliodes attenuata* (hop flea beetle) and also from *Orobanche ramosa*. Resistance was introduced by back crossing with Southern hemp. Resistance is always acquired from the female parent.

Currently dioecious populations are only used for breeding purposes. The most important selections at present are several types of so called Yuzhnaya (abbreviated: USO). Average yields of these varieties are 6–8 tons straw and up to 30% bast fiber. Higher fiber content (up to 40%) is supposed to be possible but causes lodging and a decrease of fiber quality. Hybrid F1 varieties are only used for breeding purposes. Hybrid seed production for large scale cultivation, as is common in Hungary, is considered to be too complicated and too expensive.

Selection for low narcotic potency was started in 1973 by Dr. Virovets. Before that time THC contents of 2% were common, at present contents of 0.1% and even of 0% occur. The content of CBD also decreased very much as a result of this selection. Varieties with low THC content are: USO14, USO31, USO16, Dneprovskaya, Zolotskaya and Kuban.

Screening and Evaluation Methods

In selection fields, plants are widely spaced in a density of 30 plants/m² with row distances of 45 cm. Fiber content and quality, seed yield, stem yield, stem length and diameter, infection by *Fusarium*, *Botrytis* and *Sclerotinia* and the concentration of narcotic compounds are the most relevant characters that are evaluated.

Stem Quality

Traditionally, textile quality parameters of stems and fibers were judged. Important fiber quality criteria are: durability against biological and mechanical agents, flexibility, ability to splice, large breaking strength, absence of impurities and an easy extraction of fibers in retting processes. A general problem in textile hemp breeding programs is that an increase of stem fiber content causes a decrease of fiber quality.

The improvement of evaluation methods of stems in order to accelerate the selection procedure is the general aim of the research of the department of technology and quality standards.

Recently a new approach in judging stem quality has been introduced, because of the possible utilization of hemp for non traditional purposes like paper pulp production.

The clarification of the relationship between plant morphology and fiber quality would allow indirect screening methods. Results of these investigations are patented and therefore not published. Although details were not discussed, we were told that only 2–3 minutes per stem is sufficient to characterize the most important parameters.

In recently developed evaluation methods fibers are treated as a complex of elementary fibrils located in amorf lignin and pectin complex. One of the methods measures the density of anatomose connections between elementary fibers. Also a method for estimating fiber lengths exists.

The characters of the xylem core are also part of the program, especially the level of adsorption and desorption are evaluated as measures for cellulose quality.

Stem parameters mentioned as being relevant to judge the quality for paper pulp production are: stem maturity, cellulose quality, level of maturity of individual fibers and uniformity of fiber length. Additionally it would be desirable if primary and secondary phloem contained the same amount of lignin (which is not the case). The higher lignin content of secondary fibers compared to primary fibers hampers a cheap production of paper pulp.

We were told that patented techniques can be bought, and in the past several patents dealing with flax were bought by French companies or institutes.

Although the main theoretical problems concerning the determination of stem quality are solved and although prototypes of the required equipment exist, the department showed interest in collaboration in the field of technical improvement of the equipment.

According to staff members of the Ukrainian Pulp and Paper Research Institute in Kiev the ideal composition of hemp stems depends on the kind of paper which is desired. In general the lignin concentration should be as low as possible and the lignin should be as easy as possible to remove. Also the xylem core should be as small as possible especially because of its difficult delignification. Although secondary bast is less desired because it causes heterogeneity in the bast pulp this problem can technically be solved. In general as much bast fiber as possible is desired. There was general agreement that it is a problem to find useful purposes for lignin and for the woody core of hemp.

Narcotic Compounds

The collection of landraces was evaluated to obtain populations with low narcotic potency. An indirect criterion for the content of the main narcotic compound delta-9 tetrahydrocannabinol (THC) is smell and stickiness of the female inflorescences. Indeed a selection lacking THC and with very low content of the other major cannabinoid cannabinol (CBD), shown to us in the field, did not possess the typical resinous smell of normal cannabis. Evaluation of THC content takes place at the stage of initial seed maturity. Ten plants out of a family group of 50 are gathered in a mixed sample and THC content in the leaf dry matter is analyzed by gas chromatography (GC).

An indirect method to predict THC content was described by Gorskhova. The density of a specified type of resin glands is used as a parameter for indirect screening of THC content. Glands are not stained while using this technique. Microscopic observation shows a dominating density of cystolithic hairs in plants with low THC content, and a domination of iron colored trichomes in plants with high THC content. This indirect technique together with thin layer chromatography (TLC) is used only in the first stages of selection. At final stages gas-liquid chromatography GLC is necessary to determine THC content. Gorshkhova's technique is suitable for selection of individual plants, for large numbers of plants it is to elaborate.

Diseases

Susceptibility for fungal diseases is solely observed in the field and never in vitro. *Botrytis* and *Sclerotinia* are not very important in the S.U. due to the continental climate. Breeding for resistance does not have high priority.

Resistance to low temperatures is not taken into account. The usual sowing time is the second half of April and damage of seedlings by late frost does not occur.

Nematodes or other soil borne diseases do not play any role in the breeding program. Hemp is believed not to suffer from these organisms. A field trial exists with a history of 60 years of hemp cultivation without rotation. If fertilizers, insecticides, organic fertilizer, micro-elements and calcium are supplied, no yield depression can be observed after such a period.

Fiber Yield

In order to increase the yield of straw and fiber two strategies were followed: 1; introducing Southern varieties (long vegetation cycle) and 2; increasing fiber yield per individual stem by a selection for long thin stems. In the second case important parameters are; diameter of stem base and stem length. Selection aims at increasing length without increasing the stem diameter. Parameters are: a coefficient calculated out of the diameter of a lower stem section and the diameter of an upper section, and a coefficient calculated out of the diameter of the stem base and the stem length. It was concluded however that a direct determination of fiber content is a more effective criterion for selection than calculated indirect parameters.

The present protocol to treat individual stems is a combination of both approaches: measurement of stem length, diameter and weight. Subsequently determination of fiber content of a representative segment of the stem and a calculation of fiber content and fiber weight of the complete stem.

GENETIC RESEARCH
Sex Expression

Existing classifications of the sexual types of hemp are not suitable for practical use in genetics and breeding. Therefore a new classification is developed. This classification is based on the theories of Grishko (1940) and Neuer (1943). Deviating from existing classifications of sexual types, male and female plants segregating from monoecious hemp are not classified as dioecious male and female type.

According to Migal's theory, sex type in dioecious hemp is determined by two genes on the sex chromosomes, which are tightly linked. Both genes have two alleles, the Y chromosome carrying allele M for male flowers and allele I for loose inflorescence. The X chromosome carrying allele F for female flowers and allele i for compact inflorescence. Allele M dominates over F and I over i. The genotype of diploid cells carried by the sex chromosomes is IiMF and iiFF.

Besides these genetic factors of sex chromosomes, all plants of dioecious and monoecious hemp have a complex set of sex determining genes on autosomes. These genes come into force when genes controlling sex on the sex chromosomes become inactive. Autosomal factors control the sex type of monoecious hemp. Inbreeding of monoecious hemp leads to 100% monoecious offspring. Crosses between dioecious and monoecious hemp give mainly dioecious (female) hemp with a small percentage monoecious hemp.

In wild dioecious hemp monoecious plants occur in a frequency ranging from 0.003 to 0.01%. Since monoeciousness is recessive and heritable in a third allele besides F and M should exist. The frequency of this allele ranges from 0.5 to 1%. It is possible that the sex chromosome becomes inactive when both chromosomes carry this allele. Inactivity of the sex chromosomes is probably not caused by mutations.

A = the factor causing differentiation of male sex organs
G = the factor causing differentiation of female sex organs
The strength (valency) can be written as AG Ag aG ag where A> and G>g.

aaGG aaGg	100% female flowers
AaGG	predominance of female flowers
AAGG AaGg aagg	50% male, 50% female flowers
AAGg	predominance of male flowers
AAgg Aagg	100% male flowers

It is not explained how loose or compact inflorescence type is determined in monoecious hemp.

Leaf Arrangement

Normally leaves on the vegetative part of the stem are arranged in opposite pairs (decussate). In the generative part leaves are arranged spirally (alternate).

Occasionally trifoliate plants appear (three leaves on one node). Selection of trifoliate plants is possible. Populations with 82% trifoliate plants were obtained. In these populations plants occur with four leaves per node, even plants with five leaves where found. In the trifoliate populations the percentage of male plants was higher than in the original population, 55% vs 45%. In the original populations also plants appear with one leaf per node. This form is not heritable.

Apomixis

At rare occasions two seedlings germinate from one seed. One of them is apomict. Often one of the two seedlings is very small. These plants appear to be haploid.

Breeding Program and Techniques

The program has three major goals. The maintenance of existing varieties, the selection of new varieties and the production of elite seed.

History

Before breeding started hemp yielded about 3–4 tons of straw per hectare and 0.7–0.8 ton of seed. One ton of straw gave about 0.1–0.15 ton of high quality fiber. In the beginning (1930s) landraces were collected. The best landraces were selected. There were two ways for increasing fiber yield. Improving the straw yield by use of Southern Hemp or selecting for a longer vegetation period. The second method did not give the wanted result, seed production declined. After a few years the progress also stopped with the first method.

The selection for a higher fiber content started. The ratio length/diameter of the stem was used as an indirect measure for fiber content. Later the fiber content was determined by retting the stem.

Fiber content increased from 15% to 30%. In breeding material even 40% was obtained.

By increasing the fiber content, the quality of the fiber declined. Therefor tests were developed to determine the fiber quality, such as purity, durability and strength. These new tests determine fiber content in a mechanical way, so that retting was no longer needed. During autumn and winter 30,000 to 40,000 can be evaluated.

In the '30s a problem occurred with the mechanization of hemp harvest. Dioecious male plants started retting on the field while female plants were still green. Italian scientists and Grischko developed equal maturing hemp. In these varieties male plants have a habitus like female plants, but these varieties were not stable. A few years later they started the development of monoecious hemp. Nowadays most of the Russian hemp varieties are monoecious.

In former days conventional mass selection was used. The last decade family selection is used.

Selection of New Varieties

The Institute selects hemp for fiber and seed production. One variety may be used for both purposes. As a seed hemp it must be early maturing and as a fiber hemp the bast fiber content must be high, with a good fiber quality. About 30% is the maximum fiber content, higher fiber content decreases quality and plants become sensitive to lodging.

The main breeding objective last decade has been decreasing THC content. The maximum content according to Soviet law is 0.2%. Most varieties have a content of about 0.1%. The institute has recently created varieties without THC. Variety Nr 42 yields 10 tons of straw or 1 ton of seed, has a fiber content from 25 to 28% and no THC. For the selection of families and populations in an early stage thin layer chromatography is used. In a later stage gas liquid chromatography is used. Individual plants are scored with the trichome method.

As basic breeding material landraces from varying origin are used. These landraces have a high fiber quality. Southern maturing hemp is used for its high straw yield and its resistance against *Psylliodes attenuata*. New dioecious material is crossed with a monoecious variety. This hybrid contains only few monoecious plants so the hybrid population is backcrossed with a monoecious variety. This population contains enough monoecious plants for further selection. This procedure is standard for the production of basic selection material. Selection takes place on a family basis. It is not clear whether full sib- or half sib families are used as a basis. Families are evaluated and selected during 10–11 years on the field. During the evaluation of the families all male plants are removed. The selections are evaluated on different locations in the country. By doing this different varieties are created for different regions.

After the period of selection a selected family becomes a variety and the variety will be multiplied for cultivation. Super elite seed is sown on an area of 0.3 hectare, selection takes place against male and inferior plants. Next year elite seed is sown on an area of 0.6 hectare, again selection takes place. Two further years of multiplication is board out to a Sovchos or Kolchos without selection. The seed then produced is used for cultivation.

Existing varieties are maintained under continuous selection. Without selection a variety will deteriorate and become dioecious in a few generations.

AGRONOMY
Fertilization and Rotation

In most cases fertilization of hemp in the Soviet Union carried out with chemical fertilizers only. Depending on the soil and the expected yield, 60 to 120 kg of N and P_2O_5 and 80 to 140 kg of K_2O are applied. Fertilization affects fiber quality by its effect on plant density. The more N fertilizer is applied, the smaller the number of plants at harvest and the larger mean plant size will be. Large plants have a lower bast fiber content than small plants.

In the Glukhov region hemp may be grown after each of the crops in the rotation (cereals, potatoes, maize, clover). Hemp is considered to be self-compatible, it sometimes is grown for 5 to 10 years continuously on the same field, with no apparent effect on yield. Fertilizer requirements however are said to be higher when hemp is grown continuously. In a field experiment as Glukhov hemp has been grown continuously for 60 years. The experiment contains fertilization levels ranging from no fertilization (yield 880 kg of stem/ha) to 40 tons of manure/ha (yield 7,000 to 8,000 kg of stem/ha). Reported weights of straw and fiber include respectively 20% and 13% moisture.

Sowing

Hemp is usually sown in the second half of April. In most cases hemp seed is treated with TMTD. On good soils 450 seeds/m^2 are sown for fiber hemp, on poor soil 500 to 550 seeds/m^2 are used. Row width is 7 to 12 cm. In a good crop of fiber hemp 300 plants/m^2 will be present at harvest. When hemp is grown for seed production, plant density at harvest varies from 30 to 180 plants/m^2, depending on the variety.

Weed Control

In fiber hemp weed control is not necessary. In seed hemp, which is sown at a lower plant density, herbicides are used. Against monocotyls: Nabu, Targa (quizalo-fop-ethyl), Zellek (manufactured by Dow), Fusilade (fluazifop, 1.5 to 2.5 l./ha) and Iloxan (diclofop, 2 to 3 l./ha).

Against dicotyls: Ballan (benefin), Dual (etolachlor), Lenacil (venzar), Pyramin (pyrazon). A mixture of Dual (1,5 l./ha) and Lenacil (1.2 1/ha) is often used.

Pests and Diseases

Two insect species (*Lepidoptera*) may cause damage to hemp: *Grapholita delineata* and *Ostrinia nubilalis*. Against both insects, *Bacillus thuringiensis* and *Trigogamma spp*. Against *Psylliodes attenuata*, the hop flea beetle, a seed treatment is available, the composition of which is secret.

Harvesting and Processing

About 70% of the hemp area of the Soviet Union is harvested for fiber only. Harvest takes place at "technical maturity," that is, when the male plants are shedding pollen. At Glukhov this stage generally is reached by the end of July or early in August. Seed ripeness occurs one month later. By the end of July a hemp crop will yield 7 to 8 tons of stem (20% humidity)/ha and 1.7 to 2 tons of bast fiber (13% humidity)/ha.

Prior to harvest, the crop will be defoliated, either by mechanical means or by spraying magnesium chlorate. Most of the hemp is dew retted, depending on the weather, dew retting may take 10 days to one month. Other common techniques are warm water retting and chemical retting. In some factories hot steam is used to separate the bast fiber from the rest of the stem. The best fiber quality is obtained from warm water retting. High quality hemp stems are typically 1.50 to 2.00 m long, their diameter (at half height) will be 5 to 7 mm.

Harvest Technology

The department of mechanization and harvest technology develops prototypes of new machines for hemp. The machines shown to us are listed here:

- **Harvester.** This machine mows the hemp and ties it into bundles without damaging (breaking or crushing) the stems. Careful handling of the stems is important when the fiber is used for textile. For hemp which is used for pulp this is less important. The machine leaves the bundles in the field to dry. This machine can handle hemp of a length of up to 3.5m.
- **Mechanical defoliator.** Research into mechanical defoliation has started in order to find an alternative to chemical defoliation.
- **A machine which turns hemp stems** in the course of dew retting.
- **A machine which picks up hemp stems** after dew retting and makes bundles.
- **A big baler** which picks up hemp from the field while driving diagonally across stems.
- **A machine which is used to unroll big bales** in the processing factory.

We were told that the lack of harvesting machines is the main factor limiting the area of hemp grown in the Soviet Union. In the republic of Uzbekistan 20,000 ha of kenaf is grown. Mechanization is similar to that used for hemp.

Pulp and Paper Technology

Among other topics, the Ukrainian Pulp and Paper Research Institute at Kiev investigates pulping, paper making, composite materials and paper recycling. A paper in English, listing in full the activities of the institute can be obtained from the authors of this report. The Institute also investigates the use of annual crops (flax, hemp, reed, rice straw) as a raw material for paper making.

Currently two pulp plants are operating in the Ukraine, both use aspen wood as raw material, they produce paper and board. The feasibility of a third pulp plant is being studied. One of the product lines of this new plant might be based on hemp bast fiber. Hemp bast pulp might be used for three paper grades:

- **Cigarette paper.** At present cigarette paper is imported. The required technology is available in the Ukraine, the pulp would consist of 50% hemp bast fiber and 50% wood.
- **Document paper (high strength, bank notes).** This paper usually is produced using the polluting Kraft method. The quality of document paper does not depend so much on fiber lengths but on the pulping and bleaching techniques used. Dr. Krotov proposes a new non-polluting method for making document paper from bast fiber. When used on the woody core this material will yield a relatively good pulp. The method is described in a paper (in English) which can be obtained from the authors of this report. This new method is not yet used, as the machines which are required cannot be built in Ukraine.
- **Reinforced paper for the sausage industry.** This type of paper is currently bought from the Dexter company. The technology required for making sausage paper is being developed at the Leningrad (St. Petersburg) pulp and paper institute. For this paper grade the fibers should be as long and strong as possible.

Dr. Krotov thinks that the conservation of wet hemp stems ("ensiling," as is considered in the Dutch hemp program) prior to processing in the pulp factory is a viable option, as appropriate conservation products are available. These chemicals will conserve the hemp stems and initiate the pulping process. The institute would be interested to cooperate with Dutch researchers on this topic. In order to be best suited for paper production, hemp stems should contain as much bast and as little wood as possible. The woody core of the hemp stem is relatively hard to delignify (relative to aspen). A lower lignin content in the wood would therefore be desirable. Experiments carried out in cooperation with the research institute at Glukhov have shown that the crop development state at harvest has little effect on the delignification process of the woody core.

Closing Remarks

Literature, seed material and results will possibly be exchanged. For example CPRO-DLO has evaluated a collection of hemp accessions, including some Russian varieties. It would be interesting to compare results obtained in the Soviet Union with those obtained under Dutch conditions. This report will be handed to colleagues involved in the Dutch National Hemp Program which will probably lead to contacts on other fields of research besides breeding and agronomy. It would be a pleasure for us if a countervisit to Holland could be arranged in the future.

Fiber Hemp in the Ukraine, 1993

by H. M. G. van der Werf

THE INSTITUTE OF BAST CROPS at Glukhov in the Ukrainian Republic was established in 1931 by the government of the Soviet Union as the All-Union Institute of Bast Crops. During the first 60 years of its existence the institute investigated breeding, agronomy, mechanization, processing and economy of fiber hemp. In 1991, when the Soviet Union was dismantled and Ukraine became independent, the Institute obtained its current name and shifted its focus from research mainly on hemp to research on both flax and hemp.

Yields of straw and seed reported in this report include 20% and 13% moisture, respectively.

Area of Hemp

In the 1950s 140,000 hectares (ha) of hemp was grown in the Ukraine, 500,000 ha were grown in Russia. In 1993 about 8,000 ha was left in the Ukraine, the area of hemp in Russia was estimated at 35,000 to 40,000 ha. Nowadays, hemp is a very small crop, its area of cultivation continues to decline. In the current economic difficulties food crops are of more concern to the Ukrainian government than fiber crops.

Cultivars

The latitude of Glukhov is 52 degrees: London and Rotterdam are situated at about the same latitude. This means that the flowering date of a cultivar will be similar in Glukhov, the Netherlands and the south of England. The Bast Crops Institute at Glukhov has produced a range of monoecious hemp cultivars, of different flowering dates. Early-flowering cultivars reach technical maturity (the optimum stage for harvest of the stem only) at the beginning of August, late cultivars reach technical maturity towards the end of August. When grown for the production of both stem and seed, the optimum harvest date is about one month after technical maturity. Straw yields vary between 6 tons (metric) per hectare (t/ha) for an early cultivar to up to 9 t/ha for a late cultivar. Seed yields vary between more than 1 t/ha for an early cultivar to 0.5 t/ha or less for a late cultivar.

In the breeding program fiber quality is an important factor. Many of the cultivars which have a high fiber content in the stem have been found to have larger fiber bundles than the older cultivars which have a low fiber content. Large fiber bundles are undesirable as they decrease fiber fineness, one of the most important quality parameters for cordage and textile purposes. Attempts are made now to obtain cultivars which combine high fiber content and high fiber quality (E L Pashin, personal communication). The content of fiber (extracted by retting) in the straw varies between 25% and 30% depending on the cultivar. THC content is about 0.1% in many cultivars, some of the latest cultivars contain no THC at all.

Rotation

In the Glukhov region hemp may be grown after each of the crops in the rotation (cereals, potatoes, maize, clover). An experiment conducted during 10 years by Borisienko has shown that straw yield of hemp is affected by the preceding crop (Senchenko & Demkin 1972). Average straw yield was 5.6 t/ha after lupins; after potatoes, silage maize, winter wheat, clover and pea hemp straw yields were 5.1 t/ha; but after 4 years of continuous hemp growing straw yield of hemp was only 4.2 t/ha. Still, hemp is considered to be relatively self-compatible, it sometimes is grown for 5 to 10 years continuously on the same field. By this practice its yield is affected negatively, but the reduction in yield is relatively small compared to that found in other crops when grown continuously. Fertilizer requirements are said to be higher when hemp is grown continuously. In a field experiment at Glukhov hemp has been grown continuously for 60 years. The experiment contains fertilization levels ranging from no fertilization (yield 880 kg/ha of straw) to 40 t/ha of manure (yield 7,000 to 8,000 kg/ha of straw).

Fertilization

In most cases fertilization of hemp is carried out with chemical fertilizers only. Depending on the soil and the expected yield, about 120 kg/ha of N, 90 kg/ha of P_2O_5 and 80 to 140 kg of K_2O are applied. Uptake by the crop depends on yield.

A hemp crop fertilized with 20 t/ha of manure and 60 kg/ha of N, 45 kg/ha of P_2O_5 and 45 kg of K_2O yielded 6.6 t/ha of above-ground dry matter when harvested at flowering, stem yield was 5.4 t/ha of dry matter. At flowering contents of N, P_2O_5 and K_2O in the dry matter of the stem were 0.97%, 0.27% and 1.64% respectively; in the dry matter of the leaves contents were 3.28%, 0.70% and 2.25% respectively (Shatun 1975).

A hemp crop fertilized with 30 t/ha of manure and 60 kg/ha of N, 60 kg/ha of P_2O_5 and 60 kg/ha of K_2O yielded 6.5 t/ha of straw and 0.8 t/ha of seed when harvested at seed ripeness (Bedak 1979). With the same amount of manure but with 120 kg/ha of N, P_2O_5 and K_2O it yielded 7.9 t/ha of straw and 1.3 t/ha of seed. In both cases the seed contained 6.2% N, 3.3% P_2O_5 and 1.2% K_2O in its dry matter.

A mower cuts and binds the hemp stalks and drops them for drying in the field.

Sowing

Grenikov & Tollochko (1953) state that emergence of seed will occur at temperatures between 1–2° C and 45° C, optimum temperature for germination is 30–35° C. Hemp is most resistant to frost in the seedling stage, seedlings survive a short frost of up to -8 to -10° C (Grenikov & Tollochko 1953). After the seedling stage but before the beginning of flowering hemp plants support frosts of up to -5 to -6° C (Senchenko & Timonin 1978). A frost of -1° C at flowering will decrease seed yield and seed quality (Senchenko & Demkin 1972).

Senchenko & Demkin (1972) recommend to sow hemp when the soil temperature reaches 8 to 10° C, in the Glukhov area this corresponds to the second half of April. When sown at the end of April the cultivar US-6 yielded 5.3 t/ha of straw and 1.1 t/ha of seed. Sown 10, 20 or 30 days later, straw yield s were 5.2, 4.4 and 3.4 t/ha respectively, seed yields were 1.0, 0.7 and 0.5 t/ha respectively (Senchenko & Demkin 1972).

Generally hemp seed is treated with TMTD to prevent fungal diseases. For the production of stem only, 450 seeds per square meter (m^2) are sown on good soils, on poor soils 500 to 550 seeds/m^2 are used. Row width is 7 to 12 cm. In a good crop of fiber hemp about 300 plants/m^2 will be present at harvest. When hemp is grown for the production of seed and stem, optimum plant density at harvest varies from 30 to 180 plants/m^2, depending on the cultivar. At low plant densities row width will be 30 to 45 cm, to permit inter-row cultivation.

Recommended sowing depth is 3–4 cm when the seedbed is sufficiently moist, 4–5 cm when the seedbed is dry (Senchenko & Timonin 1978).

Weed control

In fiber hemp weed control generally is not necessary, as weeds are suppressed by the crop. The competitive potential of hemp relative to weeds increases with the plant density of the hemp crop. In a non-fertilized hemp crop straw yield was lower and weight and number of weeds was larger than in a well-fertilized hemp crop (Katsov 1967). The 4-year crop rotation: potato, hemp, sugar beet, silage maize was conducted during 10 years either without any form of weed control in any of the

Photo by Hayo van der Werf

Workers remove the hemp fiber from the decorticator for further processing.

crops, or with effective chemical weed control in each crop whenever necessary. In the absence of weed control, the yields of sugar beet, potato, silage maize and hemp were reduced to 24%, 30%, 40% and 85% respectively of the yields which were obtained when weeds were controlled effectively throughout the rotation (Tarasov 1975). This result nicely demonstrates the exceptional potential of hemp to suppress weeds and to give good yields at a level of weed infestation which strongly reduces yield in other crops.

When hemp is grown mainly for the production of seed, it is sown at a low plant density, and weed control may be necessary. This can be done mechanically using an inter-row cultivator or herbicides can be used. Herbicides used against grassy weeds are: Targa (quizalofopethyl), Fusilade (fluazifop), Iloxan (diclofop) and Dual (etolachlor). Against broad-leaved weeds the following herbicides are used: Ballan (benefin) and Lenacil (venzar). A mixture of Dual (1.5 liters/hectare) and Lenacil (1.2 l/ha) is often used when both grassy and broad-leaved weeds are present.

Pests and Diseases

Two insect species (Lepidoptera) may cause damage to hemp: *Grapholita delineata* and *Ostrinia nubilalis*. Against both insects, *Bacillus thuringiensis* and *Trigogamma spp.* are used. Against *Psylliodes attenuata*, the hop flea beetle, a seed treatment is available, the composition of which is secret.

Harvesting

About 70% of the hemp area is harvested for fiber only. In this case the crop is harvested when fiber quality is best: at "technical maturity." At this development stage the male plants have completely finished flowering and the first ripe seeds are found on female plants. Depending mainly on the cultivar technical maturity will occur between the beginning and the end of August. The remaining 30% of the hemp area is harvested for seed and fiber at the so-called stage of "biological maturity," when between 50% and 75% of the seeds are ripe and seed yield is maximal. Biological maturity occurs about one month after technical maturity. In fact, the maximum amount of seed is present somewhat later, when all seeds are ripe. But at this stage seed losses during harvest are very large and fiber quality is less than when 50% to 75% of the seeds are ripe.

Different harvesting machines are used, depending on the product harvested (stem only or stem and seed) and on method of retting (dew or water retting). Harvest at technical maturity (i.e. for stem only) followed by dew retting is the most common practice. A special machine cuts the hemp and lays it down in swaths for dew retting). Depending on the weather the stems will be retted in 10 to 30 days, to ensure homogeneous retting the swath can be turned over during this period, using a special machine. When the hemp is sufficiently retted it is picked up and baled using a modified big-baler which keeps the stems parallel to each other. The stems lose most of their leaves during retting and while being picked up.

The best fiber quality is obtained from water retting. When the crop is to be water retted, the harvesting machine makes sheaves instead of laying the stems in a swath. The sheaves are dried in the field.

If the crop is harvested for both stem and seed the machine which is used for cutting the hemp is equipped with a threshing unit which takes off the seed prior to making sheaves or to laying the stems in a swath. Most of the machines for hemp harvest are available for export.

Processing

Prior to the extraction of fiber from the stem, retted hemp is kept in stacks outdoors). Retted hemp can be kept in this way for one year or more without a negative effect on fiber quality. The extraction of long fiber from the retted stems is done with breaking and scutching lines similar to those used for the processing of retted flax. This process yields short fiber and woody core as by-products. Long and short fiber are processed into string, rope, cord and cables, burlap or non-woven textile products. The woody core is used for the production of particle boards and building blocks. The building blocks contain 70 litre of cement, 70 litre of sand and 860 litre of woody core per cubic meter.

This pile of hemp stalk photographed in the summer of 1993. Consumer demand had not yet kicked in and there was still a surplus of raw farm goods. This pile has been rumored to have been removed for use in the last year.

Prices of hemp products have been low in recent years. In the Ukraine, the retted long hemp fiber is sold for about $200/ton, the woody core is sold for less than $20/ton.

Pulp and Paper Technology

Among other topics, the Ukrainian Pulp and Paper Research Institute at Kiev investigates pulping, paper making, composite materials and paper recycling. The institute also investigates the use of annual crops (flax, hemp, reed, rice straw) as a raw material for paper making.

Currently two pulp plants are operating in the Ukraine, both use aspen wood as raw material, they produce paper and board. The feasibility of a third pulp plant is being studied. One of the product lines of this new plant might be based on hemp bast fiber. Hemp bast pulp might be used for three paper grades:

Cigarette paper. At present cigarette paper is imported. The required technology is available in the Ukraine, the pulp would consist of 50% hemp bast fiber and 50% wood.

Document paper (high strength, bank notes). This paper usually is produced using the polluting Kraft method. The quality of document paper does not depend so much on fiber lengths but on the pulping and bleaching techniques used. Dr. Krotov of the Pulp and Paper Research Institute proposes a new non-polluting method for making document paper from bast fiber. When used on the woody core, this material will yield a relatively good pulp. The method is described in a paper (in English) which can be obtained from the author of this report. This new method is not yet used, as the machines which are required cannot be built in the Ukraine.

Reinforced paper for the sausage industry. This type of paper is currently bought from the Dexter company. The technology required for making sausage paper is being developed at the St. Petersburg pulp and paper institute. For this paper grade the fibers should be as long and strong as possible.

Dr. Krotov thinks that the wet anaerobic storage of hemp stems ("ensiling," as is considered in the Dutch hemp program) prior to processing in the pulp factory is a viable option, as appropriate conservation products are available. These chemicals will conserve the hemp stems and initiate the pulping process.

In order to be best suited for paper production, hemp stems should contain as much bast and as little wood as possible. The woody core of the hemp stem is relatively hard to delignify (relative to aspen). A lower lignin content in the wood would therefore be desirable. Experiments carried out in cooperation with the research institute at Glukhov have shown that the crop development stage at harvest has little effect on the delignification process of the woody core.

Concluding remarks

The visit to the Institute of Bast Crops was very much worth while. I was impressed by the vast amount of practical and scientific knowledge on hemp which has been accumulated by the researchers working at the Institute over the past 60 years. The area of hemp in the world has been decreasing for more than 100 years. However, it seems a turning point might be close, and hemp area might stabilize and possibly increase. The knowledge available at the Bast Crops Institute may facilitate this "hemp revival," some of that knowledge can be found in this report. Continuing contacts between "new" hemp researchers outside the Ukraine and their more experienced colleagues at Glukhov will be beneficial to hemp research and, hopefully, to hemp production, world wide.

Hemp: From Today Into Tomorrow

by Chris Conrad

THIS BOOK MARKS a particular moment in the history of cannabis hemp. Five years ago few people even thought of cannabis as a commercial industrial resource. Today scores of new hemp businesses have emerged, hundreds of new products are on the market, and there is a perceptible surge in public support for the crop.

With an estimated 50,000 commercial uses to choose from, it will take a long time just to work through all the possibilities. Some at present appear more likely to be profitable than others, hence more viable for investment; but there remains the possibility of scientific or engineering breakthroughs that could alter that relationship. Given these variables, it is only natural for researchers to form differing opinions. One difficulty in resolving the question of hemp's modern value is that the available data is filled with reports on yields and applications that are difficult to reconcile. It will take substantial investment to properly investigate matters.

Let's weigh rhetoric against reality for an honest assessment of the useful hemp plant. My years of research indicate that restoring commercial access to hemp will not be an overnight miracle cure-all for society's ills; but intelligently developing hemp and other sustainable resources with appropriate technology will help us find long term solutions to many of our most pressing environmental, economic and social problems.

Five Years that Changed the World

In 1989, sterile hemp birdseed and hemp twine were virtually the only legal cannabis products that could still be purchased in America. That year I formed the Business Alliance for Commerce in Hemp, or BACH, with a five year plan to advance these goals: restore industrial hemp in manufacture, allow prescription medical marijuana, and regulate the production and sale of cannabis for adult use. This project coincided with a grassroots revival of a global cannabis reform movement, to the seeming dismay of both the drug legalizers, who had avoided discussing industrial hemp for years, and hemp industries who had sought to distance themselves from the marijuana debate. However, the holistic public relations approach has actually benefitted both groups.

Since then, the market has expanded to include a wide assortment of quality products being commercially produced by scores of large and small, independent companies, and a research patch has been grown in southern California. One can buy hundreds of separate hemp items: cookies, candies, cloth, clothing and accessories, macrame, carpet, stationery, paper products, soaps, cosmetics, pouches, soft luggage, and so on.

The BACH strategy combines a business association with an outreach program of local representatives who promote hemp's merits to a targeted community network. It set about changing the way people talk and think about cannabis. By first restoring the plant's true name, hemp, BACH began to carefully re-educate targeted business interests, ecologists, farmers, health care professionals, political activists, media outlets, human rights groups, etc., to stimulate a convergence of interests for hemp restoration. The growing coalition is profiting from shared experience, and growing together, but along separate tracks.

While some hemp purists insist on using 100% hemp in their products, others use hemp in combination with other materials like cotton, beads, leather, metals, recycled materials—even synthetic fibers—in the interests of utility, price and other market concerns. Hemp will always be special for many of us, but will hopefully soon be so widely used, and so fully integrated into the blend of materials, that even we may have to read product labels to find it. The more hemp is assimilated, the more secure our future becomes.

The New Global Roundup

The European Community comprises a potential global powerhouse for hemp agriculture in part because its subsidy on hemp entices farmers, and the Frankfort Resolution chips away at the Berlin Wall of prohibition. The crucial next step is to keep a supply available and growing until more profitable markets emerge, probably fairly rapidly over the next five years, then leveling off in pace after the turn of the millennium.

Several promising start-ups in the U.K. are growing hemp or marketing products. The vigorous interest some Germans are giving the prospect of "hanf" restoration adds a dynamic new force for modern hemp processing systems. Germans developed the Dresden cottonization process in the 1920s and had a hemp program in the Second World War. They may also be a formidable player in hemp farming.

France and Spain continue to produce "chanvre" and "canamo," respectively, and have advanced their technologies. They closely guard their processes as trade secrets, and limit their applications to the more expensive specialty fiber market. By manipulating the supply, these national industries artificially inflate market prices, and have been quite comfortable with the status quo.

Dutch "hennep" advocates now face another reality: good intentions and good yields are not enough; markets and infrastructure are also necessary. Farmers are eager to produce this cash crop, and the Netherlands is a hotbed of research and development. Over 100 hectares of hemp were harvested in 1994, and the question of the moment is what to do with all those stalks. The longer term task is to design the redeploy processing mills to satisfy the modern market demand for finished consumer goods.

Former Soviet satellite states have lowered output and still labor under outdated production methods and technology. Hungary has made significant progress in producing higher quality consumer goods, both as garment quality textiles and in paper products. Their advances are set against the backdrop of new initiatives in the Ukraine and Kazakhstan, forming a region that sprawls from Europe to China. These countries have little idea of modern global market demands and how or where to get the equipment and information to make rapid progress. Short on both capital and consumer goods, these countries export hemp now, but could concentrate on developing a vertical hemp industry to satisfy their own domestic needs for food, clothing, housing and paper.

China remains the most diversified source of value added and finished hemp goods such as paper and fabrics. Thailand has become a new gateway to Laotian and Cambodian hemp. The hemp belt regions of India and South America remain unexplored but could be interesting new sources of hemp products.

Hemp Caught in an American Time Warp

There is a difference in attitude between researchers and institutions abroad and those on this continent, which can be loosely summarized as European traditionalism versus Yankee "can do" bravado. That is why so many products originate in the States—entrepreneurial Americans are more willing to give it a try and see what happens instead of talking themselves out of making the effort. Combining hemp's versatility with American ingenuity and modern technology could result in significant progress in a relatively short time.

The U.S. and Canada comprise the largest market for and source of finished hemp goods, but pose unique problems for their industries to overcome. Unfortunately, American hemp has been blacklisted for over a half century; a formidable obstacle. Canada issued its first commercial research license this year, but the U.S. research crop was destroyed by zealous prohibition agents.

We must undertake full restoration of large-scale, vertical hemp industries, so we can reap the benefits of this sustainable "new" resource. However, hemp is not a "new" resource at all, but a very ancient one. Our ancestors left a solid groundwork of knowledge on which to build. Looking over the historical record, it is clear that hemp has been used for many thousands of years in a wide range of consumer goods. It has been an extremely productive crop and has been profitably grown throughout the temperate and tropical zones. As a traditional farm crop, hemp is well suited to American climate and conditions.

Much of the excitement and innovation that marked the U.S. hemp renaissance of the early 20th century was deliberately crushed by the

Marijuana Tax Act of 1937, and its brief revival during the Second World War was wrapped in a cloak of national security, then quietly laid to rest. During these two phases hemp was processed into the widest range of products; paper and textiles, plastics, fiberboard, auto body parts, and energy to power mills while generating a 50% energy surplus.

The machinery and blueprints for those sophisticated and efficient systems have long been lost, or perhaps still languish in corporate research and development files, or rot away on the shelves of the Patent Office, waiting for a national emergency to convince bureaucrats to again reverse policy and promote the development of this time-honored resource. What has become of the factory prototypes and working farm equipment produced during the forward push of those heady times? With patent rights now expired, this line of research could be a gold mine for future exploration.

Why Hemp?

Hemp offers a once in a century investment opportunity: it is an easily produced commercial resource, it is underdeveloped and in high demand. At once it offers financial prosperity while protecting posterity. Governments and parents have a duty to provide for the well being of society and future generations that outweighs any impulse for short term profits by exploitation and environmental degradation. Other crops should be used if they are better for particular conditions and applications and can be grown in a non-polluting agriculture-based economy.

Why not some other crop? The argument that farmers will only grow a crop if it is the most profitable simply does not hold up, or all farms would be mono-cultural and everyone would be growing marijuana. Obviously there are other concerns that determine where people put their energies.

Sustainable economics means regional productivity and self-sufficiency growing from the ground up. A stable supply could develop rapidly due to hemp's profuse annual output. Hemp is versatile and easy to grow. Only one or two years are needed to establish stable, acclimatized seed lines on enough land area to support small scale industrial development. Large scale demand can probably be met within five to ten years.

The pulp industry's demand is so tremendous that it can immediately consume as much hemp as anyone can produce. As for fuel production, the relative cleanliness of sulfur-free biomass combined with saved fossil fuels and intact forests will benefit us all. Not all energy should come from a single source, and conservation is a critical factor. Many energy crops should be developed, especially indigenous annuals. On-site conversions of hemp plant matter for mill power is one practical way to cut factory energy consumption costs, offset waste disposal and eliminate fuel transportation costs to and from the facility. This advantage reduces vehicle traffic, and surrounding hemp fields will remove CO_2 seasonally, with obvious benefit to air quality.

This illustrates one of many applications for hemp that may not be seen as commercially profitable, but are so ecologically beneficial as to merit development. Others include eliminating weeds, preventing erosion, restructuring soil, helping re-establish forests, providing shade, nesting and feeding materials for wildlife, as green manure, for drug content, to add beauty, etc. And hemp certainly is hardy.

Cannabis is grown in the Rif mountains of Morocco on land that will not support other crops (i.e., marginal land), and has been grown for millennia in certain regions of India and China. Its sustainability is amply illustrated by the large wild patches that U.S. prohibition agents still find throughout the Midwest. In August 1994, for example, a "drug eradication" task force destroyed a naturalized, 14-acre patch of wild Minnesota hemp. These plants had grown untended on the same soil since the Second World War or earlier, with a mean height from eight to ten feet. Such cases are common, and make it difficult to accept claims that hemp is a heavy feeding, soil depleting crop. Returning roots, foliage and seeds to the soil is a key part of that annual natural equation, but historical records show that removal of the stalks (particularly the fiber) can be balanced by crop rotation and addition of animal manure. Of course, adding fertilizer increases crop yields, and better soil and growing conditions produce better crop results. No one disputes these points, or argues for cannabis hemp mono-culture. The point that does keep being made is that hemp must be able to compete to show its true value.

Many people simply love this plant and will grow and work with hemp in the face of great adversity. When they can once again do so without government interference, it will be like the opening of a floodgate through which wonderful things will flow. This advantage is nearly unique to hemp.

Where Hemp is Going Next

Some estimates put forth by hemp enthusiasts may be overstated, but the more conservative observers could also be criticized for understanding the full potential of hemp. Most of the findings are in general agreement, and disagreements are about "a matter of degree." Whether hemp produces four times as much pulp as does timber, which U.S. Department of Agriculture Bulletin 404 contends, or not; the point is that using hemp wood for paper or construction and fabrication materials will save trees and create jobs.

Large scale production of hemp is more efficient. The small-scale production now practiced prevents hemp from being cost competitive against timber and petrochemicals. It is time for governments to level the playing field. This means instituting new policies that end political barriers to hemp. Current policies benefit foreign producers while penalizing prospective domestic producers. We need a return to true free enterprise. Don't ban other resources, just take away their taxpayer support, factor in related environmental cleanup costs, and given hemp a fair chance to compete.

Hemp is not a panacea, but should be part of a broad approach to sustainable economics. It must also include other sustainable raw materials, sound farming practices, clean technology and responsible industrial investment, production and marketing practices.

Psychoactive Cannabis

Introduction

by Ed Rosenthal

HEMP AND MARIJUANA are products of different varieties of the same plant species, *Cannabis Sativa*. In other countries, hemp is a crop considered separate from psychoactive marijuana. For instance, in France, where there is strict enforcement of marijuana laws, hemp has been grown in two areas of the country, Le Mans and Troyes in Brittany. In England, marijuana laws have remained in force while hemp production has restarted.

In the U.S., hemp and marijuana were linked legally for political reasons and considered related issues by the public. Today applications for growing industrial, non-psychoactive hemp are considered by the Drug Enforcement Administration. Therefore it is unrealistic to discuss one issue without at least a cursory glance at the other.

The marijuana issue can be separated into two components: medical and recreational use. These two issues are wisely delineated by the public. For instance, every local resolution regarding medical use has won. In San Francisco, a resolution sponsored by marijuana-gay activist, Dennis Peron[1] won by the widest margin of any proposition in the city's history, over 79%.

Although the margins of victory would not be as wide in other parts of the country, it does translate to majorities in most states. Twenty seven states have passed have passed medical marijuana laws. The reason for this is that almost nobody wants to deny a person medicine that can relieve pain or suffering.

If marijuana were to be legalized for medical use, the list of ailments and symptoms which it could be used for would be enormous. The U.S. Pharmacopia pre-prohibition had a five page discussion of its uses. These include, anti-nausea, anti-spasmodic, lowering blood pressure, treatment of glaucoma, anorexia, bulimia, tranquilizer, sedative and as anti-depressant.

Loss of profits may be the reason that many pharmaceutical companies sponsor "anti-drug" campaigns. Their incentive to oppose medical use of marijuana is well founded. Given the choice, many people would choose this simple herbal remedy rather than high priced, less effective and more contra-indicative patented pharmaceuticals.

Recreational use is much more controversial and has been used to keep all forms of *cannabis* illegal. It is not the purpose of this book to enter a debate on either the ethics of criminal or civil regulation of marijuana use or of the sociological issues surrounding it. However, under the standard definition of addiction, marijuana must be considered a relatively benign substance.

The American Psychological Association and the U.N. World Health organization list a number of characteristics to consider when determining addictive qualities.[2] These are:

1.) Loss of Control—Use of the drug more often and in larger quantity than intended.

2.) Unsuccessful attempts to quit.

3.) Excessive time seeking substance.

4.) Intoxication or withdrawal at inappropriate times.

5.) Sacrifice of other pleasures for it.

6.) Use despite knowledge of harm.

7.) Tolerance to the substance. More is required to satisfy needs.

8.) Withdrawal symptoms.

9.) Drug taking to relieve withdrawal.[3]

As shown in the charts below marijuana is not considered especially addictive and appears to be among the least serious drugs.

Ratings by Dr. Jack Henningfield, National Institute on Drug Abuse

Substance	Withdrawal	Reinforcement	Tolerance	Dependence	Intoxication
Nicotine	3	4	2	1	5
Heroin	2	2	1	2	2
Cocaine	4	1	4	3	3
Alcohol	1	3	3	4	1
Caffeine	5	6	5	5	6
Marijuana	6	5	6	6	4

1 = Most serious   6 = Least serious

Ratings by Dr. Neal L. Benowitz, U. of California, San Francisco

Substance	Withdrawal	Reinforcement	Tolerance	Dependence	Intoxication
Nicotine	3	4	4	1	6
Heroin	2	2	2	2	2
Cocaine	3	1	1	3	3
Alcohol	1	3	4	4	1
Caffeine	4	5	3	5	5
Marijuana	5	6	5	6	4

1 = Most serious   6 = Least serious

Most marijuana aficionados consider the law to be the most dangerous part of marijuana use. Comparable studies of other drug users show that they recognize the inherent dangers of the substances they use. This is a good indication that marijuana users have come to similar conclusions as addiction experts.

At some point the U.S. government will probably follow the Dutch example, tolerating use of cannabinoids. This will occur after a serious evaluation of the effects of psychoactive substance relative to the laws used to regulate it. When society finally weighs the harm and benefits of marijuana as compared with the effects of the laws the conclusion to legalize will not be difficult.

If marijuana were used only for medical purposes under strict regulations, it would become a multi-billion dollar industry. This is based on its efficacy as a medicine in treating so many medical problems. Robert Clarke and Dave Pate's chapter, "Medical Marijuana" references its many uses. They show that there is an extremely large body of data on its use as a treatment. It is clear from the article that Cannabis can serve many medical uses for humankind.

Used recreationally, the industry would grow much larger. Dale Gieringer's article, "Economics of Cannabis Legalization" uses a standard economic formula to gain a perspective on the economic potential of the industry. He shows that the potential tax revenues and enforcement savings could be quite significant.

"Economics of Marijuana" is a detailed study of the costs of prohibition and the potential economic benefits of legalization. It was written in 1981. Some of the monetary figures are low due to inflationary pressures since that time. They remain proportionally accurate, however. The article details most of the costs of the present policy and the advantages to the economy of a civil regulatory system.

These three articles show that legalization of the psychoactive form of Cannabis either for medical use only or for medical and recreational use would result in considerable benefit to the country. Since the European countries have started to move to a harm reduction paradigm regarding drugs, it is only natural that they are changing the laws regarding Cannabis use. In the future, during a different swing of the pendulum, the laws in the U.S. will change. A major industry will literally be born overnight.

Medical Marijuana

by Robert C. Clarke and David W. Pate

CANNABIS IS A PLANT with worldwide distribution, yielding fiber and food, as well as a psychoactive drug. The flowers have been used as a medicine for millennia. Investigation of its major chemical components has revealed their utility for the treatment of a wide variety of diseases. *Delta*-9-tetrahydrocannabinol is currently approved as an oral prescription drug for the treatment of nausea and vomiting associated with cancer chemotherapy and for appetite stimulation in cases of *anorexia* associated with AIDS. However, many patients find that smoking *cannabis* offers a superior route of administration and therefore illicitly self-medicate.

Introduction

For those not familiar with marijuana and in need of it for medical purposes, the prospect of consuming an illicit drug may seem rather daunting. However, marijuana is used by 20–30 million people in the U.S. and many times that number worldwide, under completely uncontrolled circumstances, with little apparent harm. It is the world's fourth most popular recreational drug behind caffeine, alcohol and nicotine. Unlike these latter drugs, *cannabis* in not addictive and no one in

(Note: This article appeared in the Journal of the International Hemp Association, *Vol. 1 No. 1, June 1994)*

the several thousand year history of its use is known to have died from its effects.

The intent of this article is to provide the prospective medical user with an introduction to this drug as a possible therapeutic option. The basis of our subject start with the realization that this much-discussed drug, like many of the others we consume, is from a plant with an interesting natural history.

Cannabis, the Plant

Cannabis is a dioecious annual producing approximately equal numbers of male and female plants. Marijuana comes from the flower-associated bracts of female *Cannabis*. The male plant is much less useful for this purpose. Almost all of the *Cannabis* found worldwide is classified as *Cannabis sativa*. Many taxonomists argue that *C. indica* and *C. ruderalis* are also valid species names (Emboden 1974, Schultes *et al.* 1974) although this remains controversial (Small and Cronquist 1976). However, even accounting for these additional species, 95% of the cultivated *Cannabis* in the world would still be classified as *Cannabis sativa*.

As it grows well at low temperatures, *Cannabis* is well adapted to temperate climates (van der Werf 1994). Ancient northern Asian and European societies used *Cannabis* mostly for its fiber and seed. It is also an aggressive weed plant at higher latitudes worldwide. South Asian and African cultures used *Cannabis* mostly for its drug content, and the frost-free climates allowed more time for development of the psychoactive resin. Intense levels of ambient ultraviolet radiation and of insect predation in the tropics may also have contributed to a natural selection for these drug types (Pate 1983). In any case, *Cannabis* has evolved into two basic races. Plants grown for fiber and seed are universally called "hemp." Cannabis grown for its drug content is commonly called "marijuana" or "drug *Cannabis*." Its female flower bracts are covered with numerous small resin glands containing the pharmacologically active cannabinoids (Fig. 1) that are unique to this genus.

FIGURE 1.

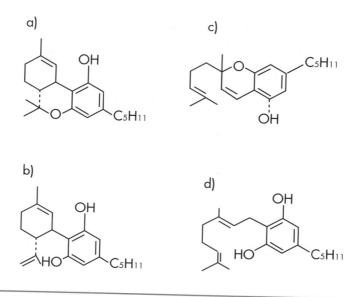

a)

c)

b)

d)

Some cannabinoids, a) THC, delta-9-tetrahydrocannabinol;
b) CBC, cannabichromene; c) CBD, cannbidiol; d) CBG, cannabigerol.

Most of the psychoactive properties of marijuana can be attributed to its content of a cannabinoid (Fig. 1a) named *delta*-9-tetrahydrocannabinol (THC). In some literature, it is designated as *delta*-9-tetrahydrocannabinol due merely to a conflict between two methods of naming chemicals, but it is the very same molecule. Modern hemp varieties are nearly devoid of THC and, therefore, cannot be practically diverted into the drug trade. Hemp has been heavily selected for high fiber content, high stalk yield, high seed yield, and low (<0.3%) inflorescence THC content (DeMeijer et al. 1992). Drug-type *Cannabis* varies widely in THC content from approximately 1–2% in unselected strains to over 10% in the best modern varieties (Watson 1994). It is not feasible to 'get high' on hemp, and most marijuana produces very little low-quality fiber. Hemp should never be confused with marijuana, as their roles cannot be reversed.

Cannabis, the Medicine

Cannabis has been recognized for centuries as a valuable therapeutic agent. Folk uses of *Cannabis* include treatment of insomnia, inflammation, various psychoses, digestive disorder, depression, rheumatism, migraine, neuralgia, fatigue, constipation, diarrhea, parasites, appetite disorders and it has also been employed by women to facilitate childbirth, stimulate lactation, and relieve menstrual cramping (Mechoulam 1986). These traditions continue in every region where *Cannabis* is available. Modern Western *Cannabis* users also frequently claim relief from many of these same medical complaints.

Cannabis or THC have been used experimentally to effectively lower the elevated intraocular pressure of glaucoma (Adler and Geller 1986) and have shown potential for the treatment of alcoholism (Rosenburg 1976) and drug dependence (Hine *et al.* 1975). THC has been used as a bronchodilator for the relief of asthma symptoms (Graham 1986) and may also be effectively used as an analgesic for pain relief (Segal 1986). It has even been shown to have antibacterial properties (Van Klingeren and Ten Ham 1976).

The low toxicity of THC is best indicated by its widespread use with very few reports of anything even approaching an overdose. Occasionally, people may get too 'high' for their psychic comfort, but their bodies continue to function fairly normally. The dosage sufficient to kill half of the organisms tested (LD_{50}) for orally ingested THC is approximately 1 g/kg of body weight. Simply interpreted, this means an average sized human would have to consume 50–100 g of pure THC to reach the LD_{50} level. Since high-potency *Cannabis* contains approximately 10% THC, a person would have to eat at least 500–1,000 grams of this marijuana before having a 50% chance of death. A 1 gram marijuana cigarette of 10% THC *Cannabis* contains 100 mg of THC and is usually shared among several smokers. Clinically effective oral doses for the relief of nausea start at 5–10 mg. This means that, even accounting for pyrolytic decomposition and smoke loss, there is a several-thousandfold difference between an effective does of THC and a potentially lethal one! For alcohol, this difference is only about twentyfold. Other common non-prescription drugs, such as aspirin, have similar relatively narrow margins of safe use. Research into the actions of the natural cannabinoids led to the creation of many artificial ones based on variations of their basic molecular structure. However, none of these artificial compounds are currently approved for medical use in the U.S. Nabilone proved to be toxic to laboratory test animals and in 1978, human tests were suspended, although it is available in Canada, Switzerland and the United Kingdom as Cesamet,® Levonathrodal, another synthetic cannabinoid analog, was not approved for use in the U.S., also following incidents of toxicity in test animals.

Other natural cannabinoids (Fig. 1b–d), such as cannabichromene (CBC), cannabidiol (CBD) and cannabigerol (CBG) have been shown to have potential therapeutic value, and can be isolated from both non-psychoactive as well as psychoactive *Cannabis* varieties, Epilepsy, multiple sclerosis, dystonias, and other neurological disorders have been experimentally treated with CBD (Consroe and Snider 1986). CBD has also been shown to relieve anxiety, especially the minor anxiety occasionally associated with the medical use of THC (Zuardi *et al.* 1982). CBC, CBD, and CBG and related analogs have been shown to have anti-microbial action (ElSohly *et al.* 1982, Van Klingeren and Ten Ham, 1976). These non-psychoactive compounds are generally not restricted by international regulations prohibiting *Cannabis* and THC.

Various delivery systems for these cannabinoids, such as suppositories, time release encapsulation, eye drops, nasal sprays, aerosols, topical ointments, and transdermal patches will eventually become available. Several such cannabinoid delivery systems have already been patented (*e.g.*, ElSohly 1990, Hussain 1984).

The only cannabinoid medicine currently available in the U.S. is a synthetic THC encapsulated in sesame oil (generically known as 'Dronabinol'). It is sold under the trade name Marinol® as a Schedule II controlled substance (allowing restricted prescription, similar to morphine and cocaine) and was afforded a narrow, specific legal exemption from the Schedule I status of other *Cannabis* products (forbidden from clinical use). It has been accepted and prescribed in the United States since 1985 as an anti-emetic to treat the nausea associated with cancer chemotherapy (Levitt 1986). Use as an appetite stimulant to correct the weight loss related to *anorexia* in AIDS patients was approved by the

U.S. Food and Drug Administration on December 22, 1992 (Anonymous 1992). THC is not a cure for cancer or AIDS, but helps to relieve suffering and improve quality of life, perhaps prolonging the lives of those afflicted. THC may also eventually win approval as a general appetite stimulant for *anorexia nervosa* and other appetite disorders.

Before other cannabinoids or *Cannabis* can become available to patients in the U.S., they must be similarly rescheduled. This also applies to the non-psychoactive compounds or even an otherwise identical, by *plant*-derived THC medicine! On April 29, 1991, the UN Commission on Narcotic Drugs decided that *delta*-9-tetrahydrocannabinol should be transferred from Schedule I to Schedule II of the 1971 Convention on Psychotropic Substances to facilitate its therapeutic use. Similar rescheduling in each member country would allow doctors to prescribe it as a medicine and permit easier research. This has already been accomplished in England and Germany. Patients claim there is an acute need to reform the laws concerning other *Cannabis* products, especially in response to the medical plight of thousands of cancer and AIDS patients. If economic incentives could be created by liberalizing outdated anti-*Cannabis* laws and streamlining new drug registration and testing procedures for AIDS related medicines, several new *Cannabis* medicines would appear on the market within the next few years.

Currently, in the U.S., the cost of a single dose of Marinol® ranges between $4.00 and $8.00 and the average patient cost ranges from $12.00 to $32.00 per day. Since Marinol® is expensive, narrowly prescribed and often less effective than crude *Cannabis* preparations, potent sinsemilla-type (seedless) marijuana remains the most viable form of *Cannabis* medicine, despite the fact that its illegality artificially inflates its cost. Physicians learned as much from their patients and began to publish guidebooks on the appropriate medical use of *Cannabis* (*e.g.*, Roffman 1982), which is most often smoked or consumed in baked goods.

In some respects, it may be unfortunate that *Cannabis* has played such a prominent role in the American media's coverage of the counterculture movement since the 1960s. The popularization of *Cannabis* as the drug of choice increased its exposure to the general public, but government disinformation promoted the mainstream culture's confusion of it with hard drugs. It has been difficult for even the more knowledgeable patients and practitioners to view *Cannabis* as a genuine medicine rather than merely a recreational drug. Of course, many doctors are also reluctant to suggest *Cannabis* use because it is illegal. Marinol® is too expensive for many patients to afford and orally ingested anti-emetics are of questionable value because their application must be carefully timed to avoid vomiting the drugs. Many patients who both smoke *Cannabis* and swallow Marinol® report that THC absorbed through the lungs offers more immediate relief, better dose titration, fewer side-effects and shorter duration of action.

Conclusions

For millennia, *Cannabis* has been used as an effective medicine. Modern research has revealed that clear potential for this plant and its cannabinoid products to resume their place in the pharmacopoeia. Further work is urgently needed to determine how *Cannabis* can be best utilized as a clinical tool. Meanwhile, cancer and AIDS patients and members of the medical marijuana movement have taken responsibility for their own health and self-medicate without a doctor's prescription.

Economics of Cannabis Legalization

by Dale Gieringer, Ph.D.

MARIJUANA LEGALIZATION offers an important advantage over decriminalization in that it allows for legal distribution and taxation of cannabis. In the absence of taxation, the free market price of legal marijuana would be extremely low, on the order of five to ten cents per joint. In terms of intoxicating potential, a joint is equivalent to at least $1 or $2 worth of alcohol, the price at which cannabis is currently sold in the Netherlands. The easiest way to hold the price at this level under legalization would be by an excise tax on commercial sales. An examination of the external costs imposed by cannabis users on the rest of society suggests that a "harmfulness tax" of $.50–$1 per joint is appropriate. It can be estimated that excise taxes in this range would raise between $2.2 and $6.4 billion per year. Altogether, legalization would save the taxpayers around $8–$16 billion, not counting the economic benefits of hemp agriculture and other spinoff industries.

The Case for Legalization

As drug war hysteria subsides it becomes increasingly clear that there must be a serious re-examination of the laws prohibiting marijuana. The decriminalization of soft drugs has now emerged as an active political issue in Australia, England, France, Germany, Italy, and Switzerland. The policies being considered range from "decriminalization," or repeal of criminal penalties for private use and cultivation of cannabis, to full "legalization," in which cannabis is commercially sold like alcohol, tobacco and other commodities.

Decriminalization has enjoyed impressive support from a succession of official panels, including the Presidential Commission on Marijuana, the California Research Advisory Panel, and the Canadian Le Dain Commission. Decriminalization was also officially the policy of the state of Alaska from 1976 through 1990, when it was narrowly overturned in a referendum. The basic appeal of decriminalization is to reduce the harm of criminal punishment and respect personal freedom and privacy, while avoiding offensive commercialization. The basic flaw in decriminalization is that it does not make allowance for pot users who cannot or will not grow their own. The result is to create an illicit black market for cannabis that is neither regulated nor taxed, leaving many of the same basic enforcement problems as prohibition.

These problems can be avoided by legalization, under which cannabis could be legally sold, taxed and regulated like alcohol or tobacco. (It should be noted that legalization need not involve the evils of commercialization, given suitable restrictions on advertising). The world presently has no example of a completely legalized cannabis market, since this is forbidden by the Single Convention Treaty on Narcotics. The nearest approximation may be seen in the Netherlands, which officially tolerates the possession and sale of up to 30 grams of hashish or marijuana in coffeehouses, although distribution and manufacture are technically illegal and large-scale traffickers are punished. The apparent success of the Dutch in controlling hard drug abuse without a major hashish abuse epidemic has led a league of 15 European cities to endorse the principle of legalized cannabis in the so-called Frankfurt Resolution. An important advantage of legalization is to open the door to taxation of marijuana—a potentially valuable source of public revenue—while eliminating the need for an illegal market.

In the following, we will examine more closely the economics of a legalized cannabis market.

The Cheapest Intoxicant

In an untaxed free market, cannabis ought to be as cheap as other leaf crops. Bulk marijuana might reasonably retail at the price of other medicinal leaf herbs, around $.75–$1.50 an ounce. Premium grades might be compared to fine teas, which range up to $2 per ounce, or to pipe tobacco, which retails for $1.25–$2.00. High grade domestic sinsemilla might however cost somewhat more, due to the relatively lower yield of cannabis compared to tea and tobacco, and the high level of U.S. labor costs. Cultivation expert Ed Rosenthal estimates that domestic labor costs could be as high as $5 per ounce for top grades from boutique gardeners. Advertisements from medical catalogs indicate that cannabis cost about $2.50–$5 per pound in 1929–30.[1] Adjusting for inflation, this works out to $1.20–$2.40 per ounce, a breathtaking 100- to 300-fold reduction from today's illicit prices, which range from $100–$200 per ounce for low-grade Mexican to $400–$600 per ounce for high-grade sinsemilla.

It is useful to translate these prices to a per-joint basis, where one joint is defined to represent the standard dosage of marijuana. The number of joints in an ounce depends on the potency of the product involved, where potency is measured in terms of the concentration of tetrahydrocannabinol (THC), the chief psychoactive ingredient in marijuana. THC potencies typically range from 2–3% for low-grade leaf to 10% or more for premium sinsemilla buds. We will define a standard dose of THC to be that contained in the government's own marijuana joints, which NIDA supplies to researchers and selected human subjects. These consist of low-quality 2.5%–3% potency leaf rolled into cigarette-sized joints of 0.9 grams, yielding a 25 milligram dose of THC. The same dose can be had in a slender one-third or one-quarter gram joint of 10–12% sinsemilla. A typical joint has been estimated to weigh about 0.4 grams.[2] Taking this as a standard, we will define a "standard joint" to be 0.4 grams of average-quality 6% buds. Thus an ounce of "standard pot" equals 60 joints, an ounce of 12% sinsemilla 120, and an ounce of government pot only 30 joints. Due to the fact that the price of marijuana tends to be proportional to potency, the price of a one-quarter gram joint of $600-per-ounce sinsemilla is about the same as a one-gram joint of $150-per-ounce low-grade import, that is around $6.

We have seen that, in the absence of taxation, the price of legal marijuana would be cut by a factor of 100 or more. At this rate, a joint costing $6 today would cost about 6¢ in a free legal market. It therefore appears that marijuana would be a very cheap bargain compared to other intoxicants, including alcohol.

The free-market price of joints can also be calculated by comparison to tobacco cigarettes, which would probably cost about the same to manufacture. Cigarettes now sell at an average of $1.83 per pack, or 9¢ per cigarette, one-quarter of which represents federal and state taxes.[3] There is no reason to think that joints could not be sold for the same price under legalization.

At a nickel per joint, marijuana would be a uniquely economical intoxicant. For only one-half dollar per day, a marijuana user could nurse a whopping ten-joint per day habit. It may be doubted whether public opinion would tolerate so low a price for marijuana. On one hand, it would invite extensive abuse. Parents would no doubt object against making a serious marijuana habit so affordable for their young. Moreover, cheap marijuana would also pose a serious challenge to the alcohol industry, a powerful political interest, whose products are over ten times as expensive. In order to make legalization politically palatable, it would almost certainly be necessary to raise the price through taxation or regulation.

Putting a Value on Cannabis

One way to estimate a reasonable price for marijuana is to evaluate it in comparison to the major competing intoxicant, alcohol. While it is impossible to make an exact comparison between pot and booze, since their duration and effects are different and dosages vary from person to person, a joint might be roughly equated to an intoxicating dose of alcohol—between one and two ounces, or two to four drinks. Thus one joint might be worth two to four 12-oz. beers or $1/3–2/3$ bottle of wine. These are currently sold on grocery shelves at a minimum price of around $1.50–$2.50. It may therefore be concluded that a reasonable minimum price for marijuana should be around $1.50–$2.50 a joint, with higher prices for premium grades. This works out to $90–$150 per ounce for standard 6% potency marijuana.

Coincidentally, this price range is in line with that presently seen in the Netherlands, where coffeehouses sell hashish and sinsemilla by the gram for 4 to 15 guilders, or $2.15–$8.10.[4] Taking the cheaper grade to yield two joints per gram and the premium grade four, this works out to $1 to $2 per joint. The fact that the Dutch have not been plagued by widespread cannabis abuse and indeed believe they have obtained public health benefits from their system provides reassurance that this price level is realistic.[5]

It should be noted that Dutch prices are inflated by the fact that cannabis remains illegal, not by any form of legal taxation (though the state does tax cannabis indirectly through the sales tax on cafes). Although Dutch authorities tolerate a number of small-scale domestic producers, international traffickers and domestic distributors are both subject to busts at the whim of the police. As a result, Dutch consumers pay inflated black market prices. This is not necessarily the optimal model for marijuana price control, since the lion's share of the profits go to illicit traffickers.

In a legalized market, the easiest way to maintain marijuana prices would appear to be through some form of excise tax, as presently imposed on alcohol and tobacco. This could conveniently be assessed on licensed manufacturers or wholesalers, like the federal tax on cigarettes. Aside from a strict prohibition against sales to unlicensed distributors, cultivators need not be directly regulated. Excise taxes have the advantage of being easy to enforce, since they involve a relatively small number of distributors. The latter in turn pass the tax along with a markup, magnifying the price increase throughout the distribution chain.

Another way to control the market would be to tax or regulate cultivation. However, experience shows that it is no easy task to track down and regulate marijuana growers. More so than alcohol or tobacco, marijuana lends itself easily to small-scale home cultivation and production. The problem therefore arises as to how to treat home cultivation in the legal market. Clearly, the sale of untaxed home marijuana must be banned. In theory, home cultivation could also be taxed and licensed in order to maintain high prices. However, it seems unlikely that such requirements could be enforced in a world of legalized marijuana. The policing of home growers would appear to require many of the most odious and objectionable techniques of current marijuana enforcement, such as helicopter surveillance, snooping on homes and spying on garden stores.

The most practical policy is thus likely to be the one most consistent with principles of personal freedom and civil liberties, namely to let Americans grow their own cannabis at home, just as they might grow tomatoes, apples or grapes or brew beer or wine. The inducements to home cultivation should not be exaggerated: in Alaska, where it was the one legal way to get marijuana before 1991, pot continued to be sold illicitly at prices around $250 an ounce, proof that many pot smokers are quite disinclined to grow on their own. Nonetheless, home cultivation would effectively put a lid on the amount marijuana could be taxed, since consumers would be induced to grow their own if prices rose too high.

Another possible way to limit marijuana abuse would be to regulate consumers directly, for instance, by requiring "user's licenses" for the right to buy or use marijuana, as proposed by Kleiman.[6] By charging fees for these licenses, the state could raise tax revenues. User fees are apt to be more costly to administer than excise taxes, since they must be collected from a much wider population. More importantly, they are also apt to be unenforceable, given the ease with which unlicensed users can grow their own at home. One situation in which user fees might be attractive would be under a regime of decriminalization, where commercial sales were illegal. Consumers might then be allowed to purchase a license to consume and grow marijuana for personal use. In this system, licenses would afford the one opportunity for the government to derive tax revenues from marijuana, while an active marijuana surveillance program would still be needed to prevent commercial sales and unlicensed use.

The problem of cannabis enforcement was first rigorously addressed one hundred years ago by the British Indian Hemp Drugs Commission.[7] The commission concluded that cannabis prohibition was not practicable, and that the best solution was to tax it to the extent possible. After examining the different regulatory systems in various provinces of India, the Commission especially recommended the system in Bengal, where cannabis was taxed more rigorously than in other provinces by means of a system of excise fees and vendors' licenses. Noting that hemp drugs tended to be much cheaper than liquor, the Commission argued that cannabis was undertaxed.[8] It also noted that there were regions where cannabis grew wild, in which it was virtually impossible to control traffic in bhang, a low-potency beverage made from leaves. Cannabis remained legal in India until 1989 under provisions of the Single Convention Treaty on Narcotics.

Computing a Harmfulness Tax

The question might well be asked from a libertarian free-market perspective why cannabis (or other drugs) should be taxed in the first place. Why should government concern itself with regulating what is in essence a private decision, that is, what kind of drugs to ingest? Why shouldn't prices simply be settled by supply and demand?

The best answer is that marijuana consumption may impose costs on innocent third parties who do not consume it. According to standard economic theory, such "external costs" may be compensated by means of a harmfulness tax.[9] Examples of external costs of drug abuse include increased insurance costs, accidents affecting third parties, and drug-induced violence and criminality. In principle these costs must be distinguished from "internal costs" that fall on the user, such as ill-health, reduced personal income, poor achievement, etc. Because users already pay for the latter, there is no sense in making them pay again through a tax.

From a non-libertarian, public health perspective, higher taxes are often justified simply as a disincentive to prevent people from over-indulging in what is presumably an unhealthy habit. This argument is most persuasive in the case of highly addictive drugs such as nicotine, where naive users run a high risk of getting themselves trapped in an unhealthy habit due to initial misjudgment. Punitive taxation appears less justifiable in the case of cannabis, not only because it has low addictivity, but also because of the ease with which home growers can evade excessive taxes.

In the following discussion, we will examine the external costs of marijuana abuse as the basis for a prospective harmfulness tax. At the outset, it should be noted that much further epidemiological research is needed to accurately assess the costs of marijuana; nonetheless, it is possible to hazard a guess at their magnitude. Overall, the general scientific consensus is that marijuana has definite deleterious effects, though less so than alcohol or tobacco. In the words of the California Research Advisory Panel: "An objective consideration of marijuana shows that it is responsible for less damage to society and the individual than are alcohol and cigarettes."[10]

From a physiological standpoint, the major health risk of heavy marijuana use appears to be respiratory harm due to smoking.[11] A recent epidemiological study by the Kaiser Permanente Center for Health Research found that daily cannabis smokers had a 19% higher rate of respiratory complaints.[12] Aside from cases of passive smoking, these must be counted as internal costs, except to the extent that they may raise group health insurance costs for others. (There are actually good grounds to believe that legalization would reduce the costs of respiratory damage from marijuana smoking by encouraging the development of better smoke filtration technology, the substitution of more potent, less smoke-producing varieties of marijuana, and the substitution of oral preparations for smoked marijuana.)

More important than the respiratory harm of marijuana is the increased risk of accidents due to mental impairment. In the Kaiser study, this emerged as the number one hazard of marijuana use, with daily users reporting a 30% higher rate of injuries than non-users. Presumably, these injuries reflected an increased risk of accidents that might also involve third parties. Hence, accidents should probably be counted as the major external cost of marijuana use. Other concerns, such as amotivation, poor school performance and the controversial "gateway drug" syndrome are more properly classified as internal costs.

In order to quantify the external costs of marijuana, it is useful to consider those of alcohol and tobacco. These are shown in Table 1, based on an analysis by W. Manning et al.[13] aimed at estimating the appropriate level of taxation for alcohol and cigarettes. Manning's analysis shows how the health costs imposed on the insurance system by tobacco- and

TABLE 1.—EXTERNAL COSTS OF DRUG USE

	CIGARETTES (pack of 20)*	ALCOHOL (1 excess oz.)*	MARIJUANA (1 joint)
Net Health Costs	$ 0.15 smoking diseases $ 0.23 passive smoking	$ 0.26	$ 0.01–.02 smoking
Accidents		$0.93	$0.38-0.93
Total	$0.38	$1.19	$0.40-0.95

* Source: Manning et al., "The Taxes of Sin: Do Smokers and Drinkers Pay Their Way?," JAMA 261:1604-9.

alcohol-related illness tend to be counterbalanced by the fact that smokers and drinkers die younger, and therefore collect fewer pension and retirement benefits.

In the case of tobacco, Manning estimates the gross cost of medical care for smoking-related diseases at 26¢ a pack, or just over one penny per cigarette. This turns out to be largely compensated by savings in retirement pensions and nursing home care for smokers. The final balance is highly sensitive to technical assumptions about the economic discount rate, and can even be made to show net external benefits at interest rates under 3%. Manning's final net estimate of 15¢ per pack assumes a 5% interest rate.

By estimating the equivalency between joints and cigarettes, one can translate these costs to marijuana. On a weight-for-weight basis, pot smokers inhale about four times as much noxious tars as cigarette smokers;[14] as we have seen, however, the average joint weighs about half as much as a cigarette. Also, cannabis lacks nicotine, a leading factor in tobacco-related heart disease. It seems reasonable on this basis to suppose that a joint is equal to less than two cigarettes, putting the net external cost of marijuana smoking at under 1.5¢ per joint.

One fault in Manning's accounting of external costs is that it excludes the costs of second-hand smoking, which he estimates at 23¢ per pack, on the questionable grounds that these costs are mainly internal to the users' families. We treat them here as external costs instead. There are grounds to think that passive smoking is of much less concern with cannabis since pot smokers emit less smoke than cigarette smokers. It therefore seems reasonable to conclude that the total smoking-related costs of active and passive pot smoking are unlikely to exceed two cents per joint.

Turning to alcohol, Manning concludes that the net medical-less-pension costs of alcoholism-related disease are 26¢ for every "excess ounce" of alcohol, which is defined to mean an ounce in excess of one per day (Manning does not try to account for the possibility that moderate consumption may actually extend life). These costs turn out to be greatly outweighed by the cost of alcohol-related accidents, which he estimates at 93¢ per excess ounce. This figure includes traffic accidents to third parties caused by drunken drivers, but does not appear to include other alcohol-related accidents. Also missing from Manning's account are the external costs of alcohol-related violence. Altogether, Manning concludes that the total cost of alcohol is $1.19 per excess ounce, or 48¢ per ounce when averaged over all alcohol drunk.

While the cost of alcohol seems clearly dominated by accidents, it is unclear how to relate these to marijuana. The burden of expert opinion appears to be that marijuana is less of an accident risk than alcohol, though this is disputed.[15] Studies of fatal car accidents indicate that, at least on the road, marijuana tends to be a secondary risk factor compared to alcohol.[16] On the other hand, one survey of trauma patients found that, with respect to all accidental injuries, cannabis may be every bit as much a risk factor as alcohol.[17] In terms of intoxicating potential, one joint probably lies between one ounce and one excess ounce of alcohol. At the high end, if one equates a joint with one excess ounce, the accident costs of pot would be 93¢ per joint. More reasonably, one could equate a joint with an "average" ounce of alcohol, the accident costs of which work out to 38¢. There are reasons to favor a lower external cost on marijuana relative to alcohol, notably the fact that marijuana tends to suppress violence, whereas alcohol tends to aggravate it. From this perspective alone, an overall shift from alcohol to marijuana may be desirable.

In conclusion, one can reasonably argue that marijuana should be assessed a harmfulness tax of 40¢ to 95¢ per joint—or, say, 50¢–$1 in round figures. Experience indicates these taxes would probably be magnified at least twofold in the market, resulting in a minimum retail price of $1–$2 per joint.[18] Happily, this is consistent with the target price range we derived previously.

Different lines of reasoning thus converge to argue that cannabis should be taxed at 50¢ to $1 per joint. That is $15–$30 per ounce for low-grade 3% leaf or $30–$60 per ounce for 6% standard cannabis. Ideally, the tax rate per ounce should be proportional to THC potency. In practice, this could be implemented through a schedule of fixed product categories similar to those used for alcohol (beer, wine and hard liquor). These categories might include: (1) leaf (potency <3%), (2) standard blend cannabis (4–10% potency), and (3) high-grade sinsemilla or hashish (potency >10%). Other cannabis-based products, such as hashish, hash oil, tonics and foodstuffs, could be taxed according to their leaf or bud content. It should be noted that low-grade leaf, though harsh for smoking, could play a valuable role in the market as a source for cooked preparations and extracts, which are likely to play an increasing role in the market as health-conscious consumers seek to avoid smoking.

Revenues From Legalization

Assuming a tax of 50¢ or $1 per joint, we can venture a rough estimate of the revenues that could be raised from legalized cannabis. According to the 1991 National Household Survey on Drug Abuse, some 19.5 million Americans used marijuana at least once in the year, of whom 5.3 million used at least once a week and 3.1 million daily. About one-half of the latter are thought to be multiple-daily users, who can be expected to make up the bulk of total consumption.[19] Assuming the mean consumption of all daily users is two or three joints per day, current national consumption can be figured to exceed 7 to 10 million joints per day, or 1200 to 1800 metric tons of 6% THC cannabis per year. These figures may well be low, since the Household Survey underestimates actual use. A considerably higher estimate is given by Kleiman, who puts 1986 consumption at the equivalent of 2700 metric tons of 6% THC cannabis; other trafficking-based estimates range as high as 4700 tons.[20]

Consumption would surely expand further in a legal market where joints were freely and cheaply available. At the height of marijuana's popularity around 1979, consumption was over twice that of today. One factor that could significantly expand the demand for legal cannabis in the future would be the development of mild cannabis beverages like bhang, which traditionally constituted the bulk of demand in India. It is therefore not unreasonable to forecast ultimate consumption at 15–30 million joints per day, or 2,750–5,500 metric tons of 6% THC cannabis per year.

The obvious question remains what portion of consumption would be absorbed by home growers. As we have seen, it is probably hopeless to limit personal use cultivation. Home growing would naturally be most attractive to heavy users with little money, who probably account for a major share of consumption. At $2 per joint, a three-joint per day habit would cost over $2000 a year, a hefty incentive for any home gardener. It therefore seems likely that home cultivation would absorb a substantial portion of the consumption of multiple daily users, who are estimated to account for 60% of the total market.[21]

We shall estimate the size of the commercial cannabis market by posing two price scenarios. (1) Given a 50¢ excise tax and a minimum price of $1 per joint, we will assume that home growing absorbs 20% of consumption (that is, one-third of the consumption of multiple daily smokers), leaving a commercial demand of 12–24 million joints per day. This works out to about $2.2 to $4.4 billion per year in tax revenues. (2) Given a $1 excise tax and a price over $2 per joint, we assume commercial consumption would be cut by 40% to 918 million joints, yielding $3.2 to $6.4 billion per year. We conclude that revenues from cannabis excise taxes might range from $2.2 to $6.4 billion per year. This is comparable to the revenues currently raised through the federal tax on alcohol ($8 billion) and cigarettes ($5 billion).

By comparison, in the Netherlands, a nation of 15 million people, total domestic sales of soft drugs have been estimated at under 1 billion guilder, or $500 million.[22] Extrapolating this to the U.S. population, one arrives at total retail sales of about $8 billion. If one-half of this went to taxes, one would get $4 billion per year.

Similarly, in Bengal, with a population of 50 million, the Indian Hemp Drugs Commission reported total tax revenues from ganja of 24 million rupees in the year 1892–3, or about $10 million (1892 dollars).[23] Extrapolated fivefold to the current U.S. population, this would work out to $700 million in 1992 currency. The tax on ganja was about 8 rupees per kilo in Bengal, or just 4¢ per joint in current dollars.[24] Were the tax increased tenfold to the level we have proposed, revenues would presumably increase to $7 billion, minus a substantial amount due to decreased demand from higher prices.

In addition to excise taxes, states could impose sales taxes on cannabis. Unlike excise taxes, sales taxes would be proportional to final retail price, including the added markup for premium brands. Just like alcohol, it can be expected that marijuana would often be sold for substantially more than its minimum price: in a hotel bar, a good sinsemilla joint might well go for $5. Assuming average retail prices of $1.50–$2.50 per joint, and sales taxes between 4% and 6%, the total revenues raised might range from $200 million to $1.3 billion.

In addition, legalization would create numerous revenue-generating spinoff industries, such as coffee houses, gardening equipment and paraphernalia. The city of Amsterdam, with a million people, boasts 300 coffee houses retailing cannabis.[25] Translated to the U.S, this would amount to over 60,000 retailers and 100,000 jobs.

Finally, the legalization of cannabis would also permit the agriculture of hemp, a versatile source of fiber, protein, biomass and oil, which was once one of America's top crops. Hemp production might well rival that of other leading crops such as cotton or soy beans, which are currently on the order of $6–10 billion per year.

On the other side of the ledger, legalization would save the considerable economic and social costs of the current criminal prohibition system. Current federal drug enforcement programs run at $13 billion per year. State and local programs are probably of similar or greater magnitude: in California, the Legislative Analyst's Office estimated the cost of state drug enforcement programs at around $640 million per year in 1989–90, plus perhaps twice as much more in local expenditures.[26] A sizable chunk of these costs involve cannabis, which accounts for 30% of drug arrests nationwide. Legalization of cannabis would also divert demand from other drugs, resulting in further savings. If legalization reduced current narcotics enforcement costs by one-third to one-fourth, it might save $6–$9 billion per year.

TABLE 2—ECONOMIC BENEFITS OF CANNABIS LEGALIZATION

Excise Taxes	$2.2–$6.4 Billion
Sales Taxes	$0.2–$1.3 Billion
Enforcement Savings	$6–$9 Billion
Hemp Industry	$6–$10 Billion
Others	Spinoff industries Reduced hard-drug and alcohol abuse

The economic benefits of marijuana legalization are summarized in Table 2. The total direct savings to government in taxes and enforcement come to some $8–$16 billion per year. These figures are somewhat lower than those sometimes bandied about in public discourse, as both legalizers and prohibitionists have a tendency to make consumption estimates that are, in our opinion, inflated. Nonetheless, the benefits of legalization seem both substantial and undeniable, and deserve to be taken seriously.

Economics of Marijuana

by Ed Rosenthal

In 1977 the DEA estimated that the marijuana industry grossed $48,000,000,000.[1] In 1981 we estimate real gross income at $43,000,000,000. It is probably among the top 15 industries in the United States based on dollar volume.[2]

About two thirds of the marijuana sold in this country is imported.[3] Principal exporting nations producing marijuana for the U.S. are Colombia, Mexico, Thailand and Jamaica. Total marijuana imports come to about $3.2–4 billion.[4]

If marijuana were legal, the risk factor incidental to contraband substances would be eliminated, so that the cost of the substance would probably go down significantly. The marijuana industry is one of the only truly competitive industries in the United States. The price of the substance is determined solely by supply and demand. There is easy entrance and exit from the market; that is, anyone can become a dealer or quit dealing.

There are no cartels or interests which control a significant percentage of market share (at least domestically); there are no monopolies or oligarchies as are found in most industries in the U.S. where 2 to 5 corporations control a significant share of the market. Although not engaged in anti-competitive practices, in reality these companies set prices higher than one finds in a truly competitive market.

Part of the price that consumers pay is a "premium" for the risk factor associated with pursuing an illegal enterprise. To make it worth the risk, there must be a higher profit potential than in legal businesses or there would be no incentive to enter the market. The sellers are compensated directly by the government since dealers pay virtually no taxes on their profits. In higher tax brackets, that alone could be significant.

If the risk were eliminated through regulation, part of the premium now paid to dealers would be paid to the government as excise tax. Uneconomic factors associated with illegal enterprises would be eliminated.

When prohibition was eliminated, the cost of alcohol plummeted to about a third of its black market cost. When formerly contraband substances were re-introduced into the legal marketplace, their cost was reduced between 30–80%; for example, costs of abortions were reduced about 80% and prices of formerly banned books reduced about 30%.

Using a conservative estimate of 50% reduction in marijuana prices to the consumer if it were regulated, the marijuana industry based on present users would gross $22 billion a year. Under a regulatory model there would probably be a slight increase in usage because of increased availability so that the industry could probably yield somewhere between $30–35 billion a year. Federal excise, manufacturing taxes, licenses, and fees could generate about $7–9 billion a year. It has been observed that marijuana is one of the largest tax-exempt industries in the country today and regulation would end that exemption.[5]

State licensing, taxes and fees could generate about $4–6 billion a year. And these are only the direct revenues that could be generated by regulation. Indirect revenues, from taxes generated by sales of paraphernalia, recreational establishments, and new industries, would increase the totals considerably. New cannabis-related industries might include seed and nursery stock, specialized grower's supplies, cultural events, video and movie documentaries, nightclubs and food related products.

The ripple effect of the marijuana industry has already spread to various communities. In the 1960s, Humboldt County, California, was considered economically depressed. Its main industry, logging, had virtually closed down. With no new major legal industries, Humboldt is now considered one of California's most prosperous areas although the reported per-capita income of the residents does not reflect that prosperity. The county is in the heart of sinsemilla country and all the businesses in the county are supported by growers' spending. Land values have also increased astronomically.

Several states and the federal government have recently sought to "tax" the profits of the marijuana industry by seizing profits and other valuables used in the commission of illegal acts or purchased by virtue of the gains of them, but this new source of revenue can easily be abused by the authorities and lead to further corruption of the system. One can easily imagine that government agents might seek to entrap or frame an individual who has property or valuables desired by the government. Given prosecution's leeway regarding entrapment, the government would be able to successfully pick on virtually any property holder in the United States.

The authority to confiscate property is based on a 1970 federal law allowing the seizure of land and property gained as a result or proved to be involved in illegal drug trafficking. Once local authorities make an arrest under state law, the local U.S. attorney seeks a forfeiture order which is granted by a federal judge. Once forfeited, the land becomes government property and could be sold at auction after the destruction of the marijuana crop.

The efforts to seize growers' land gives cultivators a disincentive to use their own property. Instead, they seek out public lands on which to plant. This has become such a serious problem that Senate hearings were held September 29, 1982, by the Forestry Subcommittee of the Agriculture Committee to discuss it. At the hearing, Frank Monastero, administrator for operations of the DEA said that "the amount cultivated on federal lands is increasing and is now between 30 and 50% of the total [marijuana cultivated in the United States].[6]

F. Dale Robertson of the U.S. Forest Service has said, "Almost every national forest reported marijuana cultivation during the 1981 growing season."[7]

At least 1,500,000 people are employed full or part time in the marijuana industry. Their total net income probably comes to about $22,000,000,000 a year. There are approximately 65,000,000 Americans who regularly or occasionally light up a joint. Obviously, all marijuana-use statistics are extrapolated from small samples or are best estimates. The NAS Study cites statistics showing that 19.6% of the adult population has used marijuana and 68% of young adults between 18–25 have tried it. The total U.S. population is currently about 230,000,000. Of those 65,000,000, approximately 1 out of every 4 or 5 people (about

13–16 million) purchase marijuana regularly. Twenty-five percent of the users grow their own or homegrown cultivated by friends. Twenty-five percent smoke only when turned on by someone else. Each purchase serves approximately 2 consumers. The others receive it as gifts, share it with friends, or cultivate it. The average retail dealer has approximately 15–20 customers so that there are about 1 million retail dealers. There are approximately 200,000 people who cultivate commercially, 300,000 people in wholesale distribution, and approximately 50,000 involved in importing or distribution on a high level. If the average retail dealer's medial wage is figured at $10,000 per year (many are part timers), their total net income comes to about $10,000,000,000 a year.

The small percentage of the market which the domestic crop holds makes it the fourth largest domestic agricultural crop after corn, soybeans and wheat.[8] A more impressive statistic is given in *Newsweek*'s article "Guns, Grass—and Money," which claims that marijuana is the third largest cash crop grown domestically, after corn and soybeans. Estimated gross revenues to marijuana farmers comes to $8.5–10 billion a year or 5–6.2% of total legal gross revenues which came to $166.7 billion in 1981.[9]

As a percentage of net farm income, marijuana revenues are even higher. On $10 billion revenue, estimated profits are $6.5 billion. The average pound is sold for $1,000–$1,200 by the farmer. In 1981 total farm income came to $25.1 billion; marijuana as a percentage of net farm income came to 25.9%.

Most farmers do not grow marijuana; the laws leave only a small minority to reap the harvest. As with any industry which functions outside the mainstream economy, this one is molded into some unusual patterns. While large farms are being foreclosed at near record levels, marijuana farmers who grew 25–50 plants sometimes earn $30,000–$50,000 a year.

It would seem that allowing farmers to grow marijuana would help save many small farms and provide many jobs since marijuana farming and preparation are very labor-intensive. Some farmers have already begun cultivating marijuana: "$2,000 for one marijuana plant sure beats the price of beans and corn," according to C.C. Maddox of the Missouri State Patrol. Another lawman, Sheriff Yale Jarvis of Washington County,

Iowa, said, "If you put out one acre of marijuana, you can make more than on your entire farm operation."[10]

The group that probably profits most by the marijuana laws per capita are the lawyers. Even a simple possession bust is liable to cost the victim $500 to $2,000 in legal fees. Attorney Norman Kent said that in south Florida, "Misdemeanors start at $1,000. Felonies start at $2,500. A fortune of wasted money." Interviewed October 28, 1982. Mr. Kent is a graduate of the Hofstra School of Law on Long Island, a former law professor and is currently in private practice in Ft. Lauderdale, Florida. Cases in which the prosecution tries to prove distribution or conspiracy cost much more.

For the most part, marijuana users have little experience with the judicial system, so that they are often prey to incompetent attorneys who overcharge them or who do not represent them properly.

Over $125,000,000,000 is billed per year for legal fees in defense of marijuana cases. $125,000,000,000 is a conservative estimate. There are 400,000 arrests. If each person arrested uses a lawyer and the average cost for legal fees is $300–$2,000, billings will be between $120,000,000 and $800,000,000. Of course, not everyone is lucky enough to hire a private lawyer. If only 20% or 80,000 people who are arrested use private legal services at an average cost of $1000, a total of $80,000,000 would be billed. Sales cases are much more costly to the defendant; total billings for these types of cases comes to more than for possession cases.

The government agencies most affected by law enforcement are the various federal and state police and customs agencies which use about $2.7 billion a year on enforcement attempts. The total cost of law enforcement, including police protection, judicial, legal, defense, and corrections services for the year 1979 was $25.9 billion.[11]

Total arrests in the U.S. in 1981 were 8,512,697. There were 400,300 marijuana arrests in 1981, or 4.7% of all arrests. 4.7% of $25.9 billion is $1.2 billion. However, the specialized law enforcement arms such as the DEA, the use of the military and many specialized eradication teams bring up the cost by at least $1.5 billion. On this very same issue, NORML estimates that over $3 billion in law enforcement resources are spent annually on marijuana arrests and prosecution.[12]

Since these agencies function with a total budget which has been eroded by inflation and the mounting tide of lawlessness, money spent on marijuana enforcement detracts from the total monies available to fight violent crime.

The California Bureau of Narcotic Enforcement (BNE) has field offices in seven California counties. In fiscal year 1979–1980 they made a total of 2,269 drug-related arrests. In 1980 the total BNE budget came to $8,221,000, or about $3,623 per arrest. The Buy-Program, using 12,348.5 agent hours, made 292 arrests thereby expending 42 agent hours per arrest.[13] This does not include the cost of legal proceedings, incarceration, or police fringe benefits. Fringe benefits alone are generally figured at three times salary. A truer accounting figure of arrest costs would be much higher.

There are over 20 federal agencies enlisted in the fight against marijuana use. These include: FBI, CIA, DEA, Immigration & Naturalization Department, Navy, Air Force, Army, Agriculture Department, Customs, Post Office, U.S. Forestry Service, Department of Education, Department of Health and Welfare, Coast Guard, IRS, NASA, Commerce Department, Interstate Commerce Commission, National Institutes of Mental Health, and the Treasury Department.

Costs of enforcement include costs of educational programs, arrests, incarceration and judicial proceedings but they do not reflect the indirect costs of those laws. Not surprisingly, in 1976 when the state of California decriminalized penalties for marijuana possession of one ounce or less, they estimated they may have saved as much as $74 million per year over what the state had previously been spending to enforce the laws.

In 1970, an act of Congress created the formation of what is now called the "Shafer Commission," an inquiry group specifically charged to examine the usage of marijuana in the United States. The commission's purpose was to investigate the increasing use of marijuana and make recommendations for governmental action. It was so-named because Raymond Shafer, former governor of Pennsylvania, headed the commission. In March, 1972, the commission issued their report to the public, entitled *Marijuana: A Signal of Misunderstanding, the Technical Papers of the First Report of the National Commission on Marijuana and Drug Abuse*. It was a massive and comprehensive effort, published in two volumes of 1,252 pages. At the time of its release, it was widely hailed by human rights activists, lawyers, and members of the medical community for its fair and logical conclusions and suggestions. President Richard M. Nixon said that he tossed the report in a wastebasket without reading it. In an interview with Governor Shafer on January 20, 1983, he said, "I am proud of that report. I stand by it and I am satisfied that it helped to initiate change in the laws."

Probably as a direct result of the recommendations of the Shafer Commission Report, 13 states with 50% of the nation's population decriminalized marijuana to varying extents. According to their figures, over 82% of those individuals arrested for marijuana law violations had jobs or went to school, and fully 87% of them were permanent residents of their localities.[14]

The average marijuana arrestee who does not make bail, about 40%: is incarcerated about 45 days before trial and loses 30 days of work due to the arrest. Figuring the arrestees' income at a median salary of $8,853 per year. Mean income for U.S. workers is $10,429; median income is $8,853.[15]

The arrestee loses $1,062.36 in salary and the country loses $169,977,600 in productivity.

There is no doubt that the marijuana industry is here to stay and is part of this nation's economic life. This industry, unlike almost every other, is subject to no government regulation regarding consumer protection, quality of product, distribution, import controls and taxation.. If the government keeps the marijuana industry illegal it will continue to produce revenue and profits, but the U.S. economy will continue to be the loser. If it remains unregulated the economic benefits will not accrue to society. The industry will persist as a costly expense to the taxpayers who pay for the judicial and penal systems. No tax revenue will be generated from what is presently a $43 billion a year industry. The government will continue to give the marijuana industry the biggest tax exemption in the history of the United States. But the revenue losses from industries now illegal, such as hemp cultivation, are incalculable.

Summary

by Ed Rosenthal

A LIE CAN ONLY BE USED for so long before cracks appear in its smooth surface. Truth's roots go deep to support the young shoot as it hits light. Even after a seventy year "big lie" propaganda campaign, the truth could not be buried. The book, *The Emperor Wears No Clothes* and Jack Herer's long-running author tour renewed interest in the subject.

Now that hemp is actually an issue on the table, it is extremely important that there is a reliable source of information on the subject. That is the purpose of this book: to provide a factual, reality based report on hemp.

The authors have expressed their varied perspectives. Dave West's history showed how restrictions were used to eliminate hemp as a serious industrial crop. This conspiracy of special interests used fear and deception to stop hemp cultivation for most of the twentieth century. Even with the force of industry and government opposed to it, truth willed out. The hemp industry is flourishing in the U.S. based upon imports of cloth, seed and now fiber. Retail demand has been a strong impetus.

Some of the authors express doubts about some of the theories in Herer's book. David Walker's partial literature review questions hemp's biomass potential. Lynn Osburn, a researcher and editor of *The Emperor*, defends his theory. "Hemp Realities" presents tables showing biomass potential of many domesticated plants. The essay concludes that hemp has a great future, but not as a biomass plant.

Despite controversy regarding its use as biomass, hemp's potential contributions to humanity continue to brighten. Reports on the fiber, seed and wood substitute potential indicate a renewable resource from a reliable crop. As the costs of other cellulose based materials rise, hemp will become more competitive.

Hemp has some qualities not found in other materials. The fiber is the longest and one of the strongest in the plant kingdom. The seeds contain essential oils which are especially well balanced for human health. They also have a high protein content. The hurd can be used as a wood substitute for processed boards and animal bedding as well as paper. As research resumes after a 70 year hiatus many more uses are sure to be found.

The national reports show hemp at the cusp. Except in France, where the cigarette paper industry has gradually expanded, hemp production was in decline all over the world. Hemp hit its nadir around 1992 and has been in an upward curve since. In 1994 total acreage and production was higher than ever before. This trend will continue as more manufacturers find uses for hemp products. Consumer response to hemp products has been warm.

Hemp Today was written as the hemp industry was being reborn. Most of the reports will remain current for only a few years. Yet it serves an extremely important service: to present a realistic assessment of hemp and the hemp industry now and in the near future. The fact that the writers disagree is actually a positive sign. It shows an industry growing large enough to accommodate widely divergent views and perspectives.

In a few years we will probably be viewing a much different industry. Hemp will be grown in Canada and the U.S. as well as Europe, Asia and Australia. It will become a major agricultural commodity and raw material for food processors, fiber and pulp industries. Hemp will be a prime candidate for use as a hybrid product combining an agricultural product with industrial processing. New technologies not yet foreseen will insure its continued use.

Appendix

Appendix
Selection of Articles

by Ed Rosenthal

THE ARTICLES IN THE APPENDIX were chosen for their relevance to modern hemp investigations. The information they contain provides an invaluable backgound for further research.

In choosing these articles we sifted through an incredible wealth of documents. Hemp treatises date back to the seventeenth century. However, the more recent material, from the early twentieth century is probably of most interest.

"Hemp," the 1913 Dept. of Agriculture *Yearbook* article, written by Lyster H. Dewey, is one of the most accurate monographs written on hemp cultivation and processing. Although harvesting and processing methods have changed, most of the article's descriptions remain relevant.

"Hemp" by B.B. Robinson, *Farmer's Bulletin 1935*, was revised by the Dept. of Agriculture in 1952. Although it covers much of the same ground as Dewey's "Hemp," it shows the modernization of farming techniques. The article is cited in some of the articles in the book.

U.S.D.A. Bulletin #404 by Jason Merrill was written in 1916. It was in response to the warnings by forest researchers that trees were being harvested at three times the rate they were growing. The *Bulletin* is cited as a reference in *The Emperor Wears No Clothes* and is important in showing that the government knew about the potential of hemp as a paper source.

The European Economic Community (EEC) agreement on hemp is a description of the requirements hemp must meet to be legally grown there.

The EEC offers a seed oil subsidy which makes hemp production very attractive to farmers.

The Isochanvre article shows how hemp can be used as a building material. The company has produced material used to build ovver 800 structures. This is a promising new material for construction.

"Revolutionizing An Industry," a 1921 *Scientific American* article, shows that the high labor costs associated with hemp were being tackled early in the century.

The "New Billion Dollar Crop," an article printed in *Popular Mechanics* Magazine in 1937 shows that even a half century ago one of the major obstacles to efficient hemp production was solved. It implies that the industry could have supplied a natural renewable resource to meet many of the country's industrial and commercial needs.

"Hemp Wood as a Papermaking Material" by C.J. West from the *Paper Trade Journal*, shows that there was intensive research in hemp papermaking more than 70 years ago. The technology had already been developed. It was only the interests of the mill and forest owners which prevented its use.

"Hemp for Victory" was a film produced by the Dept. of Agriculture to induce farmers to grow hemp during WWII, when supplies of imported fibers were cut off. The text of the film paints a bright picture of hemp as a crop. This transcript was taken directly from the film. Fifty years later, the words ring true.

ARTICLE REPRINTED FROM
YEARBOOK OF THE U.S. DEPARTMENT OF AGRICULTURE 1913

Hemp

By Lyster E. Dewey,
Botanist in Charge of Fiber-Plant Investigations,
Bureau of Plant Industry.

Introduction

The two fiber-producing plants most promising for cultivation in the central United States and most certain to yield satisfactory profits are hemp and flax. The oldest cultivated fiber plant, one for which the conditions in the United States are as favorable as anywhere in the world, one which properly handled improves the land, and which yields one of the strongest and most durable fibers of commerce, is hemp. Hemp fiber, formerly the most important material in homespun fabrics, is now most familiar to the purchasing public in this country in the strong gray tying twines one-sixteenth to one-fourth inch in diameter, known by the trade name "commercial twines."

Name

The name "hemp" belongs primarily to the plant *Cannabis sativa.* (Pl. XL, fig. 1.) It has long been used to designate also the long fiber obtained from the hemp plant.(Pl. XL, fig.4.) Hemp fiber, being one of the earliest and best-known textile fibers and until recent times the most widely used of its class, has been regarded as the typical representative of long fibers. Unfortunately, its name also came to be regarded as a kind of common name for all long fibers, until one now finds in the market quotations "Manila hemp" for abaca, "sisal hemp" for sisal and henequen, `"Mauritius hemp" for Furcreaea fiber, "New Zealand hemp" for phormium, "Sunn hemp" for Crotalaria fiber, and "India hemp" for jute. All of these fibers in appearance and in economic properties are unlike true hemp, while the name is never applied to flax, which is more nearly like hemp than any other commercial fiber.

The true hemp is known in different languages by the following names: *cannabis*, Latin; *chanvre*, French; *cañamo*, Spanish; *canhamo*, Portuguese; *canapa*, Italian; *canep*, Albanian; *konopli*, Russian; *konopj* and *penek*, Polish; *kemp*, Belgian; *hanf*, German; *hennup*, Dutch; *hamp*, Swedish; *hampa*, Danish; *kenevir*, Bulgarian; *ta-ma*, *si-ma*, and *tse-ma*, Chinese; *asa*, Japanese; *nasha*, Turkish; *kanabira*, Syrian; *kannab*, Arabic.

Importance of Hemp

Hemp was formerly the most important long fiber, and it is now used more extensively than any other soft fiber except jute. From 10,000 to 15,000 tons are used in the United States every year. The approximate amount consumed in American spinning mills is indicated by the following table, showing the average annual importations[1] and estimates of average domestic production of hemp fiber for 35 years:

Average annual imports and estimates of average annual production of hemp fiber in 5-year periods from 1876 to 1910, inclusive, and from 1911 to 1913, inclusive:

Years	Imports	Production in United States	Total
	Tons	Tons	Tons
1876 to 1880	459	7,396	7,855
1881 to 1885	5,393	5,421	10,814
1886 to 1980	10,427	8,270	18,697
1891 to 1805	4,962	5,631	10,593
1806 to 1900	4,985	5,177	10,162
1901 to 1905	4,577	6,175	10,752
1906 to 1910	6,375	5,150	11,525
1911 to 1913	5,982	5,100	11,082

There are no statistics available, such as may be found for wheat, corn, or cotton, showing with certainty, the acreage and production of hemp in this country. The estimates of production in the production in the foregoing table are based on the returns of the commissioner of Agriculture of Kentucky for earlier years with amounts added to cover the production in other States, and on estimates of hemp dealers for more recent years. While these figures can not be regarded as accurate statistics, and they are probably below rather than above the actual production, especially in the earlier years, they indicate a condition well recognized by all connected with the industry. The consumption of hemp fiber has a slight tendency to increase, but the increase is made up through increased importation, while the domestic production shows a tendency toward reduction.

Production in United States Declining

This falling off in domestic production has been due primarily to the increasing difficulty in securing sufficient labor to take care of the crop;

secondarily, to the lack of development of labor-saving machinery as compared with the machinery for handling other crops and to the increasing profits in raising stock, tobacco, and corn, which have largely taken the attention of farmers in hemp-growing regions.

The work of retting, breaking, and preparing the fiber for market requires a special knowledge, different from that for handling grain crops, and a skill best acquired by experience. These factors have been more important than all others in restricting the industry to the bluegrass region of Kentucky, where the plantation owners as well as the farm laborers are familiar with every step in handling the crop and producing the fiber.

An important factor, tending to restrict the use of hemp, has been the rapidly increasing use of other fibers, especially jute, in the manufacture of materials formerly made of hemp. Factory-made woven goods of cotton or wool, more easily spun by machinery, have replaced the hempen "homespun" for clothing; wire ropes, stronger, lighter, and more rigid, have taken its place in standing rigging for ships; abaca (Manila hemp), lighter and more durable in salt water, has superseded it for towing hawsers and hoisting ropes; while jute, inferior in strength and durability, and with only the clement of cheapness in its favor, is usurping the legitimate place of hemp in carpet warps, so-called "hemp carpets," twines, and for many purposes where the strength and durability of hemp are desired.

The introduction of machinery for harvesting hemp and also for preparing the fiber, together with the higher prices paid for hemp during the past three years, has aroused an interest in the industry, and many experiments are being tried with a view to the cultivation of the crop in new areas.

BOTANICAL STUDY OF HEMP

The Plant

The hemp plant, *Cannabis sativa* L.,[2] is an annual, growing each year from the seed. It has a rigid, herbaceous stalk, attaining a height of 1 to 5 meters (3 to 16 feet), obtusely 4-cornered, more or less fluted or channeled, and with well-marked nodes at intervals of 10 to 50 centimeters (4 to 20 inches). When not crowded it has numerous spreading branches, and the central stalk attains a thickness of 3 to 6 centimeters (1 to 2 inches), with a rough bark near the base. If crowded, as when sown broadcast for fiber, the stalks are without branches or foliage except at the top, and the smooth fluted stems are 6 to 20 millimeters (1/4 to 3/4 inch) in diameter. The leaves, oppo-

site, except near the top or on the shortened branches, appearing fascicled, are palmately compound and composed of 5 to 11—usually 7—leaflets. (Pl. XLI, fig. 1.) The leaflets are dark green, lighter below, lanceolate, pointed at both ends, serrate, 5 to 15 centimeters (2 to 6 inches) long, and 1 to 2 centimeters (3/8 to 3/4 inch) wide. Hemp is dioecious, the staminate or pollen-bearing flowers and the pistillate or seed-producing flowers being borne on separate plants. The staminate flowers (Pl. XL, fig. 2) are borne in small axillary panicles, and consist of five greenish yellow or purplish sepals opening wide at maturity and disclosing five stamens which discharge abundant yellow pollen. The pistillate flowers (PL. XL, fig. 3) are stemless and solitary in the axils of the small leaves near the ends of the branches, often crowded so as to appear like a thick spike. The pistillate flower is inconspicuous, consisting of a thin, entire, green calyx, pointed, with a slit at one side, but remaining nearly closed over the ovary and merely permitting the two small stigmas to protrude at the apex. The ovary is one seeded, developing into a smooth, compressed or nearly spherical achene (the "seed"), 2.5 to 4 millimeters (1/10 to 3/16 inch) thick and 3 to 6 millimeters (1/88 to 1/4 inch) long, from dark gray to light brown in color and mottled (Pl. XLI, fig. 2). The seeds cleaned for market nearly always include some still covered with the green, gummy calyx. The seeds vary in weight from 0.008 to 0.027 gram, the dark-colored seeds being generally much heavier than the light-colored seeds of the same sample. The light-colored seeds are often imperfectly developed. Dark-colored and distinctly mottled seeds are generally preferred.

The staminate plants are often called the flowering hemp, since the pistillate flowers are rarely observed. The staminate plants die after the pollen is shed, but the pistillate plants remain alive and green two months later, or until the seeds are fully developed.

The Stalk

The hemp stalk is hollow, and in the best fiber-producing types the hollow space occupies at least one-half the diameter. The hollow space is widest, or the surrounding shell thinnest, about midway between the base and the top of the plant. The woody shell is thickened at each node, dividing the hollow space into a series of partly separated compartments. (Pl. XLI, fig. 4.) If the stalk is cut crosswise a layer of pith, or thin-walled tissue, is found next to the hollow center, and outside of this a layer of wood composed of hard, thick-walled cells. This layer, which forms the "hurds," is a very thin shell in the best fiber-producing varieties. It extends clear across the stem below the lowest node, and in large, coarse stalks grown in the open it is much thicker and the central hollow relatively smaller. Outside of the hard woody portion is the soft cambium, or growing tissue, the cells of which develop into the wood on the inside, or into the base that bark o the outside. It is chiefly through this cambium layer that the fiber-bearing bast splits away from the wood in the processes of retting and breaking. Outside of the cambium is the inner bark, or bast, comprising short, thin-walled cells filled with chlorophyll, giving it a green color, and long thick-walled cells, making the bast fibers. These bast fibers are of two kinds, the smaller ones (secondary bast fibers) toward the inner portion making up rather a short, fine fibers, many of which adhere to the wood or hurds when the hemp is broken, and the coarser ones (primary bast fibers) toward the outer part, extending nearly throughout the length of the stalk. Outside of the primary bast fiber is a continuation of the thin-walled chlorophyll-bearing cells free from fiber, and surrounding all is the thin epidermis.

The Fiber

The hemp fiber of commerce is composed of the primary bast fibers, with some adherent bark and also some secondary bast fiber. The bast fibers consist of numerous long, overlapping, thick-walled cells with long, tapering ends. The individual cells, almost too small to be seen by the unaided eye, are 0.015 to 0.05 millimeter (1/1000 to 13/1000 inch) in diameter, and 5 to 55 millimeters (3/16 to 2 1/8 inches) long. Some of the bast fibers extend through the length of the stalk, but some are branched, and some terminate at each node. They are weakest at the nodes.

Relationships

The hemp plant belongs to the mulberry family, Moraccae, which includes the mulberry, the Osage orange, the paper mulberry, from the bast of which the tapa of the South Sea Islands is made, and the hop, which contains a strong bast fiber. Hemp is closely related to the nettle family, which includes ramie, an important fiber-producing plant of Asia, and several species of nettles having strong bast fibers.

The genus Cannabis is generally regarded by botanists as monotypic, and the one species *Cannabis sativa* is now held to include the half dozen forms which have been described under different names and which are cultivated for

Fig. 17—Chinese character ma, the earliest name for hemp.

different purposes. The foregoing description refers especially to the forms cultivated for the production of fiber.

HISTORY

Early Cultivation in China

Hemp was probably the earliest plant cultivated for the production of a textile fiber. The "Lu Shi," a Chinese work of the Sung dynasty, about 500 A.D., contains a statement that the Emperor Shen Nung, in the twenty-eighth century B.C., first taught the people of China to cultivate "ma" (hemp) for making hempen cloth. The name ma (fig 17) occurring in the earliest Chinese writings designated a plant of two forms, male and female, used primarily for fiber. Later the seeds of this plant were used for food.[3] The definite statement regarding the staminate and pistillate forms eliminates other fiber plants included in later times under the Chinese name ma. The Chinese have cultivated the plant for the production of fiber and for the seeds, which were used for food and later for oil, while in some places the stalks are used for fuel, but there seems to be no record that they have used the plant for the production of the narcotic drugs bhang, charas, and ganga. The production and use of these drugs were developed farther west.

Cultivation For Narcotic Drugs

The use of hemp in medicine and for the production of the narcotic drug Indian hemp, or cannabis, is of interest in the paper only because of its bearing on the origin and development of different forms of the plant. The origin of this use is not definitely known, but the weight of evidence seems to indicate central Asia or Persia and a date many centuries later than its first cultivation for fiber. The name *bhanga* occurs in the Sanskrit "Atharvavéda" (about 1400 B.C.), but the first mention of it as a medicine seems to be in the work of Susruta (before the eighth century A.D.), while in the tenth century A.D. its intoxicating nature seems to have been known, and the name "indracana" (Indra's food) first appears in literature.[4] A further evidence that hemp, for the production of fiber as well as the drug, has been distributed from central Asia or Persia is found in the common origin of the names used. The Sanskrit names "bhanga" and "gangika," slightly modified to "bhang" and "ganja," are still applied to the drugs, and the roots of these words, "ang" and "an," recur in the names of hemp in all of the Indo-European and modern Semitic languages, as bhang, ganja, hanf, hamp, hemp, chanvre, canamo, kannab, cannabis.[5]

Hemp in India

Northern India has been regarded by some writers as the home of the hemp plant, but it seems to have been unknown in any form in India before the eighth century, and it is now thought to have been introduced there first as a fiber plant. It is still cultivated to a limited extent for fiber in Kashmir and in the cool, moist valleys of the Himalayas, but in the warmer plains regions it is grown almost exclusively for the production of the drugs.[6]

Hemp was not known to the Hebrews nor to the ancient Egyptians, but in medieval times it was introduced into North Africa, where it has been cultivated only for the drug. It is known in Morocco as "kif," and a small form, 1 to 3 feet high, cultivated there has been described as a distinct variety, *Cannabis sativa kif*.[7]

Introduction into Europe

According to Herodotus (about 450 B.C.), the Thracians and Scythians, beyond the Caspian Sea, used hemp, and it is probable that the Scythians introduced the plant into Europe in their westward migration, about 1500 B.C., though it seems to have remained almost unknown to the Greeks and Romans until the beginning of the Christian era. The earliest definite record of hemp in Europe is the statement that "Hiero II, King of Syracuse (270 B.C.), bought hemp in Gaul for the cordage of his vessels."[8] From the records of Tragus (1539 A.D.), hemp in the sixteenth century had become widely distributed in Europe. It was cultivated for fiber, and its seeds were cooked with barley and other grains and eaten, through it was found dangerous to eat too much or too frequently. Dioscorides called the plant *Cannabis sativa*, a name it has continued to bear to the present time, and he wrote of its use in "making the stoutest cords" and also of its medicinal properties.[9] Nearly all of the early herbalists and botanical writers of Europe mention hemp, but there is no record of any further introduction of

importance in the fiber industry until the last century.

Introduction of Chinese Hemp into Europe

In 1846 M. Hébert sent from China to the Museum at Paris some seeds of the "tsing-ma" great hemp, of China. Plants from this seed, grown at Paris by M. L. Vilmorin, attained a height of more than 15 feet, but did not produce seeds. In the same year M. Itier sent from China to M. Delile, of the Garden at Montpellier, France, seeds of a similar kind of hemp. These seeds were distributed in the southern part of France, where the plants not only grew tall, some them measuring 21 feet, but they also produced mature seeds. M. Delile called this variety *Cannabis chinensis*[10] and the one from the seeds sent by M. Hébert, he called *C. gigantea*.[11] These two forms of hemp were regarded as the same by M.L. Vilmorin, who states that they differ very much in habit from the common hemp of Europe, which was shorter and less valuable for fiber production. We are also told that this chanvre de Chine did not appear to be the same as the chanvre de Piedmont,[12] the tall hemp of eastern France and northern Italy, the origin of which has sometimes been referred to this introduction, but this may have originated in a previous introduction, since *Cannabis chinensis* is mentioned as having been in the Botanical Garden at Vienna in 1827. In the same statement, however, *C. sativa pedemontana* is described as a distinct variety.[13] Particular attention is called to the introduction of this large Chinese hemp into Europe, since it was doubtless from the same source as the best hemp seed now brought from China to the United States.

Introduction into South America

Hemp from Spain was introduced into Chile about 1545.[14] It has been largely grown in that country, but at present its cultivation is confined chiefly to the fertile lands in the valley of the Rio Aconcagua, between Valparaiso and Los Andes, where there are large cordage and twine mills. The fiber is all consumed in these mills.

Introduction into North America

Hemp was introduced into New England soon after the Puritan settlements were established, and the fact that it grew "twice so high" as it did in old England was cited as evidence of the superior fertility of the soil of New England.[15] A few years later a writer in Virginia records the statement that "They begin to plant much Hempe and flax which they find growes well and good."[16]

The cultivation of hemp in the New England colonies, while continued for some time in Massachusetts and Connecticut, did not attain as much importance as the cultivation of flax for supplying fiber for household industry. In the South hemp received more attention, especially from the Virginia Legislature, which passed many acts designed to promote the industry, but all in vain.[17]

The cultivation of hemp seems to have been a flourishing industry in Lancaster County, Pa., before the Revolution. An elaborate account of the methods then employed in growing hemp, written about 1775 by James Wright, of Columbia, Pa.,[18] was recently published as an historical document. The methods described for preparing the land were equal to the best modern practice, but the hemp was pulled by hand instead of cut. Various kinds of machine brakes had been tried, but they had all "given Way to one simple Break of a particular Construction, which was first invented & made Use of in this country." The brief description indicates the common hand brake still in use in Kentucky.

Early Cultivation in Kentucky

The first crop of hemp in Kentucky was raised by Mr. Archibald McNeil, near Danville, in 1775.[19] It was found that hemp grew well in the fertile soils of the bluegrass country, and the industry was developed there to a greater extent than it had been in the eastern colonies. While it was discontinued in Massachusetts, Virginia, and Pennsylvania, it has continued in Kentucky to the present time. In the early days of this industry in Kentucky, fiber was produced for the homespun cloth woven by the wives and daughters of the pioneer settlers, and an export trade by way of New Orleans was developed. In 1802 there were two extensive ropewalks in Lexington, Ky., and there was announced "a machine, moved by a horse or a current of water, capable, according to what the inventor said, to break and clean eight thousand weight of hemp per day."[20] Hemp was later extensively used for making cotton-bale covering. Cotton bales were also bound with hemp rope until iron ties were introduced, about 1865. There was a demand for the better grades of hemp for sailcloth and for cordage for the Navy, and the industry was carried on more extensively from 1840 to 1860 than it has been since.

Extension of the Industry to other States

Hemp was first grown in Missouri about 1835, and in 1840 1,600 tons were produced in that state. Four years later the output had increased to 12,500 tons, and it was thought that Missouri would excel Kentucky in the production of this fiber. With the unsatisfactory methods of cleaning the fiber on hand brakes and the difficulties of transporting the fiber to the eastern markets, hemp proved less profitable than other crops, and the industry was finally abandoned about 1890.

Hemp was first grown at Champaign, Ill., about 1875. A cordage mill was established there for making twines from the fiber, which was prepared in the form of long tow by a large machine brake. The cordage mill burned and the industry was discontinued in 1902 because there was no satisfactory market for the kind of tow produced.

In Nebraska, hemp was first grown at Fremont in 1887 by men from Champaign, Ill. A binder-twine plant was built, but owing to the low price of sisal, more suitable for binder twine, most of the hemp was sold to eastern mills to be used in commercial twines. After experimenting with machine brakes the company brought hand brakes from Kentucky and colored laborers to operate them. The laborers did not stay, and the work was discontinued in 1900. Some of the men who had been connected with the company at Fremont began growing hemp at Havelock, near Lincoln, in 1895. A machine for making long tow, improved somewhat from the one at Champaign, was built. Further improvements were made in the machine and also in the methods of handling the crop, but the industry was discontinued in 1910, owing to the lack of a satisfactory market for the kind of tow produced.

Hemp was first grown on a commercial scale in California at Gridley, in Butte County, by Mr. John Heaney, who had grown it at Champaign and who devised the machine used there for making long tow. Mr. Heaney built a machine with some improvements at Gridley, and after three disastrous inundations from the Feather River moved to Courtland, in the lower Sacramento Valley, where the reclaimed lands are protected by dikes. The work is now being continued at Rio Vista, in Solano County, under more favorable conditions and with a machine still further improved. The hemp fiber produced in California is very strong and is generally lighter in color than that produced in Kentucky.

In 1912 hemp was first cultivated on a commercial scale under irrigation at Lerdo, near Bakersfield, Cal., and a larger acreage was grown there in 1913. The seed for both crops was obtained in Kentucky.

Introduction of Chinese Hemp into America

In 1857 the first Chinese hemp seed was imported. It met with such favor that some of this seed is said to have brought $10 per quart. [21] Since that time the common hemp of European origin has given place in this country to the larger and better types from China.

Geographical Distribution

The original home of the hemp plant was in Asia, and the evidence points to central Asia, or the region between the Himalayas and Siberia. Historical evidence must be accepted rather than the collection of wild specimens, for hemp readily becomes naturalized, and it is now found growing without cultivation in all parts of the world where it has been introduced. Hemp is abundant as a wild plant in many localities in western Missouri, Iowa, and in southern Minnesota, and it is often found as a roadside weed throughout the Middle West. De Candolle[22] writes of its origin as follows:

The species has been found wild, beyond a doubt, south of the Caspian Sea (De Bunge); in Siberia, near the Irtysch; and in the Desert of Kirghiz, beyond Lake Baikal, in Dahuria (Government of Irkutsh). It is found throughout central and southern Russia and south of the Caucasus, but its wild nature here is less certain. I doubt whether it is indigenous in Persia, for the Greeks and Hebrews would have known of it earlier.

Hemp is now cultivated for the production of fiber in China, Manchuria, Japan, northern India, Turkey, Russia, Austria-Hungary, Italy, France, Belgium, Germany, Sweden, Chile, and in the United States. It is grown for the production of the drugs bhang, ganja, kif, marihuana, hasheesh, etc., in the warm, arid, or semiarid climates of India, Persia, Turkey, Algeria, central and southern Africa, and in Mexico, and for the production of seed for oil in China and Manchuria.

In the United States hemp is now cultivated in the blue-grass region of Kentucky within a radius of 50 miles of Lexington; in the region of Waupun, Wis.; in northern Indiana; near Lima, Ohio; and at Lerdo and Rio Vista, Cal. There are numerous small experimental plats in other places.

The principal countries producing hemp fiber for export are Russia, Italy, Hungary, and Roumania. China and Japan produce hemp fiber of excellent quality, but it is nearly all used for home consumption. Hemp is not cultivated for fiber in the Tropics or in any of the warm countries.

The historical distribution of hemp, as nearly as may be traced from the records, and the areas where hemp is now cultivated are indicated in the accompanying map.

Varieties

Hemp, cultivated for three different products—fiber from the bast, oil from the seeds, and resinous drugs from the flowers and leaves—has developed into three rather distinct types or groups of forms. The extreme, or more typical, forms of each group have been described as different species, but the presence of intergrading forms and the fact that the types do not remain distinct when cultivated under new conditions make it impossible to regard them as valid species.

There are few recognized varieties in either group. Less than 20 varieties of fiber-producing hemp are known, although hemp has been cultivated for more than 40 centuries, or much longer than either cotton or corn, both of which now have hundreds of named varieties.

China

The original home of the hemp plant was in China, and more varieties are found there than elsewhere. It is cultivated for fiber in nearly all parts of the Chinese Republic, except in the extreme south, and over a wide range of differences in soil and climate with little interchange of seed, thus favoring the development and perpetuation of varietal differences.

The variety called "ta-ma" (great hemp) is cultivated chiefly in the provinces of Chekiang, Kiangsu, and Fukien, south of the Yangtze. In the rich lowland soils, often in rotation with rice, but not irrigated, and with a warmer and longer growing season than in Kentucky, this hemp attains a height of 10 to 15 feet. The seed is dark colored, usually well mottled, small, weighing about 1.2 grams per hundred. The internodes of the main stem are 6 to 10 inches long; the branches long and slender, usually drooping at the ends; the leaves large; and the pistillate flowers in small clusters. Seed brought from China to Kentucky in recent years is mostly of this variety. When first introduced it is too long in maturing to permit all of the seeds to ripen.

The most important fiber plant of western China is the variety of hemp call "hoa-ma." It is grown in the province of Szechwan and as a winter crop on the plans of Chengtu in that province. It is shorter and more compact in its habit of growth and earlier in maturing than the ta-ma of the lowlands.

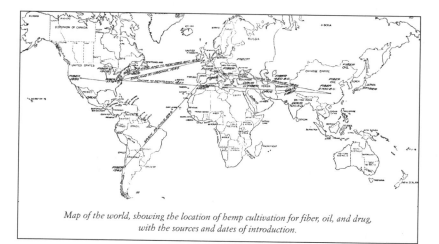

Map of the world, showing the location of hemp cultivation for fiber, oil, and drug, with the sources and dates of introduction.

A variety called "shan-ma-tse" is cultivated in the mountain valleys in the provinces of Shansi and Chihli, in northern China. Its fiber is regarded as the best in North China, and in some respects as superior to that of ta-ma, though the yield is usually smaller. The plants attain a height of 6 to 9 feet, with a very thin woody shell, short ascending branches, rather small leaves, and larger seeds in larger clusters than those of ta-ma. Imported seed of this variety, grown in a trial plat in Kentucky, produced plants smaller in size and maturing earlier than Kentucky hemp.

In the mountains both north and south of Ichang in central China a variety called "t'ang-ma" (cold hemp) is cultivated primarily for the production of seeds, from which oil is expressed. It is a very robust form, with stalks 6 to 12 feet high and 2 to 4 inches in diameter. These stalks are used for fuel, and occasionally a little fiber is stripped off for domestic use.

In Manchuria two distinct kinds of hemp are cultivated. One, called "hsien-ma," very similar to the shan-ma-tse of northern China, is grown for fiber. It attains a height of 8 to 9 feet, and required nearly 150 days from seeding to full maturity. The other, called "shem-ma," is grown for oil-seed production. It attains a height of 3 to 5 feet and is ripe with fully matured seeds in less than 100 days. The branches usually remain undeveloped, so that the clusters of seeds are borne in compact heads at the tops of the simple stalks. (Pl. XLII, fig. 1.) It is said that in Manchuria these two forms remain distinct without crossing or producing any intergrading forms.

The Chinese name "ma" (fig. 17), originally applied only to the true hemp (*Cannabis sativa*), is now used as a general term to designate early all textile plants in China.[23] This general use leads to nearly as much confusion among English-speaking people in China as does the unfortunate use of the name hemp as a synonym for fiber in this country. The staminate hemp plant is called "si-ma," and the pistillate plant "tsu-ma." Flax, cultivated to a limited extent in northern China, is called "siao-ma" (small hemp), but this name is also applied to small plants of true hemp. Ramie, cultivated in central and southern China, is "ch'u-ma" or "tsu-ma." China jute, cultivated in central and northern China and in Manchuria and Chosen (Korea), is called "tsing-ma," or "ching-ma," and its fiber, exported from Tientsin, is called "pei-ma." India jute, cultivated in southern China and Taiwan, is called "oi-ma." The name "chih-ma" is also applied in China to sesame, which is not a fiber plant.

Japan

Hemp, called "asa" in the Japanese language, is cultivate chiefly in the provinces or districts of Hiroshima, Tochigi, Shimane, Iwate, and Aidzu, and to a less extent in Hokushu (Hokkaido) in the north and Kiushu in the south. It is cultivated chiefly in the mountain valleys, or in the north on the interior plains, where it is too cool for cotton and rice and where it is drier than on the coastal plain. That grown in Hiroshima, in the south, is tall, with a rather coarse fiber; that in Tochigi, the principal hemp-producing province, is shorter, 5 to 7 feet high, with the best and finest fiber, and in Hokushu it is still shorter.

Seeds from Hiroshima, Shimane, Aidzu, Tochigi, and Iwate were tried by the United States Department of Agriculture in 1901 and 1902. The plants showed no marked varietal differences. They were all smaller than the best Kentucky hemp. The seeds varied from light grayish brown, 5 millimeters (1/5 inch) long, to dark gray, 4 millimeters (1/6 inch) long. The largest plants in every trial plat were from Hiroshima seeds, and these seeds were larger and lighter colored than those of any other variety except Shimane, the seeds of which were slightly larger and the plants slightly smaller.

Hemp is cultivated throughout the greater part of Russia, and it is one of the principal crops in the provinces of Orel, Kursk, Samara, Smolensk, Tula, Voronezh, and Poland. Two distinct types, similar to the tall fiber hemp and the short oil-seed hemp of Manchuria, are cultivated, and there are doubtless many local varieties in isolated districts where there is little interchange or seed. The crop is rather crudely cultivated, with no attempt at seed selection or improvement, and the plants are generally shorter and coarser than the hemp grown in Kentucky. The short oil-seed hemp with slender stems, about 30 inches high, bearing compact clusters of seeds and maturing in 60–90 days, is of little value for fiber production, but the experimental plants, grown from seed imported from Russia, indicate that it may be valuable as an oil-seed crop to be harvested and thrashed in the same manner as oil-seed flax.

Hungary

The hemp in Hungary has received more attention in recent years than that in Russia, and this has resulted in a better type of plants. An experimental plat grown at Washington from Hungarian seed attained a height of 6 to 10 feet in the seed row. The internodes were rather short, the branches numerous, curved upward, and bearing crowded seed clusters and small leaves. About one-third of the plants had dark-purple or copper-colored foliage and were more compact in habit than those with normal green foliage.

Italy

The highest-priced hemp fiber in the markets of either America or Europe is produced in Italy,[24] but it is obtained from plants similar to those in Kentucky. The higher price of the fiber is due not to superior plants, but to water retting and to increased care and labor in the preparation of the fiber.

Four varieties are cultivated in Italy:

(1) "Bologna," or great hemp, called in France, "chanvre de Piedmont," is grown in northern Italy in the provinces of Bologna, Ferrara, Roviga, and Modena. In the rich alluvial soils and under the intensive cultivation there practiced this variety averages nearly 12 feet in height, but it is said to deteriorate rapidly when cultivated elsewhere.

(2) "Cannapa picola," small hemp, attaining a height of 4 to 7 feet, with a rather slender reddish stalk, is cultivated in the valley of the Arno in the department of Tuscany.[25]

(3) "Neapolitan," large seeded.

(4) "Neapolitan," small seeded.

The two varieties of Neapolitan hemp are cultivated in the vicinity of Naples, and even so far up on the sides of Vesuvius that fields of hemp are occasionally destroyed by the eruptions of that volcano.

Seed of each of these Italian varieties has been grown in trial plats at Washington, D.C., and Lexington, Ky. The Bologna, or Piedmont, hemp in seed rows attained a height of 8 to 11 feet, nearly as tall as Kentucky seed hemp grown for comparison, but with thicker stalks, shorter and more rigid branches, and smaller and more densely clustered leaves. The small hemp, cannapa picola, was only 4 to 6 feet high. The large-seeded Neapolitan was 7 to 10 feet high, smaller than the Bologna, but otherwise more like Kentucky hemp, with more slender stalks and more open foliage. The small-seeded Neapolitan, with seeds weighing less than 1 gram per 100, rarely exceeded 4 feet in height in the series of plats where all were tried.

France

Hemp is cultivated in France chiefly in the departments of Sarthe and Ille-et-Vilaine, in the valley of the Loire River. Two varieties are grown, the Piedmont, from Italian seed, and the common hemp of Europe. The former grows large and coarse, though not as tall as in the Bologna regions, and it produces a rather coarse fiber suitable for coarse twines. The latter, seed of which is sown at the rate of 1-1/2 to 2 bushels per acre, has a very slender stalk, rarely more than 4 or 5 feet high, producing a fine flaxlike fiber that is largely used in woven hemp linens.

The common hemp of Europe, which includes the short hemp of France, is also cultivated to a limited extent in Spain, Belgium, and Germany. It grows taller and coarser when sown less thickly on rich land, but it never attains the size of the Bologna type.

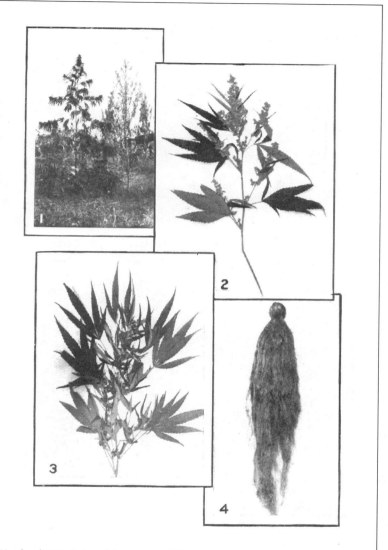

Yearbook U.S. Dept. of Agriculture, 1913.
PLATE XL.—HEMP, PLANT AND FIBER.

Fig. 1—Pistillate plant, left; staminate plant, right.
Fig. 2—Staminate flowers.
Fig. 3—Pistillate flowers.
Fig. 4—Fiber in the form in which it leaves the farm.

Yearbook U.S. Dept. of Agriculture, 1913.
PLATE XLI.—DETAILS OF HEMP PLANT.

Fig. 1—Leaf, one-third natural size.
Fig. 2—Seeds, natural size.
Fig. 3—Roots, showing strong taproot.
Fig. 4—Sections of stalk, showing woody shell slightly thickened at the nodes.

Chile

Chilean hemp, originally from seed of the common hemp of Europe, has developed in three and a half centuries into coarser plants with larger seeds. When sown broadcast for fiber in Chile the plants attain a height of 6 to 8 feet, and when in checks of drills for seed they reach 10 to 12 feet.

Hemp from Chilean seed (S.P.I. No. 24307), grown at the experiment stations at Lexington, KY., and St. Paul, Minn., in 1090, was 4 to 9 feet high in the broadcast plats and about the same height in the seed drills. It matured earlier than hemp of Chinese origin. Its leaves were small and crowded, with the seed clusters near the ends of slender, spreading branches. The fiber was coarse and harsh. The seeds were very large, 5 to 6 millimeters long, and weighed about 2 grams per 100.

Turkey

A variety of hemp, intermediate between the fiber-producing and the typical drug-producing types, is cultivated in Asiatic Turkey, especially in the region of Damascus, and to a limited extent in European Turkey. This variety, called Smyrna, is about the poorest variety from which fiber is obtained. It is cultivated chiefly for the narcotic drug, but fiber is also obtained from the stalks. It grows 3 to 6 feet high, with short internodes, numerous ascending branches, densely crowded foliage of small leaves, and abundant seeds maturing early. It seems well suited for the production of birdseed, but its poor type, combined with prolific seed production, makes it a dangerous plant to grow in connection with fiber crops.

India

Hemp is cultivated in India over an area of 2,000 to 5,000 acres annually for the production of the narcotic drugs known as hashish, charras, bhang, and ganja. Some fiber is obtained, especially from the staminate plants, in the northern part of Kashmir, where the hemp grown for the production of charras is more like the fiber types than that grown for bhang farther south.

Plants grown by the Department of Agriculture at Washington from seed received from the Botanical Garden in Sibpur, Calcutta, India, agreed almost perfectly with the description of *Cannabis indica*[26] written by Lamarck more than a century ago. (Pl. XLII, fig. 2) They were distinctly different in general appearance from any of the numerous forms grown by this department from seed obtained in nearly all countries where hemp is cultivated, but the differences in botanical characters were less marked. The Indian hemp differed from Kentucky hemp in its more densely branching habit, its very dense foliage, the leaves mostly alternate, 7 to 11 (usually 9) very narrow leaflets, and in its nearly solid stalk. It was imperfectly dioecious, a character not observed in any other variety. Its foliage remained green until after the last leaves of even the pistillate plants in Kentucky hemp had withered and fallen. It was very attractive as an ornamental plant but of no value for fiber.

Arabia and Africa

Hemp somewhat similar to that of India, but generally shorter, is cultivated in Arabia, northern Africa, and also by some of the natives in central and southern Africa for the production of the drug, but not for fiber. In Arabia it is called "takrousi," in Morocco "kief" or "kif," and South Africa "dakkan." None of these plants is suitable for fiber production.

Kentucky

Practically all of the hemp grown in the United States is from seed produced in Kentucky. The first hemp grown in Kentucky was of European origin, the seed having been brought to the colonies, especially Virginia, and taken from there to Kentucky. In recent years there has been practically no importation of seed from Europe. Remnants of the European types are occasionally found in the shorter, more densely branching stalks terminating in thick clusters of small leaves. These plants yield more seed and mature earlier than the more desirable fiber types introduced from China.

Nearly all of the hemp now grown in Kentucky is of Chinese origin. Small packets of seed are received from American missionaries in China. These seeds are carefully cultivated for two or three generations in order to secure a sufficient quantity for field cultivation, and also to acclimate the plants to Kentucky conditions. Attempts to produce fiber plants by sowing imported seed broadcast have not given satisfactory results. Seed of the second or third generation from China is generally regarded as most desirable. This Kentucky hemp of Chinese origin has long internodes, long, slender branches, opposite and nearly horizontal except the upper ones, large leaves usually drooping and not crowded, with the seeds in small clusters near the ends of the branches. Small, dark-colored seeds distinctly mottled are preferred by the Kentucky hemp growers. Under favorable conditions Kentucky hemp attains a height of 7 to 10 feet when grown broadcast for fiber and 9 to 14 feet when cultivated for seed.

Improvement by Seed Introduction

Without selection or continued efforts to maintain superior types, the hemp in Kentucky deteriorates. As stated by the growers, the hemp "runs out." The poorer types of plants for fiber are usually the most prolific seed bearers, and they are often earlier in maturing; therefore, without selection or roguing, the seed of these undesirable types increases more rapidly than that of the tall, late-maturing, better types which bear fewer seeds. New supplies are brought from China to renew the stock. Owing to the confusion of names the seed received is not always of a desirable kind, and sometimes jute, China jute, or ramie seeds are obtained. When seed of the ta-ma variety is secured and is properly cultivated for two or three generations there is a marked improvement, but these improved strains run out in less than 10 years.

The numerous trials that have been made by the Department of Agriculture with hemp seed from nearly all of the sources mentioned and repeated introductions from the more promising sources indicate that little permanent improvement may be expected from mere introduction not followed by breeding and continued selection. In not instance, so far as observed, have any of the plants from imported seed grown as well the first year as the Kentucky hemp cultivated for comparison. Further introduction of seed in small quantities is needed to furnish stock for breading and selection. The most promising varieties for introduction are ta-ma and shan-ma-tze, from China; Hiroshima and Tochigi, from Japan; Bologna, from Italy; and improved types from Hungary.

Improvement by Selection

Kentucky hemp is reasonably uniform, not because of selection, or even grading the seeds, but because all types have become mixed together. Nearly all the seed is raised in an limited area. Hemp being cross-fertilized, it is more difficult to keep distinct types separate than in the case of wheat, flax, or other crops with self-pollinated flowers, but it is merely necessary to isolate the plants cultivated for seed and then exercise care to prevent the seed from being mixed. Until 1903 no well-planned and continued effort seems to have been undertaken in this country to produce an improved variety of hemp. At that time the results of breeding by careful selection improved varieties of wheat and flax at the Minnesota Agricultural Experiment Station

were beginning to yield practical returns to the farmers of that State. Mr. Fritz Knorr, from Kentucky, then a student in the Minnesota College of Agriculture, was encouraged to take up the work with hemp. Seed purchased from a dealer in Nicholasville, Ky., was furnished by the United States Department of Agriculture. The work of selection was continued until 1909 under the direction of Prof. C.P. Bull, agronomist at the station. Points especially noted in selecting plants from which to save seed for propagation were length of internode, thinness of shell, height, and tendency of the stems to be well fluted. The seasons there were too short to permit selection for plants taking a longer season for growth. The improved strain of hemp thus developed was called Minnesota No. 8. Seed of this strain sown at the experiment station at Lexington, Ky., in 1910 and 1911 produced plants more uniform than those from unselected Kentucky seed, and the fiber was superior in both yield and quality. A small supply of this seed, grown by the Department of Agriculture at Washington, D.C., in 1912, was distributed to Kentucky hemp-seed growers in 1913, and in every instance the resulting seed plants were decidedly superior to those from ordinary Kentucky seed.

Seed selection is practiced to a limited extent on some of the best hemp-seed farms in Kentucky. Before the seed-hemp plants are cut the grower goes through the field and marks the plants from which seed is to be saved for the seed crop of the following year. Plants are usually selected for height, lateness, and length of internodes. Continued selection in this manner will improve the type. Without selection continued each season, the general average of the crop deteriorates.

Climate

Hemp requires a humid temperate climate, such as that throughout the greater part of the Mississippi Valley. It has been grown experimentally as far north as Saskatoon, in northwestern Canada, and as far south as New Orleans, La., and Brunswick, Ga.

Temperature

The best fiber-producing types of hemp require about four months free from killing frosts for the production of fiber and about five and one-half months for the full maturity of the seeds. The climatic conditions during the four months of the hemp-growing season in the region about Lexington, Ky., are indicated by the following table:

Yearbook U.S. Dept. of Agriculture, 1913.

PLATE XLII.—DIFFERENT TYPES OF HEMP AND SEED HEMP.

Fig. 1—Manchurian oil-seed hemp.

Fig. 2—India drug-producing hemp on left; Kentucky fiber-producing hemp in seed rows on right.

Fig. 3—Hemp-seed field in Kentucky River Valley, walled in with ledges of lime rock.

Yearbook U.S. Dept. of Agriculture, 1913.
PLATE XLIII.—SEED HEMP AND MALADIES.

Fig. 1—Shock of seed hemp curing.
Fig. 2—Seed-hemp plant attacked by fungus disease.
Fig. 3—Branched broom rape, parasite on hemp roots.

TEMPERATURE AND RAINFALL IN THE HEMP-GROWING REGION OF KENTUCKY[1]

| Month | Temperature. | | | Precipitation. | | |
| | Mean | Absolute maximum | Absolute minimum | Mean | Total amount driest year | Total amount wettest year |
	°F	°F	°F	Inches	Inches	Inches
May	64	91	32	3.6	3.7	4.7
June	73	95	42	4.2	3.7	7.4
July	76	103	51	4.0	2.6	3.1
August	75	96	51	3.8	3.7	7.3
Mean for 4 months	72	—	—	3.9	—	—
Annual mean	55	—	—	42.5	—	—

[1] Henry, Alfred Judson. *Climatology of the United States.* U.S. Department of Agriculture, Weather Bureau, Bulletin Q, p. 762, 1906.

Hemp grows best where the temperature ranges between 60° and 80° F., but it will endure colder and warmer temperatures. Young seedlings and also mature plants will endure with little injury light frosts of short duration. Young hemp is less susceptible than oats to injury from frost, and field of hemp ready for harvest have been uninjured by frosts which ruined fields of corn all around them. Frosts are injurious to nearly mature plants cultivated for seed production.

Rainfall

Hemp requires a plentiful supply of moisture throughout its growing season, and especially during the first six weeks. After it has become well rooted and the stalks are 20 to 30 inches high it will endure drier conditions, but a severe drought hastens it maturity and tends to dwarf its growth. It will endure heavy rains, or even a flood of short duration, on light, well-drained soils, but on heavy, impervious soils excessive rain, especially when the plants are young, will ruin the crop.

In 1903, a large field of hemp on rich, sandy-loam soil of alluvial deposit, well supplied with humus, near Gridley, Cal., was flooded to a depth of 2 to 6 inches by high water in the Feather River. The hemp had germinated but a few days before and was only 1 to 3 inches high. The water remained on the land about three days. The hemp started slowly after the water receded, but in spite of the fact that there was no rain from this time, the last of March, until harvest, the last of August, it made a very satisfactory crop, 6 to 12 feet in height. The soil, of porous, spongy texture, remained moist below the dusty surface during the entire growing season.

An experimental crop of about 15 acres on impervious clay and silt of alluvial deposit, but lacking in humus, in eastern Louisiana was completely ruined by a heavy rain while the plants were small.

The total average rainfall during the four months of the hemp-growing season in Kentucky is 15.6 inches, as shown in the table, and this is distributed throughout the season. When there is an unusual drought in that region, as in 1913, the hemp is severely injured. It is not likely to succeed on upland soils in localities where corn leaves curl because of drought before the middle of August.

Irrigation

In 1912, and again in 1913, crops of hemp were cultivated under irrigation at Lerdo, Cal. The soil there is an alluvial sandy loam of rather firm texture, but with good natural drainage and not enough clay to form a crust on the surface after flooding with water. The land is plowed deeply, leveled, and made up into irrigation blocks with low borders over which drills and harvesting machinery may easily work. The seed is drilled in the direction of the fall, so that when flooded the water runs slowly down the drill furrows. Three irrigations are sufficient, provided the seed is sown early enough to get the benefit of the March rains. The fiber thus produced is strong and of good quality.

Weather for Retting and Breaking

Cool, moist weather, light snows, of alternate freezing and thawing are favorable for retting hemp. Dry weather, not necessarily free from rain but with a rather low relative humidity, is essential for satisfactory work in breaking hemp. The relative humidity at Lexington in January, February, and March, when most of the hemp is broken, ranges from 62 to 82 per cent. The work of breaking hemp is rarely carried on when there is snow on the ground. The work of collecting and cleaning hemp seed can be done only in dry weather.

SOIL

Soils in the Hemp-Growing Region of Kentucky

The soil in most of the hemp fields of Kentucky is of a yellowish clay loam, often very dark as a result of decaying vegetable matter, and most of it overlying either Lexington or Cincinnati limestone. There are frequent outcroppings of lime rock throughout the region. The soil is deep, fertile, well supplied with humus, and its mechanical condition is such that it does not quickly dry out or become baked and hard. The land is rolling, affording good natural drainage.

Hemp Soils in other States

In eastern Nebraska, hemp has been grown on a deep clay-loam prairie soil underlain with lime rock. In some of the fields there are small areas of gumbo soil, but hemp does not grow well in these areas. In California, hemp is cultivated on the reclaimed lands of alluvial deposits in the lower valley of the Sacramento River. This is a deep soil made up of silt and sand and with a very large proportion of decaying vegetable matter. These rich, alluvial soils, which are never subject to drought, produce a heavier growth of hemp than the more shallow upland soils in Kentucky. In Indiana, crops of hemp have been grown in the Kankankee Valley on peaty soils overlying marl or yellow clay containing an abundance of lime. These lands have been drained by large open ditches. There is such a large proportion of peat in the soil that it will burn for months if set on fire during the dry season, yet this soil contains so much lime that when the vegetation is cleared away Kentucky bluegrass comes in rather than sedges. It is an alkaline rather than an acid soil. The large amount of peat gives these soils a loose, spongy texture, well adapted to hold moisture during dry seasons. Water remains in the ditches 6 to 10 feet below the surface nearly all summer, and the hemp crops have not been affected by the severe drought which has injured other crops on the surrounding uplands. In southeastern Pennsylvania, and in Indiana, Wisconsin, and Minnesota, the best crops, producing the largest yields of fiber and fiber of the best quality, have been grown on clay-loam upland soils. In some instances, however, the upland crops have suffered from drought.

Soils Suited to Hemp

Hemp requires for the best development of the plant, and also for the production of a large quantity and good quality of fiber, a rich, moist soil having good natural drainage, yet not subject to severe drought at any time during the growing season. A clay loam of rather loose texture and containing a plentiful supply of decaying vegetable matter or an alluvial deposit alkaline and not acid in reaction should be chosen for this crop.

Soils to be Avoided

Hemp will not grow well on still, impervious, clay soils, or on light sandy or gravelly soils. It will not grow well on soils that in their wild state are overgrown with either sedges or huckleberry bushes. These plants usually indicate acid soils. It will make only a poor growth on soils with a hardpan near the surface or in fields worn out by long cultivation. Clay loams or heavier soils give heavier yields of strong but coarser fiber than are obtained on sandy loams and light soils.

Effect of Hemp on the Land

Hemp cultivated for the production of fiber, cut before the seeds are formed and retted on the land where it has been grown, tends to improve rather than injure the soil. It improves its physical condition, destroys weeds, and does not exhaust its fertility.

Physical Condition

Hemp loosens the soil and makes it more mellow. The soil is shaded by hemp more than by any other crop. The foliage at the top of the growing plants makes a dense shade and, in addition, all of the leaves below the top fall off, forming a mulch on the ground, so that the surface of the soil remains moist and in better condition for the action of soil bacteria. The rather coarse taproots (Pl. XLI, fig. 3), penetrating deeply and bringing up plant food from the subsoil, decay quickly after the crop is harvested and tend to loosen the soil more than do the fibrous roots of wheat, oats, and similar broadcast crops. Land is more easily plowed after hemp than after corn or small grain.

Crops	Nitrogen	Phosphoric acid	Potassium
	(Pounds)	*(Pounds)*	*(Pounds)*
Hemp (yielding 1,000 pounds of clean fiber)[1]	62.7	33.2	101.3
Corn (50 bushels and 1 1/2 tons of stover)[2]	74.0	11.5	35.5
Wheat (25 bushels of grain, 1 1/4 tons of straw)[2]	48.0	8.0	24.0
Oats (50 bushels of grain, 1 1/4 tons of straw)[2]	48.5	8.0	34.0
Sugar beets (20 tons of roots)[2]	100.0	18.0	157.0
Cotton (yielding 400 pounds of lint)[1]	29.2	22.5	35.3

1 *Jaffa, M. E. Composition of the Ramie Plant. California Experiment Station Bulletin, p. 91, 1891.*
2 *Hopkins, Cyril G., and Pettit, James H. The Fertility in Illinois Soils. Illinois Experiment Station Bulletin 123, p. 180, 1908.*

Hemp Destroys Weeds

Very few of the common weeds troublesome on the farm can survive the dense shade of a good crop of hemp. If the hemp makes a short, weak growth, owing to unsuitable soil, drought, or other causes, it will have little effect in checking the growth of weeds, but a good, dense crop, 6 feet or more in height, will leave the ground practically free from weeds at harvest time. In Wisconsin, Canada thistle has been completely killed and quack-grass severely checked by one crop of hemp. In one 4-acre field in Vernon county, Wis., where Canada thistles were very thick, fully 95 per cent of the thistles were killed where the hemp attained a height of 5 feet or more, but on a dry, gravelly hillside in this same field where it grew only 2 or 3 feet high, the thistles were checked no more than they would have been in a grain crop. Some vines, like the wild morning-glory and bindweed climb up the hemp stalks and secure light enough for growth, but low-growing weeds can not live in a hemp field.

Hemp does not Exhaust the Fertility of the Soil

An abundant supply of plant food is required by hemp, but most of it is merely borrowed during development and returned to the soil at the close of the season. The amounts of the principal fertilizing elements contained in mature crops of hemp, as compared with other crops, are shown in the accompanying table.

The data in the table indicate that hemp requires for its best development a richer soil than any of the other crops mentioned except sugar beets. These other crops, except the stalks of corn and the tops of beets, are entirely removed from the land, thus taking away nearly all the plant food consumed in their growth. Only the fiber of hemp is taken away from the farm and this is mostly cellulose, composed of water and carbonic acid.

The relative proportions by weight of the different parts of the hemp plant, thoroughly air dried, are approximately as follows: Roots 10 per cent, stems 60 per cent, and leaves 30 per cent.[27] The mineral ingredients of these different parts of the hemp plant are shown in the following table:

Ash ingredients of the leaves, stalks, and roots of the hemp plant, carbonic acid excluded, 100 parts dried material in each case.[1]

Ingredients	Leaves	Stalks	Roots
Lime	4.992	0.949	0.713
Magnesia	.585	.194	.291
Potash	2.858		
Soda	.024	1.659	1.829
Phosphoric acid	.947	.447	.531
Sulphuric acid	.226	.040	.047
Chlorin	.017	.019	.014
Silica	.575	.035	.077
Percentage of ash	10.224	3.343	3.502

1 *Peter, Robert. Chemical Examination of the Ash of Hemp and Buckwheat Plants. Kentucky Geological Survey, p. 12, 1884.*

The foliage, constituting nearly one-third of the weight of the entire plant and much richer in essential fertilizing elements than the stalks, all returns to the field where the hemp grows. The roots also remain and, together with the stubble, they constitute more than 10 per cent of the total weight and contain approximately the same proportions of fertilizing elements as the stalks. The leaves and roots therefore return to the soil nearly two-thirds of the fertilizing elements used in building up the plant.

After the hemp is harvested it is spread out on the same land for retting. In this retting process nearly all of the soluble ingredients are washed out and returned to the soil. When broken in the field on small hand brakes, as is still the common practice in Kentucky, the hurds, or central woody portion of the stalk, together with most of the outer bark, are left in small piles and burned, returning the mineral ingredients to the soil. Where machine brakes are used the hurds may serve an excellent purpose as an absorbent in stock yards and pig pens, to returned to the fields in barnyard manure.

The mineral ingredients permanently removed from the farm are thus reduced to the small proportions contained in the fiber. These proportions, calculated in pounds per acre and compared with the amounts removed by other crops, are shown in the table below.

The hemp fiber analyzed was in the ordinary condition as it leaves the farm. When washed with cold water, removing some but not all of the dirt, the ashy residue was reduced more than one-third, and the total earthy phosphates were reduced nearly one-half. The amount of plant food actually removed from the soil by hemp is so small as to demand little attention in considering soil exhaustion. The depletion of the humus is the most important factor, but even in this respect hemp is easier on the land than other crops except clover and alfalfa. The fact that hemp is often grown year after year on the same land for 10 to 20 years, with little or no application of fertilizer and very little diminution in yield, is evidence that it does not exhaust the soil.

Rotation of Crops

In Kentucky, hemp is commonly grown year after year on the same land without rotation. It is the common practice in that State to slow hemp after bluegrass on land that has been in pasture for many years, or sometimes it is sown as the first crop on recently cleared timberland. It is then sown year after year until it ceases to be profitable or until conditions favor the introduction of other crops. On the prairie soils in eastern Nebraska and also on the peaty soils in northern Indiana, more uniform crops were obtained after the first year. On some of the farms in California hemp is grown in rotation with beans. Hemp is recommended to be grown in rotation with other farm crops on ordinary upland soils suited to its growth. In ordinary crop rotations it would take about the same place as oats. If retted on the same land, however, it would occupy the field during the entire growing season, so that it would be impossible to sow a field crop after hemp unless it were a

	Mineral ingredients removed from the soil by hemp, wheat, corn, and tobacco, calculated in pounds, per acre.[1]			
Ingredients.	Hemp Fiber In 800 pounds	Wheat: In 20 bushels	Corn: In 50 bushels	Tobacco, including stalks: In 1,000 pounds
Lime	7.872	1.63	0.22	68.00
Magnesia	1.128	2.43	3.61	8.67
Potash	.968	5.45	8.06	69.73
Soda	.096	.13	6.22	6.80
Phosphoric acid	2.080	9.12	11.85	8.13
Sulphuric acid	.232	.08	(2)	8.40
Chlorin	.016	.35	(2)	1.06
Silica	.736	.41	.71	5.86
Total ash	13.128	19.60	30.67	176.65

1 Peter, Robert. *Chemical Examination of the Ash of Hemp and Buckwheat Plants. Kentucky Geological Survey, p. 17, 1884.*
2 Not estimated.

crop of rye. The growing of rye after hemp has been recommended in order to prevent washing and to retain the soluble fertilizing element that might otherwise be leached out during the winter. This recommendation, however, has not been put in practice sufficiently to demonstrate that it is of any real value. Hemp will grow well in fertile soil after any crop, and it leaves that land in good condition for any succeeding crop. Hemp requires a plentiful supply of fertilizing elements, especially nitrogen, and it is therefore best to have it succeed clover, peas, or grass sod. If it follows wheat, oats, or corn, these crops should be well fertilized with barnyard manure. The following crop rotations are suggested for hemp on fertile upland soils:

Hemp leaves that ground mellow and free from weeds and is therefore recommended to precede sugar beets, onions, celery, and similar crops which require hand weeding. If hemp is grown primarily to kill Canada thistle, quackgrass, or similar perennial weeds, it may be grown repeatedly on the same land until the weeds are subdued.

Fertilizers

Hemp requires an abundant supply of plant food. Attaining in four months a height of 6 to 12 feet and producing a larger amount of dry vegetable matter than any other crop in temperate climates, it must be grown on a soil naturally fertile or enriched by a liberal application of fertilizer. In Europe and in Asia heavy applications of fertilizers are used to keep the soils up to the standard for growing hemp, but in the United States most of the hemp is grown on lands that fertility of which has been exhausted by centuries of cultivation. In Kentucky, where the farms are well stocked with horses and cattle, barnyard manure is used to maintain the fertility of the soils, but it is usually applied to other crops and not directly to hemp. In other States no fertilizer has been applied to soils where hemp is grown, except in somewhat limited experiments.

Barnyard Manure.—The best single fertilizer for hemp is undoubtedly barnyard manure. It supplies the three important plant foods, nitrogen, potash, and phosphoric acid, and it also adds to the store of humus, which appears to be more necessary for hemp than for most other farm crops. If other fertilizers are used, it is well to apply barnyard manure also, but it should be applied to the preceding crop, or at the latest, in the fall before the hemp is sown. It must be well rotted and thoroughly mixed with the soil before the hemp seed is sown, so as to promote a uniform growth of the hemp stalks. Uniformity in the size of the plants of other crops is of little consequence, but in hemp it is a matter of prime importance. An application of coarse manure in the spring, just before sowing, is likely to result in more injury than benefit. The amount that may be applied profitably will vary with different soils. There is little danger, however, of inducing too rank a growth of hemp on upland soils, provided the plants are uniform, for it must be borne in mind that stalk and not fruit is desired. On soils deficient in humus as the result of long cultivation, the increased growth of hemp may well repay for the application of 15 to 20 tons of barnyard manure per acre. It would be unwise to sow hemp on such soils until they had been heavily fertilized with barnyard manure.

Commercial Fertilizers.—On worn-out soils, peaty soils, and possibly on some alluvial soils, commercial fertilizers may be used with profit in addition to barnyard manure. The primary effect to be desired from commercial fertilizers on hemp is a more rapid growth of the crop early in the season. This rapid early growth usually results in a greater yield and better quality of fiber. The results of a series of experiments conducted at the agricultural experiment station at Lexington, Ky., in 1889 led to the following conclusions:[28]

(1) That hemp can be raised successfully on worn bluegrass soils with the aid of commercial fertilizers.

First year	Second year	Third year	Fourth year	Fifth year
Hemp	Corn	Wheat	Clover	Grass and pasture
Do	Sugar Beets Potatoes or Onions	Do	Do	Do
Corn	Peas or Beans	Hemp	Barley or Oats	Clover

(2) That both potash and nitrogen are required to produce the best results.

(3) That the effect was the same, whether muriate or sulphate was used to furnish potash.

(4) That the effect was about the same, whether nitrate of soda or sulphate of ammonia was used to furnish nitrogen.

(5) That a commercial fertilizer containing about 6 per cent of available phosphoric acid, 12 per cent of actual potash, and 4 per cent of nitrogen (mostly in the form of nitrate of soda or sulphate of ammonia) would be a good fertilizer for trial.

The increased yield and improved quality of the fiber on the fertilized plats compared with the yield from the check plat, not fertilized, in these experiments would warrant the application of nitrogen at the rate of 160 pounds of nitrate of soda or 120 pounds of sulphate of ammonia per acre, and potash at the rate of about 160 pounds of either sulphate or muriate of potash per acre.

On the rich alluvial soils reclaimed by dikes from the Sacramento River at Courtland, Cal., Mr. John Heaney has found that an application of nitrate of soda at the rate of not more than 100 pounds per acre soon after sowing and again two weeks to a month later, or after the first application has been washed down by rains, will increase the yield and improve the quality of the fiber.

Leguminous Crops or Green Manure.— Beans grown before hemp and the vines returned to the land and plowed under have given good results increased yield and improved quality of fiber on alluvial soils at Courtland, Cal. Clover is sometimes plowed under in Kentucky to enrich the land for hemp. It must be plowed under during the preceding fall, so as to become thoroughly rotted before the hemp is grown.

Hemp as a Green Manure.—In experiments with various crops for green manure for wheat in India, hemp was found to give the best results.[29] In exceptionally dry seasons, as in 1908 and 1913, many fields of hemp do not grow high enough to be utilized profitably for fiber production. They are often left until fully mature and then burned. Better results would doubtless be obtained if the hemp were plowed under as soon as it could be determined that it would not make a sufficient growth for fiber production. Mature hemp stalks or dry hurds should not be plowed under, because they rot very slowly.

Diseases, Insects, and Weeds

Hemp is remarkably free from diseases caused by fungi. In one instance at Havelock, Nebr., in a low spot where water had stood, nearly 3 per cent of the hemp plants were dead. The roots of these dead plants were pink in color and a fungous mycelium was found in them, but it was not in a stage of development to permit identification. The fungus was probably not the primary cause of the trouble, since the dead plants were confined to the low place and there was no recurrence of the disease on hemp grown in the same field the following year.

A fungus described under the name *Dendrophoma marconii* Cav. was observed on hemp in northern Italy in 1887.[30] This fungus attacked the plants after they were mature enough to harvest for fiber. Its progress over the plant attacked and also the distribution of the infection over the field were described as very rapid, but if the disease is discovered at its inception and the crop promptly harvested it causes very little damage.

In the fall of 1913 a disease was observed on seed hemp grown by the Department of Agriculture at Washington. (Pl. XLIII, fig 2.) It did not appear until after the stage of full flowering of the staminate plants and therefore after the stage for harvesting for fiber. A severe hailstorm had bruised the plants and broken the bark, doubtless making them more susceptible to the disease. The first symptoms noted in each plant attacked were wilted leaves near the ends of branches above the middle of the plant, accompanied by an area of discolored bark on the main stalk below the base of each diseased branch. In warm, moist weather the disease spread rapidly, killing a plant 10 feet high in five days and also infesting other plants. It was observed only on pistillate plants, but the last late-maturing staminate plants left in the plat after thinning the earlier ones were cut soon after the disease was discovered.[31]

In a few instances insects boring in the stems have killed some plants, but the injury caused in this manner is too small to be regarded as really troublesome.

Cutworms have caused some damage in the late-sown hemp in land plowed in the spring, but there is practically no danger from this source in hemp sown at the proper season and in fall-plowed land well harrowed before sowing.

A Chilean dodder (*Cuscuta racemosa*) troublesome on alfalfa in northern California was found on the hemp at Gridley, Cal., in 1903. Although it was abundant in some parts of the field at about the time the hemp was ready for harvest, it did not cause any serious injury.

Black bindweed (*Ploygonum convolvulus*) and wild morning glory (*Convolvulus sepium*) sometimes cause trouble in low, rich land by climbing up the plants and binding them together.

The only really serious enemy to hemp is branched broom rape (*Orobanche ramosa*). (Pl. XLIII, fig. 3.) This is a weed 6 to 15 inches high, with small, brownish yellow, scalelike leaves and rather dull purple flowers. The entire plant is covered with sticky glands which catch the dust and give it a dirty appearance. Its roots are parasitic on the roots of the hemp. It is also parasitic on tobacco and tomato roots.[32] Branched broom rape is troublesome in Europe and the United States, but is not known in Asia. Its seeds are very small, about the size of tobacco seed, and they stick to the gummy calyx surrounding the hemp seed when the seed-hemp plants are permitted to fall on the ground in harvesting. There is still more opportunity for them to come in contact with the seed of hemp grown for fiber. The broom rape is doubtless distributed more by means of lint seed (seed from overripe fiber hemp) than by any other means. When broom rape becomes abundant it often kills a large proportion of the hemp plants before they reach maturity. As a precaution it is well to slow only well-cleaned seed from cultivated hemp and insist on a guaranty of no lint seed. If the land becomes infested, crops other than hemp, tobacco, tomatoes, or potatoes should be grown for a period of at least seven years. The seeds retain their vitality several years.[33]

Hemp-Seed Production

All of the hemp seed used in the United States for the production of hemp for fiber is produced in Kentucky. Nearly all of it is obtained from plants cultivated for seed for the fiber crop are of the fiber-producing type and not the type commonly obtained in bird-seed hemp. Old stocks of hemp seed of low vitality are often sold for bird seed, but much of the hemp seed sold by seedsmen or dealers in bird supplies is of the densely branching Smyrna type.

Lint Seed

In some instances seed is saved from hemp grown for fiber but permitted to get overripe before cutting. This is known as lint seed. It is generally regarded as inferior to seed from cultivated plants. A good crop is sometimes obtained from lint seed, but it is often lacking in vigor as well as germinative vitality, and it is rare that good crops are obtained from lint seed of the second or third generation.

Cultivated Seed

Nearly all of the cultivated seed is grown in the valley of the Kentucky River and along the creeks

tributary to this river for a distance of about 50 miles above High Bridge. The river through this region flows in a deep gorge about 150 feet below the general level of the land. The sides of this valley are steep, with limestone outcropping, and in some places perpendicular ledges of lime rock in level strata. (Pl. XLII, fig. 3.) The river, which overflows every spring, almost covering the valley between the rocky walls, forms alluvial deposits from a few rods to half a mile in width. The seed hemp is grown on these inundated areas, and especially along the creeks, where the water from the river backs up, leaving a richer deposit of silt than along the banks of the river proper, where the deposited soils are more sandy. There is a longer season free from frost in these deep valleys than on the adjacent highlands. Instead of having earlier frosts in the fall, as may be usually expected in lowlands, the valley is filled with fog on still nights, thus preventing damage from frost. For the production of hemp seed a rich, alluvial soil containing a plentiful supply of lime and also a plentiful supply of moisture throughout the growing season is necessary. The crop also requires a long season for development. The young seedlings will endure light frosts without injury, but a frost before harvest will nearly ruin the crop. A period of dry weather is necessary after the harvest in order to beat out and clean the seeds.

Preparation of Land

The land is plowed as soon as possible after the spring floods, which usually occur in February and early in March. After harrowing, it is marked in checks about 4 or 5 feet each way. Hemp cultivated for seed production must have room to develop branches. (Pl. XL, fig. 1.)

The seed is planted between the 20th of March and the last of April—usually earlier than the seed is sown for the production of fiber. It is usually planted by hand, 5 to 7 seeds in a hill, and covered with a hoe. In some instances, planters are used, somewhat like those used for planting corn, and on some farms seeders are used which plant 1 or 2 drills at a time 4 or 5 feet apart. When planted in drills it is usually necessary to thin out the plants afterwards. One or two quarts of seed are sufficient to plant an acre. Less than one quart would be sufficient if all the plants were allowed to grow.

Cultivation

On the best farms the crop is cultivated four times—twice rather deep and twice with cultivators with fine teeth, merely stirring the surface.

When the first flowers are produced, so that the staminate plants may be recognized, all of these plants are cut out except about one per square rod. These will produce sufficient pollen to fertilize the flowers on the pistillate, or seed-bearing plants, and the removal of the others will give more room for the development of the seed-bearing plants.

Harvest

The seed-bearing plants are allowed to remain until fully mature, or as long as possible without injury from frost. They are cut with corn knives, usually during the first half of October, leaving the stubble 10 to 20 inches high. The plants are set up in loose shocks around one or two plants which have been left standing. The shocks are usually bound near the top with binder twine. They are left in this manner for two or three weeks, until thoroughly dry. (Pl. XLIII, fig.1.)

Collecting the Seed

When the hemp is thoroughly dry, men (usually in gangs of five or six, with tarpaulins about 20 feet square) go into the field. One man with an ax cuts off the hemp stubble between four shocks and clears a space large enough to spread the tarpaulin. The other men pick up an entire shock and throw it on the tarpaulin. They then beat off the seeds with sticks about 5 feet long and 1-1/2 inches in diameter. (Pl. XLIV, fig. 1.) When the seed has been beaten off from one side of the shock the men turn it over by means of the sticks, and after beating off all of the seed they pick up the canvas, and then treat another shock in the same manner. They will beat off the seed from four shocks in 15 to 20 minutes, securing 2 or 3 pecks of seed from each shock. While this seems a rather crude way of collecting the seed, it is doubtless the most economical and practical method that may be devised. The seed falls so readily from the dry hemp stalks that it would be impossible to move them without a very great loss. Furthermore, it would be very difficult to handle plants 10 to 14 feet high, with rigid branches 3 to 6 feet in length, so as to feed them to any kind of thrashing machine.

Cleaning the Seed

The seed and chaff which have been beaten on the tarpaulin are sometimes beaten or tramped to break up the coarser bunches and stalks, and in some instances they are rubbed through coarse sieves in order to reduce them foils to be put through a fanning mill. The seed is then partly cleaned by a fanning mill in the field and afterwards run once or twice through another mill

with finer sieves and better adjustments of fans. Even after this treatment it is usually put through a seed-cleaning machine by the dealers. There has recently been introduced on some of the best seed-hemp farms a kind of homemade thrashing machine, consisting essentially of a feeding device, cylinder, a concaves, attached to a rather large fanning mill, all being driven by a gasoline engine. (Pl. XLIV, fig. 2.) The hemp seed is fed to this machine just as it comes from the tarpaulin after beating off from the shock. It combines the process of breaking up the chaff into finer pieces and the work of fanning the seed in the field, and it performs this work more effectively and more rapidly.

Yield

Under favorable conditions the yield of hemp seed ranges from 12 to 25 bushels per acre. From 16 to 18 bushels are regarded as a fair average yield.

Cost of Seed Production

The hemp-seed growers state that it costs about $2.50 per bushel to produce hemp seed, counting the annual rental of the land at about $10 per acre. With the introduction of improved machinery for cleaning the hemp this cost may be somewhat reduced, since it is estimated that the ordinary methods of rubbing the seed through sieves or beating it to reduced the chaff to finer pieces the cost from beating it off the shock to delivering it at the market is about 50 cents per bushel. These estimates of cost are based on wages at $1.25 per day.

Prices

The price of hemp seed, as sold by the farmer during the past 10 years, has ranged from $2.50 to $5 per bushel. The average farm price during this period had been not far from $3 per bushel. Hemp seed is sold by weight, a bushel weighing 44 pounds.

CULTIVATION FOR FIBER
Preparation of the Land

Fall plowing on most soils is generally regarded as best for hemp, since the action of the frost in winter helps to disintegrate the particles of soil, making it more uniform in character. In practice, hemp land is plowed at any time from October to late seeding time in May, but hemp should never be sown on spring-plowed sod. The land should be plowed 8 to 10 inches in order to give a deep seed bed and opportunity for root development. Plowing either around the field or from the

Yearbook U.S. Dept. of Agriculture, 1913.
PLATE XLIV.—COLLECTING SEED AND RETTING STALKS.

Fig. 1—Beating off seed from an entire shock of seed hemp.
Fig. 2—Homemade hemp seed-cleaning machine.
Fig. 3—Spreading fiber hemp for retting.

Yearbook U.S. Dept. of Agriculture, 1913.
PLATE XLV.—CUTTING HEMP.

Fig. 1—Cutting hemp by hand, about three-fourths acre per day.
Fig. 2—Self-rake reaper, mostly used; cuts about four acres per day.
Fig. 3—Mowing machine with bar to bend over hemp; cuts about six acres per day.

Yearbook U.S. Dept. of Agriculture, 1913.
PLATE XLVI.—BREAKING HEMP.

Fig. 1—The hand brake, cleans about 100 pounds of fiber per day.
Fig. 2—Shock of hemp, tied in bundles for stacking.
Fig. 3—Machine brake which has produced 9,000 pounds of fiber in one day.
Fig. 4—Machine brake which separates and cleans the tow and the line fiber at the
    same time.

center is recommended, since back furrows and dead furrows will result in uneven moisture conditions and more uneven hemp. Before sowing, the land is harrowed to make a mellow seed bed and uniform level surface. Sometimes this harrowing is omitted, especially when hemp is grown on stubble ground plowed just before seeding. Harrowing or level in some manner is recommended at all times, in order to secure conditions for covering the seed at a uniform depth and also to facilitate close cutting at harvest time.

SEEDING
Methods of Seeding

Hemp seed should be sown as uniformly as possible all over the ground and covered as nearly as possible at a uniform depth of about three-fourths of an inch, or as deep as 2 inches in light soils. Ordinary grain drills usually plant the seed too deeply and in drills too far apart for the best results. Uniform distribution is sometimes secured by drilling in both directions. This double working, especially with a disk drill, leaves the land in good condition. Ordinary grain drills do not have a feed indicator for hemp seed, but they may be readily calibrated, and this should be done before running the risk of sowing too much or too little. Fill the seed box with hemp seed, spread a canvas under the feeding tubes, set the indicator at a little less than one-half bushel per acre for wheat, and turn the drivewheel as many times as it would turn in plowing one-tenth acre; then weigh the seed that has fallen on the canvas. If the land is to be tilled in both directions, one-half bushel each way, the drill, should feed 2.2 pounds for one-tenth acre. One method giving good results is to remove the lower sections of feeding tubes on grain drills and place a flat board so that the hemp seed falling against it will be more evenly distributed, the seed being covered either by the shoes of the frill or by a light harrow. Good results are obtained with disk drills, roller press drills, and also with the end-gate broadcast seeder. Drills made especially for sowing hemp seed are now on the market, and they are superseding all other methods of sowing hemp seed in Kentucky. Rolling after seeding is advised, in order to pack the soil about the seed and to secure a smooth surface for cutting, but rolling is not recommended for soils where it is known to have an injurious effect.

Amount of Seed

Hemp is sown at the rate of about 3 pecks (33 pounds) per acre. On especially rich soil 1-1/2 bushels may be sown with good results, and on poor land that will not support a dense, heavy crop a smaller amount is recommended. If conditions are favorable and the seed germinates 98 to 100 percent, 3 pecks is usually sufficient.

When kept dry, hemp seed retains its germinative vitality well for at least three or four years, but different lots have been found to vary from 35 to 100 percent and it is always well to test the seed before sowing.

Time of Seeding

In Kentucky, hemp seed is sown from the last of March to the last of May. The best results are usually obtained from April seeding. Later seedings may be successful when there is a plentiful rainfall in June. In Nebraska, hemp seed was sown in April, May, or sometimes as late as June. In California, it is sown in February or March; in Indiana and Wisconsin, in May. In general, the best time for sowing hemp seed is just before the time for sowing oats in any given locality.

After the seed is sown, the hemp crop requires no further care or attention until the time of harvest.

HARVEST
Time

In California, hemp is cut late in July or in August; in Kentucky, Indiana, and Wisconsin it is cut in September. The hemp should be cut when the staminate plants are in full flower and the pollen is flying. If cut earlier, the fiber will be finer and softer but also weaker and less in quantity. If permitted to become overripe, the fiber will be coarse, harsh, and less pliable, and it will be impossible to ret the stalks properly.

METHODS OF HARVESTING
Harvesting by Hand

In Kentucky, a small portion of the hemp crop is still cut by hand with a reaping knife or hemp hook. (Pl. XLV, fig. 1.) This knife is somewhat similar to a long-handled corn cutter. The man cutting the hemp pulls an armful of stalks toward him with his left arm and cuts them off as near the base a possible by drawing the knife close to the ground; he then lays the stalks on the ground in a smooth, even row, with the butts toward him, that is, toward the uncut hemp. An experienced hand will cut with a reaping knife about three-fourths of an acre a day. The hemp stalks are allowed to lie on the ground until dry, when they are raked up by hand and set up in shocks until time to spread for retting.

Harvesting with Reapers

Sweep-rake reapers are being used in increasing numbers for harvesting hemp in Kentucky and in all other localities where hemp is raised. (Pl. XLV, fig.2.) While not entirely satisfactory, they are being improved and strengthened so as to be better adapted for heavy work. Three men, one to grind sections, one to drive, and one to attend to the machine, and four strong horses or mules are required in cutting hemp with a reaper. Under favorable conditions, from 5 to 7 acres per day can be cut in this manner. This more rapid work makes it possible to harvest the crop more nearly at the proper time. The stalks, after curing in the gavel, are set up in shocks, usually without binding into bundles unless they are to be stacked.

Harvesting with Mowing Machines

In some places, hemp is cut with ordinary mowing machines. (Pl. XLV, fig.3.) A horizontal bar nearly parallel with the cutting bar, the outer end projecting slightly forward, is attached to an upright fastened to the tongue of the machine. This bar is about 4 feet above the cutting bar and about 20 inches to the front. It bends the hemp stalks over in the direction the machine is going. The stalks are more easily cut when thus bent away from the knives and, furthermore, the bases snap back of the cutting bar and never drip through between the guards to be cut a second time, as they often do when cut standing erect. With a 5-1/2 foot mowing machine thus equipped, one man and one team of two horses will cut 6 to 8 acres per day. The work is regarded as about equal to cutting a heavy crop of clover. The hemp thus cut all falls in the direction the machine is going, the tops overlapping the butts of the stalks. The ordinary track clearer at the end of the bar clears a path, so that the stalks are not materially injured either by the horses or the wheels of the machine at the next round.

The hemp stalks are then left where they fall until retted, or in places where the crop is heavy the stalks are turned once or twice to secure uniform curing and retting. When sufficiently retted the stalks are raked up with a 2-horse hayrake, going crosswise of the swaths, and then drawn, like hay, to the machine brake. This is the most inexpensive method for handling the crop. It is impossible to make clean, long, straight fiber from stalks handled in this manner, and it is not recommended where better methods are practicable. It is worthy of more extended use, however, for handling short and irregular hemp, and

hundreds of acres of hemp now burned in Kentucky because it is too short to be treated in the regular manner might be handled with profit by this method. There may be nearly as much profit in 3-1/2-cent fiber produced at a cost of 2 cents per pound as in 5-cent fiber produced at a cost of 3 cents, provided the land rent is not too large an item of cost.

Need for Improvement in Hemp Harvesters

The most satisfactory hemp-harvesting machines now in use are the self-rake reapers, made especially for this purpose. They are just about as satisfactory for hemp now as the similar machines for wheat and oats were 30 years ago. More efficient harvesting machinery is needed to bring the handling of this crop up to present methods in harvesting corn or small grain. A machine is needed which will cut the stalks close to the ground, deliver them straight and not bruised or broken, with the butts even, and bound in bundles about 8 inches in diameter. A modified form of the upright corn binder, arranged to cut a swath about 4 feet wide, is suggested. Modified forms of grain binders have been tried, but with rather unsatisfactory results. Green hemp 8 to 14 feet high can not be handled successfully by grain binders; furthermore, the reel breaks or damages a large proportion of the hemp. The tough, fibrous stalks, some of which may be an inch in diameter, are more difficult to cut than grain and therefore require sharp knives with a high motion.

A hemp-reaping machine is also needed that will cut the hemp and lay it down in an even swath, as grain is laid with a cradle. The butts should all be in one direction, and the swath should be far enough from the cut hemp so as not to be in the way at the next round. A machine of this type may be used where it is desired to ret the hemp in the fall immediately after cutting. It might be used for late crops in Kentucky, or generally for hemp farther north, where there is little danger of "sunburn" after the hemp is harvested.

Stacking

Hemp stalks which are to be stacked are bound in bundles about 10 inches in diameter, with small hemp plants for bands, before being placed in shocks. (Pl. XLVI, fig.2.) They are allowed to stand in the shock from 10 to 15 days, or a sufficient length of time to avoid danger of heating in the stack. The bundles are hauled from the shocks to the stacks in rather small loads of half a ton or less on a low rack or sled. Three men with a team and low wagon to haul the stalks can put up two hemp stacks of about 8 tons each in a day.

A hemp stack must be built to shed water. It is started much like a grain stack with a shock, around which the bundles are placed in tiers, with the butts sloping downward and outward. The stack is kept higher in the center and each succeeding outer tier projects slightly to a height of 5 or 6 feet, when another shock is built in the center, around which the bundles are carefully placed to shed water and the peak capped with an upright bundle. A well-built stack may be kept four or five years without injury.

Hemp which has been stacked rets more quickly and more evenly, the fiber is usually of better quality, and the yield of fiber is usually greater than hemp retted directly from the shock. Hemp is stacked before retting, but not after retting in Kentucky. Staking retted hemp stalks for storage before breaking is not recommended in climates where there is danger of gathering moisture. Retted stalks may be stored in sheds where they will be kept dry.

Care in Handling

Hemp stalks must be kept straight, unbroken, and with the butts even. They must be handled with greater care than is commonly exercised in handling grain crops. When a bunch of loose stalks is picked up at any stage of the operation, it is chucked down on the butts to make them even. The loose stalks, or bundles, are handled by hand and not with pitchforks. The only tool used in handling the stalks is a hook or rake, in gathering them up from the swath.

Retting

Retting is a process in which the gums surrounding the fibers and binding them together are partly dissolved and removed. It permits the fiber to be separated from the woody inner portion of the stalk and from the thin outer bark, and it also removes soluble materials which would cause rapid decomposition if left with the fiber. Two methods of retting are practiced commercially, viz, dew retting and water retting.

Dew Retting

In this country dew retting is practiced almost exclusively. The hemp is spread on the ground in thin, even rows, so that it will all be uniformly exposed to the weather. In spreading hemp the workman takes an armful of stalks and, walking backward, slides them sidewise from his knee, so that the butts are all even in one direction and the

layer is not more than three stalks in thickness. (Pl. XLIV, fig.3.) This work is usually paid for at the rate of $1 per acre, and experienced hands will average more than 1 acre per day. The hemp is left on the ground from four weeks to four months. Warm, moist weather promotes the retting process, and cold or dry weather retards it. Hemp rets rapidly if spread during early fall, provided there are rains, but it is likely to be less uniform than if retted during the colder months. It should not be spread early enough to be exposed to the sun in hot, dry weather. Alternate freezing and thawing or light snows melting on the hemp give most desirable results in retting. Slender stalks one-fourth inch in diameter or less ret more slowly than coarse stalks, and such stalks are usually not overretted if left on the ground al winter. Hemp rets well in young wheat or rye, which hold the moisture about the stalks. In Kentucky most of the hemp is spread during December. A protracted January thaw with comparatively warm rainy weather occasionally results in overretting. While this does not destroy the crop, it weakens the fiber and causes much loss. When retted sufficiently, so that the fiber can be easily separated from the hurds, or woody portion, the stalks are raked up and set up in shocks, care being exercised to keep them straight and with the butts even. They are not bound in bundles, but a band is sometimes put around the shock near the top. The work of taking up the stalks after retting is usually done by piecework at the rate of $1 per acre.

Water Retting

Water retting is practiced in Italy, France, Belgium, Germany, Japan, and China, and in some localities in Russia. It consists in immersing the hemp stalks in water in streams, ponds, or artificial tanks. In Italy, where the whitest and softest hemp fiber is produced, the stalks are placed in tanks of soft water for a few days, then taken out and dried, and returned to the tanks for a second retting. Usually the stalks remain in the water first about eight days and the second time a little longer.

In either dew retting or water retting the process is complete when the bark, including the fiber, readily separates from the stalks. The solution of the gums is accomplished chiefly by certain bacteria. If the retting process is allowed to go too far, other bacteria attack the fiber. The development of these different bacteria depends to a large extent upon the temperature. Processes have been devised for placing pure cultures of specific bacteria in the retting tanks and then keeping the temperature and air supply at the best for their development.[34] These methods, which seem to give promise of success, have not been adopted in commercial work.

Chemical Retting

Many processes for retting or for combined retting and bleaching with chemicals have been devised, but none of them have given sufficiently good results to warrant their introduction on a commercial scale. In most of the chemical retting processes it have been found difficult to secure a soft, lustrous fiber, like that produced by dew or water retting, or completely to remove the chemicals so that the fiber will not continue to deteriorate owing to their injurious action.

One of the most serious difficulties in hemp cultivation at the present time is the lack of satisfactory method of retting that may be relied upon to give uniform results without injury to the fiber. An excellent crop of hemp stalks, capable of yielding more than $50 worth of fiber per acre, may be practically ruined by unsuitable weather conditions while retting. Water retting, although less dependent on weather conditions than dew retting, has not thus far given profitable results in this country. The nearest approach to commercial success with water retting in recent years in America was attained in 1906 at Northfield, Minn. where after several years of experimental work, good fiber, similar to Italian hemp in quality, was produced from hemp retted in water in large cement tanks. The water was kept in circulation and at the desired temperature by a modification of the Deswarte-Loppens system.

Steaming

In Japan, where some of the best hemp fiber is produced, three methods of retting are employed —dew retting, water retting, and steaming, the last giving the best results. Bundles of hemp stalks are first immersed in water one or two days to become thoroughly wet. They are then secured vertically in a long conical box open at the bottom and top. The box thus filled with wet stalks is raised by means of a derrick and swung over a pile of heated stones on which water is dashed to produce steam. Steaming about three hours is sufficient. The fiber is then stripped off by hand and scraped, to remove the outer bark. The fiber thus prepared is very strong, but less flexible than that prepared by dew retting or water retting.

Breaking

Breaking is a process by means of which the inner, woody shell is broken in pieces and removed,

leaving the clean, long, straight fiber. Strictly speaking, the breaking process merely breaks in pieces the woody portions, while their removal is a second operation properly called scutching. In Italy and in some other parts of Europe the stalks are broken by one machine, or device, and afterwards scutched by another. In this country the two are usually combined in one operation.

Hand Brakes

Hand brakes (Pl. XLVI, fig.1), with little change or modification, have been in use for many generations, and even yet more than three-fourths of the hemp fiber produced in Kentucky is broken out on the hand brake. This simple device consists of three boards about 5 feet long set edgewise, wider apart at one end than the other and with the upper edges somewhat sharpened. Above this a framework, with two boards sharpened on the lower edges, is hinged near the wide end of the lower frame, so that when worked up and down by means of the handle along the back these upper boards pass midway in the spaces between the lower ones. A carpenter or wagon maker can easily make one of these hand brakes, and they are sold in Kentucky for about $5.

The operator takes an armful of hemp under his left arm, places the butts across the wide end of the brake near the hinged upper part, which is raised with his right hand, and crunches the upper part down, breaking the stalks. This operation is repeated several times, moving the stalks along toward the narrow end so as to break the shorter pieces, and when the hemp appears pretty well broken the operator takes the armful in both hands and whips it across the brake to remove the loosened hurds. He then reverses the bundle and breaks the tops and cleans the fiber in the same manner.

The usual charge for breaking the hemp on the hand brake in this manner is 1 cent to 1-1/2 cents per pound. There are records of 400 pounds being broken by one man in a day, but the average day's work, counting six days in a week, is rarely more than 75 pounds. In a good crop, therefore, it would require 10 to 15 days for one man to break an acre of hemp. The work requires skill, strength, and endurance, and for many years there has been increasing difficulty in securing laborers for it. It is plainly evident that the hemp industry can not increase in this country unless some method is used for preparing the fiber requiring less hand labor than the hand brake.

Machine Brakes

Several years ago a brake was built at Rantoul, Ill., for breaking and cleaning the fiber rapidly, but producing tow or tangled fiber instead of clean, straight, line fiber, such as is obtained by the hand brake. This machine consisted essentially of a series of fluted rollers followed by a series of beating wheels. Machines designed after this type, but improved in many respects, have been in use several years at Havelock, Nebr., and first at Gridley, then at Courtland and Rio Vista, Cal. These machines have sufficient capacity and are operated at comparatively small costs, the hurds furnishing more than sufficient fuel for the steam power required, but the condition of the fiber produced is not satisfactory for high-class twines and it commands a lower price than clean, long straight fiber.

The Sanford-Mallory flax brake, consisting essentially of five fluted rollers with an interrupted motion, producing a rubbing effect, has been used to a limited extent for breaking hemp. This machine, as ordinarily made for breaking flax, is too light and its capacity is insufficient for the work of breaking hemp.

A portable machine brake (Pl. XLVI, fig. 4) has been used successfully in Kentucky during the past two years. It has a series of crushing and breaking rollers, beating and scutching devices, and a novel application of suction to aid in separating hurds and tow. The stalks are fed endwise. The long fiber, scutched and clean, leaves the machine at one point, the tow, nearly clean, at another, and the hurds, entirely free from fiber, at another. It has a capacity of about 1 ton of clean fiber per day.

Another portable machine brake has been in use in California during the past two years, chiefly breaking hemp that has been thoroughly air dried but not retted. This hemp, grown with irrigation, becomes dry enough in that arid climate to break well, but this method is not practicable in humid climates without artificial drying. The stalks, fed endwise, pass first through a series of fluted or grooved rollers and then through a pair of beating wheels, removing most of the hurds, and the fiber, passing between three pairs of moving scutching aprons, each pair followed by rollers, finally leaves the machine in a kind of continuous lap folded back and forth in the baling box.

A larger machine (Pl. XLVI, fig. 3), having the greatest capacity and turning out the cleanest and most uniform fiber of any of the brakes thus far brought out, has been used to a limited extent during the past eight years in Kentucky, California, Indiana, and Wisconsin. This machine weighs about 7 tons, but it is mounted on wheels and is drawn about by a traction farm engine, which also furnishes power for operating it. The stalks are fed sidewise in a continuous layer 1 to 3 inches thick, and carried along so that the ends, forced through the slits, are broken and scutched simultaneously by converging revolving cylinders about 12 and 16 feet long. One cylinder, extending beyond the end of the other, cleans the middle portion of the stalks, the grasping mechanism carrying them forward being shifted to the fiber cleaned by the shorter cylinder. The cylinders break the stalks and scutch the fiber on the under side of the layer as it is carried along, and the loosened hurds on the upper side are scutched by two large beating wheels just as it leaves the machine. The fiber leaves the machine sidewise, thoroughly cleaned and ready to be twisted into heads and packed in bales. This machine with a full crew of 15 men, including men to haul stalks from the field and other to tie up the fiber for baling, has a capacity of 1,000 pounds of clean, straight fiber of good hemp per hour. It does good work with hemp retted somewhat less than is necessary for the hand brake, and it turns out more uniform and cleaner fiber. For good work it requires, as do all the machines and also the hand brakes, that the hemp stalks be dry. If the atmosphere is dry at the time of breaking, the hemp may be broken directly from the shocks in the field, but in regions with a moist atmosphere, or with much rainy weather, it would be best to store the stalks in sheds or under cover, and with a stationary plant it might be economical to dry them artificially, using the hurds for fuel. Extreme care must be exercised in artificial drying, however, to avoid injury to the fiber.

Improvement needed in Hemp-Breaking Machines

While hemp-breaking machines have now reached a degree of perfection at which they are successfully replacing the hand brakes, as the thrashing machines half a century ago began replacing the flail, there is still room for improvement. This needed improvement may be expected as soon as hemp is grown more extensively, so as to make a sufficient demand for machinery to induce manufacturers to invest capital in this line. For small and scattered crops a comparatively light, portable machine is desirable, requiring not more than 10 horsepower and not more than four or five laborers of average skill for its operation. It should prepare the fiber clean and straight, ready to be tied in hanks for baling, and should have a capacity of at least 1,000 pounds of clean fiber per day. For localities where hemp is grown more abundantly, so as to furnish a large supply of stalks within short hauling distance, a larger machine operated in a stationary central plant by a crew of men trained to their respective duties, like workers in a textile mill, will doubtless be found more economical. Artificial retting and drying may also be used to good advantage in a central plant.

The hemp growers of Europe have adopted machine brakes more readily than the farmers in this country, and the hemp industry in Europe is most flourishing and most profitable where the machines are used. Most of the hemp in northern Italy is broken and scutched by portable machines. Machines are also used in Hungary, and the machine-scutched hemp of Hungary is regularly quoted at $10 to $15 per ton higher than that prepared by hand. These European machines may not be adapted to American conditions, but, together with American machines which are doing successful work, they sufficiently contradict the frequent assertion of hemp growers and dealers that "no machine can ever equal the hand brake."

Sorting

On many hemp plantations the stalks are roughly sorted before breaking, so that the longer or better fibers will be kept separate. The work of sorting can usually be done best at this point, short stalks from one portion of a field being kept separate from the longer stalks of another portion and overretted stalks from stalks with stronger fiber. Sometimes the men breaking the hemp sort the fiber as it is broken. An expert handler of fiber will readily work it into two or three grades by feeling of it as it leaves the hand brake or the breaking machine. It is a mistaken policy to suppose that the average price will be higher if poor fiber is mixed with good. It may be safely assumed that the purchaser fixing the price will pay for a mixed lot a rate more nearly the value of the lowest in the mixture, and he can not justly do otherwise, for the fiber must be sorted later if it is to be used to the best advantage in the course of manufacture.

Packing Fiber for Local Market

The long, straight fiber is put up in bundles, or heads, 4 to 6 inches in diameter and weighing 2 to 4 pounds. (Pl. XL, fig.4) The bundle of fiber is twisted and bent over, forming a head about one-third below the top end. It is fastened in this form by a few strands of the fiber itself, wound tightly around the neck and tucked in so that it may be readily unfastened without cutting or becoming tangled. Three ropes, each about 15 feet long, twisted by hand from the hemp tow, are stretched on the ground about 15 inches apart. The hanks of fiber are piled crosswise ont these ropes with the heads of the successive tiers alternating with the loose ends, which are tucked in so as not to become tangled. When the bundle thus built up is about 30 inches in diameter, the ropes are drawn up tightly by two men and tied. These bundles weigh about 200 pounds each. Most of the hemp leaves the farm in this form. Hemp tow, produced from broken or tangled stalks and fiber beaten out in cleaning the long straight hemp, is packed into handmade bales in the same manner.

Hackling

In Kentucky, most of the hemp is sold by the farmers to the local dealers or hemp merchants. The hemp dealers have large warehouses where the fiber is stored, sorted, hackled, and baled. The work of hackling is rarely done on the farms. The rough hemp is first sorted by an expert, who determines which is best suited for the different grades to be produced. A quantity of this rough fiber, usually 112 or 224 pounds, is weighed out to a workman, who hackles it by hand, one head at a time. The head is first fastened and the fiber shaken out to its full length. It is then combed out by drawing it across a coarse hackle, beginning near the top end and working successively toward the center. When combed a little beyond the center, the bundle of fiber is reversed and the butt end hackled in the same manner. The coarse hackle first used consists of three or four rows of upright steel pins about 7 inches long, one-fourth of an inch thick, and 1 inch apart. The long fiber combed out straight on this hackle is called "single-dressed hemp." This may afterwards be treated in much the same manner on a smaller hackle with finer and sharper needles set closer together, splitting and subdividing the fibers as well as combing them out more smoothly. The fiber thus prepared is called "double-dressed hemp," and it commands the highest price of any hemp fiber on the American market.

The work of hackling is paid for at a certain rate per pound for the amount of dressed fiber produced. The workman therefore tries to hackle and dress the fiber in such a manner as to produce the greatest possible amount of dressed fiber and least amount of tow and waste. The dressed fiber is carefully inspected before payment is made, and there are few complaints from manufacturers that American dressed hemp is not up to the standard.

A large proportion of the hemp purchased by the local dealers is sold directly to the twine and cordage mills without hackling or other handling except carefully sorting and packing into bales.

Baling

The bales packed for shipment are usually about 4 by 3 by 2 feet. The following table gives the approximate weights per bale:

Average weight per bale of hemp for shipment to mills.

Class of hemp.	Pounds.
Tow	450
Rough	500
Single dressed	800
Double dressed	900

When cleaned by machine brakes the fiber is often baled directly without packing it in the preliminary handmade bales. In this way it has sometimes escaped the process of careful sorting and had brought unjust criticism on the machines. This cause for criticism may easily be avoided by exercising a little more care in sorting the stalks, and, if necessary, the cleaned fiber.

Yield

The yield of hemp fiber ranges from 400 to 2,500 pounds per acre. The average yield under good conditions is about 1,000 pounds per acre, of which about three-fourths are line fiber and one-fourth is tow. The yield per acre at different stages of preparation may be stated as follows:

Stalks:	Pounds.
Green, freshly cut	15,000
Dry, as cured in shock	10,000
Dry, as after dew retting	6,000
Long fiber, rough hemp	750
Tow	250

If the 750 pounds of long fiber is hackled, it will yield about 340 pounds of single-dressed hemp, 180 pounds shorts, 140 pounds fine tow, and 90 pounds hurds and waste.

The average yields in the principal hemp-producing countries of Europe, based on statements of annual average yields for 5 to 10 years, are as follows:

	Pounds.
Russia	358
Hungary	504
Italy	622
France	662

The yield is generally higher in both Europe and the United States in regions where machine brakes are used, but this is due, in part at least, to the better crops, for machine brakes usually accompany better farming.

Cost of Hemp-Fiber Production

The operations for raising a crop of hemp are essentially the same as those for raising a crop of wheat or oats up to the time of harvest, and the implements or tools required are merely a plow, disk, drill or seeder, a harrow, and a roller, such as may be found on any well-equipped farm. Estimates of the cost of these operations may therefore be based upon the cost of similar work for other crops with which all farmers are familiar. But the operations of harvesting, retting, breaking, and bailing are very different from those for other farm crops in this country. The actual cost will, of course, vary with the varying conditions on different farms.

Hemp can not be economically grown in areas of less than 50 acres in any one locality so as to warrant the use of machinery for harvesting and breaking. The following general estimate is therefore given for what may be considered the small practical area:

Estimated cost and returns for 50 acres of hemp.

Cost:

Plowing (in fall) 50 acres, $2 per acre	$100
Disking (in spring), 50 cents per acre	25
Harrowing, 30 cents per acre	15
Seed, 40 bushels, delivered, $4.50 per bushel	180
Seeding, 40 cents per acre	20
Rolling, 30 cents per acre	15
Self-rake reaper for harvesting	15
Cutting with reaper, $1 per acre	50
Picking up from gavels and shocking, $10 per acre	50
Spreading for retting, 41.50 per acre	50
Picking up from retting swath and setting in shocks, $1.40 per acre	70
Breaking 50,000 pounds fiber, including use of machine brake, 1-1/2 cents per pound	750
Baling 125 bales (400 pounds each), including use of baling press, $1.40 per bale	175
Marketing and miscellaneous expenses	150
Total cost	1,750

Returns:

Long fiber, 37,500 pounds, 6 cents per pound	2,250
Tow, 12,500 pounds, 4 center per pound	500
Total returns	2,750

It is not expected that a net profit of $20 per acre, as indicated in the foregoing estimate, may be realized in all cases, but the figures given are

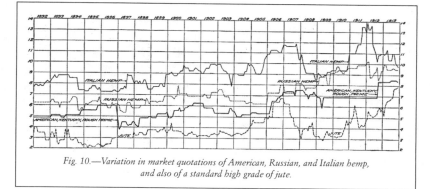

Fig. 10.—Variation in market quotations of American, Russian, and Italian hemp, and also of a standard high grade of jute.

regarded as conservative where all conditions are favorable.

Market

All of the hemp produced in this country is used in American spinning mills, and it is not sufficient to supply one-half of the demand. The importations have been increasing slightly during the past 20 years, while there has been a decided increase in values. The average declared value of imported hemp, including all grades, for the 4,817 tons imported in 1893, was $142.31 per tons, while in the fiscal year 1913 the importations amounted to 7,663 tons with an average declared value of $193.67 per ton. There have been some fluctuations in quotations, but the general tendency of prices of both imported and American hemp has been upward. (Fig. 19.) The quotations for Kentucky rough prime, since October, 1912, have been the highest recorded for this standard grade. Furthermore, the increasing demand for this fiber, together with the scarcity of competing fibers in the world's markets, indicates a continuation of prices at high levels.

Effect of Tariff

So far as can be determined from the record of importations and prices since 1880, the earliest available statistics, the changes in the rate of import duty on hemp have had no appreciable effect on the quantity imported, on the declared import value[35] of the fiber, or on the quantity produced or the price of American hemp in this country. (Fig. 20) The tariff acts of 1870, 1883, and 1590, in force until 1894, imposed a duty of $25 per ton on line hemp. From 1894 to 1899 hemp was on the free list, and from 1899 to 1913 it was dutiable at $22.50 per ton.

The importations reached a high level in 1899, when hemp was extensively used for binder twine. From that year onward henequen from Yucatan and abaca from the Philippines replaced hemp in binder twine, while jute from India replaced it completely for cotton-bail covering. The increasing demand for hemp for commercial twines has resulted in higher prices for both imported and American hemps, but this demand has been met in this country neither by importation nor by production. There are not accurate statistics of acreage or production in the United States, but there has been a general decline from about 7,000 tons in 1880 to about 5,000 in 1913. The average annual production during the period of free importations, 1894 to 1899, was about 5,000 tons, but slightly less than that of the previous 10 years and about the same as the average of the period of dutiable hemp since then.

The present tariff, 1913, with hemp on the free list, has not been in force long enough to indicate any appreciable effect.

Location of American Mills

Some hemp from the larger farms is sold directly to the spinning mills, but most of that produced in this country passes through the hands of local dealers in Kentucky. The hemp imported is purchased either directly from foreign dealers by the mills or through fiber brokers in New York and Boston.

There is one twine mill at Frankfort, Ky., on the western edge of the hemp-producing region, and one at Covington, Ky., opposite Cincinnati, but aside from the comparatively small quantities used by these mills and a little used in the mill at Oakland, Cal., practically all the hemp fiber is shipped away from the States where it is produced. There are 28 mills in this country using

American hemp, most of them in the vicinity of Boston or New York, as indicated on the accompanying map[36] (fig. 21). In most of these mills other soft fibers, such as jute, China jute, and flax, are also used and many of them are also engaged in the manufacture of twines and cordage from the hard fibers—sisal, henequen, abaca (manila), phormium, and Mauritius.

Uses

Hemp is used in the manufacture of tying twine, carpet warp, seine twine, sails, standing rigging, and heaving lines for ships, and for packing. It has been used to some extent for binder twine, but at the relative prices usually prevailing it can not well compete with sisal and abaca for this purpose. Binder twine made of American hemp and India jute mixed has been placed upon the market. This twine is said to give excellent results because it is more smooth and uniform than twine made of hard fiber. The hemp fiber is tougher and more pliable than hard fibers, and the twine is therefore more difficult to cut in the knotter. Hemp is also used to a limited extent for bagging and cotton baling. Only the tow and cheaper grades of the fiber can compete with other fibers for these purposes. The softer grades of hemp tow are extensively used for oakum and packing in pumps, engines, and similar machinery. It endures heat, moisture, and friction with less injury than other fibers except flax, used for these purposes. Hemp is especially adapted by its strength and durability for the manufacture of carpet warp, hall rugs, aisle runners, tarpaulins, sails, upholstery webbing, belt webbing, and for all purposes in textile articles where strength, durability, and flexibility are desired. Hemp will make fabrics stranger and more durable than cotton or woolen fabrics of the same weight, but owing to its coarser texture it is not well suited for clothing and for many articles commonly made of cotton and wool.

Competing Fibers

The principal fibers now competing with American-grown hemp are Russian and Hungarian hemp, cotton, and jute. Italian hemp, being water retted, is not only higher in price but it is different in character from the American dew-retted hemp, and it is used for certain kinds of twines and the finer grades of carpet warp for which American hemp is not well suited. Twine made of Italian hemp may, of course, be used sometimes where American hemp twine might serve just as well, but owing to its higher price it is not likely to be used as a substitute, and it can not compete to the disadvantage of American hemp.

Russian and Hungarian hemp, chiefly dew retted, is of the same character as American hemp and is used for the same purposes. Russian hemp is delivered at the mills in this country at prices but little above those of rough hemp from Kentucky. Most of the Russian and Hungarian hemp imported is of the better grades, the poorer grades being retained in Europe, where many articles are made of low-grade hemp that would be made of low-grade cotton in this country.

In some years, owing to unsuitable weather conditions for retting Kentucky hemp or to greater care in handling Russian hemp and to care in grading the hemp for export from Russia, much of the Russian hemp of the better grades has been stronger and more satisfactory to twine manufacturers than American hemp placed on the market at approximately the same price. It is used for mixing with overretted and weak American hemp to give the requisite strength to twine.

Cotton is now used more extensively than all other vegetable fibers combined. The world's supply of cotton is estimated in round

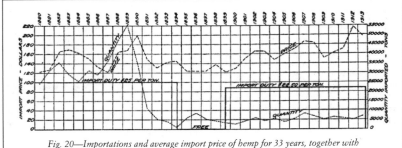

Fig. 20—Importations and average import price of hemp for 33 years, together with changes in the rate of import duty.

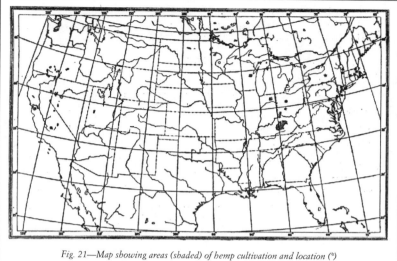

Fig. 21—Map showing areas (shaded) of hemp cultivation and location (*) of hemp spinning mills in the United States.

numbers at 5,500,000 tons, valued at nearly $1,000,000,000. The total supply of all other fibers of commerce—hemp, flax, jute, China jute, ramie, sisal, abaca, phormium, Mauritius fiber, cabuya, mescal fiber, and Philippine maguey—amounts annually to about 3,300,000 tons, valued at about $350,000,000. Cotton, therefore, so greatly overshadows all other textile fibers that it may scarcely be regarded as competing directly with any one of them. Cotton is prepared and spun on different kinds of machines from those used for preparing and spinning long fibers. Cotton is not mixed with hemp and is rarely spun in the same mills where hemp is used. Cotton twines do, however, compete with hemp tying twines, and cotton is largely used for carpet warp, where hemp, with its superior strength and durability, would give better service. Less than a century ago hemp and flax were used more extensively than cotton, but the introduction of the cotton gin, followed by the rapid development of machinery all along the line for preparing and spinning cotton fiber, while there has been no corresponding development in machinery for preparing and spinning hemp or other long fibers, has given cotton the supremacy among vegetable fibers. There is little probability that hemp will regain the supremacy over cotton, even with improved machinery for handling the crop and spinning the fiber, because cotton is better adapted to a wide range of textile products. Hemp should, however, regain many of the lines where it will give better service than cotton.

Jute is the most dangerous competitor of hemp. Jute is produced in India from the bast or inner bark of two closely related species of plants, jute (*Corchorus capsularis*) and nalta jute (*Corchorus olitorius*). These plants are somewhat similar in appearance to hemp, though not at all related to it. They are grown on the alluvial soils in the province of Bengal, India, and to a much less extent in other parts of India, southern China, and Taiwan (Formosa). More than 3,000,000 acres are devoted to this crop, and the annual production is approximately 2,000,000 tons of fiber, valued at $150,000,000. The plants are pulled by hand, water retted in slow streams or stagnant pools, and the fiber cleaned by hand without the aid of even crude appliances as effective as the hand brake for hemp. Jute fiber thus prepared, cleaner, softer, and more easily spun than Kentucky rough-prime hemp, is delivered in New York at an average price of about 4 cents per pound for the better grades. Jute butts, consisting of the coarser fiber cut off at the base, 5 to 10 inches long, are sold in this country at 1 to 2 cents per pound. Most of the long jute fiber comprising the "light jute" grades are of a light straw color, white the "dark jutes," also called "desi jute," are of a dark, brownish gray. The fresh

Reactions of hemp and jute.[1]

Test	Hemp	Jute.
Schweitzer's	Clean fiber dissolved	Bluish color, more or less distinct swelling
Iodin and sulphuric acid	Greenish blue to pure blue	Yellow to brown
Anilin sulphate	Faint yellow	Golden yellow to orange
Warming in weak solution of nitric acid and potassium chromate, then washing and warming in dilute solution of soda ash and washing again; place on microscopic slide, and when dry add drop of glycerol. Use polariscope (dark field).	Uniform blue or yellow	Prismatic colors

1 *Matthews, J. Merritt. The Textile Fibers, p. 349, 1908.*

fiber of both kinds when well prepared is lustrous, but with age it changes to a dingy, brownish yellow.

Fresh jute fiber is about two-thirds as strong as hemp fiber of the same weight, but jute lacks durability and rapidly loses its strength even in dry air, while if exposed to moisture it quickly goes to pieces. It is not suitable for any purpose where strength or durability is required.

Jute is used most extensively for burlaps, gunny bags, sugar sacks, grain sacks, wool sacking, and covering for cotton bales. Hemp has been used for all of these purposes, but the cheaper jute fiber now practically holds the entire field in the manufacture of coverings for agricultural products in transit. This is a legitimate field for jute, where it constitutes a "gift package," generally to be used but once, but even in this field hemp may regain some of its uses where it is found that jute does not give sufficient strength or durability.

Jute is often used as an adulterant or as a substitute for hemp in the manufacture of twines, webbing, carpet warp, and carpets. The careless use of the name hemp to indicate jute aids in facilitating this substitution. Twine made of pure jute fiber is sold as "hemp twine" in the retail stores in Lexington, Ky., in the heart of the hemp-growing region. Many of the so-called hemp carpets and hemp rugs are made only of jute, and they wear out quickly, whereas as carpet made of hemp should be as durable as one made of wool. Jute is substituted for hemp very largely in the manufacture of warp for carpets and rugs, a purpose for which its lack of strength and durability makes it poorly fitted. It is to the interest of the purchaser of manufactured articles as well as to the producer of hemp and the manufacturer of pure hemp goods that the line between hemp and jute be sharply drawn. Unfortunately, the difference in the appearance of the fibers by which they may be distinguished is not as strongly marked as the differences between their strength and wearing qualities.

Tests for Distinguishing between Jute and Hemp

There are no satisfactory tests for these fibers without the aid of a microscope and chemical reagents. A ready, but uncertain, test consists in untwisting the end of twine or yarn. Jute fiber thus unwound is more fuzzy and more brittle than hemp. The two fibers may be distinguished with certainty with a microscope and chemical reagents, as indicated by the differences in the table which follows:

At the present high prices of jute (fig. 4), resulting from increasing demands in foreign markets and a partial failure of the crop in India, jute could not compete successfully with hemp were it not that manufacturers are using it in established lines of goods, and further, that they are uncertain about securing supplies of hemp.

Summary

Hemp is one of the oldest fiber-producing crops and was formerly the most important.

The cultivation of hemp is declining in the United States because of the (1) increasing difficulty in securing sufficient labor for handling the crop with present methods, (2) lack of labor-saving machinery as compared with machinery for handling other crops, (3) increasing profits in other crops, (4) competition of other fibers, especially jute, and (5) lack of knowledge of the crop outside of a limited area in Kentucky.

Hemp was cultivated for fiber in very early times in China.

The history of the distribution of hemp from Asia to other continents indicates its relationships and the development of the best fiber-producing types.

Hemp is cultivated in warm countries for the production of a narcotic drug, but for fiber only in moderately cool and humid temperate regions.

Very few well-marked varieties of hemp of fiber-producing types have been developed.

The climate and soils over large areas in the valley of the Mississippi and its tributaries and in the Sacramento and San Joaquin Valleys in California are suited for hemp.

Hemp improves the physical condition of the soil, destroys weeds, and when retted on the ground, as is the common practice, does not exhaust fertility.

Hemp is recommended for cultivation in regular crop rotations to take the place of a spring-sown grain crop.

Fertilizers are not generally used in growing hemp, but barnyard manure applied to previous crops is recommended.

Hemp is rarely injured by insects or fungous diseases.

Broom rape, a root parasite, is the most serious pest in hemp.

Practically all of the hemp seed used in the United States is produced in Kentucky.

The best seed is obtained from plants cultivated especially for seed productions, but some seed is obtained from broadcast overripe fiber crops.

The land should be well plowed and harrowed, so as to be level and uniform.

The seed should be sown early in spring by any method that will distribute and cover it uniformly.

Some hemp is still cut by hand in Kentucky, but the use of machinery for harvesting the crop is increasing.

Dew retting is regarded as the most practical method in this country.

Hand brakes for preparing the fiber are still used, but they are being replaced by machines.

The price of hemp has been generally increasing during the past 30 years.

About 30 different spinning mills in the United States, beside dealers in oakum supplies, offer a market for raw hemp fiber.

The market would expand if manufacturers could be assured of larger supplies.

India jute, often retailed under the name hemp, is the most dangerous competitor of hemp.

Footnotes

1   Computed from reports of the Bureau of Navigation and commerce, U.S. Treasury Department, and Bureau of Statistics, Department of commerce.

2   Linnaeus. Species Plantarum, ed. 1, 1027, 1753. Dioscorides. Medica Materia, libri sex, p. 147, 1537. Synonyms: Cannabis erratica paludosa Anders. Lobel. Stirpium Illstoria, 284, 1576. Cannabis indica Lamarck. Encyclopaedia, 1: 695, 1788. Cannabis macrosperma Stokes. Bot. Mat. Med., IV, 539,1812. Cannabis chinensis Delile. Ind. Sem. Hort. Monst. in Ann. Sci. Nat. Bot., 12:365, 1849. Cannabis gigantea Delile. L. Vilmorin. Rev. Hort., 5: s. 3, 109, 1851.

3   Bretschneider, E. Botanicum Sinicum, in Journal of the North China Branch of the Royal Asiatic Society, n.s., v. 25, p. 203, 1893, Shanghai.

4   Watt, Sir George. Commercial Products of India, p. 251, 1908.

5   De Candolle, Alphonse. Origin of Cultivated Plants, p. 148, 1886.

6   Watt, Sir George. Commercial Products of India, p.253, 1903.

7   De Candolle, Alphonse. Prodromus, v.16, pt. 1, 1869

8   De Candolle, Alphonse. Origin of Cultivated Plants, p.143, 1886.

9   Dioscorides. Medica Materia, libri sex, p. 147, 1537.

10 Delile, Raffenau. Index seminum horti botanici Monspeliensis. Ann. Sci. Nat. Bot., v.12, p.365,1849.

11 Vilmorin, L. Chanvre de Chine. Rev. Hort. 5: s. 3, p. 109, 1831.

12 PEpin. Sur le chanvre de Chine. Rev. Hort. 1: s. 3, p.199, 1847.

13 De Candolle, Alphonse. Prodromus, v.16, pt.1, p.31, 1869.

14 Husbands, José D.   U.S. Department of Agriculture, Bureau of Plant Industry, Bulletin 153, p. 42, 1909.

15 Morton, Thomas. New English Canaan, p. 64, 1632. In Force, Peter, Tracts and Other Papers, v. 2, 1838.

16 Virginia, printed for Richard Wodenoth, 1649. In Force, Peter, Tracts and Other Papers, v. 2, 1838.

17 Moore, Brent. A Study of the Past, the Present, and the Possibilities of the Hemp Industry in Kentucky, p. 14, 1905.

18 New Era, Lancaster, Pa., June 24, 1905.

19 Moore, Brent. A Study of the Past, the Present, and the Possibilities of the Hemp Industry in Kentucky, p. 16, 1905.

20 Michaux, F. Andre. Travels to the West of the Alleghanies, p. 152, 1805. In Thwaites, Early Western Travels, v. 3, p. 200, 1904.

21 Moore, Brent.   The Hemp Industry in Kentucky, pp. 60–61, 1905.

22 De Candolle, Alphonse. Origin of Cultivated Plants. p. 148, 1886.

23 Bretschneider, E.   Botanicum Sinicum, p. 203, 1893.

24 Bruck, Werner F. Studien fiber den Hansbau in Italien, p. 7, 1911.

25 Dodge, Charles Richards. Culture of Hemp in Europe. U.S. Department of Agriculture, Fiber Investigations, Report No. 11, p. 6, 1989.

26 Lamarck. Encyclopedie, v. 1, p. 695, 1788.

27 Peter, Robert. Chemical Examination of the Ash of Hemp and Buckwheat Plants. Kentucky Geological Society, p. 12, 1884.

28 Scovel, M.A.   Effect of Commercial Fertilizers on Hemp. Kentucky Agricultural Experiment Station, Bulletin 27, p. 3, 1890.

29 Report of Cawnpore Agricultural Station, United Provinces, India, for 1908, p. 12.

30 Cavara, Fridiano, Appunti de Patologia Vegetal. Atti dell" Institute Botanico dell' Universita de Pavia, s. 2, v. 1, p. 425, 1888.

31 This fungus was not in a stage permitting identification, but cultures for further study were made in the Laboratory of Plant Pathology.

32 Garman, II. The Broom-Rape of Hemp and Tobacco. Kentucky Agricultural Experiment Station, Bulletin 24, p. 16, 1890.

33 Garman, H. The Broom-Rapes. Kentucky Agricultural Experiment Station, Bulletin 105, p. 14, 1903.

34 Rossi, Giacomo. Macerazione della Canapa. Annali della Regia Scuola Superiore de Agricultura de Portici, s. 2, v. 7, p. 1–148, 1907.

35 Declared value at port of shipment.

36 Some of the mills are so close together around New York and Boston that it is impossible to indicate each one by a separate star.

Hemp

Caution

The hemp plant contains the drug marihuana. Any farmer planning to grow hemp must comply with certain regulations of the Marihuana Tax Act of 1937. This involves registration with the farmer's nearest Internal Revenue Collector and the payment of a fee of $1. Although the fee is small, the registration if mandatory and should not be neglected, as the penalty provisions for not complying with the regulations are very severe. The registration must be renewed each year beginning July 1. This so-called "license" permits a farmer to obtain viable hemp seed from a registered firm dealing in hemp, to plant and grow the crop, and to deliver mature, retted hemp stalks to a hemp mill.

Washington, D.C.
Issued January 1943
Slightly Revised April 1952

Hemp

by B. B. Robinson, Senior Agronomist
Division of Cotton and Other Fiber Crops
and Diseases
Bureau of Plant Industry, Soils, and Agricultural
Engineering
Agricultural Research Administration

Hemp is a fiber used in making twines and light cordage. It is also used as an extender for imported cordage fibers, particularly abaca, sisal, and henequen. The size of the hemp industry, therefore, is greatly influenced by the availability of imported cordage fibers.

Hemp is not a hard crop to grow. It should be planted on the most product land on the farm—land that would make 50 to 70 bushes of corn per acre.

The crop is planted with a grain drill and harvested with special machinery rented from hemp mills.

It is allowed to lie on the ground until the outer part of the stalks has rotted, freeing the fibers. This process is called dew retting.

The most important step in hemp farming is to stop the retting process at the proper time.

This bulletin tells how to grow and harvest hemp. For more information write to the Bureau of Plant Industry, Soils, and Agricultural Engineering, United States Department of Agriculture, or to your State experiment station, or consult your county agent.

What it is

Hemp is an annual plant that grows from seed each year, and therefore it can be brought readily into production. It produced twice as much fiber per acre as flax, the only other fiber that is its equal in strength and durability and that is known to be suitable for culture and preparation on machinery in this country.

When hemp seed is sown thickly for fiber production, the plants usually grow from 5 to 8 feet tall. However, when the plants are thinly spaced in rows for seed production, they may, under favorable conditions, reach a height of 12 to 16 feet. If the plants are not crowded, they become much branched and are bushy. Uniform stems approximately 3/8 inch in diameter and 5 to 8 feet long are especially desired for fiber production, because they can be handled well by the harvesting and processing machinery available in this country.

Hemp is a dioecious plant, that is, the staminate (male) and pistillate (female) flowers are borne on separate plants, rather than both on one plant. The flowers of the two types of plants are different, but the male plant is easily distinguished from the female, as the anthers are about the size of a wheat kernel. The male plants die soon after discharging their pollen; this is usually almost 3 to 6 weeks before the female plants mature seed and die.

The fiber of commerce ranges from 4 to 8 feet in length and has the appearance of a flat, line ribbon. It lies very close to the epidermis or skin of the plant. Spinners desire the fiber ribbon 1/10 inch or less in width. The long strands of fiber are called "line" fiber to distinguish them from "tow" fiber, which consists of shorter, broken, tangled pieces.

It Grows Well in the Corn Belt

Hemp is recommended as a good crop for the Corn Belt States, because of their favorable climatic and soil conditions.

Most fiber producing varieties of hemp require a frost-free growing season of 5 months or longer to product seed and approximately 4 months for fiber production. Hemp will endure light frosts in the spring and survive frosts in the fall better than corn. It grows best when well supplied with moisture throughout its growing season and especially in its early stages of growth. Drought conditions, if accompanied by light temperatures, appear to hasten maturity before the plants are fully grown.

The vegetative growth of hemp should be uniform. This growth is noticeably affected if the soil is flooded or saturated with moisture for too long a period. The leaves turn yellow, and the plants die. Rainfall, well distributed during the growing season, is, therefore, desirable for uniform vegetative growth. Hemp should be planted only on well-drained soils and not on flat, heavy, imperious soils.

Climate is important and only in the growth of the plant but also in the preparation of the crop after harvest. It influences the method used in handling the crop and the labor requirements, which determine the cost of production. In the United States the common practice (known as dew retting) is to cut the crop and let it lie on the ground. Exposure to the weather causes the fiber in the outer part of the stem to separate. Light snows and alternate freezing and thawing seem to improve or make the retting more uniform.

HOW TO GROW IT

Soils and Fertilizers

Hemp should not be grown on poor soils. To obtain good yield and fiber of high quality, it is necessary to have a growth of uniform stalks 6 to 8 feet long. Short stalks, from poor nonfertile soils, seldom produce a high quality fiber.

Fiber hemp grows successfully on soils of the Clarion., Tama., Carrington, Maury, Hagerstown, and Miami series, which, in general, are deep, medium-heavy loams, well-drained, and high in organic matter. Artificially drained areas of the Webster, Brookston, and Maumee series also give satisfactory yields. These soils are among the most productive soils of the Corn Belt. They produce average yields of 50 to 70 bushels of corn per acre. If land will not produced from 50 to 70 bushels of corn per acre, it should not be planted to hemp for fiber production.

Muck or peat soils are not recommended for the production of high quality hemp fiber. The quantity of fiber produced per acre on these soils may be very high, but experience has demonstrated that the fiber lacks strength, which is the first requirement of hemp fiber for good cordage.

The inexperienced farmer usually gets advice from an experienced hemp-mill superintendent in the selection of the right soil. In fact, the farmer's contact to grow hemp usually specifies the exact field that it has been mutually agreed should be used for the hemp crop. This type of supervision by the company contracting for hemp has helped to prevent many crop failures.

Hemp should not be grown continuously on the same soil, for the same reasons that many other crops are not adapted to such practices. In Wisconsin, fields previously used for a cultivated crop are selected for hemp planting in preference to ones upon which small grains have been grown. In Kentucky, bluegrass soil, if obtainable, is selected. Old pastures plowed up are well suited for hemp culture. Fields previously cropped to soybeans, alfalfa, and clover are excellent for hemp. A good rotation is to follow corn with hemp, and in Kentucky a fall cereal may follow the hemp.

Although hemp requires a rich soil, it does not remove from the farm an excess of plant-food material. Nearly all the leaves on the hemp plants, containing much of the plant nutrients removed from the soil, fall off during the growth and maturing of the plant. The remaining leaves may drop off in the field during the process of retting. Further, the plant stems have almost 20 percent in weight of soluble and decomposed materials, which leach out upon the fields, and the stubble may be plowed under. The plant in this manner returns to the land a large part of the plant nutrients that it removes during its growth.

Commercial fertilizers may be used to advantage on soils that are not well supplied with organic matter. Ordinarily, the best fertilizer for hemp is barnyard manure, but commercial fertilizer can be used to advantage to supplement manure. Lime applications may be supplied on acid soils to advantage. Consult your county agent for recommendations as to amounts of fertilizer and lime to apply.

Seed

The period of flowering of the hemp plant may extend over several weeks, and as a result the seed does not all mature at one time. Hemp seed for sowing frequently contains some immature green to yellowish-green seeds that may not germinate well. Good hemp seed for sowing should be relatively free of such seeds and should germinate 90 percent or better. As the oil content of hemp seed usually ranges between 29 and 34 percent, the seed should be kept cool and dry, as it spoils rapidly under warm and damp conditions. Hemp seed seldom retains its germinating power well enough to be used for seed after 2-years' storage.

When to Plant

Hemp should be planted in the spring just before corn. In a program calling for small spring grains and corn, the farmer should plan to plant his hemp between the time he plants his small grains and the corn.

Seeding

Hemp grown for seed production should be sown in rows or hills. The hills are commonly spaced 3 by 5 feet, with 6 to 10 seeds to the hill, planted not more than 1/2 inch deep. The plants are thinned to 3 to 5 to a hill. If care is taken to save seed, about 1-1/2 pounds will sow an acre. Most farmers use more seed, and frequently the crop is replanted because of late floods or failure to obtain good stands.

Hemp grown for fiber should be sown with a broadcast seeder or with a grain drill. A drill with 4 inches between drill tubes is preferred to one with 6 inches or more. The seed should not be planted deeper than 1 inch, and a depth of 1/2 inch is preferred. If the seed is planted deep, the hemp seedling is not capable of pushing its way to the surface of the ground. A slight crust on the ground frequently results in a poor stand. If the seedbed is loose, disks on a seed drill may cut too deep into the soil and the seed will be sown more than 1 inch deep. In such cases, to make certain that the disks do not cut too deep into the seedbed, they should be tied to the seed box.

A standard bushel of hempseed weighs 44 pounds. The rate of seeding hemp for fiber production ranges between 3 and 5 pecks of seed per acre. In Kentucky, where hemp is hand-broken, it has been the practice to sow 3 pecks (33 pounds) per acre. However, when the hemp is to go to the mill, 1 bushel per acre gives a product that is better suited to milling. Wisconsin and other Corn Belt farmers have commonly sown 5 pecks per acre. The lighter rate of seeding in Kentucky produces larger stalks. These stalks are easily broken, and the fiber is easily prepared by the hand breaking methods that have been used there since colonial days. Machine methods of breaking and scutching to prepare the fiber are used in Wisconsin, and recently to some extent in Kentucky. The machines will handle finer stems, and the sowing of 5 pecks is advisable where hemp is to be prepared by machine.

A good practice is planting hemp for fiber production is to sow around the edge of the field next to the fence a 16- to 18-foot width of small grains, which may he harvested before the hemp. Space is thus provided for the harvester to enter

the field and begin cutting without injuring the hemp. It also prevents hemp plants at the edge from growing too rank. Uniform plants are necessary for uniform fiber quality.

Culture

Fall plowing in Wisconsin gives better results with hemp than spring plowing.

Hemp for fiber production requires little or no cultivation or care after planting until the harvest; but if after seeding and before the seedlings emerge the ground crusts badly it may be advisable to roll the field to break the crust. Hemp for seed production should be cultivated the same as corn; that is, sufficiently to keep back the weeds. Spudding out Canada thistles where they appear in dense stands in hemp fields should be done when the hemp is only a few inches high. In most cases hemp will compete well with weeds, if the hemp gets off to a good start.

Varieties to grow

The fiber hemp grown in the United States by the early colonists was of European origin; but our present hemp, commonly known as Kentucky or domestic hemp, is of Chinese origin. Few importations of hempseed have been made in recent years for commercial plantings, as imported seed has not proved as productive under domestic conditions as Kentucky hemp.

Enemies

In the United States there are no hemp diseases of economic importance, and hemp has not been seriously affected by insects. The European corn borer and similar stem-boring insects occasionally kill a hemp stem. However, they have not proved important, perhaps because hemp has not been grown to any extent in the sections of the United States where the European corn borer is a serious pest. Seedling plants are frequently attacked by cutworms and white grubs after spring plowing of sod land.

Broom rape is a small weed 6 to 15 inches high that is parasitic on the roots of hemp, tobacco, and tomatoes. It usually grows in clumps and has purpose flowers, which produce many very small seeds. These adhere to the waxy flower parts surrounding the hempseed and are distributed in this manner. Broom rope can be can be very serious on hemp if proper control measures are not followed. Only well-cleaned hempseed and seed from fields containing no broom rape should be sown.

Hemp has been recommended as a weed control crop. Its dense, tall growth helps to kill out many common weeds. The noxious bindweed, a member of the morning glory family, is checked to some extent by hemp. Unfortunately, bindweed and several other species of morning glory have seeds so near the same size and weight of hemp seed that mixtures obtained in producing hempseed are carried to the field planted for fiber production. In growing hemp for seed all vine weeds of this type found on the hemp stalks should be removed before the hemp plants begin to produce seed.

HARVESTING

Time to Harvest

Hemp is harvested for seed production when the plant on being shaken sheds most of its seed. This occurs when the seeds are fully mature on the middle branches. The seeds will mature on the lower branches first and on the top of the plant last. The common method of harvesting hemp for seed production is to cut it by hand and shock it to permit more seed to mature and cure before threshing. The harvesting should be in the early morning or on damp days when the seeds do not shatter so much as they do in the warmer and drier part of the day. Threshing of the seed hemp should be done on dry afternoons. It threshing, the seed shocks should be placed on large canvas cloths 24 by 24 feet and then be beaten with long sticks to remove the seed.

Hemp is harvested for fiber production when the male plants are in full flower and are shedding pollen. By harvesting before the male plants die, the retting of both male and female plants is more uniform, as both types of plants are still green and growing. The harvesting period may extend for 2 weeks or longer. Very early harvested hemp may produce a finer and softer fiber than that harvested later, but it is usually weaker. The fiber from hemp that has been harvested so late that many seeds have matured does not possess so good a cordage and textile characteristics as fiber from hemp harvested earlier. Hemp stalks should be relatively free of leaves except a few at the very top before harvesting. This is important when hemp is shocked after harvest, as it makes the top of the shock smaller so that less rain can enter the shock.

Machinery

Harvesting methods vary with locality and climate. In Kentucky, hemp may grow to a height of 15 feet or more. These long stalks are difficult to handle with machinery. Self-rake reapers have been used in harvesting hemp for many years, and

they probably do better work with very tall hemp than any other machine now available. A modified rice binder, which cuts and binds the hemp into bundles, is also available, although difficulty in handling the very tall hemp may be experienced. This latter type of machine can be used for short hemp in areas such as Kentucky, where hemp must be shocked within a few days after harvest to avoid sunburn.

In the northern part of the Corn Belt the hemp usually does not grow so tall and therefore can be handled more easily with machines. During the first World War hemp harvesting machinery was developed. These harvesters in one operation cut up an 8- or 9-foot swatch and elevate the stalks to a quarter-circle platform where they are turned automatically and dropped or spread on the ground for retting. The butts of the stems all lie in the same direction and are relatively even. The thickness of the layer of stalks in the swath influences the speed and uniformity of the dew retting. Machines of this type because of their labor economy, are recommended for use in the Northern States, where hemp can be safely spread for retting when harvested. Hemp harvesters are usually owned by the hemp mills. They are rented to the individual farmers, who usually furnish the motive power and the labor to run the harvesters.

Retting

Retting is the partial rotting of the hemp stock. It permits the fiber in the stalk to separate easily in long strands from the woody core. The fiber strands break if unretted stems are bent or broken.

In this country the usual practice is to ret hemp by allowing it to lie on the ground, where it is exposed to rain and dew. This method is called dew retting.

Dew retting is dependent upon dews and rains to furnish the moist conditions necessary for the growth of the molds that cause the retting. In warm, moist weather the retting may require 1 to 2 weeks, but usually 4 to 5 weeks is required for retting in Kentucky and Wisconsin. Hemp has remained spread under snow in Wisconsin until spring without serious injury, but more often hemp left under snow all winter is overretted and ruined.

Underretting and Overretting

If hemp stalks are lifted from the ground before they are sufficiently retted, the fiber will not separate easily from the woody hurds (small pieces of the woody core of the plant) in milling. However, if the retting is permitted to go too far, the fiber separates very readily from the core, but the adhesive substance between the individual fiber cells in the long strand breaks down and the fiber is weak. Hemp further overretted produces mostly short broken strands of fiber called tow fiber, which is less valuable than the long parallel strands of fiber called line fiber.

Sunburning

In Kentucky, hemp spread immediately to ret after harvest is apt to sunburn or sunscald. It is common belief that the hot, bright days in August and September is some way cause deterioration of the fiber if spread for retting. Sunburned fiber is uneven in color, usually has less strength, and possible is drier and more harsh than fiber not sunburned. In order to avoid sunscalding, the hemp is shocked after being harvested and not spread for retting until the cooler days of November. In locations having climatic conditions similar to those prevailing in Wisconsin, sunscald of hemp is rare.

Turning Stalks

In dew retting the spread stalks should be turned once or more during the retting period. This aids in bleaching the stalks and results in fiber of more uniform color and quality. The turning is done by workmen using bent poles approximately 8 to 10 feet in length. The poles are pushed under the head cuts of stalks in the swath, and the stalks are turned over without moving the butt ends.

In turning the straw the workmen start in the middle of the field turning the first swath into vacant center space. The second swath will be turned to lie where the first swath had been, and so on.

Care should be exercised in turning to prevent the stalks from tangling. The more hemp is handled, the more tangled the stalks may become. Tangled hemp is more difficult to process and produces a high proportion of tangled, short, tow fiber.

Testing the End Point of the Ret

A few days too long in the field may make the difference between retting and rotting. Therefore, it is most important that inexperienced farmers obtain the assistance of the hemp mill superintendent or an experienced grower in determining when to stop the retting.

Dry hemp stalks should be tested when possible to determine the degree of retting. Three to six stalks are taken in both hands and bent back and forth to perform the break test. If properly retted, the fiber should not break when the woody core

breaks. The hurds should fall free of the fiber in the breaking and shaking between one's hands. If the hemp is only partly retted, some hurds will adhere to the loosened fiber. Unretted hemp fiber is usually green or light yellow. Dew-retted hemp is usually slate grey or black.

After the fiber is broken free, its strength should be tested by breaking a small strand between the fingers. A small strand of fiber not twisted and almost 3/32 inch wide should break with great difficulty and with a decided snap. If it is very weak and breaks with little or no snap the hemp is probably fully overretted or may have been grown under unfavorable cultural conditions.

An indication that the retting end point is near is that the hemp makes "bowstrings." In a small percentage of the stems, less than 1 to 5 percent under certain conditions, the middle of the stalks appear to ret first. The fiber comes free from the middle and forms a string fastened at the top and bottom of the stem, not unlike a bowstring. If bowstring stems are found, a sample of the hemp should be taken to the hemp mill superintendent as soon as possible for verification of the retting end point. The bowstring condition is only a supplementary aid in determining when to stop the retting, and it may or may not occur in proper dew-retted hemp.

Some experienced hemp producers use the peeling test for determining the degree of retting. This is accomplished by peeling the fiber away from the butt ends of the stems. If properly retted, the fiber should peel freely from the woody core of the stem. If the hemp is not sufficiently retted, the fiber will break after a few inches have been peeled. This free peelage stage is desirable for breaking hemp on hand breaks. Where hemp is to be processed by machinery the retting need not progress quite so far as is necessary for hand breaking.

Picking Up the Retted Stalks

Hemp stalks may be picked up by hand. This methods has been used from early times and is satisfactory where labor is plentiful. However, in this country it is being replaced by machine pick up binders.

In picking up the straw by hand, small sticks about 3 feet long with a single steel or wooden hook on the end are used. The hemp is raked into bunches with these implements, and usually tied. Hemp fiber bands are used in tying the bundles. An inexpensive "buck" may be used to bunch the hemp, or it may be bunched with a pitchfork.

The most efficient method is to use the pick-up binder. These machines, drawn by tractors, cover about an acre an hour. They pick up the retted hemp stalks and tie them into bundles in one operation. The machines are part of the modern hemp-mill equipment and are rented to farmers.

Dew-retted hemp is usually shocked after being picked up. The hemp remains in the shock until it is transported to the mill.

Extra Care Insures Extra Profits

The farmer's job is done when he delivers the hemp to the mill. All further processing to prepare the fiber is part of the milling operation. However, it is of interest to both farmers and mill operators to attempt to keep the hemp stalks and fiber well butted. This means keeping the butt ends of the stalks or fiber in a bundle all even. Every time the hemp stalks are handled, care should be taken to see that this is done. If the hemp stalks are well butted in the bundle when processed, the milling operations can be carried out more economically. Tangled, uneven bundles are more difficult and require more time to handle. The yield of high-value long-life fiber is much greater if the stalks are well butted.

Hemp stalks are considered most desirable if they are less than half an inch in diameter. The thickness of a pencil is frequently used to illustrate the size of desirable stalks. The larger diameter stalks have a lower percentage of fiber than finer stems, are harder to break, and produce more tow fiber.

Hemp stalks grown on unproductive soil usually contain a lower percentage of fiber, and this fiber may be coarse, harsh, and of low strength, so that it breaks into tow in milling.

Stalks underretted frequently must be run through the mill breaker a second or third time to remove the remaining hurds. This increases the milling labor costs, and the resultant fiber may be reduced to a low grade.

Yields

Hemp yields have been extremely variable when this crop has been planted in new areas by inexperienced farmers. In Wisconsin and Kentucky, where only experienced farmers have grown the crop in recent years, the yields have not varied a great deal. The crop has been reasonably dependable and has not often been injured by storms or droughts.

The average yields per acre for experienced farmers are approximately 2-1/4 to 2-1/2 tons of air-dry retted hemp stalks; 850 pounds total fiber. Under the Wisconsin machine milling system the yields may average 450 pounds line fiber and 400 pounds two fiber; under the Kentucky hand-breaking system they may average 775 pounds Kentucky rough and 76 pounds tow.

If hemp is planted for seed production, the average yields per acre are approximately 15 bushels or 660 pounds, on bottom land, and 12 bushels on uplands.

U.S. DEPARTMENT OF AGRICULTURE

Bulletin No. 404

The hemp stalk grown in a broadcast crop for fiber production is from one-eighth of an inch in diameter and from 4 to 10 feet tall. The stalk is hollow, with a cylindrical woody shell, thick near the base, where the stalk is nearly solid, and thinner above, where the hollow is relatively wider.

In the process of breaking, the woody cylinder inside of the fiber-bearing bark is broken into pieces one-half of an inch to 3 inches long and usually split into numerous segments. The thicker or lower sections are split less than the think-shelled upper ones, and they are often left quite solid.

Pith, Wood, and Fiber

The inner surface of the hurds usually bears a layer of pith, consisting of thin-walled cells nearly spherical or angular, but not elongated. They are more or less crushed and torn. They are probably of little value for paper, but they constitute less than 1 percent of the weight of the hurds. The principal weight and bulk consist of slender elongated woody cells. The outer surface is covered with fine secondary fibers composed of slender elongated cells, tougher than those of the wood but finer and shorter than those of the hemp fiber of commerce. No method has been devised thus far which completely separates from the hurds all of the long fiber. From 5 to 15 percent of the weight of the hurds consists of hemp fiber, in strands from 3 inches to 8 feet in length. Some fragments of the bark, made up of short cubical cells, usually dark in color, cling to the strands of fiber.

Character of Hurds Affected by Retting

Nearly all of the hemp in the United States is dew retted. The stalks are spread on the ground in swaths, as grain is laid by the cradle. The action of the weather, dew, and rain, aided by bacteria, dissolves and washes out the green coloring matter (chlorophyll) and most of the gums, leaving only the fibrous bark and the wood. The plants in this process lose about 60 percent of their gram weight, or about 40 percent of their air-dry weight.

The stalks are sometimes set up in shocks to cure before retting, and after retting they are set up in shocks to dry. Each time the stalks are handled they are chucked down on the ground to keep the butts even. In these operations sand and clay are often driven up into the hollow at the base of the stalks, and this dirt, which often clings tenaciously, may constitute an objectionable feature in the use of hemp hurds for paper stock.

In Italy and in most localities in Russia and Austria-Hungary where hemp is extensively cultivated, it is retted in water, but water retting has never been practiced in the United States except to a limited extent before the middle of the last century. Hurds from water-retted hemp are clean and softer than those from dew-retted hemp.

The fiber is sometimes broken from dry hemp stalks without retting. The hurds thus produced contain a small percentage of soluble gums, chiefly of the pectase series. Comparatively little hemp is prepared in this manner in America.

Process retting by means of weak solutions of chemicals or oils in hot water is practiced to a limited extent. The hurds from these processes may contain traces of the chemicals or oils and also soluble gums in greater degree than those of the dew-retted or water-retted hemp.

Proportion of Hurds to Fiber and Yield Per Acre

The yield of hemp fiber varies from 400 to 2,500 pounds per acre, averaging 1,000 pounds under favorable conditions. The weight of hurds is about five times that of the fiber or somewhat greater from hemp grown on peaty soils. A yield of 2-1/2 tons of hurds per acre may be taken as a fair average.

Hurds Available From Machine-Broken Hemp

Hemp hurds are available only from hemp which is broken by machines, when the hurds may be collected in quantity in one place. Most of the hemp in Kentucky is still broken by hand brakes. These small brakes are moved from shock to shock, so that the hurds are scattered all over the field in small piles of less than 50 pounds each, and it is the common practice to set fire to them as soon as the brake is moved. It would be difficult to collect them at a cost which would permit their use for paper stock.

Where machine brakes are used, the hemp stalks are brought to the machine as grain is brought to a thrashing machine, and the hurds accumulate in large piles, being blown from the machine by wind stackers.

Machine brakes are used in Wisconsin, Indiana, Ohio, and California, but only a limited extent in Kentucky. Five different kinds of machine brakes are now in actual use in this country, and still others are used in Europe. All of the best hemp in Italy, commanding the highest market prices paid for any hemp, is broken by machines. The better machine brakes now in use in this country prepare the fiber better and much more rapidly than the hand brakes, and they will undoubtedly be used in all localities where hemp raising is introduced as a new industry. They may also be used in Kentucky when their cost is reduced to more reasonable rates, so that they may compete with the hand brake. Hemp-braking machines are being improved and their use is increasing. The hemp-growing industry can increase in this country only as machine brakes are developed to prepare the fiber. A profitable use for the hurds will add an incentive to the use of the machine brake.

Present Uses of Hemp Hurds

Hemp hurds are used to a limited extent for barn-yard litter and stable bedding, as a substitute for sawdust in packing ice, and, in rare instances for fuel. They are not regarded as having a commercial value for any of these uses, though they are doubtless worth at least $1 per ton on the farm when used for table bedding. They are a waste product, without value for other purposes which might compete with their use for paper stock.

Present Supplies of Hurds Available

During the last season, 1915, about 1,500 acres of hemp have been harvested outside of Kentucky and in regions where machine brakes are used. Estimating the yield of hurds at 2-1/2 tons per acre, this should give a total quantity of about 3,750 tons. Large quantities of hemp from the crop of 1914, which are still unbroken in these areas, and large piles of hurds undisturbed where the machines have been used during the last two or three years, increase the total to more than 7,000 tons. Hemp is now grown outside of Kentucky in the vicinity of McGuffy, east of Lima, Ohio; around Nappanee, Elkhart County, and near Pierceton, in Kosciusko County, Ind.; about Waupun and Brandon, Wis.; and at Rio Vista and Stockton, Cal.

In Kentucky, hemp is grown in most of the counties within a radius of 50 miles of Lexington. No accurate statistics of the acreage are collected, but the crop harvested in 1915 is estimated at 7,000 acres. A machine brake will probably be used in Bourbon County and also in Clark County, but most of the hemp in Kentucky will be broken on hand brakes.

Bailing For Shipment

The hurds will have to be baled to facilitate handling in transportation and to economize storage space at the paper mills. The bales will need to be covered with burlap or some material to keep them from shaking out. They may be baled in the same presses that are used for baling hemp fiber, but care must be exercised to avoid breaking the press, for the hurds are more resistant than hemp fiber. A bale of hemp 2 by 3 by feet weighs about 500 pounds. A bale of hurds of the same size will weight about one-third less, or approximately six bales per ton.

Rough hemp fiber as it is shipped from the farm is not covered; therefore, the covering material must be purchased especially for the hurds. A piece of burlap about 36 by 48 inches placed on either side of the bale will be sufficient, but these pieces, weight about 3 pounds each, cost about 40 cents a pair. Baling rope, in addition to jute covering, will cost at least 5 cents per bale, making the total cost of covering and ties $2.70 or more per ton. Possibly chip board, costing about $33 per ton, or not more than 5 cents for the two pieces for each bale, may be used in place of burlap. Chip board, burlap, and also rope ties may all be used for paper stock. Burlap covers might be returned, to be used repeatedly until worn out, but chip board could not be used more than once.

Cost of Baling

If burlap covers are used the cost of baling, including covering, ties, use of baling press, power, and labor will amount to at least 50 cents per bale, or about $3.75 per ton. If chip board can be used the cost may be reduced to about $2 per ton. The cost of hauling and loading on the cars will vary from $1 to $3 per ton, depending upon the distance and the roads. The farmer must therefore receive from $4 to $6 per ton for the hurds, baled, on board cars at his home station.

Summary

Hemp hurds are the woody inner portion of the hemp stalk, broken into pieces in removing the fiber.

They are not used at present for any purpose that would complete with their use for paper.

Hurds are available only from machine-broken hemp, for the cost of collecting them from the hand brakes would be too great.

About 7,000 tons are now available in restricted localities in Ohio, Indiana, Wisconsin, and California.

The quantity is likely to increase as the use of machine brakes increases.

The hurds may be baled in hemp-fiber presses, with partial burlap covers like those on cotton bales, or possibly chip-board covers.

It is estimated that the farmers may deliver the bales on board cars profitably at $4 to $6 per ton.

The Manufacture of Paper From Hemp Hurds

by Jason J. Merrill,
Paper Plant Chemical, Paper-Plant Investigations

The purpose of this paper is to report upon preliminary tests which were conducted to determine the paper-making value of hemp hurds, a crop waste of the hemp-fiber industry.

The search for plant materials capable of being utilized in paper manufacture is a comparatively recent but world-wide activity which has for its object the husbanding of present sources of paper-stock supply by the substitution of new materials for some of these which re rapidly becoming less plentiful and more costly.

The abstract idea of utilizing that which is at present a waste can ply no important role in such activities, the successful commercial outcome of which must be based on the three fundamental factors—market or demand for product, satisfactory raw material, and cost.

Since hemp hurds are to be treated in this report as a raw material for the manufacture of book and printing papers, the qualities, supply, probable future, and cost of the material will be considered in comparison with wood, with which it must compete. There seems to be little doubt that the present wood supply can not withstand indefinitely the demands placed upon it, and with increased scarcity economy in the use of wood will become imperative. This effect is already apparent in many wood-using industries, and although the paper industry consumes only about 3 percent of the total forest cut, it is probable that it will be affected through this company. Our forests are being cut three times as fast as they grow, and as wood becomes more expensive proper growing and reforesting will receive more attention. Thus, naturally, a balance will be established between production and consumption, but as this condition approaches its limiting values the price of wood may rise to such levels that there will be a demand for other raw materials.

The use of waste paper in conjunction with chemical wood pulp has increased to enormous proportions, and it is probably that the increase will continue. Although it is a cheaper raw material than wood, it is reasonable to suppose that as the wood supply decreases nd the price of wood pulp advances, the price of waste paper will advance somewhat proportionately.

In view of these conditions it is advisable to investigate the paper-making value of the more promising plant materials before a critical situation arises. To be of substantial value the investigations should include not only a determination of the quality and quantity of pulp and paper which the material is capable of producing, but should embrace a consideration of such relevant factors as agricultural conditions, farm practice, assembling conditions, transportation, and probably future supply.

Certain cultivated plants seem particularly promising, because in the harvesting of the regular crop that portion which might be utilized for paper manufacture necessarily is either wholly or partially assembled. To this class of plants belong corn, broom corn, sorghum, sugar cane, bagasse, flax, hemp, and the cereal straws.

It is generally conceded that the employment of different raw materials would probably yield products of a somewhat different quality than those now prevailing in the markets, but the qualities of papers and the public demands are so diversified and numerous that this possible objection should not be serious. Ten years ago sulphur manufacturers would not accept consignments of spruce logs if they contained over 5 percent of fir, while today many manufacturers tolerate 50 percent. Rope papers are found to contain not only jute, but when this raw materials is not plentiful, chemical pulp of various kinds. "Linen paper" is often no more than a trade term. Not long ago printing papers were made entirely from chemical wood pulp, but today if it is desired to secure paper which is free from ground wood the specifications must so stipulate. Writing papers, formerly made entirely from rags, now are likely to contain either chemical or even ground-wood pulp unless the specifications prohibit it. Without doubt, many paper manufacturers have maintained certain papers up to a fixed standard for a long series of years, but it is equally true that composition has lowered the standard of a great many papers, some of which had acquired a distinctive recognition. The employment of plant fibers will not necessarily lower the present quality of papers, but if their employment does result in products whose qualities are somewhat different from our so-called standard papers it does not necessarily follow that such papers will not find a ready market.

Factors Justifying an Investigation of Hemp Hurds

Hemp hurds form a crop waste, in that they necessarily are produced in the raising and preparation of hemp fiber, and their present use and value are comparatively insignificant.

The assembling of the hurds may be affected with economy, since the area in which hemp is handled with the use of machine brakes is restricted. Although it must be stated that the present annual supply would not be sufficient to justify the installation of a pulp mill nor would its transportation to existing mills appear feasible, it is expected that the available annual tonnage, especially in certain general sections, will increase, due to the increased use of the machine brake. The present tonnage is approximately as follows: In the region of Ohio and Indiana, 2,500 tons; in the Wisconsin section 1,000 tons; in the California region, 1,400 tons.

In years of adverse weather conditions there are often large areas of hemp which are not harvested on account of its poor quality; there are also large areas of cut hemp which become over-retted, due to inclement weather. It has been suggested by some of the hemp raisers that this large amount of material might be utilized as a paper stock. In these cases the cost of the whole material would probably be somewhat higher than that of the hurds, because either all or part of the cost of harvesting and the total cost of breaking would have to be borne by the paper maker. Moreover, the quality of this material would be so very irregular and the supply so uncertain that it probably would not appeal to the paper manufacturer.

Without doubt, hemp will continue to be one of the staple agricultural crops of the United States. The wholesale destruction of the supply by fire, as frequently happens int he case of wood, is precluded by the very nature of the hemp-raising industry. Since only one year's growth can be harvested annually the supply is not endangered by the pernicious practice of overcropping, which has contributed so much to the present high and increasing cost of pulp wood. The permanency of the supply of hemp hurds thus seems assured.

The favorable location geographically of the hemp regions in relation to the pulp and paper industry is a factor of considerable importance. The Kentucky region is not at present in a position to supply hurds, as machine methods have not been adopted there to any appreciable degree. The Ohio and Indiana region, which at present has the greatest annual tonnage, with the prospect of an increase, is situated south of the Wisconsin and Michigan wood-pulp producing region and at a distance from the eastern wood-pulp producing regions; therefore, it is in a favorable position to compete in the large Ohio and Indiana markets. Since, as will be shown, the hurd pulp acts far more like soda poplar stock than sulphite stock, competition would be

strongest from the eastern mills; in fact, the hurd stock might very possibly meet with favor as a book-stock furnish in the Michigan and Wisconsin paper mills, which are within the sulphite fiber-producing region. Because of its very close proximity to paper mills, this latter possibility applies with far greater force to the Wisconsin hemp region, where a considerable extension of the hemp industry is anticipated.

HEMP HURDS AS PAPER-MAKING MATERIAL

Character of the Material

As received from Pierceton, Ind., the hurds consisted of a mixture of tangled hemp bast fibers and pieces of broken wood of the hemp stalk. No reliable data were secured as to the proportion of bast fiber in the total shipment of 4 tons, although two hand separations of small representative samples gave results averaging 8 percent. The chemical character of the material was such and the quantity was so small that any appreciable variation of the proportion should not affect materially the treating process finally adopted, yet its presence in varying proportions undoubtedly would modify to some extent the quality of the resulting paper product. Since the length of the ultimate bast fiber averages about 22 mm. and the length of the ultimate hemp wood fiber averages 0.7 mm. it is natural to assume that the bast fiber would tend to increase the strength of paper produced from the hurds.

The broken pieces of wood contained in the hurds varied in length from more particles which were somewhat finer than sawdust to pieces about 3-1/2 inches long, exceptional pieces being found which measured 6 inches in length. The majority of the long pieces were between 2 and 3 inches in length. In thickness the pieces ranged from one-eighth of an inch, in case they were derived from the base of the hemp stalks, to about one sixty-fourth of an inch in those pieces which were derived from the top and branches of the stalks. In cross section the pieces often were found to be a quarter or half of the rounded rectangular woody shell of the stalk, although there appeared to be no regularity in this respect.

From the pulp-maker's standpoint the great irregularity in thickness, length, and mass of the woody pieces militate decidedly against economy in pulp production. The smaller pieces reduce by chemical treatment sooner than the larger fragments and are thereby over-treated, which results in a lower yield of cellulose fiber and a product composed of under-treated and overtreated fibers, the production and use of which are not satisfactory or economical. It probably would be found more satisfactory, therefore, to screen or sort the hurds and treat the various sizes separately and differently.

Associated with the hurds was a small quantity of chaff and dirt, composed chiefly of sand, soil, particles of hemp leaves and flowers, and other extraneous matter. The sand and soil were present because of the practice of placing the stalks in shocks in the field, the butts of the stalks being in contact with the soil. It is a simple matter, however, to remove the chaff and dirt by sieving, and this practice was followed in most of the paper tests conducted with this material.

Character of the Tests

Because of the similarity of hemp hurds to other materials which have been tested by the Office of Paper-Plant Investigations, semi-commercial tests were conducted in cooperation with a paper manufacturer without preliminary laboratory tests. Laboratory pulp and paper tests are regarded only as a preliminary to semi-commercial tests and therefore are not employed unless the material in question presents new features which should resolve investigation before large-sized tests are undertaken.

The advantages of cooperative mill tests are many, among which may be mentioned the counsel and advice of the mill management and employees, the services of specialized and skilled labor, facilities for comparing the processes and the results of tests with commercial processes and results, and the use of commercial or semi-commercial types and sizes of machinery. Tests conducted in this manner and on this scale are of a different quality than is possible in those conducted in a laboratory, and the results are susceptible of commercial interpretation with a fair degree of reliability. It is found, in general, that the cost of securing such equipment and service for a complete and comprehensive test does not exceed $500, while the installation of an equally satisfactory equipment alone would cost at least $50,000 and in many cases very much more. Tests conducted in this manner constitute a direct demonstration to the manufacturer, and the results obtained are found to carry more weight when presented to other manufacturers for consideration.

It is well known that the method of conducting tests necessarily varies with the size of the test. In the matter of yield determination, for example, laboratory tests may be on such a small scale that the weighing and sampling of the resulting cellulose fibers may be conducted by means of chemical laboratory apparatus and analytical balance, while in tests involving a matter of 5 to 10 pounds of material larger and different types of equipment are necessary. When the tests are so increased in size as to employ 300 or 400 pounds, still other types of equipment are necessary for the treatment of the material and for a determination of the yield of fiber. In tests involving tons of material the equipment involves the use of machines. Accuracy in degree of control and in results will vary materially with the size of the test. As the size of the test increases, certain factors will vary in a beneficial manner, while others will vary in a detrimental manner, so it is a question for each investigator to decide, after taking all factors into consideration, as to the size of test which will give the most satisfactory results. In work of this nature it is found, on the whole, that better results are obtained in large tests, although the control of the factors and the determination of the yield of fiber are more difficult than in smaller tests.

In the tests described in this bulletin, the Department of Agriculture employed a rotary digester of its own design, comprising a shell 5 feet 5 inches in length by 4 foot in diameter, capable of holding about 300 pounds of air-dry hurds. It is believed that a test of this size is large enough to give satisfactory results and that the results are susceptible of commercial interpretation, while at the same time they are sufficiently small for complete control and to afford fiber-yield figures which are both accurate and reliable. Two such rotary charges gave enough fiber for one complete paper-making test.

Operations Involved in a Test

A complete test on hurds comprises seven distinct operations, and the method will be described, operation by operation, in the order in which they were conducted.

Sieving—The hurds for the first test were not sieved to remove sand and dirt, but the resulting paper was so dirty that sieving was practiced in all subsequent tests. The hurds were raked along a horizontal galvanized-iron screen, 15 feet long and 3 feet wide, with 11-1/2 meshes per linear inch, the screen being agitated by hand from below. Various amounts of dirt and chaff could be removed, depending on the degree of action, but it was found that if much more than 3 percent of the material was removed it consisted chiefly of fine pieces of wood with practically no additional sand or dirt; in most of the tests, therefore, the material was screened so as to remove approximately 3 percent. It became apparent that a finer screen would probably serve as well and effect a saving of small but good hurds.

Cooking—Cooking is the technical term for the operation by which fibrous raw materials are reduced to a residue of cellulose pulp by means of chemical treatment. In these tests about 300 pounds of hurds were charged into the rotary with the addition of a caustic-soda solution, such as is regularly employed in pulp mills and which tested an average of 109.5 grams of caustic soda per liter, or 0.916 pound per gallon, and averaged 85 percent causticity. Sufficient caustic solution was added to furnish 25 or 30 percent of actual caustic soda, calculated on the bone-dry weight of hurds in the charge. After closing the rotary head, it was started rotating at the rate of one-half revolution per minute, and in about five minutes steam at 20 pounds per square inch was admitted at such a rate that the charge was heated in one hour to 170°C, which is the theoretical equivalent of 100 pounds of steam pressure per square inch. It was found, however, that when the temperature reached 70°C, the pressure was usually 115 or 120 pounds instead of 100 pounds, due to air and grass inclosed in the rotary. At this point the rotary was stopped and steam and air relieved until the pressure dropped to 100 pounds, or a solid steam pressure. The temperature was maintained at this point for the number of hours required to reduce the hurds, which was found to be about five, after which the rotary was stopped and steam relieved until the pressure was reduced to zero, when the head was removed and the stock was emptied into a tank underneath, measuring 5-1/2 by 6 by 2 feet deep, where it was drained and washed. Samples of waste soda solution or "black liquor," which were taken from some of the "cooks" for analysis, were drawn while the stock was being thus emptied into the drainer.

Determination of yield—For determining the yield of cellulose fiber the stock in the drain tank was washed with water until free from waste soda solution, when, by means of a vacuum pump communicating with the space between the bottom and the false perforated bottom, the water was sucked from the stock, leaving the fiber with a very uniform moisture content throughout its entire mass and in a condition suitable for removing, sampling, and weighing for a yield determination. Tests have shown that it is possible to sample and calculate the yield of bone-dry fiber within 0.05 percent of the actual amount.

It has been found that stocks from different materials vary greatly in their ability to mat in the drain tank, thereby enabling a good vacuum to be obtained, some stocks permitting a 26-inch vacuum to be obtained, while other will not permit more than 5 inches. For this reason the moisture contact of the stock will vary from 65 to 85 percent.

Washing and bleaching—Washing and bleaching were performed for the purpose of bleaching the brown-colored cooked stock to a white product, since it was regarded as highly probable that the fiber would be suitable for book-paper manufacture. The colored stock was charged into a 400-pound beating and washing engine of regular construction and washed about one hour, the cylinder washer being covered with 60-mesh wire cloth in order to remove fine loose dirt and chemical residues. The washer was then rinsed, the stock heated by steam to about 40°C, and a solution of commercial bleaching powder was added in the quantity judged to be necessary, after which the stock was pumped to a large wooden tank, to remain and bleach overnight. If the stock was bleached sufficiently white it was drained and washed from bleach residues, and if not more bleach was added until a good color was obtained. The bleaching powder used was estimated to contain 35 percent of available chlorine, as this is the commercial practice, and the amount required was calculated to the bone-dry weight of the unbleached stock. More bleach is required for undercooked stock than for stock which is properly cooked or overcooked; therefore, the percentage of bleach required in an indication of the quality of the cooked stock. Since bleaching is usually more expensive than cooking, it is desirable to cook to such a degree that the consumption of bleach will be held within certain limits, depending on the raw materials used and the quality of paper to be produced. In these tests it was desirable so to cook the hurds that the consumption of bleach would not be over about 10 percent of the fiber.

Furnishing—Furnishing is the operation of charging the beating engine with the desired kind or kinds of fiber in the proper proportion and amount and the adding of such loading and sizing agents as may be necessary. As shown in the record of results, the furnish in these tests consisted of hurd stock alone and of various proportions of hurds, sulphite fiber, and soda fiber. The percentage to be given in the record of the furnishes refer to the percentage of the total fiber furnish, and this likewise applies to the loading and sizing agents. In case sulphite or soda fiber was used, the commercial product in the dry state was charged into the beating engine and disintegrated, after which the hurd stock was added in the wet condition.

Beating—Beating is that operation concerning which the paper makes often say "there is where the paper is really made," and although the statement may not be literally true it contains a great deal of truth. It is the operation whereby the fibers are separated from each other, reduced to the proper lengths, and put in such a physical or chemical condition that they felt properly and form into a satisfactory shoot. It is probable that the quality of the sheet depends more upon the proper beater action than upon any other single operations. The action consists in drawing a water suspension of the fiber between two sets of rather blunt knives, one set being located in the bottom of a circulating trough and the other set on the periphery of a roll revolving just above the former set of knives. It is during this operation that the loading and sizing agents are incorporated and the whole furnish is tinted either to produce a satisfactory white or the desired color.

The term "paper making," as used in this publication, means the operation of forming the finished sheet of paper from stock which has been furnished and prepared in the beater. In these tests a 30-inch Fourdrinier machine of regular construction was used, a machine which often is used for the production of paper for filling regular commercial orders. The machine is designed to cause the water suspension of fibers to flow on to a traveling wire cloth, whereby the water drains away. More water is removed by passing the wet sheet through a series of press rolls, after which the sheet is dried on steam-heated drums and passed through polished iron rolls, which impart a finish to the sheet. A Jordan refining machine was employed in conjunction with the machine to improve further the quality of the fiber, and a pulp screen was used in order to remove coarse and extraneous materials from the fiber.

Description of Tests

The nature of each complete paper test and the dependence of each operation on the others were such that it does not seem advisable to submit the results of the seven tests in tabular form.

Discussion of the various cooks will be given in connection with the descriptions of those paper tests in which the stocks from the cooks were used, since a stock and its cooking condition can be judged adequately only after it has been put through the various processes and into the finished sheet of paper.

The first test consisted in making four separate cooks, Nos. 283, 291, 295, and 296, of approximately 300 pounds each, dividing the total stock into two parts and making two separate paper tests. The first test was make primarily in order to learn some of the qualitative characteristics of the stock and to get the machinery equipment adjusted properly. The yield of fiber was not determined in this preliminary test, since the knowledge of it was not essential at this stage of the work. The cooked stock which was emptied into the drainer to be washed free from black liquor was composed largely of whole pieces of hurds, but only slight pressure between the fingers was required to crush the pieces. In the case of wood, this condition ordinarily would indicate undercooking, but might not in the case of hurds. Further observation on the action of the cooked stock during subsequent processes was necessary in order to judge of its quality or the suitability of the cooking conditions. The total cooked stock, about 500 pounds, was divided into two portions of 200 and 300 pounds, respectively, and work was continued on them separately. The 200-pound test, designated as run No. 135, was put into a 350-pound washing engine, washed one hour, and given a total light bleach of 2-1/2 hours. The washing removed a great amount of dirt, but the engine did not reduce the hurd stock as much as was desired. After heating the stock in the heater to 40°C, it was bleached with bleaching-powder solution, 94 gallons at 0.418 pound bleach per gallon, equivalent to 19.7 percent of the fiber. This percentage of bleach is regarded as too high for stock intended for book-paper manufacture, and subsequent cooks therefore were given harder treatment in order to reduce this figure. After draining and washing free from bleach residues, the stock was furnished in the beater with 13 percent of clay, 1 percent of resin size, and 2.5 percent of alum, was tinted blue, given one hour's light brush, and pumped to the stock chest. When running it on the paper machine, the Jordan refiner seemed to have little effect in reducing shives of undertreated wood, which indicated further the necessity of harder cooking. The furnish acted well on the paper machine at 70 feet per minute, but appeared somewhat too "free" on the wire. The paper produced from this test is of very low quality, due to the improper preparation of the stock, lack of sufficient bleach, the use of too small an amount of blue tinting, and the presence of an excessive amount of dirt, sand, and shives. The excessive amount of dirt and sand suggested the sieving of the hurds before cooking, and this was performed in all subsequent cooks. The finish of the sheet is very poor, due to the fact that the calendar stock was composed of very light rolls which did not have a satisfactory surface, yet the stock is know to be able to produce better finishes if the proper stock is employed.

Item No. 136 was made on the 300-pound portion of stock from cooks Nos. 293, 294, 295, and 296, and in essentially the same manner as run No. 135. The stock was washed one hour, but given a brush of three hours, and this brush was harder than in run No. 135. Bleach to the extent of 19.8 percent of the fiber was used, assisted by 1 pint of oil of vitriol, and the resulting color was an improvement over that of run No. 135. After adding 13.5 percent of clay and sizing with 1.1 percent of resin size, the furnish was given one-half hour's light brush, tinted, and run on the machine, which was set at 70 feet per minute. This stock acted better on the wire and gave no trouble on the machine, but it still seemed to be impossible to reduce the wood shives by manipulation of the Jordan refiner. The resulting sheet is an improvement over that produced by No. 135, but is far from satisfactory.

Item No. 138 was made from hurds which, as in all subsequent tests, were sieved on a 11-1/2-inch wire screen until practically all the loose dirt and sand was removed, which operation caused a loss averaging 3 percent of the hurds. Stock from cooks Nos. 302 and 303 was used for this run and the increased amount of caustic soda and the increase in the time of cooking gave a stock of better appearance than those of preceding tests.

The stock, amount to 231 pounds dry weight, was washed and at the same time given a light brush for one hour only, after which it was bleached with 17 percent of bleach without the addition of acid. Since the preceding paper appeared somewhat weak and had a low tearing quality, it was decided to use a furnish of 15.7 percent bleached sulphite and 84.3 percent bleached hemp-hurd stock. After loading with 13.1 percent of clay nd sizing with 1.1 percent of resin size, the furnish was given a medium brush for one hour, tinted, and run on to the machine at 70 feet per minute. The stock gave no trouble on the machine, but it was impossible to judge the effect of the Jordan refiner, because through an oversight the machine chest had not been cleaned since previous use on an unbleached yucca material. It is believed, however, that sheet No. 138 shows improvement in the preparation of the hurd pulp.

Run No. 139 was made from stock of cooks Nos. 304 and 305, in which still more caustic soda was employed and the time and temperature of cooking were increased, giving a yield of total fiber of 40.7 percent of the sieved or 39.4 percent of the universal hurds. The cooked stock still seemed to be undertreated, but it must be remembered that in working with any new raw material it is impossible to know in advance how the properly treated material should appear. A washing of one hour was given while the roll was lowered from a light to a medium brush, after which the stock was bleached with 17.1 percent of bleach without the aid of acid. Some sulphite stock improved the previous paper, this bleached stock was used in a furnish of 16.6 percent sulphite and 83.4 percent hurds, loaded with 16.7 percent clay, sized with 1.4 percent resin size, given a medium brush of two hours, tinted, and run on to the machine at 70 feet per minute. The Jordan refiner seemed to have little effect in reducing shives and was therefore left "just off." No trouble was experienced with the stock on the machine, and the sheet is an improvement over previous samples.

Run No. 140 was made from cooks Nos. 306 and 307, in which more caustic soda was employed than in any previous cooks and at a higher concentration, the fiber yields of which averaged 37.3 percent of the unsieved hurds. Not much improvement was apparent in the cooked stock, in spite of the increased severity of cooking. The stock was washed and given a medium brush for one hour, bleached with 11.9 percent of bleach, assisted with one-half pint of oil of vitriol, and made into a furnish of 14.9 percent sulphite and 85.1 percent of the hurd stock. After loading with 14.7 percent of clay and sizing with 1.28 percent of resin size, the furnish was given two hours' medium brush, tinted, and run on to the paper machine at 70 feet per minute. Again the Jordan refiner did not seem to resolve the wood shives sufficiently, and it was left "just off." No trouble which could be attributed to the stock was experienced on the paper machine. The color of the resulting paper is due to the use of too little blue in tinting and probably in some measure to the use of too low a percentage of bleach.

Run No. 141 was made from the stock of cooks Nos. 308 and 109 in practically the same manner as run No. 140. The stock was washed and brushed one hour, bleached (the record of the amount of bleach was lost), made into a furnish of 14.7 percent of sulphite and 83.3 percent of hurd stock, loaded with 14.9 percent of clay, sized with 1.26 percent of resin size, given one hour at a medium brush, tinted, and run on to the machine. The Jordan refiner was able to reduce the wood shives to a somewhat greater degree than in previous runs and was held at a medium brush. The stock acted well on the machine and produced a sheet of better quality than any preceding, with the exception of the color, which was due to using too small a quantity of blue.

Among the cooks made for run No. 143 are Nos. 312 and 313, in which the concentration of the caustic soda was raised to 113 and 116 grams per liter and the percentage employed was also increased. In spite of these increases the stock from these two cooks did not show any appreciable improvement when dumped from the rotary. Stock from cooks Nos. 310, 311, and 312 was given a medium brush and washing of one hour, bleached with 10.96 percent of bleach, made into a furnish consisting of 15.3 percent of sulphite and 84.4 percent of hurd stock, loaded with 16.2 percent of clay, sized with 1.28 percent of resin size, given a medium brush for one hour, tinted, and pumped into the stock chest. Stock from cooks Nos. 313 and 314 was treated in exactly the same manner, except that 11.4 percent of bleach wa used. It was pumped to the stock chest and mixed with the furnished stock from cooks Nos. 310, 311, and 312. A medium Jordan brush was given the stock and it acted well on the paper machine, which was speeded up to 75 feet per minute. There seems to be a tendency in the hurd stock to crush a little at the "dandy roll," and although the marks are not removed by the calendar stock which was employed in those tests it was found that one "nip" on the super calenders renders them practically imperceptible and it is believed that the proper size and weight of calendar stock would entirely remove these markets. All of the papers produced up to this point are somewhat lacking in the bulk desired in a book paper; therefore, in the two following runs sodapoplar stock was included in the furnishes.

In run No. 143 stock from books Nos. 315 and 316 was given a medium brush and washing for one hour and was medium brushed for one hour more, bleached with 11.3 percent of bleach assisted with one-half pint of oil of vitriol, made into a furnish of 16.5 percent of sulphite, 22.3 percent of soda poplar, and 61.3 percent of hurd stock, loaded with 22 percent of clay, sized with 1.38 percent of resin size, given a hard brush for one hour, tinted very strongly, and pumped to the stock chest. This stock was beaten to a greater extent than in previous runs. The stock was run on the paper machine at a speed of 75 feet per minute, using a medium Jordan brush, and no trouble whatsoever was experienced. Not over 2 pounds of "broke" was produced during the

whole run, and that was in the "threading" of the machines. The color of the sheet is entirely satisfactory for many uses. The wood shives apparently were reduced to a satisfactory degree. Experienced paper makers commented very favorable on the running of this furnish and the quality of the paper produced.

Run No. 144 was intended as a duplicate of run No. 143. Stock from cooks Nos. 317 and 318 was given a medium brush and washing for one hour and a further medium brush of one hour, bleached with 11.4 percent of bleach, and made into a furnish composed of 15.5 percent of sulphite, 23.5 percent of soda poplar, and 61 percent of hurd stock, loaded with 21.4 percent of clay, sized with 1.17 percent of resin size, hard brushed for one hour, tinted by the expert colorer of the company, and pumped to the stock chest. Stock from cooks Nos. 319 and 320 was treated in exactly the same manner except that the stock was bleached with 12.1 percent of bleach and pumped to the stock chest to mix with the former furnish. The stock acted very well on the machine, which was speeded to 75 feet per minute, with the Jordan refiner set at a medium brush. The sheet is as good, if not better, than that of run No. 143, and it is also a good illustration of the extent to which proper tinting will enhance the general appearance of a paper. The poor appearance of the samples of previous runs is due largely to lack of proper tinting. Various degrees of whiteness, however, are demanded by the trade.

Comparison of the Tests and Commercial Practice

In work of this nature and on this scale it is practically impossible to arrive at a cost figure which would be susceptible of commercial interpretation, and in this preliminary publication nothing will be attempted beyond a comparison of the process used with the hurds with that process commercially applied to poplar wood. The process last used with the hurds should not be regarded as final, satisfactory, or most suitable, as it has been shown that progress was being made up to the conclusion of the work.

In comparing the method using hurds with the method of handling poplar wood, a difference is apparent on the delivery of raw material at the mill. Ordinarily, poplar is received at the mill in the form of logs about 4 feet in length, which may be stored in piles in the open. Hurds very likely would be received baled, and it would seem advisable to store them under cover for the following reasons: (a) baled hurds would probably absorb and retain more water during wet weather than logs of wood, thereby causing excessive dilution of the caustic liquor; (b) prolonged excessive dampness might create heating and deterioration unless the hemp were properly retted; (c) wet hurds could not be sieved free from sand and chaff. Should further work show that the first two reasons need not be taken into consideration, the third objection might be overcome by sieving the hurds before baling. Even then, it is probable that baled hurds stored in the open would accumulate and retain considerable dirt from factory chimneys, locomotives, and wind. Chocked pulp wood exposed in the open invariable suffers from these causes.

In the preparation of the raw material for the digesters there is likewise considerable differences between hurds and poplar wood. The former apparently requires only a moderate sieving to remove sand and chaff, which operation doubtless would require only a small amount of labor and the installation of some simple machinery of low power consumption. In preparing poplar for digestion, the 4-foot logs are chipped by a heavy, comparatively expensive chipper of high power consumption, after which the chips are sorted by sieving, the large pieces being rechipped. There would be a noteworthy difference in the installation, operating, and depreciation costs of the two equipments, and this difference would counterbalance to a considerable extent the difference in cost of raw material storage.

It is possible that in the use of the chip loft more care would have to be exercised in using hurds because of the tendency of the bast fiber to cause lodgements, but this should not be considered a serious difficulty.

The weight of hurds which are capable of being charged into a rotary is a decidedly unfavorable factor. The weight of a cubic foot of hurds varies somewhat with the proportion of best fiber, but average about 5.4 pounds, which, compared with a cubic foot of poplar chips at 8.93 pounds, represents a digester charge of 60.5 percent of the weight of a poplar-wood charge, or, in terms of fiber capacity, the hurds charge would yield 38.6 percent as much fiber as the wood charge. The hurds upon being baled for transportation may be broken and crushed to such a degree that the weight of the charge may be increased, and it might be found possible to increase the charge weight by stosining or by the employment of tamping devices. This small weight of charge constitutes one of the most serious objections to the use of hurds in paper manufacture.

In those tests in which the most satisfactory results were obtained, the cooking conditions were 29.5 percent of caustic soda at a concentration of 107 grams per liter and a causticity of 34.0 percent acting at a temperature of 170°C for five hours, or a total time of seven hours. The steam condensation in the rotary used for these tests was abnormally high, due to the fact that the steam supply pipe was uncovered for a considerable distance and the rotary was entirely uncovered. It is believed, therefore, that a larger amount of caustic was necessary than would otherwise have been the case. This belief is strengthened by the quality of the waste liquor from one of the later cooks, which gave on analysis 16.85 grams per liter of free caustic soda and showed a causticity of 27.75 percent. These data show that only 67.3 percent of the total caustic employed was actually consumed in the cooking operation, which percentage is lower than obtains in practice. The stock from this cook was bleached with 11.5 percent of bleach. But even as the figures stand, the comparison with poplar cooking practice is as follows: 29.5 percent caustic soda used as against 22 to 25 percent; 107 grams per liter as against 100 to 110; 84 percent causticity it little different than obtains in practice; 170°C is about commercial practice; five hours as pressure as against four to six hours; seven hours' total time as against possibly six to eight hours; 11.5 percent bleach as against 8 to 10 percent. Thus, it is evident that the cooking conditions employed were slightly more severe and expensive than those in commercial use with poplar wood.

The yield of total fiber obtained from the hurds may be placed at 35 percent of bone-dry fiber calculated on the bone-dry weight of hurds used, or 33.1 percent of air-dry fiber calculated on air-dry hurds. The yield of bleached fiber was not determine in this preliminary work, but may be safely estimated as 30 percent, which is low when compared with a yield of almost 47 percent of bone-dry bleached fiber from bone-dry poplar wood. It is believed quite possible that satisfactory cooking conditions may be found which will give a higher yield than was obtained during these tests. The stock should be classed as easy bleaching, and 11.4 percent of bleach is a satisfactory figure, although a little high.

As to beating cost, in the last two and most satisfactory tests the total washing and beating time was three hours, which maybe almost an hour more than ordinarily is used in making papers of this grade, although the practice varies to a considerable extent.

In regard to furnish, there is such a diversity of practice that it is difficult to make a comparison, but it the hurd stock can be produced as cheaply as soda-poplar stock, the furnish used in these last two tests should be regarded as satisfactory to the book and printing paper manufacturer.

The finish of the paper was not all that might be desired, but that was due almost entirely to the calendar stock available for the work, which was composed of nine light rolls, many of which were about 6 inches in diameter and which had not been reground for some time. From a small test on a large calendar stock it was readily shown that the paper product is capable of taking a satisfactory finish.

This comparison, satisfactory in many respects, develops two factors which are decidedly unfavorable to hemp hurds, namely, raw material storage and digester capacity, and they must be taken into full account in considering the paper-making value of this material, although it should be recognized that investigation may result in the material improvement of these conditions. Moreover, it is not at all improbable that further investigations would develop more satisfactory treating conditions and more suitable furnish compositions, and the belief in this possibility is strengthened by the fact that material progress was being made at the conclusion of this preliminary work.

Every tract of 10,000 acres which is devoted to hemp raising year by year is equivalent to a sustained pulp-producing capacity of 40,500 acres of average pulp-wood lands. In other words, in order to secure additional raw material for the production of 25 tons of fiber per day there exists the possibility of utilizing the agricultural waste already produced on 10,000 acres of hemp lands instead of security, holding, reforesting, and protecting 40,500 acres of pulp-wood land.

The annual growth per acre, although decidedly in favor of hurds, has little bearing on the project, because the utilization of the hurds is subordinate to the raising of hemp, and the paper manufacturer probably could afford to use only hurds resulting from the hemp industry.

Physical Tests of the Papers Produced

Samples of paper produced in the seven tests were submitted to the Leather and Paper Laboratory of the Bureau of Chemistry.

There is no system of numerically recording the general appearance and "look through" of a paper, but it can be stated that only papers Nos. 143 and 144 are satisfactory in these respects, the other samples being more or less thickly specked with shives. The general character and taste of these papers correspond very closely with No. 1 machine-finish printing paper, according to the specifications of the United States Government Printing Office, which call for a sheet not exceeding 0.0035 inch in thickness, strength not less than 12 points, free from unbleached or ground wood pulp, and ash not over 10 percent. The strength factor of such papers is almost 0.28. The ash should not be over 10 percent for this grade of paper, but in spite of the larger amount used the physical tests are sufficiently high. It is to be noted that the physical tests in samples Nos. 138 and 142, inclusive, are higher than in Nos. 143 and 144, in which 23 percent of soda poplar was used, which shows clearly that hemp-hurd stock imparts strength and folding endurance to a greater extent than does soda-poplar stock. From these preliminary tests it would be concluded, therefore, that hemp-hurd stock acts similarly to soda-poplar stock, but will produce a somewhat harder and stronger sheet and one of higher folding endurance. Undoubtedly, there is more dirt in the samples than would be tolerated by the trade, but this was to be expected, since in this preliminary work the new material sieved by hand screens instead of by automatic machines which would sieve more thoroughly.

Conclusions

There appears to be little doubt that under the present system of forest use and consumption the present supply can not withstand the demands placed on it. By the time improved methods of forestry have established an equilibrium between production and consumption, the price of pulp wood may be such that a knowledge of other available raw materials may be imperative.

Semicommercial paper-making tests were conducted, therefore, on hemp hurds, in cooperation with a paper manufacturer. After several trials under conditions with a paper manufacturer which are regarding as favorable in comparison with those used with pulp wood, paper was produced which received very favorable comment both from investigators and from the trade and which according to official tests would be classed as a No. 1 machine-finish printing paper.

ARTICLE REPRINTED FROM

COMMISSION REGULATION (EEC) NO. 1164/89 OF 28 APRIL 1989

Laying Down Detailed Rules Concerning the Aid for Fibre Flax and Hemp

THE COMMISSION OF THE EUROPEAN COMMUNITIES

Having regard to the Treaty establishing the European Economic Community,

Having regard to Council Regulation (EEC) No. 1308/70 of 29 June 1970 on the common organization of the market in flax and hemp[1], as last amended by Regulation (EEC) No. 3995/87[2], and in particular Articles 2 (6) and 4 (5) thereof,

Whereas Council Regulation (EEC) No. 619/71[3], as last amended by Regulation (EEC) No. 2059/84[4], lays down general rules for the grant of aid for flax and hemp; whereas it is the responsibility of the Commission to lay down the relevant implementing rules;

Whereas, if the aid scheme is to operate properly, it must be possible to distinguish flax grown mainly for fibre from that grown mainly for seed; whereas this aim may be achieved by specifying the seeds from which the two types of flax may be grown; whereas to the same end the varieties of hemp the tetrahydrocannabinol content of which does not exceed the limits laid down in Regulation (EEC) No. 619/71 should be indicated on the one hand and the way that content is to be recorded should be determined on the other hand;

Whereas, Article 4 of Regulation (EEC) No. 619/71 requires Member States to introduce supervisory arrangements to ensure that the product for which aid is requested satisfies the requirements for the grant of such aid; whereas the declarations of areas sown and the aid applications to be sent in by the producers must therefore contain the minimum particulars necessary for such supervision; whereas, in order to simplify the operation of the aid scheme, provision should be made, where the producer has concluded a cultivation contract for fibre flax, for his application to be accompanied by a copy of that contract;

Whereas Article 5 of Regulation (EEC) No. 619/71 provides for spot checks of the declarations and aid applications referred to above; whereas, in order to be effective, such checks must be made of a significant number of declarations and applications; whereas uniform provisions should be laid down for the grant of the aid where the areas recorded during a check differ from those indicated in declarations of areas sown in aid applications;

Whereas, having regard to the existing arrangements in Member States, the said States should be required, when granting aid for fibre flax in cases where no cultivation contract has been concluded, to apply a system of production certificates or of registered contracts; whereas if such a system is to operate effectively, the minimum amount of information which must appear in such certificates should be specified;

Whereas uniform provisions should be laid down for payment of the aid;

Whereas Article 2 of Regulation (EEC) No. 1308/70 provides that, in order to promote sales of flax products, Community measures to encourage the use of flax fibre and products obtained from such fibres can be adopted;

Whereas, in the interests of sound management, schemes to promote the use of flax fibres to be approved by the Commission should be carried out as part of a detailed programme to be drawn up following consultation of the Member States and, where appropriate, those working in this field; whereas, with the same aim, provision should be made for the practical execution of the schemes in accordance with procedures to their specific technical characteristics;

Whereas the previous proposals presented under the agreed procedures must be assessed according to criteria that will permit the best possible selection; whereas, to that end, open or restricted invitation to tender appears to be the most appropriate procedure; whereas, however, for schemes which call for an in-depth knowledge of the flax industry, direct negotiation with the trade and interbranch organizations may be considered the most suitable procedure;

Whereas the Member States should be informed of the Commission's choices and of the progress of the schemes selected;

Whereas for the sake of clarity Commission Regulation (EEC) No. 771/74[5], as last amended by Regulation (EEC) No. 2807/88[6], should be repealed and it should be replaced by this Regulation;

Whereas the measures provided for in this Regulation are in accordance with the opinion of the Management Committee for Flax and Hemp,

HAS ADOPTED THIS REGULATION:

Article 1

The aid referred to in Article 4 of Regulation (EEC) No. 1308/70 shall be granted for fibre flax and hemp produced in the Community in accordance with the rules laid down in the Articles below.

Article 2

Aid shall be granted for flax grown from the seed varieties:

— specified in Annex A, or
— currently under review by Member States' authorities for inclusion in the catalogue of flax varieties intended mainly for the production of fibre.

Article 3

Aid shall be granted only in respect of areas of hemp which have been sown with the varieties of seed listed in Annex B.

2. For the purposes of monitoring compliance with the conditions laid down in the first paragraph of Article 3 (1) of Regulation (EEC) No. 619/71, applications for aid for hemp shall be accompanied by a copy of the official label drawn up pursuant to Council Directive 69/208EEC,[7] or provisions adopted on the basis of that Directive, for the seed used, or by any other document recognized as being equivalent by the Member State concerned.

3. The determination of the tetrahydrocannabinol content and sampling for the purpose of determining such constant shall be carried out in accordance with the method described in Annex C.

4. The Member States concerned shall pay the aid only where the area harvested and the quantity of seed shown in one of the documents referred to in paragraph 2 correspond.

Article 4

Aid shall be granted only in respect of areas:

(a) which have been completely sown and harvested and on which normal cultivation work has been carried out; and
(b) for which a declaration of areas sown has been made in accordance with Article 5.

Article 5

1. Except in cases of *force majeure*, all growers of fibre flax and hemp shall submit a declaration of the areas sown, in the case of flax not later than 30 June and in the case of hemp not later than 15 July. However, for the 1989/90 marketing year the declaration shall be submitted not later than 15 July and 31 July respectively.

2. If the area recorded proves to be smaller than that indicated in the declaration, the person making the declaration must forward the figures on the area recorded to the competent authorities, within the time-limits laid down in paragraph 1.

3. Such declaration shall include:

— the surname, first name(s) and address of the person making the declaration,
— the species together with, for flax, the main purpose for which it is sown, and the variety sown,
— the area sown, in hectares and ares,
— the cadastral register number of the areas sown, or a reference recognized as equivalent by the body responsible for checking the area.

4. A declaration relating to an area of at least three hectares shall be admissible only if:

— it has been endorsed by a body designated by the Member State concerned or,
— it is accompanied by a document certifying to satisfaction of the Member State concerned that the declaration is accurate.

Member States may provide that declarations relating to an area of less than three hectares shall be admissible only if they have been endorsed by a body designated by them.

Article 6

1. The checks provide for in Article 5 of Regulation (EEC) No. 619/71 shall be carried out on at least 5% of the declarations of areas sown referred to in Article 5 and on a representative percentage of the aid applications provided for in Article 8, having regard to the geographical distribution of the areas concerned.

2. Where significant irregularities arise relating to 6% or more of the checks carried out, the Member States shall notify the Commission thereof forthwith and shall state what measures have been adopted.

Article 7

If the checks provided for in Article 5 of Regulation (EEC) No. 619/71 show that the area declared is:

(a) less than that ascertained during the checks, the area ascertained shall be used;
(b) greater than that ascertained during the checks, the area used shall be the ascertained area minus the difference between the area

originally declared and that ascertained, without prejudice to any penalties laid down under national law, except where the difference is considered justified by the Member State concerned; in that case the area ascertained shall be used.

Member States shall notify the Commission of the measures taken for the application of this Article.

Article 8

1. All growers of fibre flax or hemp shall submit an aid application not later than 30 November for flax and 31 December for hemp.

However, except in cases of *force majeure*, if the application is lodged:

— before the end of the month following that indicated in the first subparagraph, 66% of the aid provided for in Article 4 of Regulation (EEC) No. 1308/70 shall be granted,

— before the end of the second month following that month, 33% of that aid shall be granted.

2. Aid applications shall contain:

— the surname, first name(s) and address of the applicant,

— a declaration in hectares and ares of the areas harvested, and the cadastral register number of those areas, or a reference recognized as equivalent by the body responsible for checking the areas,

— details of the place where the produce concerned is stored or, if it has been sold and delivered, the name, first name(s) and address of the purchaser.

3. Where the producer satisfies the requirements of Article 3a (b) of Regulation (EEC) No. 619/71, the aid application shall be accompanied by a copy of the cultivation contract referred to in that Article, except where such contract has been registered with the competent authority.

4. Without prejudice to paragraph 5, if the area in respect of which the aid is applied for is greater than that indicated in the declaration of areas sown, the latter area shall be used.

5. If the checks provided for in Article 5 of Regulation (EEC) No. 619/71 show that the area in respect of which the aid is applied for is:

(a) less than that ascertained during the checks, the area ascertained shall be used;

(b) greater than that ascertained during the checks, without prejudice to any penalties provided for under national law and the provisions of (c), the area used shall be the ascertained area minus the difference between the area in respect of which the aid is applied for and that ascertained, except where the difference is considered justified by the Member State concerned; in the latter case the area ascertained shall be used;

(c) greater than that ascertained during the checks and if, for the person making the declaration in question, the areas indicated in the declarations or applications have been reduced during the same marketing year or the preceding one in accordance with Article 7 or point (b) of this paragraph, except where the difference is considered justified by the Member State concerned, the aid application shall be rejected.

Member States shall notify the Commission of the measures taken for the application of this paragraph.

Article 9

For the purposes of granting aid for flax, where the producer does not satisfy the requirements of Article 3a (b) of Regulation (EEC) No. 619/71, the Member State concerned shall apply a system of production certificates or registered contracts.

Article 10

1. Where a Member State applies a system of production certificates as provided for in Article 9, for each hectare or part of a hectare in respect of which entitlement to aid has been recognized, a certificate representing half of the amount of the aid shall be issued to the grower.

2. In cases where, at the end of the marketing year:

(a) no contract as referred to in Article 3 (2) of Regulation (EEC) No. 619/71 has been concluded, or the producer has himself processed the flax into straw or had it processed on his behalf, the certificate shall be retained by the producer;

(b) such a contract has been concluded, the certificate shall be given to the buyer,

On the presentation of a properly completed certificate, half of the aid shall be paid to the person concerned. This certificate must be submitted not later than 31 December following the end of the marketing year concerned.

3. Certificates shall contain at least the following particulars:

- the surname, first name(s) and address of the grower,
- the area concerned,
- the amount of aid to be paid,
- the surname, first name(s) and address of the recipient of the aid,
- the signature of the producer and of the recipient of the aid,
- where the certificate is submitted by the producer, evidence that he satisfies one of the conditions laid down in Article 3 (2)(a) of Regulation (EEC) No. 619/71.

Article 11

Where a Member State applies a system of registered contracts as provided for in Article 9, then:
(a) where a contract as referred to in Article 3 (2) of Regulation (EEC) No. 619/71 has been concluded before the end of the marketing year, half of the aid shall be paid to the purchaser;
(b) where no such contract has been concluded by the date in (a), or where it is proved that the producer himself processes the flax into straw or has it so processed on his behalf, the whole of the aid shall be paid to the producer.

Article 12

Member States shall pay the aid for flax and hemp before 1 March following the end of the marketing year concerned.

Article 13

1. The Commission shall adopt, on the basis of the general programme referred to in Article 2 (4) of Regulation (EEC) No. 1308/70, a detailed programme of the measures referred to in paragraph 1 of that Article which it intends to take. Such programmes may cover more than one marketing year.
2. For the purposes of drawing up the detailed programme, the Commission:
- shall consult the Management Committee for Flax and Hemp,
- may consult the Advisory Committee on Flax and Hemp.
3. When drawing up its detailed programme the Commission shall:
- give details of cooperation, if any, with trade and inter-branch organizations in the sector,
- take account of promotional measures that have been carried out or are planned in this industry.

Article 14

1. Without prejudice to paragraph 2 below, the measures referred to in Article 2 (2) of Regulation (EEC) No. 1308/70 and contained in the detailed programme shall be carried out following the issue of open or restricted invitations to tender. Open invitations to tender shall be published in the *Official Journal of the European Communities*.
2. The measures referred to in the first indent of Article 2 (2) of Regulation (EEC) No. 1308/70 relating to technical or trade information or public relations which require, by virtue of their specific or technical nature, specialized knowledge regarding the use of flax fibres and products obtained from them, shall be carried out by the restricted tendering procedure. However, they shall be carried out by direct negotiation between the Commission and the trade or inter-branch organizations where those organizations alone have the necessary qualifications.
3. Expenditure on the measures referred to in paragraph 2 may not exceed 30% of the amount allocated for the measures referred to in the first indent of Article 2 (2) of Regulation (EEC) No. 1308/70.

Article 15

1. For the purposes of assessing the various tenders submitted by the interested parties, the Commission shall take into account:
- their quality and cost,
- the extent to which they meet the aims of the various measures envisaged,
- the level of specialization and of experience of the contractor in the field covered by the measure envisaged,
- measures already completed or in progress in the field in question.

In addition, the Commission shall take account:
(a) in the case of tenders relating to the measures provided for in the first indent of Article 2 (2) of Regulation (EEC) No. 1308/70, of the commercial and financial guarantees offered by the tenderer;
(b) in the case of tenders relating to the measures provided for in the second indent of Article 2 (2) of Regulation (EEC) No. 1308/70:
- of the scientific reputation of the party concerned,
- of the possible market for the products concerned,
- of the foreseeable period within which results will be obtained.

2. The Commission shall select the tenders. To that end it may consult bodies or persons specializing in the subject, and in particular the trade or inter-branch organizations in the industry. The Commission shall conclude contracts. It informs the Management Committee for Flax and Hemp at regular intervals of contracts concluded and of the progress of the measures.

Article 16

Payment of the price agreed in the contract shall be made by the Commission in instalments in relation to the progress of the work.

A contract performance guarantee may be required.

Payment of the balance and, where appropriate, release of the guarantee by the Commission shall be the subject to its ascertainment that the obligations under the contract have been met.

Article 17

1. Regulation (EEC) No. 771/74 is hereby repealed.
2. In all Community instruments in which reference is made to Regulation (EEC) No. 771/74 or to Articles of that Regulation, such references shall be construed as references to this Regulation or to the corresponding Articles thereof.

Article 18

This Regulation shall enter into force on the third day following that of its publication in the *Official Journal of The European Communities.*

It shall apply to fibre flax and hemp produced as from the 1989/90 marketing year.

This regulation shall be binding in its entirety and directly applicable in all Member States.

Done at Brussels, 28 April 1989.

For the Commission
Ray MAC SHARRY
Member of the Commission

Annex A

List of varieties of flax grown mainly for fibre

Ariane	Nanda
Astella	Natasja
Belinka	Nynke
Berber	Opaline
Fanny	Regina
Hera	Saskia
Laura	Silva
Lidia	Thalassa
Marina	Viking
Mira	

Annex B

List of varieties of hemp eligible for aid

Carmagnola	Felina 34
CS	Ferimon
Delta-Llosa	Fibranova
Delta-405	Firbimon 24
Fedora 19	Firbimon 56
Fedrina 74	Futura

Annex C

COMMUNITY METHOD FOR THE QUANTITATIVE DETERMINATION OF Delta-9 THC (TETRAHYDROCANNABINOL) IN CERTAIN VARIETIES OF HEMP

1. **Purpose and Scope**

This method permits quantitative determine of Delta-9 tetrahydrocannabinol (Delta-9 THC) in certain varieties of hemp (*Cannabis sativa* L.) for the purpose of checking that the conditions laid down in Article 3 (1) of Regulation (EEC) No. 619/71 are fulfilled.

2. **Principle**

Quantitative determination of Delta-9 THC by gas chromatography (GC) after extraction with a suitable solvent.

3. **Apparatus.**

— gas chromatography equipment with a flame ionization detector.

— glass column 2,50 m long and 3,2 mm in diameter (1,8") packed with a suitable support impregnated with a stationary phase phenyl-methyl-silicon (e.g. OV 17 at 3%).

4. **Sampling and Reduction of Sample**

Sampling

In a standing crop of a given variety of hemp, take not less than 500 plants, preferably at different points but not from the edges of the crop. Samples should be taken during the day after flowering has finished.

The pooled samples should be representative of the lot.

The plant material is then left to dry at ambient air temperature.

Reduction

Reduce the sample, obtained as described, to 500 stalks; the reduced sample should be representative of the original sample. Divide the reduced sample into two portions.

Send one portion to the laboratory which is to determine the Delta-9 THC content. Keep the other portion for counter-analysis if necessary.

5. Reagents

— petroleum ether (40/65°), or a solvent of comparable polarity,
— tetrahydrocannabinol Delta-9 THC), pure for chromatographic purposes,
— solution of 0,1% (w/v) androstene-3-17-dione in ethanol, pure for chromatographic purposes.

6. Preparation of Test Sample

For the purposes of Delta-9 THC determination, retain the upper third of the plants in the portion of the sample received. Stems and seeds must be removed from the plant material retained.

Dry the material in an oven, without exceeding 40°C, to obtain a constant weight.

7. Extraction

Reduce the material obtained as described in point 6 to a semi-fine powder (sieve of 1,000 meshes per cm²).

Take 2,0 g of well-mixed powder and extract with 30–40 ml petroleum ether (40–65°C). Leave for 24 hours, then shake in a mechanical shaker for one hour, and then filter. The extraction process is carried out twice under the same conditions. Evaporate the petroleum ether solutions to dryness. Dissolve the residue in 10,0 ml of petroleum ether. The prepared extract is used for quantitative analysis by gas chromatography.

8. Quantitative Analysis by Gas Chromatography

(a) Preparation of assay solutions

The extraction residue dissolved in 10,0 ml of petroleum ether is subjected to quantitative analysis to determine the Delta-9 THC content. This is performed with the aid of an internal standard and calculation of the peak areas.

Evaporate to dryness 1,0 ml of the petroleum ether solution. Dissolve the residue in 2,0 ml of a solution of 0,1% androstene-3-17-dione in ethanol (internal standard with a retention time distinctly higher than that of other cannabinoids, and in particular twice that of Delta-9 THC).

Calibration Ranges

0,10, 0,25, 0,50, 1,0 and 1,5 mg of Delta-9 THC in 1 ml of a solution of 0,1% androstene-3-17-dione in ethanol.

(b) Experimental conditions

Oven temperature:	240°C
Injector temperature:	280°C
Detector temperature:	270°C
Nitrogen flow rate:	25 ml/min,
Hydrogen flow rate:	25 ml/min,
Air flow rate:	300 ml/min,
Volume injected:	1 Êl of the final ethanol solution.

The relative retention time of Delta-9 THC is calculated in relation to the andostene.

9. Expression of the Results

The result is expressed in g of Delta-9 THC per 100 g of the laboratory sample dried to constant weight.

The result is subject to a tolerance of 0,03 g per 100 g.

Footnotes

Commission Regulation (EEC) No. 1164/89 of 28 April 1989

1   OJ No. L 146, 4. 7. 1970, p. 1.
2   OJ No. L 377, 31. 12. 1987, p. 34.
3   OJ No. L 72, 26. 3. 1971, p. 2.
4   OJ No. L 191, 19. 7. 1984, p. 6.
5   OJ No. L 92, 3. 4. 1974, p. 13.
6   OJ No. L 251, 10. 9. 1988, p. 13.
7   OJ No. L 169, 10. 7. 1969, p. 3.
8   OJ No. L 153, 13. 6. 1987, p. 1.

ARTICLE REPRINTED FROM
COUNCIL REGULATION (EEC) NO.
3698/88 OF 24 NOVEMBER 1988

Laying Down Special Measures for Hemp Seed

THE COUNCIL OF THE EUROPEAN
COMMUNITIES,

Having regard to the Treaty establishing the
European Economic Community, and in particular Article 43 thereof,

Having regard to the proposal from the
Commission[1],

Having regard to the opinion of the European Parliament[2]

Having regard to the opinion of the Economic and Social Committee,

Whereas the production of hemp seed is of
important to the economy of certain regions in
the Community; whereas, in order to promote the
expansion of this crop, which is subject to direct
competition from hemp seed imported from third
countries duty free, provision should be made for
appropriate support;

Whereas for this purpose the marketing of
Community production must ensure producers a
fair income; whereas to this end aid should be
granted for hemp seed produced in the
Community; whereas, in view of the characteristics of the crop, a system for laying down the aid
on a flat-rate basis should be provided for;

Whereas provision should be made to ensure
that expenditure incurred by Member States as a
result of the obligations arising out of the application of this Regulation falls within the financial
responsibility of the Community in accordance
with the regulations on the financing of the common agricultural policy;

Whereas certain varieties of hemp contain
substances which may harm human health;
whereas therefore the aid should be granted only
for hemp presenting adequate guarantees as to
the content of intoxicating substances in the
product as harvested;

Whereas, in order to ensure that the measures
provided for in this Regulation are applied under
optimum conditions during the 1988/89 marketing year, transitional measures are necessary;

whereas therefore a flat-rate aid per hectare
should be granted for that marketing year.

HAS ADOPTED THIS REGULATION:

Article 1

1. Every year before 1 August, an aid for hemp
seed falling within CN codes ex 1207 99 10 and
1207 99 91 shall be fixed for the Community, for
the following marketing year, in accordance with
the procedure laid down in Article 43 (2) of the
Treaty. The aid shall be fixed at a level which is
fair to producers, account being taken of the supply requirements of the Community.

2. The aid shall be granted only for seed of varieties providing certain safeguards to be determined in respect of the content of intoxicating
substances in the product harvested.

3. The aid shall continue to apply throughout
the marketing year in question; this shall cover
the period 1 August to 31 July, unless otherwise
decided by the Council acting by a qualified
majority on a proposal from the Commission.

Article 2

1. The aid shall be granted for a production figure obtained by applying an indicative yield to
the surface areas sown and harvested. The indicative yield may be differentiated taking into
account the yield ascertained in the major producing areas in the Community. The indicative
yield shall relate to a product of sound and merchantable quality.

2. The Council, acting by a qualified majority
on a proposal from the Commission, shall lay
down general rules in accordance with which the
aid shall be granted and the rules for verifying
areas sown and harvested within the Community
with a view to establishing eligibility for the aid.

3. The following shall be determined in accordance with the procedure laid down in Article 38
of Regulation No. 136/66/EEC[3], as last amended
by Regulation (EEC) No. 2210/88[4]:

(a) the indicative yield;

(b) detailed rules for the application of this
    Article.

Article 3

The Member States and the Commission shall
communicate to each other the information necessary for the application of this Regulation. This
information shall be decided upon in accordance
with the procedure laid down in Article 38 of
Regulation No. 136/66/EEC. Detailed rules concerning the communication and dissemination of
this information shall be adopted in accordance
with the same procedure.

Article 4

The provisions on the financing of the common agricultural policy shall apply to the system of aid provided for in this Regulation.

Article 5

1. By way of derogation from Article 2, the aid for hemp seed in respect of the 1988/89 marketing year shall be 250 ECU/hectare. The aid shall be granted to the producer in respect of the areas eligible for the aid provided for in Article 4 of Regulation (EEC) No. 1308/70,[5] as last amended by Regulation (EEC) No. 3995/87,[6] where the producer demonstrates to the satisfaction of the Member State concerned that normal operations for harvesting the seed have been carried out.

2. The operative event within the meaning of Article 5 of Regulation (EEC) No. 1676/85,[7] as last amended by Regulation (EEC) No. 1636/87,[8] as regards eligibility for the aid for hemp seed for the 1988/89 marketing year shall be deemed to have occurred on 1 September 1988.

Article 6

This Regulation shall enter into force on the day of its publication in the *Official Journal of the European Communities*.

It shall apply for the first time to hemp seed harvested during the 1988/89 marketing year.

This Regulation shall be binding in its entirety and directly applicable in all Member States.

Done at Brussels, 24 November 1988.

For the Council
The President
V. KEDIKOGLOU

Footnotes

Council Regulation (EEC) No. 3698/88 of 24 November 1988 laying down special measures for hemp seed

1 OJ No. C 276, 26. 10. 1988, p. 5.
2 Opinion delivered on 18 November 1988 (not yet published in the Official Journal).
3 OJ No. 172, 30. 9. 1966, p. 3025/66.
4 OJ No. L 197, 16. 7. 1988, p. 1.
5 OJ No. L 146, 4. 7. 1970, p. 1.
6 OJ No. L 377, 31. 12. 1987, p. 34.
7 OJ No. L 164, 24. 6. 1985, p. 1.
8 OJ No. L 153, 13. 6. 1987, p. 1.

ARTICLE REPRINTED FROM
CHÈNEVOTTE HABITAT

Isochanvre
[Insuhemp]
Nature is an architect!

France Périer

Rot resistant and non-flammable

Isochanvre is made from the cellulose part of hemp which has been specifically treated in order to **mineralize the saps and resins**. Isochanvre can thus be used in construction because it is **fire and water resistant** (see minutes of the Centre Scientifique et Technique du Batiment)

From the mineralized plant

France Perier has developed this unique process for mineralizing plant saps and resins, and defined the necessary binding agents (natural limes) and their proportions for the different applications. Several **closed patents have been registered**.

It is very important to emphasize that this mineralization process and the products used are **all natural**. The production process is not harmful to the environment, there is no toxic gas released, no polluting fumes, no noise pollutions, no release of polluted water... The binding agents used with Isochanvre Construction are also all natural. Isochanvre is a **100% environmentally sound product**. From its beginning to its eventual return to nature, Isochanvre is ever so close to nature. **Even the kraft paper packaging** has been developed to be re-used in construction. (See details in the Chänevotte Habitat technical data, page 4).

Two **Isochanvre products** are marked in three-ply kraft paper bags (100 litres or 10 kg):

—**Isochanvre Isolation** [*insulation*] which is used directly and may be poured or blown. Applications: **roof trussing, floors, partition walls, backing**.

—**Isochanvre Construction** which is mainly used with naturallines, and for flagstones with CPA 55 which is a pure cement (without additives) as certified by manufacturers. Applications: **flagstones, walls, floor leveling, insulative coatings, insulating mortar for stone walls, etc...** (See technical data)

From basement to roof trussings:

It is possible to **do it all** with the two isochanvre products. From basement to roof trussings, from inside to outside, the house can be redesigned in Isochanvre to **the best quality** in housing.

The use of Isochanvre Construction is **cost-efficient and simplifies work** on the construction site. For example, for a conventional wall, we use a 20 cm thick block (concrete or brick), plus a screen wall, insulation, a vapor barrier and plaster. However, or an Isochanvre wall, **20 cm total thickness is enough** as the wall is monolithic.

We have only one single crib-work operation, and a simple coating instead of the plaster; therefore only **two operations instead of five are needed**. Isochanvre offers the best **quality/price/versatility ratio** in construction materials; it is in fact the only "constructive insulation."

A thermal and acoustic "protector":

It gives significant acoustical protection.

Isochanvre, because of its very high thermal inertia, is **exceptionally qualified** by its very unique role as thermal **"protector"** which implies a **good thermal barrier** in addition to insulation. The current insulation materials on the market have no thermal inertia. These properties of Isochanvre have been confirmed by the Université de Rennes (Thermal Department).

Inertia means **comfort in summer** (cool inside the home: there is no longer any feelings of stuffiness in the attic rooms) ...and **significant heating cost savings** in winter. Heating is turned on a month later in the fall, and the walls remain warm...

It allows walls to breathe, thereby **avoiding condensation problems and dilapidation over time**. An Isochanvre wall covered with a coating of natural lime breathes and lives, unlike cement or lime-plaster finish on concrete. Isochanvre fits directly into the context of **an environmentally sound and healthy construction**.

Another significant advantage is that Isochanvre can be used as **a treatment for a damp or saltpetrous wall**, instead of "hiding misery" behind a dry-wall panel or an air outlet louver.

Isochanvre is the **least expensive** of natural insulation products. For a **building initially designed** in Isochanvre, the construction cost is similar to a "conventional" construction in concrete blocks or concrete (not to be confused with "traditional," meaning in "noble" materials). In the very short term, if we include heating cost savings, the cost is reduced.

Isochanvre is used in construction:

All over France as well as in the neighboring countries like **Belgium, Luxembourg, Germany, Switzerland**. New markets will soon be opening in Italy and Spain.

Since the inception of the business in 1989, 7,000 cubic meters or 700 tonnes has been sold. The volume of sales is increasing by about **50% each year**. About **150 brand new houses** have been built. **Renovations are countless**.

Under Napoléon, hemp was considered a **material of critical necessity**. It was used to make ropes, sails, and canvas. It was grown all over France, and on all types of soil. Hemp cultivation has survived through the production of cigarette paper and fine papers. Hemp cultivation is in great demand to "clean" soils, on a rotating basis every three or four years. It is currently grown under contract, just like tobacco. **One cultivated hectare** produces **6 to 8 tonnes of hemp, or 60 cubic meters of isochanvre**, which is **enough to build an "all Isochanvre" house of 135 square meters** of floor space (including insulation of all partitions and all floors!).

The original principle for the mineralization of saps and resins which has been patented by Mme France Perier can be applied to other plants. Jute, rice husks, millet, corn and other plant fibers can be made fire and water resistant with Mme France Perier's patents. Several contacts are underway to **re-utilize varied by-products**, and to help resolve the critical problem of **refuse recycling** and the replacement of the gravel required to make concrete and concrete blocks. These include extraction-related problems: defacing of nature and the pollution of underground water by refilling old gravel pits.

ARTICLE REPRINTED FROM
SCIENTIFIC AMERICAN,
JUNE 4, 1921

Revolutionizing an Industry:

HOW MODERN MACHINERY IS MINIMIZING HAND LABOR IN HEMP PRODUCTION

by George H. Dacy

Time was when the sweat of the brow, the bend in the buck and the utter fatigue of the laborers were the barometers which accurately recorded our domestic progress in hemp production. The limiting factor which restricted the culture of hemp and which prevented the rapid expansion of the industry was the human labor item. Much of the arduous, age-aiding work had to be performed by hand. Only the most robust and rugged laborers were able to stand up under the severe strain of year-round activities of this description.

Inventors devoted their most able energies toward the perfection of mechanical devices which would take the backache out of hemp breaking. Despite the combined efforts of science and industry, the practical solution of the problem eluded all these technically and practically trained sleuths until the next decade. The various early models and designs of hemp harvesting and breaking machinery, however, acted as stepping stones which gradually led to the perfection and commercialization of field implements and mill appliances which now have stabilized the business of hemp farming and which have reduced the problems connected with the culture of this crop to as simple a basis and system as those that are involved in the production of corn or the small grains.

Hemp is produced principally in this country for fiber although the foreign supplies of hemp are also utilized for seed and for medicinal purposes. In the United States, the greater part of our annual domestic supply is used in manufacturing commercial twines and wrapping cords and to a limited extent also for the manufacture of ropes and binder twine. Hemp tow is used as oakum for caulking ships and for packing in pumps, engines and other machinery. Our pre-sent production of hemp is insufficient to satisfy the demand for commercial twines so that little attempt as yet has been made to develop the other possibilities of this remarkable fiber crop. It is also valuable for the manufacture of bagging for cotton bales, for sacking of all kinds, carpets, rugs, seines, nets, fishlines, sewing threads of all description, warp for carpets, and for such fabrics as crash toweling, rough sheeting and rough clothing.

On account of its great tensile strength, its water-resistant properties and its ability to withstand wear, hemp is well suited for cordage of all kinds, for lines and ropes used in all shipping operations, for canvas, for all purposes where strength and durability rather than beauty and fineness of texture are desired. Hemp is much like flax in chemical and physical properties and this resemblance has been capitalized by the use of efficient power-drive machinery. By a process known as hackling the hemp fiber is reduced to a condition like the coarser grades of dew-retted flax and can be subsequently spun on flax-spinning machinery.

In the neighborhood of 42,000 to 45,000 acres of hemp are annually grown in this country, the yields of fiber ranging from 1,000 to 1,500 pounds to the acre. Hand labor is no longer necessary in producing and harvesting the fiber, field implements now being available which simplify the production of the crop. Specially equipped mills have been constructed and established in sections where hemp is grown on some scale for separating the fiber from the stalks. Wisconsin, which grows about 8,000 acres of hemp a year and ranks as the second state in the country in total acreage and production of the fiber, has developed her industry during the last ten years and now operates 11 of the 18 hemp mills to be found in the United States.

Hemp is an annual plant which attains a height of from 5 to 15 feet and is of value due to the fiber contained in its woody stems. The crop is seeded thickly so that the stalks will grow high and slender. The fiber obtained from the hemp is called bast fiber and is of value on account of its length, strength, pliability and general resistance to wear and tear. The system of milling the hemp known as breaking consists in separating the woody portion of the stems from the fiber.

Wisconsin's establishment in the hemp growing business is a story with a rather romantic angle. Uncle Sam appreciated that this hemp industry was tobogganing rapidly toward extinction unless he could eliminate the hand labor difficulties. Twelve years ago the National Department of

Agriculture in cooperation with the Wisconsin Agriculture College began growing hemp in Wisconsin, the soils and climate there being admirably adapted for the production of this fiber crop. As soon as it was demonstrated irrefutably that hemp would prove a success in Wisconsin, the authorities exerted every effort toward the perfection of some mechanical device for breaking the crop and reducing hand labor to a minimum. Experienced hemp growers and a large harvesting machinery company cooperated in this work and ultimately appliances were developed which efficiently performed all this work rapidly and at relatively low expense. In establishing the industry on a practical basis, Wisconsin has found that community cooperation is fundamentally essential for the practical and profitable production of hemp. Machinery for harvesting the crop is expensive and usually must be owned in partnership by a number of neighbors. The mills for separating the hemp from the woody stems cost anywhere from $10,000 to $50,000, depending on their capacity and equipment, and must be necessarily located in sections where hemp growing is a permanent business. It is essential that from 500 to 750 acres of hemp be produced annually to keep each of these mills busy. This involves the concentration of production around definite milling centers so that sufficient raw material is assured to make the operation of the mills profitable.

To a certain extent hemp is a crop which prospers only under proper conditions of soil and climate. It is not adapted for universal culture in all parts of this country but it provides propitious opportunities for successful production in territories where the local environments are favorable for its growth. It prospers in the humid sections of the temperate zones, although some of the birdseed varieties mature in from two to three months in northern Russia. For seed production, hemp demands a growing season of size months or longer while for fiber production it will mature in four months. Hemp has been produced successfully in the United States only in sections where the annual rainfall amounts to at least 30 inches. Wisconsin's climate is excellent for hemp growing as the autumn months are cool and moist, conditions which promote the efficient seasoning and retting of the fiber.

It is essential to harvest fiber hemp at the right stage of maturity or else deterioration will result. Under Wisconsin conditions, hemp harvest season occurs between September 10th and October 1st. Practically all the foreign supplies of hemp are still harvested by hand and it has only been since 1917 that an efficient mechanical harvester has been perfected and extensively used in this country. It cuts the hemp and spreads the stalks in even swaths, performing this work much better than it can be done by hand. The American hemp crop is produced by dew-retting systems, that is, exposing the hemp to rains, dews, frosts and sunshine spread out on the field which produced the crop. This effects partial decomposition so that the inner bark is loosened from the wood and the fiber can be more easily separated from the stalks. Usually it takes from four to ten weeks to dew-ret the hemp where the weather conditions are favorable. It is of maximum importance that the hemp be properly retted before being removed from the field and only the experienced grower knows exactly when this condition is reached.

Subsequently, the hemp stalks are gathered and bound in bundles which then are shocked up like corn. All this work was done by hand until 1918 when a gather-binder was invented which collects the stalks from the swath and binds them together. In regions where central breaking mills ar operated, the bundles of hemp are delivered to the mill as soon as possible after shocking where the stalks are broken immediately. Where some time must elapse before the hemp can be transported to the mill, the practice is to stack the bundles so that the crop will pass through the sweat like small grain. Experience in building stacks is necessary as where the crop is not properly stacked and the bundles are needlessly exposed to weathering, heavy losses of fiber will result.

It is necessary that hemp be wholly dry when broken and the profits from the crop often hinge on the success of this activity. Formerly, the custom was to have portable machines which journeyed itinerant-fashion from farm to farm to perform this work but weather uncertainties always markedly limited such operations so that the modern plan is to kiln-dry the stalks at the mill before they are broken. The traditional practice up to the last few years was to break the crop—crushing the wood underneath the layers of fiber so as to favor the easy separation of these two materials—with a hand brake which was a tedious, costly and strength-racking practice. The average, experienced worker could only break from 100 to 200 pounds of cleaned hemp daily by hand. Industrial science has been responsible for the making and successful operation during recent years of power brakes which accomplish the work mechanically by means of fluted rollers, and thus work more efficiently and more cheaply than hand labor. The modern hemp mill consists of a receiving room, dry kilns, breaking room with brakes, scutchers and balers, boiler room, engine and fan room.

In the dry kiln the excess moisture in the hemp stalks is removed by the use of a hot-air blast. The dry stalks are then fed into the breaking rolls where they are crushed and thence pass over a series of shakers where the loose hurds or woody portions are separated from the fiber. Then the fiber passes through scutching wheels which remove the remnant hurds. The fiber which is then fairly cleaned is baled and sold to cordage and spinning mills. Formerly, the scutching was done by hand, the uncleaned fiber being whipped over the hand brake until it was free from hurds. The present scutching machinery consists of from 2 to 4 large cylinders equipped on the exterior with wooden slats. The cylinders are stationary and revolve toward each other. As the fiber passes between the scutching cylinders, the hurds are all combed off.

The average hemp crop in Wisconsin yields from 1,000 to 1,200 pounds of fiber an acre, being higher than the production in Kentucky and only excelled by that of California. The fiber consists of long fibers, called line, which are worth about three times as much as the shorter fibers, called tow, the total fiber supply usually containing between 10 and 20 percent of tow. One thousand pounds of rough fiber will produce about 850 pounds of line and 150 pounds of tow. Usually the average well retted and dried crop of stalks amounts to three tons to the acre which will yield 20 percent by weight of rough fiber. Green hemp stalks contain almost 60 percent more water than when they are thoroughly retted and dried and hence a yield of three tons of retted stalk means an initial production of 7-1/2 tons of green material. A first class crop of hemp usually brings in a gross return of from $75 to $100 an acre while the cost of production is only about $10 or $11 more per acre than it is for a crop of small grains such as wheat. The profits from the hemp crop are large and dependable, and indications are that the industry will be materially expanded in the near future.

Before hemp or fiber can be spun into yarn, it must be either carded or hackled—submitted to combing processes by power machinery at the spinning mills. These operations remove foreign materials and reduces the fiber to finer, uniform strands. In the past, much of the Kentucky crop was hackled by hand and even today this costly method is still followed in some southern mills. However, the potential tendencies of the hemp growing and milling industry will be to make more extensive use of modern machinery which performs cheap and efficient work.

As matters stand at present, the hemp industry needs more certain sources of cheap and satisfactory seed. Kentucky bottomlands have supplied much of the seed crops used up to this time but the prices demanded for Kentucky seed are exorbitant and new sources of seed are now being developed. In some sections, a standard market classification of the locally grown fiber is prerequisite potentially if the industry is to expand without trouble. The growers must exert every effort to produce the best quality hemp while the millers must specialize in their abilities to distinguish between the different grades of hemp and so to handle the material that it will subsequently be in the best possible condition for further processing in the spinning and cordage mills.

ARTICLE REPRINTED FROM
POPULAR MECHANICS,
FEBRUARY 1938

New Billion Dollar Crop

American farmers are promised a new cash crop with an annual value of several hundred million dollars, all because a machine has been invented which solves a problem more than 6,000 years old. It is hemp, a crop that will not compete with other American products. Instead, it will displace imports of raw material and manufactured products produced by underpaid coolie and peasant labor and it will provide thousands of jobs for American workers throughout the land.

The machine which makes this possible is designed for removing the fiber-bearing cortex from the rest of the stalk, making hemp fiber available for use without a prohibitive amount of human labor.

Hemp is the standard fiber of the world. It has great tensile strength and durability. It is used to produce more than 5,000 textile products, ranging from rope to fine laces, and the woody "hurds" remaining after the fiber has been removed contains more than seventy-seven per cent cellulose, and can be used to produce more than 25,000 products, ranging from dynamite to Cellophane.

Machines now in service in Texas, Illinois, Minnesota and other states are producing fiber at a manufacturing cost of half a cent a pound, and are finding a profitable market for the rest of the stalk. Machine operators are making a good profit in competition with coolie-produced foreign fiber while paying farmers fifteen dollars a ton for hemp as it comes from the field.

From the farmer's point of view, hemp is an easy crop to grow and will yield from three to six tons per acre on any land that will grow corn, wheat, or oats. It has a short growing season, so that it can be planted after other crops are in. It can be grown in any state of the union. The long roots penetrate and break the soil to leave it in perfect condition for the next year's crop. The dense shock of leaves, eight to twelve feet above the ground, chokes out weeds. Two successive crops are enough to reclaim land that has been abandoned because of Canadian thistles or quack grass.

Under old methods, hemp was cut and allowed to lie in the fields for weeks until it "retted" enough so the fibers could be pulled off by hand. Retting is simply rotting as a result of dew, rain and bacterial action. Machines were developed to separate the fibers mechanically after retting was complete, but the cost was high, the loss of fiber great, and the quality of fiber comparatively low. With the new machine, known as a decorticator, hemp is cut with a slightly modified grain binder. It is delivered to the machine where an automatic chain conveyor feeds it to the breaking arms at the rate of two or three tons per hour. The hurds are broken into fine pieces which drop into the hopper, from where they are delivered by blower to a baler or to truck or freight car for loose shipment. The fiber comes from the other end of the machine, ready for baling.

From this point on almost anything can happen. The raw fibers can be used to produce strong twine or rope, woven into burlap, used for carpet warp or linoleum backing or it may be bleached and refined, with resinous by-products of high commercial value. It can, in fact, be used to replace the foreign fibers which now flood our markets.

Thousands of tons of hemp hurds are used every year by one large powder company for the manufacture of dynamite and TNT. A large paper company, which has been paying more than a million dollars a year in duties on foreign-made cigarette papers, now is manufacturing these papers from American hemp grown in Minnesota. A new factory in Illinois is producing fine bond papers from hemp. The natural materials in hemp make it an economical source of pulp for any grade of paper manufactured and the high percentage of alpha cellulose promises an unlimited supply of raw material for the thousands of cellulose products our chemists have developed.

It is generally believed that all linen is produced from flax. Actually, the majority comes from hemp—authorities estimate that more than half of our imported linen fabrics are manufactured from hemp fiber. Another misconception is that burlap is made from hemp. Actually, its source is usually jute, and practically all of the burlap we use is woven by laborers in India who receive only four cents a day. Binder twine is usually made from sisal which comes from Yucatan and East Africa.

All of these products, now imported, can be produced from home-grown hemp. Fish nets, bow strings, canvas, strong rope, overalls, damask, tablecloths, fine linen garments, towels, bed linen and thousands of other everyday items can be grown on American farms. Our imports of foreign fabrics and fibers average about $200,000,000 per year; in raw fibers alone we imported over $50,000,000 in the first six months of 1937. All of this income can be made available for Americans.

The paper industry offers even greater possibilities. As an industry it amounts to over $1,000,000,000 a year, and of that eighty per cent is imported. But hemp will produce every grade of paper, and government figures estimate that 10,000 acres devoted to hemp will produce as much paper as 40,000 acres of average pulp land.

One obstacle in the onward march of hemp is the reluctance of farmers to try new crops. The problem is complicated by the need for proper equipment a reasonable distance from the farm. The machine cannot be operated profitably unless there is enough acreage within driving range and farmers cannot find a profitable market unless there is machinery to handle the crop. Another obstacle is that the blossom of the female hemp plant contains marijuana, a narcotic, and it is impossible to grow hemp without producing the blossom. Federal regulations now being drawn up require registration of hemp growers, and tentative proposals for preventing narcotic production are rather stringent.

However, the connection of hemp as a crop and marijuana seems to be exaggerated. The drug is usually produced from wild hemp or locoweed which can be found on vacant lots and along railroad tracks in every state. If federal regulations can be drawn to protect the public without preventing the legitimate culture of hemp, this new crop can add immeasurably to American agriculture and industry.

Popular Mechanics Magazine can furnish the name and address of the maker of, or dealer in, any article described in its pages. If you wish this information, write to the Bureau of Information, inclosing a sampled, self-addressed envelope.

ARTICLE REPRINTED FROM
PAPER TRADE JOURNAL
OCTOBER 13, 1921

Hemp Wood as a Papermaking Material

Abstracted by C. J. West

If the composition of hemp wood as reported by Schwalbe and Becker in *Z. angew. Chem.* 32, 127 (1919) is correct, it should be a very promising raw material for paper mills. They reported a surprisingly high content of pure cellulose, namely, 51.7 per cent, while Heuser and Haug (*Z. angew. Chem.* 31, 99, 103, 166, 172 (1918) found only 43 per cent for the cellulose content of straw. Since straw has lately become an important raw material for the manufacture of pulp, it must be supposed that hemp wood, because of its higher cellulose content, would be even more suitable for this purpose.

Because of the importance of the question, B. Rassow and Alfred Zschenderlein (*Z. angew. Chem.* 34, 204-206 (1921) have reinvestigated the question of the composition of wood from hemp. The material used in the investigation consisted, first, of the product as obtained in the ordinary process of retting (from the Deutschen Hanfbaugesellschaft), and second, of a product prepared by the method of Krais (*Z. angew. Chem.* 32, 25, 160, 326; 33. 102) in which tenth normal sodium bicarbonate solution is used.

Krais' method (the "Sicherheitsröste," as Krais calls it) for the digestion of the bast fibers is readily applicable to hemp. The bast fibers dissolve completely in from three to three and a half days when the air-dry stalks are treated with a tenth normal sodium bicarbonate solution at 35 to 37° C and the resulting product shaken with hot water.

The first step in determining the suitability of the hemp wood for pulp manufacture was a study of the chemical composition of the two products. Schwalbe's scheme of analysis (*Z. angew. Chem.* 31, 50 193; 32, 125) was used; the results were as follows in the chart below.

The figures in the last two columns are the results obtained by Schwalbe and Becker. It must be remembered that these values cannot be compared in the same way that results from inorganic analysis are compared, since the methods employed do not have the same degree of precision.

The two samples analyzed by Rassow and Zschenderlein have practically the same composition. This is of great practical importance, since it indicates that the composition is independent of the method of preparation. Hemp wood resembles ordinary wood in composition, as shown by the figures obtained by Schwalbe and Becker (*Z. angew. Chem.* 32, 320) and König and Becker (*Z. angew. Chem.* 32, 157.) It resembles in particular the deciduous trees, which is seen by examining the values for pentosans and lignin, the two values which are characteristic for the difference between deciduous and coniferous trees.

Comparison of the values in the above table shows that the figures obtained by Schwalbe for crude cellulose, cellulose pentosans and pure cellulose vary considerably from those reported by Rassow and Zschenderlein. Even though the cellulose determination is not a very exact one, this fact can scarcely explain the difference between the two values for crude cellulose: 52.09 and 71.38 per cent. In attempting to explain these

Table I — Composition of Hemp Wood Shavings

	Hemp prepared by retting		Hemp prepared by Krais's method		Schwalbe's results	
	Air dry	Water free	Air dry	Water free	Air dry	Water free
Water	10.52	—	8.86	—	12.59	—
Ash	1.15	1.28	1.39	1.51	1.05	1.20
Fat and wax	2.55	2.85	3.88	4.26	1.96	2.23
Furfural	12.70	14.18	13.09	14.37	11.39	13.03
Pentosan	21.63	24.16	22.31	24.47	19.43	22.15
Crude cellulose	46.63	52.09	47.51	52.11	62.39	71.38
% of pentosan	22.12	—	22.41	—	27.57	—
Pure cellulose	36.32	40.57	36.86	40.43	45.19	51.70
Lignin	20.89	23.34	20.21	22.08	26.34	30.13

differences, the various methods for determining cellulose were compared with each other. Approximately the same results were found when varying amounts of chlorine and different methods of washing were used. The supposition that Schwalbe and Becker used an entirely different material was ruled out by analyzing some of the original material which they used, and obtaining results comparable with the lower ones here reported.

A comparison of the figures reported by Schwalbe and Becker for various woods with those of other investigators, such as König and Becker or Heuser and Sieber (*Z. angew. Chem.* 26, 801) showed that, while a part of the numbers agreed fairly well, the values for crude cellulose, cellulose pentosans and pure cellulose were consistently higher. The only explanation of this is that the crude cellulose of Schwalbe and Becker is not completely chlorinated and therefore contains considerable amounts of lignin.

Three experiments were carried out in order to determine the influence of the velocity of the chlorine stream: (1) 1 bubble in 2/3 second; (2) 1/2 bubbles per second, and (3) a lively stream. The method of Cross and Bevan as modified by Heuser and Haug was used, in which the products formed during the chlorination are washed out with 1 per cent sodium hydroxide. Hydrochloric acid is formed in the chlorination process, which, according to Heuser and Sieber, is a measure of the reactivity of the chlorine. The chlorinated product is washed with warm water (not higher than 30° C) until the filtrate is chlorine-free. The combined filtrate is warmed carefully to drive off free chlorine, and the solution of hydrochloric acid made up to volume and titrated with tenth normal sodium hydroxide. The results show that the yield of crude and pure cellulose is the same, but that the course of the reaction depends upon the velocity of the chlorine stream.

Table II

	Chlorine stream I	II	III
First chlorination	5.89	8.76	11.74
Second "	4.17	6.05	4.27
Third "	3.64	0.57	0.19
Fourth "	2.08	0.22	0.12
Total	15.78%	15.62%	16.32%

These results indicate that, in order to prepare a lignin-free crude cellulose, the fourth chlorination is necessary. They also show that even by the use of a rapid chlorine stream, as in III, there is little if any oxycellulose formed, since Heuser and Haug have shown that the amount of hydrochloric acid formed increases with the formation of oxycellulose. On the other hand, three chlorination are not sufficient, since the results show that in I, 2.08 per cent hydrochloric acid is formed on the fourth chlorination, a proof that the product still contained lignin. A fifth chlorination is not necessary because the product from the fourth dissolves to a clear solution in concentrated sulphuric acid.

The determination of crude cellulose in hemp wood, as well as in other woods, straw, flax, etc.—since these all have a similar composition—requires four chlorination periods of half an hour each, using gas stream of 1 to 2 drops per second. By this procedure it is certain that the crude cellulose contains no lignin, and at the same time, is free of celluloses. One may also follow the course of the chlorination by the change in the color of the cellulose material. As long as it contains lignin, it will have an orange color. Pure cellulose is not changed in color by the action of chlorine.

The second problem related to the method of washing the chlorinated product. Experiments were carried out with Heuser and Haug's method, using 1 per cent sodium hydroxide, and with Renker's method, in which sodium sulphite solution was used. The result's indicated that slightly better results were obtained by the first method, and it is recommended that the method be used in all cellulose determinations.

Finally, experiments were undertaken to determine the value of the hemp wood for the preparation of pulp. Cooking with water gave a product which might find use as a kraft pulp. Digestion with sodium hydroxide with sulphite liquor gave a pulp of good appearance, but containing large amounts of pentosans. The soda pulp contained as high as 20 per cent, while sulphite pulp, depending upon the manner of cooking, may contain up to 10 per cent. The Ritter-Kellner method is not suitable. Cooking for 12–13 hours at 140–150° with about 4 per cent sulphite liquor gives a pulp which, unbleached, contains 93–94 per cent crude cellulose, of which about 10 per cent is pentosans. It is not necessary to use a stronger sulphite liquor, since experiments showed that a 6 per cent liquor gave no better results.

USDA FILM:

Hemp for Victory

1942

Long ago when these ancient Grecian temples were new, hemp was already old in the service of mankind. For thousands of years, even then, this plant had been grown for cordage and cloth in China and elsewhere in the East. For centuries prior to about 1850 all the ships that sailed the western seas were rigged with hempen rope and sails. For the sailor, no less than the hangman, hemp was indispensable.

A 44-gun frigate like our cherished Old Ironsides took over 60 tons of hemp for rigging, including an anchor cable 25 inches in circumference. The Conestoga wagons and prairie schooners of pioneer days were covered with hemp canvas. Indeed the very word canvas comes from the Arabic word for hemp. In those days hemp was an important crop in Kentucky and Missouri. Then came cheaper imported fibers for cordage, like jute, sisal and Manila hemp, and the culture of hemp in American declined.

But now with Philippine and East Indian sources of hemp in the hands of the Japanese, and shipment of jute from India curtailed, American hemp must meet the needs of our Army and Navy as well as of our industry. In 1942, patriotic farmers at the government's request planted 36,000 acres of seed hemp, an increase of several thousand percent. The goal for 1943 is 50,000 acres of seed hemp.

In Kentucky much of the seed hemp acreage is on river bottom land such as this. Some of these fields are inaccessible except by boat. Thus plans are afoot for a great expansion of a hemp industry as a part of the war program. This film is designed to tell farmers how to handle this ancient crop now little known outside Kentucky and Wisconsin.

This is hemp seed. Be careful how you use it. For to grow hemp legally you must have a federal registration and tax stamp. This is provided for in your contract. Ask your county agent about it. Don't forget.

Hemp demands a rich, well-drained soil such as is found here in the Blue Grass region of Kentucky or in central Wisconsin. It must be loose and rich in organic matter. Poor soils won't do. Soil that will grow good corn will usually grow hemp.

Hemp is not hard on the soil. In Kentucky it has been grown for several years on the same ground, though this practice is not recommended. A dense and shady crop, hemp tends to choke out weeds. Here's a Canada thistle that couldn't stand the competition, dead as a dodo. Thus hemp leaves the ground in good condition for the following crop.

For fiber, hemp should be sown closely, the closer the rows, the better. These rows are spaced about four inches. This hemp has been broadcast. Either way it should be sown thick enough to grow a slender stalk. Here's an ideal stand; the right height to be harvested easily, thick enough to grow slender stalks that are easy to cut and process.

Stalks like these here on the left yield the most fiber and the best. Those on the right are too coarse and woody. For see, hemp is planted in hills like corn. Sometimes by hand. Hemp is a dioecious plant. The female flower is inconspicuous. But the male flower is easily spotted. In seed production after the pollen has been shed, these male plants are cut out. These are the seeds on a female plant.

Hemp for fiber is ready to harvest when the pollen is shedding and the leaves are falling. In Kentucky, hemp harvest comes in August. Here the old standby has been the self-rake reaper, which has been used for a generation or more.

Hemp grows so luxuriantly in Kentucky that harvesting is sometimes difficult, which may account for the popularity of the self-rake with its lateral stroke. A modified rice binder has been used to some extent. This machine works well on avenge hemp. Recently, the improved hemp harvester, used for many years in Wisconsin, has been introduced in Kentucky. This machine spreads the hemp in a continuous swath. It is a far cry from this fast and efficient modern harvester, that doesn't stall in the heaviest hemp.

In Kentucky, hand cutting is practicing in opening fields for the machine. In Kentucky, hemp is shucked as soon as safe, after cutting, to be spread out for retting later in the fall.

In Wisconsin, hemp is harvested in September. Here the hemp harvester with automatic spreader is standard equipment. Note how smoothly the rotating apron lays the swaths preparatory to retting. Here it is a common and essential practice to leave headlands around hemp fields. These strips may be planted with other crops, preferably small grain. Thus the harvester has room to make its first round without preparatory hand cutting. The other machine is running over corn stubble. When the cutter bar is much shorter than the hemp is tall, overlapping occurs. Not so good for retting. The standard cut is eight to nine feet.

The length of time hemp is left on the ground to ret depends on the weather. The swaths must be turned to get a uniform ret. When the woody core breaks away readily like this, the hemp is about ready to pick up and bind into bundles. Well-retted hemp is light to dark grey. The fiber tends to pull away from the stalks. The presence of stalks in the bough-string stage indicates that retting is well underway. When hemp is short or tangled or when the ground is too wet for machines, it's bound by hand. A wooden bucket is used. Twine will do for tying, but the hemp itself makes a good band.

When conditions are favorable, the pickup binder is commonly used. The swaths should lie smooth and even with the stalks parallel. The picker won't work well in tangled hemp. After binding, hemp is shucked as soon as possible to stop further retting. In 1942, 14,000 acres of fiber hemp were harvested in the United States. The goal for the old standby cordage fiber, is staging a strong comeback.

This is Kentucky hemp going into the dryer over mill at Versailles. In the old days braking was done by hand. One of the hardest jobs known to man. Now the power braker makes quick work of it.

Spinning American hemp into rope yarn or twine in the old Kentucky river mill at Franfort, Kentucky. Another pioneer plant that has been making cordage for more than a century. All such plants will presently be turning out products spun from American-grown hemp: twine of various kinds for tying and upholster's work; rope for marine rigging and towing; for hay forks, derricks, and heavy duty tackle; light duty firehose; thread for shoes for millions of American soldiers; and parachute webbing for our paratroopers. As for the United States Navy, every battleship requires 34,000 feet of rope. Here in the Boston Navy Yard, where cables for frigates were made long ago, crews are now working night and day making cordage for the fleet. In the old days rope yarn was spun by hand. The rope yarn feeds through holes in an iron plate. This is Manila hemp from the Navy's rapidly dwindling reserves. When it is gone, American hemp will go on duty again; hemp for mooring ships; hemp for tow lines; hemp for tackle and gear; hemp for countless naval uses both on ship and shore. Just as in the days when Old Ironsides sailed the seas victorious with her hempen shrouds and hempen sails. Hemp for victory.

Footnotes

Fiber Wars

1. *Pioneer Press*, St Paul, MN. Aug. 5, 1993. p. 1B.
2. *Prescott Journal*, Prescott, WI, Aug. 1, 1991. p. 1A.
3. *Cannabis* (in italics) is used when referring to the botanical genus; cannabis (no italics), when referring to the plants of this group in a generic sense, including hemp and marijuana types.
4. Prior to 1915, Kentucky had been the major hemp producing state, with Missouri second. The industry in Kentucky has been thoroughly covered in Hopkins, J. F. 1951. *A History of the Hemp Industry in Kentucky*. University of Kentucky Press, Lexington.
5. A broader discussion of this history and related matters can be found in: Herer, J. 1992. *The Emperor Wears No Clothes*. Queen of Clubs Publishing. Van Nuys, CA; and, Conrad, C. 1993. *Hemp—Lifeline to the Future*. Creative Xpressions Publishing. Los Angeles, CA.
6. Manila hemp (abaca, *Musa textilis*), sisal hemp (*Agave sisalana*, or henequen, Agave *fourcroydes*), Mauritius hemp (*Furcraea gigantea*), New Zealand hemp (*Phormium tenax*), sunn hemp (*Crotalaria juncea*), Indian hemp (jute, *Corchorus capsularis* or *C. clitorus*), bow-string hemp (*Sansevieria cylindrica*). (Over thirty are listed by Montgomery, B. 1954. *The Bast Fiber*. In H. R. Mauersberger (ed.), Matthews' Textile Fibers. Wiley, N.Y. p. 257-359.)
7. Dodge, Bertha. 1984. *Cotton: The Plant That Would Be King*. University of Austin Press. Texas. p. 16.
8. Scherer, J. A. B. 1916. *Cotton as a World Power*. Frederick A. Stokes Co. New York. "Who knew before the Great War, that the world's cotton crop, of which three-quarters, or thereabouts, is produced in the United States of America, exceeds in value the whole world's output of the precious metals by fifty per cent?" p. 2.
9. North, D. C. 1966. *The Economic Growth of the United States: 1790-1860*. The Norton Library, USA. p. 67.
10. Dodge,B., p. 52.
11. USDA. 1877. Flax and flax products in the United States. Report of the Statistician. p. 175.
12. Dodge, C. A. 1896. A report on the culture of hemp and jute in the United States. USDA Office of Fiber Investigations. Report No. 8. p. 21.
13. Robinson, B. B. 1943. Hemp. *Farmer's Bulletin no. 1935*. USDA.
14. Fuller, W. H. and A. G. Norman. 1944. *Nature of the flora on field-retting hemp*. Proc. Soil Sci.Soc Am. 9:101-105.
15. Bidwell, P. W. and J. I. Falconer. 1941. *History of Agriculture in the Northern United States: 1620-1860*. Carnegie Inst. Washington, D.C. p. 365.
16. Dodge, C.A. 1896, p. 16.
17. D. Wirtshafter, in this volume, mentions that Sherwin-Williams Co. was importing and growing hempseed for use in paints just before marijuana prohibition was enacted.
18. Weil, A. 1989. *Therapeutic Hemp Oil*. Natural Health, The Guide to Well-Being. Mar-Apr. Also see Proc. 55th Flax Institute of America. Fargo, ND, Jan. 27-28, 1994.

19. Comparative nutrient withdrawal of hemp and grain crops:

Crop	N (kg/ha)	P2O5 (kg/ha)	K2O (kg/ha)
Hemp (*Cannabis sativa* L.)	102.0	66.0	117.0
Maize (*Zea mays* L.) 3,000 kg grain	48.0	18.5	5.2
Wheat (*Triticum* sp.) 2,000 kg grain	42.0	21.0	12.5
Rye (*Secale cereale* L.) 2,000 kg grain	43.0	10.7	10.7
Oats (*Avena sativa* L.) 1,500 kg grain	29.0	11.5	8.9

from Dempsey, J. M. 1975. *Fiber Crops.* University of Florida Press.

20. USDA. 1940. Yearbook of Agriculture p. 213.

21. USDA. 1879 Our flax and hemp industries. Report of Commissioner of Agriculture. p. 606.

22. Benedict, M. K. 1953. *Farm Policies of the US: 1790-1959.* The 20th Century Fund, N.Y.

23. Dodge, 1896, Report No. 8. p. 15.

24. The short, tow fibers were used for oakum. Sunn hemp (*Crotalaria juncea*), another tropical fiber, competed with hemp for this market.

25. Commissioner of Agriculture. 1879. Our flax and hemp industries. *Report on Vegetable Fibers.* USDA. p. 565.

26. Dodge, C. A. 1896, p. 22.

27. Dodge, C. A. 1890. Report of the Special Agent in Charge of Fiber Investigations. Report of the Sec. of Agric. p. 453.

28. Dodge, C. A. 1893. Report of the Special Agent in Charge of Fiber Investigations. Annual Report of Department of Agriculture. p. 577.

29. Dodge, 1890, p. 455.

30. Commissioner of Agriculture, 1879, p. 582.

31. Dodge, 1893, p. 577.

32. USDA. 1905 Report of Office of Fiber Investigations. Bureau of Plant Industry. p. 145.

33. Fite, G. C. 1984. *Cotton Fields No More: Southern Agriculture 1865-1980.* The University of Kentucky Press, p. 27, 28, 85.

34. Fite, p. 34.

35. Fite, p. 84.

36. Fite, p. 34.

37. Dodge, 1893, p. 567.

38. Allen, J. L. 1900. *The Reign of Law: A Tale of the Kentucky Hemp Fields.* The MacMillan Co. Norwood, MA. p.52.

39. Dodge, C. A. 1890. *The Hemp Industry.* USDA Division of Statistics 1: 64-74.

40. Dodge, C. A. 1895, p. 216.

41. Dewey, L. H. 1901. The Hemp Industry in the United States. USDA Yearbook of Agric., p. 541-555.

42. Dodge, C. A. 1896. USDA Yearbook of Agric., p. 235.

43. USDA. 1899. Hemp. USDA Yearbook of Agriculture, p. 64.

44. USDA. 1902. USDA. Yearbook of Agric. p. 23.

45. Wright, Andrew. 1918. Wisconsin's Hemp Industry. Wisconsin Agricultural Experiment Station Bulletin # 293. p.5.

46. Wright, p. 8.

47. USDA. 1921. Annual Report of the Department of Agriculture: Hemp. p. 46.

48. Dewey, L. H. 1901. The Hemp Industry in the United States. USDA Yearbook of Agric. p. 541-555.

49. Dewey, L. H. 1943 Fiber Production in the Western Hemisphere. USDA Misc. Publication number 518.

50. USDA. Bureau of Plant Industry. Inventory of Seeds and Plants Imported. For example, nos. 35251, 37721, 38466, 62165. No. 38466: "From Sianfu, Shensi, China. Collected January 24, 1914. A variety of hemp, said to produce very strong fiber." No. 37721: "Kashgar hempseed. The hempseed was requested as the variety from which hashish or bhang is made." This type was probably sought for its widespread use in veterinary medicine. There is a clear indication from these notes as to the type and use of the cannabis being acquired that varietal difference was recognized.

51. Dodge, 1896, Report No. 8. p. 7.

52. USDA. Bureau of Plant Industry. 1917. Report of the Chief. p. 12.

53. USDA. Bureau of Plant Industry. 1918. Report of the Chief. p. 28. Water-retted hemp from Italy was the standard for quality fiber.

54. USDA. Bureau of Plant Industry. 1919. Report of the Chief. p. 21.

55. USDA. Bureau of Plant Industry. 1920. Report of the Chief. p. 26. A detailed description of four varieties developed by Lyster Dewey's federal hemp breeding program is included in the 1927 Yearbook of Agriculture.

56. USDA. 1929. Annual Reports of the Department of Agriculture: Hempseed. p. 26.

57. Dewey, L. H. 1927. Hemp varieties of improved type are result of selection. USDA Yearbook of Agric. p. 358-361.

58.Dillman, A. C. 1936. Improvement in Flax. USDA Yearbook of Agric. p. 749.

59.Dillman, 1936, p. 748.

60.Today, Canada is the largest producer of linseed oil, exporting nearly half a million tons in 1993. Markets for the industrial oil continue to decline and acreage is shifting to canola. Interest in "flax oil" as a nutritional amendment is growing.

61.USDA. 1909. Utilizing wood waste. Annual Report of Forest Service. p. 406.

62.Dewey, L. H. and J. L. Merrill. 1916. Hemp hurds as papermaking material. USDA Bulletin No. 404.

63.USDA. 1917. Bureau of Plant Industry, Annual Report: Hemp hurds. p.25.

64.Wirtshafter, D. 1994. Vanishing Act: The Story of George Schlichten. *High Times* 223:36 (March). These letters may be obtained from The Ohio Hempery, Inc., 14 N. Court St. Athens, Ohio, 45701.

65.see Zias, et al. 1993. Early medical use of Cannabis. *Nature* 363:215. Following the assassination of her husband, Mary Todd Lincoln was treated for her nervous condition with cannabis.(Meeley, M.E. Jr. and R.G. McMyrtry.1983. The Insanity File: The Case of Mary Todd Lincoln. Southern Ill. Univ. Press.)

66.Today, Wisconsin's paper industry, the largest in the country, imports into the state 30% of the pulp it uses. The rest comes from its own forests. The prospect of annual plants producing on-farm raw material for the paper industry continues to attract attention. For the North, hemp is the premier annual plant for this purpose. Moreover, since it fits well into rotations with corn, small grains and alfalfa while reducing the need for herbicides, hemp can be used as an alternative to crops with surpluses in a sustainable system of agriculture. But prohibition precludes such developments.

67.One conspiracy theory holds that newspaper magnate William Randolph Hearst was heavily invested in pulp wood woodlands and connects this to his yellow-journalistic campaign against marijuana.

68.He lists the locations as Waupon, Alto, Brandon, Fairwater (2 mills), Markesan (2 mills), Union Grove, and Iron Ridge, with plans for additional mills in Milton and Picketts. From 1921 until at least 1926, a mill owned by the Hemp Company of America, a Chicago-based corporation, was operating just outside Roberts, WI, on the western side of the state. (G. Gardiner, Roberts, WI, personal communication)

69.Wright, p. 37.

70.Wright, p. 14.

71.Dewey, L. H. 1931. Hemp fiber losing ground, despite its valuable qualities. USDA Yearbook of Agric. p. 284. The uses for hemp Dewey lists as: "Wrapping twines for heavy packages; mattress twine for sewing mattresses; spring twines for tying springs in overstuffed furniture and in box springs; sacking twine for sewing sacks containing sugar, wool, peanuts, stock feed, or fertilizer; baling twine, similar to sacking twine, for sewing burlap covering on bales and packages; broom twine for sewing brooms; sewing twine for sewing cheesecloth for shade grown tobacco; hop twine for holding up hop vines in hop yards; ham strings for hanging up hams; tag twines for shipping twines; meter cord for tying diaphragms in gas meters; blocking cord used in blocking men's hats; webbing yarns which are woven into strong webbing; belting yarns to be woven into belts; marlines for binding the ends of ropes, cables and hawsers to keep them from fraying; hemp packing or coarse yarn used in packing valve pumps; plumber's oakum, usually tarred, for packing the joints of pipes; marine oakum, also tarred for caulking the seams of ships and other water craft." p.285.

72.Butterfield, R. 1957. *The American Past.* Simon and Schuster, N. Y. p. 391.

73.Fite, p. 71.

74.Fite, p. 150.

75.Young, T. M. 1903. *The American Cotton Industry.* Chas. Scribner's Sons, N.Y., p. 106.

76.Fite, p. 184.

77.See, for example, the depiction of the destruction of the environment around the Aral Sea in the former Soviet Union which resulted from intensive cotton agriculture in that area. Ellis, W. S. and D. C. Turnley. 1990. The Aral: A Soviet Sea Lies Dying. *National Geographic* 177(2):73-93.

78.Dillman, 1936, p. 753.

79. Wright, p. 26.

80.van der Werf, H.M.G. 1991. Agronomy and Crop Physiology of Fiber Hemp, A literature Review, in this volume.

81.Secoy, D. E. and A. E. Smith. 1983. Uses of Plants in Control of Agricultural and Domestic Pests. *Econ. Bot.* 57: 28-57.

82.Fite, p. 109, a quote from the Ada, Oklahoma, *Bulletin.*

83. Wilcox, W. W. 1947. *The Farmer in the Second World War*. The Iowa State College Press. Ames, IA. p. 220.

84. Wilcox, p. 220.

85. Puterbaugh, H. L. 1964. Plant fibers—some economic considerations. *Econ. Bot.* 19(2):184-187.

86. Hale, W. J. 1934. *The Farm Chemurgic*. The Stratford Co. Boston. p. 11.

87. Fite, p. 120.

88. The American Cotton Association, The American Cotton Grower's Exchange, The American Farm Bureau Federation.

89. Fite, p. 178.

90. Fite, p. 129.

91. Agricultural Adjustment Administration. 1934. Questions and answers covering 1934 and 1935 cotton acreage reduction plan. USDA. AAA was later declared unconstitutional by the Supreme Court, but was reincarnated under the mechanism of soil conservation programs which will, for instance, pay cotton farmers $2.2 billion for 1993 and 2.4 billion for 1994 not to plant. (Congressional Budget Office estimates) The hegemony of southern interests persists in agricultural policy to the present and is reflected in such legislation as the 1985 Food Security Act: which "prohibits imposition of offsetting compliance as a condition for participation in the [subsidy] programs for rice and cotton ." (Allen, K. 1990. Agricultural Policies in a New Decade. National Center for Food and Agricultural Policy: Resources for the Future & Food and Agriculture Committee, National Planning Assoc. "Under offsetting compliance, a farmer may not participate in a government program for a given crop unless all of the farms operated by that individual are enrolled in the program for that crop. This prevents a farmer from offsetting mandated reductions in production on one farm with expanded production on other farms outside the program.")

92. Fite, p. 144.

93. Fite, p. 164.

94. USDA. 1935. Annual Reports of the Department of Agriculture, p.6.

95. Food stamps are still administered by the USDA. For a broader discussion see Solkoff, J. 1985. *The Politics of Food*. Sierra Club Books, San Francisco.

96. In the early 1960s a researcher at Berkeley was given a grant to develop a strain of *Fusarium* fungus which would be lethal to hemp, to be used for eradication.

97. Eastman, W. 1968. *The History of the Linseed Oil Industry in the United States*. T.C. Denison & Co., Inc. Minneapolis. p. 99.

98. McMillan, W. 1950. *New Riches from the Soil*. Nan Nostrand, New York, 2nd ed.

99. Hale's vision of chemurgy extended beyond the technical into all aspects of social organization. Among his proposals was a call for stronger tariffs, taxes on the wealthy, and a repeal of property taxes, which he saw as burdensome to agriculture. He aggressively attacked the oil industry, precociously pointing to the damaging effect of air pollution on lungs, and referred to the financial moguls of the day as "boobs" and "Antichrist."

100. *The Chemurgic Digest*, May 30, 1942 & Nov. 15, 1944. Hemp Industry's Future.

101. Kirby, R. H. 1963. *Vegetable Fibers*. Interscience Publ., Inc. New York. p. 61.

102. *Popular Mechanics*. 1938. The Billion Dollar Crop.

103. Although Hale recognized that the chemical industry was taking markets from agriculture, as in the cotton and wool example, he pointed out that cotton lint and wood were the prime sources of cellulose used in the manufacture of rayon. He felt the neglect of farms by a government controlled by bankers was at the root of the nation's problems.

104. George W. Carver ranks as one of the greatest chemurgists ever to live. "Carver's research program ultimately developed 300 derivative products from peanut—among them cheese, milk, coffee, flour, ink, dyes, plastics, wood stains, soap, linoleum, medicinal oils and cosmetics—and 118 from sweet potatoes, including flour, vinegar, and postage stamp glue. He also succeeded in making synthetic marble from wood pulp." *Encyclopedia Britannica*.

105. McCune, W. 1956. *Who's Behind Farm Policy?* Praeger Publ. p. 346. Media manipulation was a common practice in the Age of the Robber Barons. A glaring example can be found in the personal retrospective of reporter George Seldes regarding (FBN Director Harry Anslinger's father-in-law) Andrew Mellon's control and manipulation of the press during his divorce trial in the 1920's. (Seldes, G. 1987. Witness to a Century. Ballantine). It was business-as-usual.

106. Courtwright, D. T. 1919-82. *Dark Paradise: Opiate Addiction in America before 1940*. Harvard Univ. Press, Cambridge MA. p.117.

107. USDA. 1937. Annual Report of the Department of Agriculture, p. 7.

108. Musto, D. 1973. *The American Disease: The Origins of Narcotic Control.* Yale University Press. p. 224.

109. Dillman, 1936, p. 779.

110. Founded March 9, 1931, in Minneapolis.

111. Eastman, p.100.

112. Grinspoon, L. 1971. *Marihuana Reconsidered.* Harvard University Press. Cambridge, Mass.

113. Wellman, F. L. 1961. *Coffee: Botany, Cultivation, and Utilization.* Interscience Publ., New York. p. 23.

114. The Attorney General of Kentucky admitted that rendering such materials illegal was not the intent of the law. (G. Galbraith, personal communication)

115. Due to the efforts of John Birrenbach of the St. Paul, MN-based Institute for Hemp, who testified to the effect this change would have on the state's birdseed industry. There was also testimony from the Public Defenders Office asking that the judicial system not be clogged with young people who have been led to believe ditchweed is marijuana and get caught with a plant they've pulled up from alongside the road.

116. Subcommittee on Finance. US Senate. July 12, 1937. H.R. 6906. An act to impose an occupational excise tax upon certain dealers in marijuana, to impose a transfer tax on certain dealings in marijuana, and to safeguard the revenue therefrom by registry and recording. Subcommittee on H.R.6906. Prentiss M. Brown (Michigan), Chairman. Congressional Record.

117. Dewey, 1913, Plate XLII, Fig. 2.

118. Wright, p. 13.

119. Dempsey, J. M. 1975. *Fiber Crops.* The Univ. Presses of Florida. Gainsville.

120. Dillman, 1936, p. 761.

121. Broom-rape is a parasitic plant with a seed similar in size to hempseed which can become a problem in hemp fields. Hemp is actually a superior weed control agent.

122. Fiber types are high in cannabidiol (CBD), a nauseating but non-psychoactive chemical. The relation between fiber and herbal cannabis varieties is analogous to that between vinegar and wine.

123. USDA. 1938. Bureau of Plant Industry, Annual Report, p. 7.

124. USDA. 1939. Bureau of Plant Industry, Annual Report, p. 9.

125. *Popular Mechanics.* 1938.

126. Barre, H. W. and B. B. Robinson. 1942. Memorandum on cooperative work with the US Department of Agriculture. Cold Spring Harbor collection.

127. Warmke, H .E. 1944. Use of the Killifish, Fundulus heteroclitus, in the Assay of Marihuana. J. Amer. Pharm. Assoc. Sci. Ed. 33:122-126.

128. Bredemann, G., F. Schwanitz, and R. Van Sengbusch. 1956 Problems of modern hemp breeding with particular reference to the breeding of varieties of hemp containing little or no hashish. Bull. Narcotics 3:31-34.

129. In 1991, acreage and yields for hemp in Russia and eastern Europe were:

Country	Hectares	tons/hectare
Russia	60,000	4
Romania	24,000	4
Yugoslavia	700	8
Poland	2,500	4
Hungary	720	9

(H. Spelter, Forest Products Lab, Univ. of Wis., personal communication).Food production has tended to displace fiber crops as a priority in these countries.

130. Agra Europe #1447. July 5, 1991.

131. *Delta*-9 tetrahydrocannibinol, the principal psychoactive component of hemp's complex biochemistry, identified in 1963.

132. DeMeijer, E.P.M., H. J. van der Kamp and F. A. van Eeuwijk. 1992. Characterization of Cannabis accessions with respect to other plant characters. *Euphytica* 62: 187-200.

133. Goldstein, A. 1994. *Addiction: From Biology to Drug Policy.* W.H. Freeman & Co. NY p. 171.

134. Simmonds, N. W. 1984. *The Evolution of Crop Plants: Hemp.* Longman, London. p. 203.

135. DeMeijer, E.P.M. 1993. Hemp variations as pulp source researched in the Netherlands. *Pulp and Paper,* July: 41-43.

136. Dodge, C. A. 1895, p. 216.

137. A comprehensive analysis of the forces within society which have relegated Cannabis to its current status is beyond the scope of this history. Additional insight may be gained by consulting: Foster, S. 1991. *Echinacea: Nature's Immune Enhancer,* Healing Arts Press, Rochester, Vermont; Farnsworth, N. R. and D. D. Soejarto. 1985. Potential consequences of plant extinction in the United States on the current and future availability of prescription drugs. *Econ. Bot.* 39(3): 231-40; Drake, D. and M. Uhlman. 1993. *Making Medicine, Making Money;* Andrews and McMeel, Publ. Kansas

City; Randall, R. C. 1991. *Marijuana & Aids: Pot, Politics and PWA's in America.* Galen Press, Washington, D. C.

138. Annual Report of DuPont Chemical Co. 1937. In Herer, 1992. Today, cannabis is attacked by way of the drug connection and the generosity of major corporations ensures that this association remains intact in the public awareness. The nefarious behavior and social degradation associated with cocaine use provides indisputable evidence of the threat of drugs to the social order. Were it not for cocaine and the common label of "drugs," the cost of marijuana prohibition would be difficult to justify. In this regard, "crack" cocaine has been even more efficacious. The Criminal Justice Policy Foundation estimates that decriminalization of cannabis would create a $67 billion industry and that taxes, fees and licensing could net $20 billion a year. This does not consider the potential value of fiber hemp for fabric, building materials and paper.

139. World War II Wisconsin hemp mill sites: Clinton, Sun Prairie, De Forest, Cuba City, Darien, Union Grove, Beaver Dam, Hartford, Ripon, Brandon, Juneau and Waupon. Much of the labor was provided by German POWs and Japanese-Americans relocated from the internment camps. Many of the structures are still standing and occupied by other industries.

140. Robinson, 1943.

141. The existence of this film was denied by the USDA until it was found by Jack Herer in 1989.

142. Wis. Dept. of Agric. 1945. Wisconsin Agriculture in WW2. Crop Rep. Serv. Bull. #243. p.28.

143. Ash, A. L. 1948. Hemp: production and utilization. *Econ. Bot.* 2:158-169.

144. Reproduced in Barash, L. 1971. A Review of Hemp Cultivation in Canada. MS.

145. This address, near Loyola University, is today an apartment in a stately old building now converted into a cooperative condo. As of this writing, the author has found no more information about this Institute or the letter's author.

146. Barre and Robinson, 1942.

147. Wilcox, p. 64.

148. Wilcox, p. 222.

149. Evans, R. B. 1951. The utilization of American cotton. USDA Yearbook of Agric. p. 384.

150. Evans, p. 385.

151. Evans, p. 384.

152. Puterbaugh, p. 186.

153. "Arthur C. Dillman...has worked closely with the several State and Canadian experiment stations and with the linseed industry and the manufacturers of cigarette papers. At the beginning of the cigarette-paper industry, he suggested the use of a portable "flax break" or decorticating machine to process flax straw on the farm, thus effecting savings in the cost of shipping the bulky straw to tow mills." (Dillman, A. C. 1947. Paper from flax. USDA Yearbook of Agric. 1943-47. p. 752.)

154. Essentially due to the fact that there was more frequent replacement of northern congressmen by voters, while southern congressmen rose to committee chairs.

155. Byrom, M. H. 1951. Progress with long vegetable fibers. USDA Yearbook of Agric. p. 475.

156. Clark, T. F. 1964. Plant fibers in the paper industry. *Econ. Bot.* 19:394-405.

157. LeMahieu, P. J., E. S. Oplinger, and D. H. Putnam. 1991. *Kenaf. In Alternative Field Crops Manual.* Wisconsin Agricultural Extension Service, Madison, WI.

158. LeMahieu, et al., p. 3.

159. Puterbaugh, p. 186.

160. Weindling, L. 1947. *Long Vegetable Fibers.* Columbia Univ. Press.

161. Delafield, P. 1971. Wisconsin's 'Hemp King:' His Rise and Decline. *View* Magazine, Jan 31, 1971: 9-12.

162. Readers interested in the history of drug enforcement in the United States can find histories in Musto, D. 1973. *The American Disease: The Origins of Narcotic Control*; and Epstein, E.J. 1977. *Agent of Fear.* G.P. Putnam's Sons, NY. The latter examines the origins of the DEA in E. Howard Hunt and G. Gordon Liddy's attempt to create a presidential secret police force under the guise of attacking heroin, until its exposure with the Watergate scandal.

163. Organization for Economic Cooperation and Development. 1993. OECD schemes for the varietal certification of seed moving in international trade: List of cultivars for certification, Cannabis sativa. OECD, Paris. The following cultivars are eligible for support payments in the UK: Carmognola; CS; Delta-Llosa; Delta-405; Fedora 19; Fedrina 74; Felina 34; Ferimon; Fibranova; Fibrimon 24; Fibrimon 56; Futura.

164. Small, E., H.D. Beckstead, and A. Chan. 1975. The evolution of cannabinoid phenotypes in Cannabis. *Econ. Bot.* 29(3): 219-232.

165. Waddle, B. M. and R. F. Olwick. 1961. Producing seeds of cotton and other fiber crops. USDA Yearbook of Agric.: Seeds. p. 192.

166. Had any of the seed grown, the NSSL could not have handled it because of drug licensing requirements (Loren Weisner, NSSL, personal communication).

167. It is uncertain whether any may be found in the Vavilov collection.

168. DeMeijer, E. P. M. and L. J. M. van Soest. 1992 The CPRO Cannabis germplasm collection. Euphytica. 62:201-211.

169. USDA. 1929. Bureau of Plant Industry, Annual Report. p. 27.

170. Mankowski, J., L. Grabowska and P. Baraniecki. 1994. Hemp and flax cultivated on the soil polluted with heavy metals—A biological purification of the soil and a raw material for the pulp industry. Abstracted from: Alternative oilseed and fibre crops for cool and wet regions of Europe, a conference at Wageningen Agricultural University, The Netherlands, April 7-8, 1994

171. Martin, A. 1991. Petro-chemical alternative. Garbage 3(6):44-49 (Nov-Dec).

172. Lotz, L. A. P. 1991. Reduction of growth and reproduction of Cyperus esculentus by specific crops. Weed Research 31:153-160.

173. Latta, R.P. and B.J. Eaton. 1975. Seasonal fluctuations in cannabinoid content of Kansas marijuana. Econ. Bot. 29: 153-163.

Hemp Realities

1 Herer, Jack, The Emperor Wears No Clothes, Queen of Clubs Press, Van Nuys, CA, 1985.

2 Ibid, p. 24.

3 Abel, Ernest L. Marijuana, the First 12,000 Years. 1980. Plenum Press, New York Also in Merlin, Mark D. Man and Marijuana. 1972. Associated University Press, New Jersey.

4 World Almanac, Newspaper Enterprise Assn.,New York,1986 p. 615

Hemp as Biomass?

1 Herer, Jack, The Emperor Wears No Clothes, Van Nuys, CA, Queen of Clubs Publishing 1985

2 Osburn, Lynn, Energy Farming In America, BACH Publishing, 1989

3 Van Der Werf, Hayo, Agronomy and Crop Physiology of Fibre Hemp: A Literature Review 1991

4 Gold, Dave, Solar Gas, New Orleans, LA, Solar Age Press, 1980

5 Interview with Dave Gold, High Times

6 Van der Werf, op.cit., page 11. Figuring an average yield of 7.7 metric tons of above-ground dry matter per hectare, of which 14% is seed.

Hemp Paper Production

1 Hunter, D. Paper-making The History & Technique of an Ancient Craft, 1943, pg. 465.

2 ibid., pg. 466.

3 ibid.

4 ibid., pg. 565.

5 USDA Bulletin #404, "Hemp Hurds as a Paper-making Material."

6 Hunter, op.cit.

7 U.S.D.A. Motion Picture "Hemp for Victory," 1942.

8 Letters from Prof. Goloborodko, Director, All Union Bast Crops Institute, Glukov Ukraine.

9 U.S.D.A. Bulletin #404, Lyster Dewey, The Production and Handling of Hemp Hurds, 1916, p. 2.

10 ibid., pg. 1.

11 U.S.D.A. Motion Picture "Hemp for Victory", 1942.

12 Dewey, op. cit., pg. 2.

13 Dewey, op. cit., pg. 3-4.

14 Dewey, op. cit., pg. 2.

15 Dewey, op. cit., pg. 3.

16 Dewey, op. cit., pg. 3.

17 Letters from Prof. Goloborodko, Director, All Union Bast Crops Institute, Glukov Ukraine.

18 Dewey, op. cit., pg. 3.

19 U.S. Patent Office Patent #2,127,157; #2,108,56; 2,1976-83.

20 Dewey, op. cit., pg. 3.

21 U.S. Patent Office Patent # 2,197,683.

22 U.S. Department of Natural Resources Information Office Information on Trees used in Paper Production for the year 1990.

23 U.S. Department of Agriculture Information Services, 1991.

24 Letters from Prof. Goloborodko, Director, All Union Bast Crops Institute, Glukov Ukraine.

25 Letters from Midwest Farmers to The Institute for Hemp, 1989-1992.

26 U.S.D.A. Motion Picture "Hemp for Victory," 1942.

27 Letters from Prof. Goloborodko, Director, All Union Bast Crops Institute, Glukov Ukraine.

28 Letters from Prof. Goloborodko, Director, All Union Bast Crops Institute, Glukov Ukraine.

Hemp as a Pulp Source

1 E.P.M. de Meijer and I.J.M. van Soets, 1992, The CPRO Cannabis germ plasm collection, *Euphytica*, 62: 201-211.

2 I.M. Wood, 1981, The utilization of field crops and crop residues for paper pulp production, *Field Crop Abstracts*, 34: 557-568.

3 A. Bosia, 1975, Hemp for refiner pulp, Paper, World Research, and Development Number 1975: 37-41.

4 L. Triolo, 1980, Materie prime non legnose per l'industia certaria, italia Agricola, 1: 33-61.

5 E.P.M. de Meijer, H.J. van der Kamp and F.A. van Eeuwijk, 1992, Characterisation of Cannabis accessions (populations) with regard to cannabinoid content in relation to other plant characters, *Euphytica*, 62: 187-200.

6 G.M.C. Coonon, personal communication, 1993.

Why Hemp Seeds?

1 Erasmus, Udo. *Fats that Heal, Fats that Kill.* Alive Books, Canada, 1993, p. 291

2 Finnegan, John, Fats and Oils: Promise or Poison, the inside story about oils that nourish us and those that poison—and the new breakthrough methods of producing good oils, *California*: Elysian Arts, 1992. Rudin, Donald, M.D., and Felix, Clara, *The Omega 3 Phenomenon*, New York: Rawson Associates, 1987.

3 Erasmus, op. cit., pages 210-11.

4 Erasmus, op. cit., pages 287 and 400.

5 See for instance *Webster's New Universal Unabridged Dictionary*, 1979 Edition

6 Miller, Carol and Wirtshafter, Don. *The Hemp Seed Cookbook*. Ohio Hempery, Athens, Ohio. 1991.

Hemp in England

1 van der Werf, H.M.G., *Agronomy and Crop Physiology of Fibre Hemp, A Literature Review*, CPRO-DLO, Wageningen, Holland, 1991.

2 Ibid. p.11

3 Allen, James Lane, *The Reign of Law: a Tale of the Kentucky Hemp Fields*, Macmillan Press, New York, 1900.

4 Herer, Jack, *The Emperor Wears No Clothes*, Queen of Clubs Press, Van Nuys, CA, 1990, pp 57 - 60.

5 Abel, Ernest, *Marihuana: The First 12,000 Years*, Plenum Press, New York, 1980

6 According to David Seber in an interview 10/25/93, the price of wood chips in 1990 was $12–18, in 1991 it was $15–20, in 1992 $35–40 and in 1993 it was $55–60.

7 There is one other grower, Pete Messenger, who is growing five acres. He intends to convert the entire crop into paper at a small mill in Scotland. *Face* Magazine, Vol. 2, #61, Oct. 93, London, UK, page 102.

8 Interview with Ian Low.

9 Op. cit., *Face* Magazine, p. 101

Hemp Breeding in Hungary

1 Dioecious—Plants having either male or female flowers.

2 Kinai—Variety from Chinese origin.

3 Monoecious—Plants bearing both male and female flowers.

Psychoactive Cannabis— Introduction

1 Proposition P
November 1991
San Francisco Ballot Initiative
The people of the City and County of San Francisco recommend that the State of California and the California Medical Association restore hemp medical preparations to the list of available medicines in California. Licensed physicians shall not be penalized for or restricted from prescribing hemp preparations for medical purposes.

The term "hemp medical preparations" means all products made form hemp, cannabis, or marijuana, in all forms that are designed, intended, or used for human consumption, for the treatment of any disease, the relief of pain, or for any healing purpose, including the relief of asthma, glaucoma, arthritis, anorexia, migraine, multiple sclerosis, epilepsy, nausea, stress, for use as an antibiotic, an anti-emetic, or as any healing agent, or as an adjunct to any medical procedure for the treatment of cancer, HIV infection or herbal treatment.

2. N.Y. Times, Philip J. Hilts, Aug. 2, 1994, page B6.

3. Under this set of definitions almost anything pleasureable which a person tends to repeat can be considered addictive, including: foods (especially sweets), dangerous sports, and other peak experiences such as sexual or ecstatic. Of course, these are not necessarily substance dependent.

Economics of Cannabis Legalization

1 A 1929-30 Parke-Davis catalog advertised a 4 oz. bottle of tincture of cannabis of 20% potency for $5, which works out to the equivalent of $5 per pound at 5% potency. Another Squibb catalog of uncertain date lists powdered cannabis at $2.50/lb: from the collection of Dr. Tod Mikuriya.

2 Peter Reuter, cited in Mark Kleiman, *Marijuana: Costs of Abuse, Costs of Control,* Greenwood Press, N.Y. 1989: p 38.

3 Tobacco Institute, *The Tax Burden On Tobacco: Historical Compilation,* Washington DC 1992.

4 A.C.M. Jansen, *Cannabis in Amsterdam: A Geography of Hashish and Marihuana,* desktop publishing: Dick Coutinho, Postbus 10, 1399 ZG Muiderberg, Netherlands, 1991: p. 67.

5 A similar price range may be found in the state of South Australia, where the cultivation of fewer than 10 plants has been decriminalized to a minor misdemeanor punishable by a fine. There cannabis is sold on the black market for about $100-$150 per ounce, about one-half to one-third the price elsewhere in Australia.

6 Mark Kleiman, *Against Excess: Drug Policy for Results,* Basic Books, N.Y. 1992.

7 Report of the British Indian Hemp Drugs Commission, 1893-4, Simla, India (7 Volumes).

8 In Bombay, the Commission heard testimony that "the ordinary liquor consumer pays twice as much for what he wants as the ordinary ganja consumer would, or three times as much as the ordinary bhang drinker. I think the rates should be equalized." (Report of the British Indian Hemp Drugs Commission, 1893-4,, Vol. 1, Chap. XVI, p. 327). Even in Bengal, where taxes were higher, the Commission found that "the average allowance of liquor to the habitual consumer was "much higher than in the case of ganja." It concluded, "Judged by this test, there is room even in Bengal for increased taxation" (ibid., p. 311).

9 Lester Grinspoon, "The Harmfulness Tax: A Proposal for Regulation and Taxation of Drugs" *North Carolina Journal of International Law & Commercial Regulation* 15#3: 505-10 (Fall 1990)

10 20th Annual Report of the Research Advisory Panel Report, 1989 Commentary Section: available from Dr. Frederick Meyers, Univ. of California, San Francisco.

11 Dr. Donald Tashkin, "Is Frequent Marijuana Smoking Harmful to Health?" *Western Journal of Medicine* 158#6: 635-637 (June 1993).

12 Michael Polen, Stephen Sidney, Irene Tekawa, Marianne Sadler and Gary Friedman, "Health Care Use by Frequent Marijuana Smokers Who Do Not Smoke Tobacco," *Western Journal of Medicine* 158#6: 596-601 (June 1993).

13 Willard Manning, Emmett Keeler, Joseph Newhouse, Elizabeth Sloss, and Jeffrey Wasserman, "The Taxes of Sin: Do Smokers and Drinkers Pay Their Way?" *JAMA* 261:1604-9 (March 17, 1989).

14 TC Wu, D Tashkin, B Djahed and JE Rose, "Pulmonary hazards of smoking marijuana as compared with tobacco," *New England Journal of Medicine* 318: 347-51 (1988); William Rickert, Jack Robinson and Byron Rogers, "A Comparison of Tar, Carbon Monoxide and pH Levels in Smoke From Marihuana and Tobacco Cigarettes," *Canadian Journal of Public Health* 73: 386-391 (1982).

15 Peter Passell, "Less Marijuana, More Alcohol?" *New York Times,* June 17, 1992 p. C2.

16 D. Gieringer, "Marijuana, Driving, and Accident Safety," *Journal of Psychoactive Drugs* 20 (1): 93-102 (Jan-Mar 1988).

17 Dr. Carl Soderstrom et al., "Marijuana and Accidents: Use Among 1023 Trauma Patients," *Archives of Surgery*, 123: 733-37 (June 1988). Conceivably, alcohol may be a greater risk factor in traffic accidents because it promotes speeding, whereas pot smoking-drivers tend to slow down. On the other hand, marijuana may be more involved in other kinds of accidents where forgetfulness or loss of concentration are a risk factor.

18 In Bengal in 1892-3, excise taxes and licensing fees on ganja totaled more than 10 rupees per ser (i.e., kilo), over one-half the average retail price of 20 rupees. This appears to have represented a 10-fold increase over the free-market price of cannabis, which sold for as little as 2 rupees in other provinces where it was lightly taxed. Report of the British Indian Hemp Drugs Commission, Vol. 1, Ch. XV p.295 and Ch. XVI pp. 311-2, p.321. The U.S. cigarette tax has historically accounted for about 25%-50% of retail prices, according to the Tobacco Institute (op. cit.).

19 Among 18-25 year-olds, four-sevenths of daily users reported being multiple daily users, according to NIDA in its National Survey of Drug Abuse: Main Findings 1982.

20 M. Kleiman, Marijuana: Costs of Abuse, Costs of Control, pp. 38-9.

21 Peter Reuter, "Prevalence Estimation and Policy Formulation," *Journal of Drug Issues*, Vol 23, No. 2, 1993: p 173.

22 A.C.M. Jansen, op. cit., p. 59.

23 Report of the Indian Hemp Drugs Commission, Vol. 1, Chap. XVI, p. 312.

24 This assumes 1000 joints to the kilo, or 3% potency for Indian ganja.

25 Jansen, op. cit. p. 64

26 "Drug Use in California, 1989-1990," California Legislative Analyst's Office, Sacramento.

Marijuana Economics

1 In 1977 the Federal Drug Enforcement Administration believed that there was "a good chance that marijuana dealing does a volume of maybe 48 billion a year." This would exceed the combined amount spent in the same year on alcohol and tobacco—$46 billion. See "Cash in on Marijuana," in *This World* Magazine, Sunday, September 19, 1982 *San Francisco Examiner/Chronicle*, p. 19, by Robert Gnaizda.

2 GROSS NATIONAL PRODUCT BY INDUSTRY, 1980, IN CURRENT DOLLARS
(Billions of dollars)

1. Manufacturing	$ 591.1
2. Wholesale & Retail Trade	421.7
3. Finance, Insurance & Real Estate	392.0
4. Services	343.5
5. Government & Government Enterprises	303.4
6. Construction	119.7
7. Transportation	97.1
8. Mining	94.1
9. Agriculture, Forestry & Fisheries	77.2
10. Communications	69.0
11. Electric, Gas & Sanitary Services	68.4

3 The DEA claims 90% is imported, but virtually all experts disregard their estimate. According to Kevin Zeese, legal counsel of NORML, 66% of the marijuana is imported. In terms of dollar value, the domestic crop, which retails for 3 to 6 times the price of Colombian marijuana, far exceeds all imports. According to experts at High Times probably 50% of the marijuana consumed in this country is domestic. The discrepancy between NORML's and *High Times*' figures is based on the difference between the commercial sales and consumption of marijuana cultivated for personal use. Probably 2,000,000 marijuana smokers regularly enjoy marijuana which they, their family, or their friends have grown.] Principal exporting nations producing marijuana for the U.S. are Colombia, Mexico, Thailand and Jamaica. Total marijuana imports come to about $3.2–$4 billion.

4 This total is reached as follows: a total of 15,000–20,000 tons are consumed in the U.S. each year. About 17% of this is homegrown which never reaches a commercial market. About 8,000–12,000 tons (or two-thirds) of the rest is imported. The average cost per pound from the smuggler is about $200 ($100 for Colombian, $600 for Thai) or $400,000 per ton.

5 Report of the Tax Force on Cannabis Regulation to the Center for the Study of Drug Policy . Regulation and Taxation of Cannabis Commerce (Washington, D.C.), 12 December 1981.

6 John Fogarty, "New U.S. War on Pot Growers," *San Francisco Chronicle*, 1 October 1982, p. 1.

7 Testimony of F. Dale Robertson, Associate Chief, Forest Service of the U.S. Department of Agriculture, before the Subcommittee on Forestry, Water Resources and Environment

of the Committee on Agriculture, Nutrition and Forestry in the U.S. Senate "Concerning the Cultivation of Marijuana on Public Lands." Testimony was given on September 30, 1982.

8 Anastasia Toufexis, "Grass Was Never Greener," *Time* Magazine, 9 August 1982.

9 "Guns, Grass,and Money: America's Billion Dollar Marijuana Crop," *Newsweek*, 5 October 1982, p. 36. See also Carol Stevens, "The Legal Side of the Pot Industry," *USA Today*, 22 November 1982.

10 "Guns, Grass—and Money," *Newsweek*.

11 Sourcebook of Criminal Justice Statistics, 1981, published by the U.S. Department of Justice, Bureau of Justice Statistics, Table 1.4; also see U.S. News and World Report, 1 November 1982.

12 Marijuana in America: The Facts—A Compilation of Current Facts and Statistics about Marijuana in the U.S., prepared by NORML, 530 8th Street, S.E., Washington, D.C. 20003. Published in 1981.

13 Bureau of Narcotic Enforcement Annual Report, 1979-1980,) State of California, Department of Justice, November 1980.

14 Shafer Report, p. 657.

15 Statistical Abstract of the United States—1981, Bureau of Census: see Table 742, p. 444. The arrestee loses $1062.36 in salary and the country loses $169,977,600 in productivity.

Literature Cited

Can Hemp Save Our Planet

Alexander, A.G. 1985. *The Energy Cane Alternative*. Elsevier Science Publ. Co., New York.

Anon. 1981. *Energy Cropping Versus Food Production*. Food and Agriculture Organization of the United Nations Agricultural Services Bulletin no. 46. Rome, Italy.

Anon. 1988. *FAO Production Yearbook of 1987*. vol. 41, FAO Statistics Series no. 82, Food and Agriculture Organization of the United Nations, Rome, pp. 232-234.

Ash, Anne L. 1948. Hemp, production and utilization. *Economic Botany*, vol. 2, pp. 158-169.

Barnard, G.W. 1984. Liquid fuel production from biomass in the developing countries, an agricultural and economic perspective. In: D.L. Wise (ed.). *Bioconversion Systems*. CRC Series in Bioenergy Systems. CRC Press, Boca Raton, Florida. pp. 193-215.

Berger, J. 1969. *Hemp. The World's Major Fibre Crops: Their Cultivation and Manuring*. Centre D'Etude De L'Azore, Zurich, Switzerland, pp. 216-222.

Beutler, J.A. and A.H der Marderosian. 1978. Chemotaxonomy of Cannabis. I. Crossbreeding between Cannbis sativa and C. ruderalis, with analysis of cannabinoid content. *Economic Botany*, vol. 32, no. 4, pp. 387-394.

Cannell, M.G.R. 1988. *Biomass Forestry in Europe*. Elsevier Science Publ. Co., New York

Carr, R.H. and C.M. James. 1931. Synthesis of adequate protein in the glands of the pigeon crop. *The American Journal of Physiology*, vol. 97, pp. 227-231.

Christie, B.R. 1987. *CRC Handbook of Plant Science in Agriculture*, vol. 2, CRC Press, Boca Raton, Florida, pp. 176-177.

Clark, T.F. 1965. Plant fibers in the paper industry. *Economic Botany*, vol. 19, pp. 394-405.

Coombs, J., D.O. Hall, and P. Chartier. 1983. *Plants as Solar Collectors: Optimizing Productivity for Energy. Solar Energy R&D in the European Community*. Series E. vol. 4. D. Reidel Publ. Co., Boston.

Dacy, G.H. 1921. Revolutionizing an industry. *Scientific American*. vol 74, no. 23, 4 June 1921, pp. 446, 457, 458.

Dempsey, J.M. 1975. *Hemp. Fiber Crops*. The University Presses of Florida, Gainesville, pp. 46-89.

Dewey, L.H. and J.L. Merrill. 1916. Hemp hurds as paper-making material. *USDA Bull. no. 404* (as reproduced in Herer, 1990, pp. 118-122).

Dybing, C.D. and C. Lay. 1981. Flax. In: O.R. Zaborsky (ed.) *CRC Handbook of Biosolar*

Resources, vol. 2, CRC Press, Boca Raton, Florida, pp. 71-85.

Haarer, A.E. 1953. Hemp (Cannabis sativa). World Crops, vol. 5, no. 10, pp 445-448.

Hackleman, J.C. and W.E. Domingo. 1943. Hemp, an Illinois war crop. University of Illinois Agricultural Experiment Station Circular no. 547, 8 p.

Haney, A. and B.B. Kutscheid. 1975. An ecological study of naturalized hemp (Cannabis sativa L.) in East-Central Illinois. The American Midland Naturalist. vol. 93, no. 1, pp. 1-24.

Herer, Jack. 1990. The Emperor Wears No Clothes. HEMP Publishing, Van Nuys, CA. 182 p.

Hill, A.F. 1952. Economic Botany: A Textbook of Useful Plants and Plant Products. McGraw-Hill, NY.

Hunsigi, G. 1989. Agricultural fibers for paper pulp. Outlook on Agriculture, vol. 18, no. 3, pp. 96-103.

Isenberg, I.H. 1956. Papermaking Fibers. Economic Botany, vol. 10, no. 2, pp. 176-193.

Jain, M.C. and N. Arora. 1988. Ganja (Cannabis sativa) refuse as cattle feed. Indian J. Animal Science, vol. 58, no. 7, pp. 865-867.

Kirby, R.H. 1963. Vegetable Fibres: Botany, Cultivation, and Utilization. Interscience Publishers, New York.

Lydon, J., A.H. Teramura, and C.B. Coffman. 1987. UV-B radiation effects on photosynthesis, growth and cannabinoid production of two Cannabis sativa chemotypes. Photochemistry and Photobiology, vol. 46, pp. 201-206.

Malyon, T. and A. Henman. 1980. No marihuana: plenty of hemp. New Scientist. 13 Nov 1980, pp. 433-435.

McClure, H.E. 1943. Ecology and management of the mourning dove, Zenaidura macroura (Linn.), in Cass County, Iowa. Iowa Agricultural Experiment Station Research Bulletin, no. 310, pp. 355-415.

Monk, R.L. and S. Kresovich. 1987. New Crops Exploring the Options. In: D.O. Hall and R.P. Overend. Biomass. John Wiley & Sons, New York, pp. 103-117.

Osburn, Lynn. Date not available. Hemp for fuel. Energy Farming in America (as reproduced in Herer, 1990, pp. 136).

Parnell, C.B., Jr. 1981. Cotton. In: O.R. Zaborsky (ed.) CRC Handbook of Biosolar Resources, vol. 2, CRC Press, Boca Raton, Florida, pp. 115-122.

Pate, D.W. 1983. Possible role of ultraviolet radiation in evolution of Cannabis chemotypes. Economic Botany, vol. 37, pp. 396-405.

Payne, P.I. 1983. Breeding for protein quantity and protein quality in seed crops. In: J. Daussant, J. Mosse, J. Vaughan. Seed Proteins. Academic Press, New York, pp. 227.

Purseglove, J.W. 1966. Tropical Crops: Dicotyledons 1. John Wiley and Sons, New York, pp. 40-44.

Quimby, M.W., N.J. Doorenbos, C.E. Turner, and A. Masoud. 1973. Mississippi-grown marihuana-Cannabis sativa cultivation and observed morphological variation. Economic Botany vol. 27, pp. 117-127.

Ree, J.H. 1966. Hemp Growing in the Republic of Korea. Economic Botany vol. 20, pp. 176.

Robel, R.J. 1969. Food habits, weight dynamics, and fat content of bob-whites in relation to food plantings in Kansas. Journal of Wildlife Management, vol. 33, pp. 237-294 as cited in A. Haney, and B.B. Kutscheid. 1975. An ecological study of naturalized hemp (Cannabis sativa L.) in East-Central Illinois. The American Midland Naturalist. vol. 93, no. 1, pp. 1-24.

Robinson, B.B. 1943 (revised 1952). Hemp. USDA Farmers Bull. no. 1935.

St. Angelo, A.J., E.J. Conkerton, J.M. Dechary, and A.M. Altschul. 1966. Modification of edestin (globulin of hemp seed, Cannabis sativa) with N-carboxy-D, L-alanine anhydride. Biochimica et Biophysica Acta, vol. 121, pp. 181.

St. Angelo, A.J., L.Y. Yatsu, and A.M. Altschul. 1968. Isolation of edestin from aleurone grains of

Cannabis sativa. *Archives of Biochemistry and Biophysics*, vol. 124, pp. 199-205.

Small, E., and A. Cronquist. 1976. A practical and natural taxonomy for Cannabis. *Taxon* vol. 25, pp. 405-435.

Small, E., and H.D. Beckstead. 1973. Common cannabinoid phenotypes in 350 stocks of Cannabis. *Lloydia*, vol. 36, pp. 144-165.

Small, E., H.D. Beckstead, and A. Chan. 1975. Cannabinoid phenotypes in Cannabis. *Economic Botany*, vol. 29, pp. 219-232.

Stockwell, D.M., J.M. Dechary, and A.M. Altschul. 1964. Chromatography of edestin from Cannabis sativa at 50 degrees. *Biochimica Biophysica Acta*, vol. 82, pp. 221.

Thomas, G.W., S.E. Curl, and W.F. Bennett. 1973. *Progress and Change in the Agricultural Industry*. Kendall/Hunt Publishing Co., Dubuque, Iowa, p. 60, 62.

Turner, Jocelyn C., Paul G. Mahlberg, Vicki S. Lanyon, and Joanna Pleszczynska. 1985. A temporal study of cannabinoid composition in continual clones of Cannabis sativa L. (Cannabaceae). *Botanical Gazette*, vol. 146, pp. 32-38.

Vaughan, J.G. 1970. *The Structure and Utilization of Oil Seeds*. Chapman & Hall, London, pp. 23-27. As quoted in Quimby et al., 1973. *Economic Botany*, vol. 27, pp. 117-127.

West, C.J. 13 Oct. 1921. Hemp wood as a papermaking material. *Paper Trade Journal*, pp. 46, 48 (As reproduced in Herer, 1990).

Whigham, D.K. 1981. Soybeans. In: O.R. Zaborsky (ed.) *CRC Handbook of Biosolar Resources*, vol 2, CRC Press, Boca Raton, Florida, pp. 95-104.

Wilsie, D.P., C.A. Black, and A.R. Aandahl. 1944. Hemp Production Experiments: Cultural Practices and Soil Requirements. Iowa State College. *Agricultural Experiment Station.Agricultural Extension Service Bulletin P63*, Ames, Iowa.

Woodruff, J.G. 1981. Peanuts. In: O.R. Zaborsky (ed.) *CRC Handbook of Biosolar Resources*, vol. 2, CRC Press, Boca Raton, Florida, pp. 87-93.

Hemp Pulp and Paper Production

Abel E.L.,1980. *Marihuana, the first twelve thousand years*. Plenum Press, New York, 289 pp.

Conrad C., 1993. *Hemp, lifeline to the future*. Creative Xpressions Publishing, Los Angeles, California.

FAO 1991. The outlook for pulp and paper to 1995. Paper products, and industrial update. Food and Agricultural Organisation of the United Nations, Rome.

Hunter, D., 1957. *Papermaking, the history and technique of an ancient craft*. 2nd Ed. Albert A. Knopf.

Smook, G.A., 1982. *Handbook for pulp & paper technologists*. 2nd Ed. Angus Wilde Publications, Vancouver, B.C.

Temple, R.K.C., 1986. *China, land of discovery and invention*. Patrick Stevens, Ltd., United Kingdom.

Fiber Hemp in France

Bredemann G., K. Garber, W. Hähnke & R. von Sengbusch, 1961. Die Zächtung von monîzischen und diîzischen, faserertragreichen Hanfsorten. Zeitschrift får Pflanzenzächtung 46, 3 235-246.

Hennik S, E P M de Meijer & H M G van der Werf, 1991. Report of a visit to the All-union Scientific and Research Institute of Bast Crops, Glukhov, Ukrainian SSR. CPRO-DLO, Wageningen, 14 pp.

Meijer E P M de, H M G van der Werf & W J M Meijer,1990. Veredeling en gewaskennis van hennep in Hongarije. Reisverslag 5 en 6 juli 1990. CABO-DLO, Wageningen, 14 pp.

Paper From Dutch Hemp?

Bakker, H. and M.J.J.M. van Kemenade, 1993. Papier uit hennep van

Nederlandse grond. Eindrapportage van vier jaar henneponderzock: Samenvatting, conclusies en aanbevelingen. [Paper from hemp grown in the Netherlands. Final report of four years of research on hemp: Summary, conclusions and recommendations.] ATO-DLO, Wageningen, 37 pp.

Van Berlo J.M., 1993. Papier uit hennep van Nederlandse grond.

Eindrapportage van vier jaar henneponderzock: Business Concept en onderbouwing. [Paper from hemp grown in the Netherlands. Final report of four years of research on hemp: Business Concept and foundations.] ATO-DLO, Wageningen, 222 pp.

Fiber Hemp in the Ukraine, 1993

Bedak G R, 1979. The influence of manure and mineral fertilizers on yield and quality of monoecious hemp grown in narrow or wide rows [in Russian]. In: *Biology, cultivation and the primary processing of bast crops.* All Union Scientific and Research Institute of Bast Crops, Sumi: 62-69.

Grenikov A S & T Tollochko, 1953. *Cultivation of hemp* [in Russian]. State Editors of Agricultural Literature, Moscow, 447 pp.

Hennink S, E P M de Meijer & H M G van der Werf, 1991. *Report of a visit to the All-Union Research Institute of Bast Crops,* Glukhov, Ukrainian SSR. CPRO-DLO, Wageningen, 14 pp.

Katsov I I, 1967. Norms of sowing and ways of sowing of promising cultivars of hemp at different fertilizer levels [in Russian]. In: *Cultivation and primary processing of hemp.* Ministry of Agriculture of the USSR, Kiev, 194 pp.

Senchenko G I & A P Demkin, 1972. Methods for increasing yield and quality of hemp [in Russian]. *Journal of Agricultural Mechanization Science,* Moscow, 9: 52-59.

Senchenko G I & M A Timonin, 1978. *Hemp* [in Russian]. Kolos, Moscow, 285 pp.

Shatun B I, 1975. The influence of the conditions of nutrition on uptake of nitrogen, phosphor and potassium by hemp on a black soil in the Gorki region [in Russian]. In: *Biology, cultivation and the primary processing of hemp and kenaf.* All Union Scientific and Research Institute of Bast Crops, Glukhov, 38: 111-116.

Tarasov A V, 1975. Hemp yield and yield of other crops in a technical rotation at different growing systems [in Russian]. In: *Biology, cultivation and the primary processing of hemp and kenaf.* All Union Scientific and Research Institute of Bast Crops, Glukhov, 38: 83-88.

Medical Marijuana

Adler, M.W. and E.B. Deller, 1986. Ocular effects of cannabinoids. Pages 51-70, in R. Mechoulam, ed., *Cannabinoids as therapeutic agents,* CRC Press, Inc., Boca Raton, Florida.

Anonymous, 1992. *Wall Street Journal,* Dec. 23.

Consroe P., and S.R. Snider, 1986. Therapeutic potential of cannabinoids in neurological disorders. Pages 21-49 in R. Mechoulam, ed., *Cannabinoids as therapeutic agents,* CRC Press, Inc., Boca Raton, Florida.

De Meijer E.P.M., H.J. van der Kamp and F.A. van Fenwijk, 1992. Characterization of Cannabis accession with regard to cannabinoid content in relation to other plant characters. *Euphytica* 62: 187-200.

ElSohly M.A., 1990. Method for effecting systemic delivery of delta-9-tetrahydrocannabinol (THC) using suppository compositions containing polar THC esters. US Patent 4933363.

ElSohly H.N., C.E. Turner, A.M. Clark and M.A. ElSohly, 1982. Synthesis and antimicrobial activity of certain cannabichromene and cannabigerol related compounds, *Journal of Pharmaceutical Sciences* 71: 1319-1323.

Embodein W.A., 1974. Cannabis-a polyptic genus. *Economic Botany* 28: 304-310.

Graham J.D.P., 1986. The bronchodilator action of cannabinoids, Pages 147-158 in R. Mechoulam, ed., *Cannabinoids as therapeutic agents,* CRC Press, Inc., Boca Raton, Florida.

Hine B., E. Friedman, M. Torrelio and S. Gerson, 1975. Blockade of morphine abstinence by Delta-9-Tetrahydrocannabinol. *Science* 190: 590-591.

Hussain A.A., 1984. Nasal administration of narcotic antagonists and analgesics. US Patent 4464378.

Levitt M., 1986. Cannabinoids as antiemetics in cancer chemotherapy, Pages 71-83 in R. Mechoulam, ed., *Cannabinoids as therapeutic agents*, CRC Press, Inc., Boca Raton, Florida.

Mechoulam R., 1986. The pharmacohistory of Cannabis sativa. Pages 1-19 in R. Mechoulam, ed., *Cannabinoids as therapeutic agents*, CRC Press, Inc., Boca Raton, Florida.

Pate D.W., 1983. Role of ultraviolet radiation in evolution of Cannabis chemotype. *Economic Botany* 37: 396-405.

Roffman, R.A., 1982. *Marijuana as medicine*. Madrona Publishers, Seattle, Washington.

Rosenburg, C.M., 1976. The use of marijuana in the treatment of alcoholism. Pages 173-85 in Cohen, S. and R. Stillman, eds. *The therapeutic potential of marijuana*. Plenum Medical Book Publishing Company, New York.

Schultes R.E., W.M. Klein, T. Plowman and T.E. Lockwood, 1974. Cannabis: an example of taxonomic neglect. *Harvard Botanical Museum Leaflets* 23:337-367.

Segal M., 1986. Cannabinoids and analgesia. Pages 105-120 in R. Mechoulam, ed., *Cannabinoids as therapeutic agents*, CRC Press, Inc., Boca Raton, Florida.

Small E. and A. Cronquist, 1976. A practical and natural taxonomy for Cannabis. *Taxon* 25: 405-435.

Van der Werf, H.M.G. 1994. Crop physiology of fibre hemp (Cannabis sativa L.). Doctoral thesis. Wageningen Agricultural University, Wageningen, The Netherlands.

Van Klingeren B. and M. Ten Ham, 1976. Antibacterial activity of delta-9-THC and cannabidiol. Antonie van Leeuwenhoek *Journal of Microbiology and Serology* 42: 9-12.

Watson D.P., 1994. Personal communication.

Zuardi A.W., I. Shirakawa, E. Finkelfarb and I.G. Karniol, 1982. Action of cannabidiol on the anxiety and other effects produced by delta-9-THC in normal subjects. *Psychopharmacology* 76: 245-250.

List of Abbreviations

gm	gram	**dm**	dry matter
mg	milligram	**H**	hydrogen
kg	kilogram	**N**	nitrogen
mt	metric ton	**O**	oxygen
m	meter	**K**	potassium
cm	centimeter	**P**	phosphorus
m²	square meter	**C**	calcium
A	acre	**Mg**	magnesium
ha	hectare	**Dfl**	Dutch florins
bu	bushel	**FF**	French francs

Hemp Resource Directory

Hemp Resource Directory
Products, Information and Organizations

420 Clothing Company
304 Concord Road
Knoxville, TN 37922
(615) 984-2714; (615) 675-8712
Wholesale, Retail, Manufacturer,
Garments

A Byte Better/The Void
5443 N. Second Street
Loves Park, IL 61111
(815) 654-8484
Retail, Mail Order

Ah Hemp
1709 Solano Avenue
Berkeley, CA 94707
(510) 526-6995; (510) 526-4023 fax
Retail Store, Manufacturer, Garments

All Your Marbles
110 Main Street
Geneseo, NY 14454
(716) 235-0608
Wholesale, Retail

★ **American Hemp Mercantile**
506 Second Ave, Suite 1520
Seattle, WA 98104
(206) 340-0124; (206) 340-1086 fax
Importer, Wholesale, Retail,
Distributor, Manufacturer

Aries Arts
201 Capitola Avenue
Santa Cruz, CA 95010
(408) 476-6655
Retail Store

Baltimore Hemporium
231 W. Read Street
Baltimore, MD 21201
(410) 669-0644
Retail Store

C&S Specialty Builders Supply
23005 N. Coburg Road
Harrisburg, OR 97446
(800) 728-9488
Construction Materials

★ *Listings with stars indicate advertiser in* Hemp Today

Canadian Hemp Association
312 Adelaide Street, W #608
Toronto, Ontario
Canada M5V 1R2
(416) 977-4159; (416) 977-5116 fax
*Non-profit Environmental
Organization,
Retail Store: Friendly Stranger
(416) 977-0461*

Cannabest Inc.
1536 Monterey Street
San Luis Obispo, CA 93401
(800) 277-0510; (805) 543-0340 fax
Mail Order, Retail, Catalog

Cannabis Action Network
2560 Bancroft Way
Berkeley, CA 94704
(510) 486-1779
Organization, Information

Cannabis Clothes
P.O. Box 1167
Occidental, CA 95465
(707) 874-1104
Wholesale, Retail, Manufacturer

Cannabis Clothing
1190 Weilder, # 210
Honolulu, HI 96822
(808) 545-8686
Wholesale, Garments

Cannabis Connection
(503) 235-3583
*Wholesale, Retail, Guitar Straps,
Information*

Cannabiz Inc.
P.O. Box 272
Occidental, CA 95465
(707) 874-3449; (707) 874-2974 fax
Distributor, Garments

CB Trash
109 Commercial Dr. Bldg. 2
Bozeman, MT 59715
(406) 587-3020
Wholesale, Combat Boots

Coptic Creations
P.O. Box 293 Ucluelet
Vancouver, British Columbia
Canada V0R 3A0
(604) 726-7239
Manufacturer, Food Snacks

Cultural Repercussions
P.O. Box 1301
Bisbee, AZ 85603
(602) 230-5242; (602) 432-7425
Garments

Deep Sea Ovens
501 North 36th Street, #236
Seattle, WA 98103
(206) 344-6832
Roasted Hemp Seed

Dharma Emporium
3746 North College
Indianapolis, IN 46206
(317) 926-8255
Retail

Earth Wears
101 East Weaver Street
Carrboro, NC 27510
(919) 929-7844
Retail

Eco/Hempstore
800 Bank Street
Ottawa, Ontario
Canada K1S 3V8
(613) 567-3168; (613) 567-3568 fax
Retail Store

★ **Ecolution**
P.O. Box 2279
Merrfield, VA 22116
(703) 281-3680; (703) 281-6485 fax
Importer, Wholesale, Retail, Mail Order

Eichen Imagine Photography
P.O. Box 19099
Los Angeles, CA 90019
(213) 937-3395
Hemp photographer: products, clothing, people, cultivation

ESP
Middleway Wkshps, Summertown
Oxord, England 0X2 7LG
(011-44) 865-311151 Ph & Fax
Research, Paper

The Evanescent Press
P.O. Box 64
Leggett, CA 95585
(707) 925-6494
Manufacturer - Paper, handmade from local hemp

Everything Earthly
414 South Mill Avenue, #118
Tempe, AZ 85281
(602) 968-0650
Retail

The Eye
403 E. 4th Street
Bloomington, IN 47408
(812) 332-0048
Retail Store

Fabric Wrap
1114 Park Lane
Gulf Breeze, FL 32561
(904) 932-2332; (904) 932-5554 fax
Wholesale, Hemp Gift Bags

Forbidden Fruit
12837 Arroyo Street
Sylvan, CA 91342
(818) 837-9218
Wholesale, Distributor

Got It Covered
P.O. Box 14627
Santa Rosa, CA 95402
(707) 829-5443; (707) 829-5380 fax
Manufacturer, Retail, Accessories

★ **Great American Hemp Co.**
909 Ballard Street #B
Altamonte Springs, FL 32701
(407) 767-8513
Manufacturer, Distributor, Accessories

Great Canadian Hemporium
183 King Street, Frazier Mall, Suite 115
London, Ontario
Canada N6A 1C9
(519) 433-5267 Phone
Retail

Greener Alternative-The Eco Depot
914 Mission Street, Suite A
Santa Cruz, CA 95060
(408) 423-0701
Retail Store

★ **Greener Pastures**
2526 Alder Lane
McKinleyville, CA 95521
(707) 839-8023
Manufacturer, Accessories, Distributor

Group W Bench
1171 Chapel Street
New Haven, CT 06511
(203) 624-0683
Retail Store

H.E.M.P.
Help End Marijuana Prohibition
5632 Van Nuys Blvd., #310
Van Nuys, CA 91401
(818) 988-0285
Books

H.E.R.B.
Hemp Education Research Board
P.O. Box 7137
Boulder, CO 80306
(303) 225-8356
Research, Information Clearinghouse

H.I.L.D.A.
Hemp Initiative Legal Defense
Alliance
(303) 225-8356
Attorneys

Happy Hippie
9205 N. Western Street
Oklahoma City, OK 73114
(405) 842-1494
Retail Store

Hawaiian Hemp Co.
P.O. Box 2056
Pahoa, HI 96778
(808) 965-8600; (808) 965-6242 fax
Retail, Mail Order, Retail Store

Headcase
150 Bay Street
Jersey City, NJ 07302
(201) 420-5900; (201) 420-7101 fax
Manufacturer, Wholesale

Hemp BC
324 West Hastings Street
Vancouver, British Columbia
Canada V6B 1K6
(604) 681-4620
Retail, Wholesale, Distributor

Hemp, Book & Candle
(707) 823-4580; (707) 829-4550 fax
Distributor

The Hemp Club by Aubout Ltd.
1618 Boul St. Laurent
Montreal, Quebec
Canada H2X 2T1
(514) 842-8595; (514) 843-8722 fax
Importer, Manufacturer, Distributor,
Accessories, Garments

The Hemp Co.
72 Princess Street
Kingston, Ontario
Canada K75 1A5
(613) 547-1670
Retail Store

★ **The Hemp Connection**
P.O. Box 33
Whitethorn, CA 95589
(707) 986-7322
Manufacturer, Wholesale, Retail,
Garments

Hemp Cooperation
P.O. Box 742
Redway, CA 95560
(707) 923-5044
Speaker on herbal & ecological uses of
hemp

★ **Hemp Essentials**
P.O. Box 151
Cazadero, CA 95421
(707) 847-3642
Manufacturer, Distributor, Cosmetics

Hemp Etc. Inc.
37505 Fountain Road
Zephyrhills, FL 33541
(813) 782-5951
Retail, Wholesale, Garments, Luggage,
Accessories

Hemp Gear
4217 Inglewood Blvd., Suite 305
Los Angeles, CA 90066
(310) 398-2755
Manufacturer, Garments

Hemp Haven
7253 Lowell Blvd.
Westminster, CO 80030
(303) 429-7985
Retail, Wholesale, Mail Order

Hemp Head
428 Grantham Avenue
St. Catharines, Ontario
Canada L2M 3J1
(905) 938-2339; (905) 938-2903 fax
Manufacturer, Garments, Accessories

Hemp Hemp Hooray
P.O. Box 731
Occidental, CA 95465
(707) 874-2841
Manufacturer, Cosmetics, Skincare

Hemp Sacks
690 Nature Lane
Arcata, CA 95521
(707) 822-6972
Manufacturer, Wholesale, Hacky Sacks

Hemp Tee V
P.O. Box 426380
San Francisco, CA 94142
(415) 255-8527

Hemp Textiles International
3200 30th Street
Bellingham, WA 98225
(800) 778-HEMP; (206) 650-1684 fax
Importer, Textiles

Hemp World
P.O. Box 315
Sebastopol, CA 95473
(707) 887-7508; (707) 887-7639 fax
Journal, Books, Information

Hempman
7032 Van Nuys Blvd.
Van Nuys, CA 91405
(800) HEMPMAN
Wholesale, Distributor, Accessories, Books

Hempstead Company
2060 Placentia #B-2
Costa Mesa, CA 92627
(800) 284-4367; (714) 650-5853 fax
Manufacturer, Distributor, Mail Order, Catalog $1

Hempstead Co. Store
607 Chartres Street
New Orleans, LA 70458
(504) 529-4367
Retail Store

Hip Hemp
P.O. Box 4839
Pittsburgh, PA 15206
(412) 734-5538
Wholesale, Manufacturer

Home Grown Hats
P.O. Box 1083
Redway, CA 95560
(707) 923-5273; (707) 923-2007 fax
Manufacturer, Wholesale, Accessories-Hats & Bags

House of Hemp
P.O. Box 14603
Portland, OR 97214-0603
(800) BYE-HEMP; (503) 232-0239 fax
Manufacturer, Distributor, Textiles

★ The International Hemp
Association
P.O. Box 75007
1070 AA Amsterdam
The Netherlands
Journal, Books, Information

★ The Institute For Hemp
P.O. Box 65130
St. Paul, MN 55165
(612) 222-2628
*Mail Order, Manufacturer, Wholesale,
Retail, Information, Catalog*

It's A Beautiful Day
3916 Broadway
Kansas City, MO 64108
(816) 931-6169
Retail Store

Jamaican Style
114 22nd Street
Newport Beach, CA 92663
(800) 822-6395
Retail, Wholesale, Catalog

★ Legal Marijuana
The Hemp Store
1304 West Alabama
Houston, TX 77006
(713) 521-1134; (713) 528-HEMP fax
*Retail, Wholesale, Periodicals-Hemp
Quarterly*

Linda Kammins Salon
848 N. La Cienega Blvd. #204
Los Angeles, CA 90069
(310) 659-6257
Retail, Skincare Services & Products

Many Fantastic Colors
460 Winnetka Avenue
Winnetka, IL 60093
(708) 501-3708
Retail, Garments, Hacky Sack

Mindful Products
20095 First Street West
Sonoma, CA 95476
(707) 939-9161
Shoes

★ NW Hemp Foundation
333 SW Park Avenue
Portland, OR 97205
(503) 274-HEMP
Information Services

★ Ohio Hempery
7702 State Road 329
Guysville, OH 45735
(614) 662-HEMP; (614) 662-6446 fax
*Manufacturer, Wholesale, Distributor,
Retail*

Original Sources
P.O. Box 7137
Boulder, CO 80306
(303) 225-8356
Manufacturer-Food Products

Patt's R&R Delights
2864 Sans Pareil Street
Jacksonville, FL 32246
(904) 642-3311
Retail Store

Pipe Dreams
1376 Haight Street
San Francisco, CA 94117
(415) 431-3553
Retail

Planetary Persuasians
557 Ward Street
Nelson, British Columbia
Canada V1L 1T1
(604) 352-3844
Retail Store

Quick Trading Company
1635 East 22nd Street
Oakland, CA 94606
(510) 533-0605, (510) 535-0437 fax
Importer, distributor, wholesale, retail

Rising Star Futons
35 NW Bond Street
Bend, OR 97701
(800) 828-6711
Manufacturer, Retail

Sativa Station
232 N. LBJ
San Marcos, TX 78666
(512) 396-0580
Retail Store

Schermerhorn Bros. Co.
12922 Florence Avenue
Santa Fe Springs, CA 90670
(800) 932-9395; (310) 946-4627 fax
Importer Hemp Twine & Fabric

Shakedown Street
276 King Street West
Kitchener, Ontario
Canada N2G 1B7
(519) 570-0440
Retail

She Who Remembers
(818) 287-8254
Audio/Video Material

Simply Hemp
P.O. Box 780
Occidental, CA 95465
(707) 823-6900
Wholesale

Solutions
928 9th Street
Arcata, CA 95521
(707) 822-6972
Retail Store

Sunshine Daydream Imports
5811 Pine Tree Avenue
Panama City Beach, FL 32408
(904) 235-4090
Retail Store

Sunsports Inc.
P.O. Box 180
Stamford, CT 06904
(800) 308-HEMP; (203) 324-6651 fax
Manufacturer, Wholesale

Terra Pax
2145 Park Avenue, Suite 9
Chico, CA 95928
(916) 342-9282; (916) 342-3730 fax
*Wholesale, Manufacturer,
Miscellaneous-Luggage*

★ **The Third Stone**
520 W. Lake
Minneapolis, MN 55408
(612) 825-6120

Three Hi Guys
1420 Main Street
Seal Beach, CA 90740
(800) 775-1969; (310) 594-6072 fax
Wholesale, Manufacturer

Truth In Mj Education
P.O. Box 7036
Chico, CA 95927
Information

★ **Two Star Dog**
1526 62nd Street
Emeryville, CA 94608
(510) 655-4379; (510) 655-0209 fax
Wholesale, Retail, Garment

Tye Dye Dave
Hippie Gift Shop
P.O. Box 865
Tannerville, PA 18372
(717) 620-1982
Retail Store

★ **U.S. Hemp Bureau**
461 West Appache Trail #130
Apache Junction, AZ 85220
(800) 501-HEMP; (602) 983-7065
Wholesale, Retail, Accessories, Mail Order

US Textile
404 West Pico Blvd.
Los Angeles, CA 90015
(213) 742-0840; (213) 742-0016 fax
Manufacturer, Accessories-Hats

Used Rubber, USA
597 Haight Street
San Francisco, CA 94117
(415) 626-7855
Retail, Wholesale, Distributor

Vision Works
14 Chapman Street
Greenfield, MA 01301
(413) 772-6569
Distributor Books, Hemp Products

Whole Hemp Collective
P.O. Box 37
New Plymouth, OH 45654
(614) 385-4167; (614) 385-8526 fax
Wholesale, Retail, Distributor, Mail Order, Catalog

Wise Up! Reaction Wear
1511 West Wetmore Road
Tucson, AZ 85705
(602) 293-8005; (602) 888-6053 fax
Manufacturer, Distributor, Retail Store

Zanie's
N. 2718 Division
Spokane, WA 99207
(509) 326-8400
Retail Store

American Hemp Mercantile, Inc.™

*Importers & distributors of
quality hemp products*

Hungarian Hemp Fabric,
Twine, and Rope
Paper · Clothing · Shoes · Bags · Hats

Call or write for a free catalog
1-800-469-4367
506 Second Avenue, Suite 1323
Seattle, Washington 98104
U.S. *of* A.

Wholesale/retail orders welcome

U. S. HEMP BUREAU ™

STAND UP FOR YOUR RIGHTS IN U.S. HEMP

(MADE BY HAND IN AMERICA)
461 WEST APACHE TRAIL #130
APACHE JUNCTION, ARIZONA 85220
1-602-983-7065

MasterCard.

VISA

High Tops - Slip Ons - Low Cut - $59⁰⁰

U.S. HEMP SNEAKERS

★ These shoes are made by hand in America with the oldest, strongest fiber known to man.

★★ The Mildew and rot resistant nature of hemp fiber produces a perfect fabric for a durable, comfortable and healthier shoe.

★★★ Today the supply of true hemp fabric is rare and uncertain; it is expensive and unfortunately, many people are exploited with inferior or fake goods.

★★★★ Our products are made of the most unique and highest quality hemp fabrics on earth. We believe in extraordinary potential of this plant as a multi-purpose cash crop that will create millions of jobs and safe, quality products in America.

★★★★★ Visible proof of this versatile pant is found in our quality products. To find out more about the ever expanding line of U.S. Hemp products call us at: 1-800-501-HEMP or write to: U.S. HEMP, 461 W. Apache Trail, #130, Apache Jct., AZ 85220

NORTHWEST HEMP FOUNDATION
is your resource for:

- News and information

- Resources and contacts

- Seed money for Hemp-related businesses
  (send us a proposal for your Hemp-related idea or invention)

PLUS . . .

Watch for the **Cannabis Tax Act of 1997** - A statewide voters initiative that we are sponsoring in Oregon. For a copy of the Cannabis Tax Act or to find out how to pass legislation in your state please call:

Northwest Hemp Foundation (503) 274-HEMP

To receive one of our FREE Hemp Infopacks in the mail containing:

- over 40 pages of information about the industrial and medical uses of Hemp

- samples of Hemp cloth, Hemp string, Hemp seed and raw Hemp fiber

- printed on tree-free Hemp paper

Northwest Hemp Foundation
333 S.W. Park Avenue
Portland, Oregon 97205
(503) 274-HEMP

LEGAL MARIJUANA
THE HEMP STORE

TRADERS IN HEMP SINCE 1992
WHOLESALE INQUIRIES WELCOME

The largest selection of hemp items available anywhere, featuring clothes, paper, & oil products from **ALL POINTS EAST, AMERICAN HEMP MERCANTILE, CANNABEST, CANNABIS CLOTHES, COALITION FOR HEMP AWARENESS, CULTURAL REPERCUSSIONS, FOUR-TWENTY CLOTHING, HEAD-CASE, HEADTRIPS HATS, HEMP COLONY, HEMP CONNECTION, HEMP HERITAGE, HEMPSTEAD CO., HOME-GROWN HATS, JUST CAUSE, MINDFUL PRODUCTS, OHIO HEMPERY, SIMPLY HEMP, TREE-FREE ECO-PAPER, TWO STAR DOG, US HEMP BUREAU, USED RUBBER USA, VAN BUREN, WISE-UP REACTION WEAR**

Legal Marijuana, the Hemp Store is located at 1304 W. Alabama, Houston, TX 77006. We can be reached at 713-521-1134 (our fax# is 713- 528-HEMP). Store hours are 11:00 AM to 8:00 PM Mon-Sat, Noon to 7:00 PM on Sundays.

SUBSCRIBE TO
HEMP QUARTERLY

..products, people, and information...
an exciting overview of the growing Hemp
industry...$2 for sample issue,
$5 for one-year subscription*

name

st / po box

city / state
zip

send to HEMP QUARTERLY, 1304 W. Alabama - Houston, TX 77006

(* international rates= $4 / $10 US)

follow your heart to

Hemp...
- ◆ table linens
- ◆ checkbook covers
- ◆ medicine pouches
- ◆ lunch bags....

Greener Pastures
2526 Alder Lane
McKinleyville CA 95521
(707) 839-8023

Laura Knight

Discover yourself...

...what the ancients knew of the healing and soothing
properties of this most remarkable plant.

There is nothing like hemp seed oil for the skin.

Hemp Oil Salve

Hemp oil is combined with beeswax, goldenseal, yellow dock, comfrey root, calendula, propolis and vitamin E to create a wonderfully soothing general-purpose salve for wounds, burns, abrasions, rashes and dry skin. 1 oz. - $7

Hemp Lip Balm

Hemp seed oil combined with beeswax protects against the effects of cold and heat. $4 per jar.

Body Cream

Hemp oil, aloe, herbs and vitamins E, A and C create a luxuious body cream. 8 oz. - $8

Hemp Castile Soap

A traditional soap with hemp, coconut and virgin olive oils and aloe vera to clean and moisturize, not dry, your skin. 4 oz. - $4.95

Massage Oil

A sumptuous blend of almond, hemp and jojoba oils with vitamins E, A and C. 8 oz. - $9.75

These and other hemp-based products are custom-blended to our exact specifications. Call today for a catalog.

Ohio Hempery, Inc.

Fabric ● Seeds ● Oil ● Clothing ● Books

Orders: **1-800-BUY-HEMP**

Inquiries: (1-614) 662-4367
Fax: (1-614) 662-6446
7002 St. Rt. 329 ● Guysville, Ohio 45735

Want More Hemp Facts?

THE EMPEROR WEARS NO CLOTHES *by Jack Herer* The book that started hemp awareness. Documents the history and potential of this plant. Easy reading. *180 pages, $19.95*

MARIHUANA RECONSIDERED *by Lester Grinspoon, M.D.*
The most comprehensive assessment of the benefits and dangers of marihuana. *500 pages, $19.95*

HEMP: LIFELINE TO THE FUTURE
by Chris Conrad A thorough discussion of the plant and its history beginning 4,000 years ago and continuing through the future. *312 pages, $12.95*

HEMP TODAY *edited by Ed Rosenthal*
Printed on hemp paper, this collection of articles studies the economic and ecological benefits of hemp as proven in other countries where it is legally grown today. *300 pages, $19.95*

HEMP CAN SAVE THE PLANET T-SHIRT
Black beefy-T, indicate size L or XL, *$18.00*

HEMP FOR VICTORY   During WWII farmers were encouraged to grow hemp as part of the war effort. This film, made by the U.S. government, acknowledges the importance of hemp as a crop. VHS format. *$15.95*

CHARGE BY PHONE 1-800-428-7825 x102 or fax 1-510-533-4911

QTY	TITLE	(SIZE)	PRICE	TOTAL

Subtotal _____
CA Residents add 8 1/2% sales tax _____
UPS and Handling $5.00
P.O. Box delivery add $2 _____
TOTAL _____

Name _____

Address _____

_____

Signature _____

Enclosed: ☐ Check ☐ Money Order
☐ MasterCard ☐ Visa   Exp. Date _____
Credit Card# _____

Mail to:
Quick Trading Company P.O. Box 429477, San Francisco, CA 94142-9477

HEMP CONNECTION

HEMP CONNECTION

HEMP CONNECTION

HEMP CONNECTION

**marie mills
p.o. box 33
whitethorn
ca.   95589**

707·986·7322

100% HEMP CLOTHING
manufactured in
Northern California

wholesale & retail

mail order hemp products

HEMP CONNECTION

The Institute for Hemp

Our Goal: The Establishment of Cannabis Hemp as a Farm Crop and Annually Renewable Resource for the Production of Consumer Products

Producers of the Worlds First & Largest Catalog Devoted To Hemp Products & Information

For Nearly 1/2 a Decade Providing Accurate Information about Cannabis Hemp's Commercial Potential to people, business, media and government.

Let's Use Hemp to Help Solve our Environmental Problems

IFH Cannabis Hemp Certification Program. Assisting Hemp Consumers and Business by Certifying Products labeled as Cannabis Hemp

FOR INFO & CATALOG CALL
612-222-2628

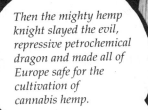

John Stahl of Evanescent Press reads HempWorld to his daughter, Garnet, while wearing the official HempWorld T-Shirt .

HempWorld T-Shirt
     Natural with Green Lettering $15.00
Subscriber T-Shirt Special $10.00
Shipping $ 3.00
12 Issues of HempWorld- USA $30.00
     International $50.00 (US)
Back Issues $ 3.00 each
     Dec.'93; Feb/Mar; June/July; Aug/Sept

Send check or money order to: HempWorld, Box 315
Sebastopol, CA   95473 Ph: 707-887-7508 Fx: 707-887-7639

The Great American Hemp Company ™
and Wax Works

**MANUFACTURER OF FINE HEMP GEAR
& ACCESSORIES:**
Hats, Caps, Wallets, Stuff Bags, Duffels
and more.

DISTRIBUTORS OF:
Yarn, Twine, Hand Made Papers, Seeds & Flour, Oils,
Soaps, Hacky Sacks, Hemp Jewelry, Books
and all kinds of other stuff.

BEESWAX & HEMP ALTERNATIVES:
Hand-Dipped Taper Candles, Scented Votives,
Tea Lights, "Log Lighters" & Filtered Wax

CUSTOM EMBROIDERY

**The GREAT AMERICAN HEMP COMPANY
663 Murphy Road
Winter Springs, Florida 32708**

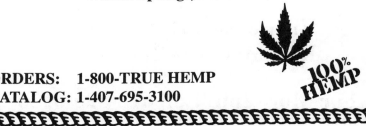

**ORDERS: 1-800-TRUE HEMP
CATALOG: 1-407-695-3100**

PROUD SPONSOR OF THE

FESTIVAL FOR PROJECT
E.A.R.T.H.

Environmental Activism
Restoring The Harmony

For More Info Call 612-825-6120

International Hemp Association

Dedicated to the advancement of Cannabis, through the dissemination of information

IHA Books Available

Influence of Marijuana on Driving
by Dr. H.W.J. Robbe, 1994, 232pp, Hard Cover
$32.00 Handling & Overland postage included

Crop Physiology of Fibre Hemp
by Dr. Hayo van der Werf,1994,165pp,Paperback
$20.00 Handling & Overland postage included

Members receive 10% off!

To Order or Join:

NAME/ORGANIZATION ——————————————————

STREET ADDRESS ————————————————————

CITY ———————————————— STATE ——————————

POSTAL CODE ———————————— COUNTRY —————————

TELE ——————————————— FAX ————————

Please enter quantity on line

—— Student Membership US $25

—— Individual Membership US $50

—— Sustaining Membership US $100

—— *Influence of Marijuana on Driving* US $32

—— *Crop Physiology of Fibre Hemp* US $20

Send this form with payment made in International Postal Money Order, American Express or Thomas Cook Money Order to:
International Hemp Association
P.O. Box 75007, 1070 AA Amsterdam, The Netherlands

DRUG EDUCATION BOOKS

CULTIVATION BOOKS

___ INDOOR MARIJUANA HORTICULTURE----------$20
___ MARIJUANA BOTANY------------------------$20
___ MARIJUANA GROWING TIPS-----------------$12
___ MARIJUANA HYDROPONICS------------------$16
___ MARIJ. GROWER'S HANDBOOK---(SPIRAL)----$23
___ MARIJUANA GROWERS GUIDE----------------$18
___ MARIJUANA GROWERS GUIDE----(SPIRAL)----$22
___ MARIJUANA GROWERS INSIDER'S GUIDE------$18
___ THE SINSEMILLA TECHNIQUE---------------$24
___ GARDENING: THE ROCKWOOL BOOK----------$15
___ THE CULTIVATORS HANDBOOK OF MARIJ.----$18
___ CASH CROP: A CLOSER LOOK---------------$20
___ CO2 TEMPERATURE AND HUMIDITY-----------$12
___ GROW YER OWN STONE--------------------$12

DRUG EDUCATION BOOKS

___ PSYCHEDELICS ENCYCLOPEDIA*------------ $24
___ PLANTS OF THE GODS--------------------$20
___ MARIJUANA RECONSIDERED----------------$19
___ LEGAL HIGHS--------------------------$10
___ OPIUM FOR THE MASSES------------------$15
___ PHARMACOTHEON*-----------------------$40
___ MARIJUANA LAW------------------------$12
___ GROWING THE HALLUCINOGENS-------------$10
___ CLANDESTINE DRUG LABORATORIES---------$15
___ RECREATIONAL DRUGS-------------------$21
___ THE ANARCHIST COOKBOOK---------------$30
___ THE ARCHAIC REVIVAL------------------$14
___ DRUG TESTING AT WORK-----------------$17
___ PSYCHEDELIC SHAMANISM----------------$20
___ PSYCHEDELIC ILLUMINATIONS: MAGAZINE---$10
___ CONTROLLED SUBSTANCES*---------------$55
___ PIHKAL: A CHEMICAL LOVE STORY*--------$22
___ COOKING WITH CANNABIS----------------$10
___ MARIJUANA CHEMISTRY------------------$19
___ ECSTASY: THE MDMA STORY--------------$17
___ SMART DRUGS & NUTRIENTS--------------$12
___ SECRETS OF METHAMPHETAMINE-----------$25
___ PSYCHEDELIC CHEMISTRY----------------$16
___ LSD MY PROBLEM CHILD-----------------$11
___ PSYCHEDELIC SHAMANISM----------------$20
___ THE COMPLETE DRUG LIBRARY------------$32
___ THE EMPEROR WEARS NO CLOTHES---------$19
___ MARIHUANA THE FORBIDDEN MEDICINE------$22
___ MARIJUANA, MEDICINE & THE LAW---------$29
___ MARIJUANA & AIDS--------------------- $12

MUSHROOM BOOKS

___ THE MUSHROOM CULTIVATOR*-------------$28
___ MUSHROOMS DEMYSTIFIED*---------------$29
___ GOURMET & MEDICINAL MUSHROOMS*-------$39
___ REISHI MUSHROOMS--------------------$15
___ THE SACRED MUSHROOM SEEKER*----------$37
___ THE NEW SAVORY WILD MUSHROOM---------$16
___ ALL THE RAIN PROMISES AND MORE-------$16
___ GROWING WILD MUSHROOMS--------------$12
___ PSILOCYBIN MAGIC MUSHROOM GUIDE-------$16
___ GROWING SHIITAKE COMMERCIALLY--------$15
___ FOOD OF THE GODS-------------------$14

MORE BOOKS

___ THE PAPER TRIP I, OR II--------------$17
___ PRIVACY: HOW TO GET IT-------------$18
___ SEX DRUGS & APHRODISIACS------------$10
___ THE RIP-OFF BOOK-------------------$12
___ MELLOW PAGES---------------------$12
___ OPIUM POPPY GARDEN----------------$14
___ AYAHUASCA ANALOGUES---------------$15
___ THE POOR MAN'S JAMES BOND*----------$22
___ THE OUTLAW'S BIBLE----------------$15
___ HIGH TIMES GREATEST HITS-----------$14
___ THE FS BOOK COMPANY CATALOG --------$2

___ # OF BOOKS-----------------------SUBTOTAL $_____
(ALL FOREIGN ADD $2 PER BOOK FOR SURFACE MAIL)

FREE SHIPPING ON ALL USA ORDERS ___N/C__

$3 PRO. FEE ON ALL CREDIT CARD ORDERS &
ORDERS UNDER $15 (SUBTOTAL)
CA. RES. ADD 7.75% TAX.   **AIR MAIL** FOR CANADA
ADD $4, EUROPE $8, PACIFIC RIM $12, **PER BOOK.**
*BECAUSE OF WEIGHT, DOUBLE THE SHIPPING RATE.

AIR MAIL ADD $2 PER BOOK (USA) _____

TOTAL $_____
VISA / MC / AMEX / DISCOVER, CHECKS (USA ONLY)
& MONEY ORDERS ARE ACCEPTED.
BOOKS ARE SOLD TO ADULTS ONLY .

MAKE CHECKS PAYABLE TO: **FS BOOK CO.**

24 HOUR FAX LINE:
1-916-771-4201
QUESTIONS :1-916-771-4203

FS BOOK CO.
PO BOX 417457 DEPT. HT
SACRAMENTO, CA
95841-7457   USA

CREDIT CARD ORDERS, CALL:
1-800-635-8883
DISCOUNT PRICES
FREE SHIPPING   FAST SERVICE
SERVING YOU SINCE 1985

Cross-strap Dress $60
Pleated Suit Pants $75
Sport Jacket $100
Thin Tie $15
Belt $15

Womans' Short Top $37
Mini-skirt w/
   Coconut Buttons $50
Flaired Tank Top $35
Full Skirt $45
Large Shoulder Bag $35

Mens' V-Neck Shirt $40
   with Mali Mud Cloth $45
Shorts $35
   with Mali Mud Cloth $40

Button-Up Shirt $45
   with Band Collar $45
   with Mali Mud Cloth $50
Drawstring Pants $50
Womans' Long Vest $60

Box Pleat Skirt $60
Woman's Dress Jacket .. $80
Bell-Bottom Pants $55

Shift (Tank Dress) $50
Oblong bag $30
Long Sleeve Button-Up Shirt $50

Crucial Creations
owner wearing Mens
Indian Curta ($55) in
wild HEMP field growing
near Iowa City, Iowa.
Plants are naturalized
survivors from the U.S.
government's
"HEMP FOR VICTORY"
campaign during
World War II.

**Crucial Creations
Cannabis**
Clothing offers
American made,
'high' fashion, quality
mens and womens
clothing made from
100% ORGANIC
CANNABIS SATIVA.
Please write or call
for a free catalog.

Wholesale inquiries
encouraged.

Crucial Creations
4550 S. 12th Avenue Suite 111
Tucson, Arizona 85714
PH#: (602) 513-6615
FAX: (602) 746-0408

1-800-HEMP-4-US

Information on the Canadian Hemp Industry was not available at the time of the first printing of <u>Hemp</u> <u>Today</u>. However, there have been several developments in Canada over the past year. The most important being the first crop grown and harvested in North America since 1947.

Hemp Line of Tillsenburg, Ontario, planted 10 acres of five different strains of hemp from Eastern Europe and France. Harvest took place in August and the crop was eagerly taken by companies in Canada and the U.S. for experimentation in particle board and paper. More acreage is expected in 1995.

✳

For THC logo merchandise, other registered logos, and custom design

IN CANADA...

✳ **The Hemp Club**
Wholesale / Catalogue...hats, bags, accessories, books
The Hemp Club,   82 Percival Ave., Montreal West, PQ. Canada H4X 1T5
(514)487-3908   FAX(514)843-8722

IN USA...

✳ **Headcase**
Wholesale licensed manufacturer of THC logo hats.
Headcase,   150 Bay Street, Jersey City, New Jersey 07302
(201)420-5900   FAX(201)420-7101

✳ **Hemp Quarterly**
Catalogue, THC...hats and acessories
Hemp Quarterly, 1304 W. Alabama, Houston, Texas 77006
(713)521-1134   FAX (713)528-4367

This page has been sponsored by The Hemp Club, Montreal